Walter Spiegelberg

HANDBUCH DER ENGLISCHEN NACHERZÄHLUNG II

WALTER SPIEGELBERG

HANDBUCH DER ENGLISCHEN NACHERZÄHLUNG II

MAX HUEBER VERLAG

ISBN 3-19-00.2150-3

4 3 2 1981 80 79 78 77
Die jeweils letzten Ziffern bezeichnen Zahl und Jahr des Drucks.
Alle Drucke dieser Auflage können nebeneinander benutzt werden.
Umschlaggestaltung: Peter Schiffelholz, Stuttgart
Gesamtherstellung: Friedrich Pustet, Regensburg
Printed in Germany

VORWORT

Vier Jahre sind seit dem Erscheinen des ersten Handbuches der englischen Nacherzählung verstrichen. Der Erfolg des Buches, die Zustimmung der Fachwelt und nicht zuletzt der häufige Ruf nach einer Fortsetzung veranlaßten mich, das HANDBUCH DER ENGLISCHEN NACHERZÄHLUNG II erscheinen zu lassen.

Es ist noch stärker gegenwartsorientiert: Es konfrontiert den Benutzer mit brennenden Tagesfragen wie Jugendkriminalität und -strafe und bezieht Spionagefälle der jüngsten Gegenwart mit ein. Auch die »science fiction« wird in größerem Maße erschlossen wie die Kriminalgeschichte höheren literarischen Ranges.

Damit wird das HANDBUCH DER ENGLISCHEN NACHERZÄHLUNG II gleichzeitig und fast ungewollt ein Buch des heutigen Englands in erzählbaren, handlungsreichen Teilaspekten, das größere Besinnung und intensivere Arbeit fordernde Texte bewußt meidet.

Es regt an, unterhält und möchte aus seiner stofflichen Fülle jedem Lernenden etwas bieten. Die fremde Sprache erscheint nicht als Selbstzweck, sondern als Mittel zum Zweck: Mit ihrer Hilfe werden spannende, geheimnisvolle, abenteuerliche Gehalte erschlossen, und somit kann die Spracherlernung aus der Eintönigkeit der täglichen Routine wenigstens zum Teil gelöst werden.

Wenn das Buch gern studiert oder auch nur zur Hand genommen wird, wenn es Aufnahmebereitschaft und Freude an der englischen Sprache steigert, hat es seine Aufgabe erfüllt.

Großhansdorf, Ostern 1971

Walter Spiegelberg

Inhaltsverzeichnis
(Approximative Wortzahlangaben)

I. UNTERSTUFE

II.. ÜBERGANG ZUR MITTELSTUFE

III. MITTELSTUFE

IV. ÜBERGANG ZUR OBERSTUFE

VIII. DIE KURZE OBERSTUFENNACHERZÄHLUNG

(Englisch als zweite oder dritte Fremdsprache)

1. What a Fright!

Tom was on holiday at the seaside. He loved to play on the sands. One day he was tired and sat on a chair. Suddenly he saw a ship sailing into the bay. The flag was the Jolly Roger. Tom knew that it was a pirate ship. Soon after, a small boat came ashore. Three pirates jumped out and quickly caught him. They put him into the boat and went back to the big ship.

Tom was taken before the pirate chief. He looked very fierce and cruel. He gave orders that Tom must walk the plank. A big plank was put over the side of the ship. They made Tom walk on it. After two steps he fell into the sea. Splash! Tom woke up in the water. The pirates were all a dream. The tide had come in and upset his chair.

Angus Maciver: *Reader—Book A*, Glasgow 1957
By permission of the publishers, Robert Gibson & Sons Ltd

VOCABULARY. *bay*: a part of the sea in a curve on the shore — *Jolly Roger*: pirates' black flag — *pirate*: sea-robber — *ashore*: on land — *fierce*: violent; very wild-looking — *walk the plank*: (of pirates' captive) walk blindfold into sea along plank laid over side of ship — *splash*: noise made by something falling into a liquid — *tide*: the rise and fall of the sea "Gezeiten".

2. The Boy Who Cried Wolf

There was once a shepherd boy who became bored with his lonely life high up the mountainside. To amuse himself he sometimes shouted, "Wolf! Wolf!" Then all the men of the village left their work in the fields below to help him. They were not very pleased when they found he was playing a joke on them. His little trick worked several times.

At last, one day a wolf really did come and attack the sheep. The boy cried out, "Wolf! Wolf!" as loud as he could. But the men in the fields went on with their work and paid no attention to his cries. They said, "He's playing tricks again!" So the wolf ate the sheep. If somebody tells lies, he is not believed even when he is telling the truth!

Elliott-Cannon: *Good Company, Book Two, Venture Fair*, London 1966
By permission of the publishers, Johnston & Bacon Ltd

VOCABULARY. *shepherd*: a man who looks after sheep — *bore*: weary or annoy — *mountain*: high hill.

3. The Old Tool Chest

Tom, Dick and Harry loved playing in the empty railway siding. There was an old chest there. It was a big wooden one in which the railway men had once kept tools. Now it was the boys' den. The chest was six feet long and four feet deep, with a lid that was held down by hasp and staple. It made a lovely place to hide in, but there was little space inside.

One evening after school, Tom, Dick and Harry went to their den. They lifted the lid, propped it open and climbed inside. Sitting on the bottom they were hidden from sight. Suddenly the lid fell with a crash and the hasp slipped over the staple. They banged on the lid, they shouted, they pushed but the lid held firm. They were trapped.

When Tom, Dick and Harry did not come home, their mothers began to get upset and telephones began to ring. Their fathers went to the police station and joined the police in an all-night search.

In the morning, on their way to school, other boys began to talk about the three missing lads.

"I bet they are in their den," said one boy. "You know, that old box in their railway siding. I'll go and tell Tom's dad." Dad and the boy ran to the siding and Dad lifted the lid of the den. There they were, tired, hungry and frightened. After a meal and a good sleep, they were none the worse for their night in their den.

(This really happened. Tom, Dick and Harry were three boys, aged eight, nine and ten, who were locked in a chest in this way.)

Meade Charlton & Zimmerman: *Panorama Book 1*, Edinburgh 1966
By permission of the publishers, Holmes McDougall Ltd

VOCABULARY. *siding*: short railway track(s) at the side of the mainline (for shunting) "Rangiergleis" — *den*: animal's hidden lying-place — *lid*: cover for a box — *hasp*: clasp or catch "Haspe, Spange" — *staple*: loop-shaped iron nail — *prop*: support — *crash*: shock of two things meeting — *slip*: move quickly, fall — *bang*: give a violent blow to — *upset*: worried; anxious — *missing*: lost.

4. The Twins Go Sailing

The twins, John and Jane, were very lucky because they lived in a seaside town, and their father, Mr Lee, had a sailing-boat. This was a dinghy 12 feet long and just over 4 feet broad, fitted with a mast and a sail.

Before setting sail they were always careful to notice the direction of the wind, and they had a look at the clouds to see what kind of weather they might expect. Yet, even with such care, accidents happen, and one happened when they least expected it.

One day the twins and their father went down to the quay. They noticed that the waves out to sea were a little stronger and higher than usual, but they soon forgot this as they made ready the boat in the shelter of the harbour. The twins took their seats, their father raised the sail, took the sheets in one hand and the tiller in the other, and they pushed off.

Just as they left the harbour, a sudden gust of wind struck them. In a moment the boat capsized. What a shock it was! One minute they were safe in the boat, and the next minute they were in the sea. But they did not lose their heads. Mr Lee had always told the twins that if they were thrown into the water they were not to try to swim to the shore, no matter how near it was. They were to cling to the boat and wait until help came.

They did as they had been told. Their life jackets kept them afloat, and very soon all three were clinging to the capsized boat.

The accident had been seen by other boats and soon there was a circle of boats around them. Willing hands hauled them aboard. Another boat took the dinghy in tow and took it back into the harbour.

Although the children were none the worse for their experience, it made them realise how necessary it is to be careful when sailing.

Andrew Scotland: *A Junior Panorama—Book Two,* London 1963
By permission of the publishers, Odhams Press Ltd

VOCABULARY. *twins*: two children born of the same mother at the same birth — *dinghy*: small open boat — *cloud*: mass of water; vapour floating above the earth — *quay*[ki:]: landing-place — *shelter*: anything that protects — *tiller*: handle of a rudder "Ruderpinne" — *gust*: sudden blast — *capsize*: upset; overturn — *cling*: stick close to — *life-jacket*: one made of cork or other light material to keep a person from sinking in the water — *afloat*: floating; resting on water — *haul*: drag, pull with force — *in tow*: being pulled by a rope or chain — *none the worse*: not in less good condition.

5. Safety Always

Mary Green lived in a little village. There was a nice playing field not far from her home, but she liked better to play with her ball on the road. Very foolishly, she thought that she would come to no harm, as there was very little traffic in that quiet village.

One day, as Mary was bouncing her ball on the road, a motor car swung round a corner, and was almost upon her before she noticed it. A passer-by saw her danger, and ran to her aid.

Too late! Mary was knocked down and her leg was badly injured. When Mary's mother arrived soon afterwards, the driver took them both in his car to the nearest hospital, which was twelve miles away.

Mary suffered much pain, and was forced to spend many weeks in bed, as she was unable to walk. She, just like Billy, learned a lesson when it was too late. As she did not wish the same to happen to any of her friends, Mary would say to them:

LOOK AT ME! DON'T PLAY ON THE ROAD.

Angus Maciver: *Reader—Book C*, Glasgow 1957
By permission of the publishers, Robert Gibson & Sons Ltd

VOCABULARY. *foolish*: silly; without sense — *bounce*: cause to spring, throw — *swing (swung)*: turn in a curve — *passer-by*: one who happens to walk that way — *aid*: help — *injure*: harm, hurt.

6. Safety First

Billy Brown lived in a big town. He had no garden in which to play, so he spent most of his time in the street. Now Billy liked very much to hang on the back of any passing motor-lorry and steal a ride. No wonder people called him "Silly Billy."

One day, he saw a motor-lorry coming down the street and, as it passed him, he sprang on the back. Not long afterwards, he jumped off, but alas! he did not see a van coming close behind him. The van-driver tried hard to stop his car in time, but it was too late. Billy was knocked down and, sad to say, his arm was broken. He suffered great pain, and had to be taken in an ambulance to hospital.

For many weeks Billy lay in bed, and felt very sorry that he had caused so much trouble. When his father and mother and friends visited him he would say

I'VE LEARNED A LESSON! NO MORE RIDES ON LORRIES FOR ME.

VOCABULARY. *motor-lorry*: strong wagon driven by petrol for carrying heavy goods — *van*: large covered wagon or car for goods — *ambulance*: van (usually motor) for carrying the sick or injured — *cause*: make happen; bring a thing about.

7. A Very Short Story

A Scotsman was going away for a holiday.

"What will you charge for taking me to the station?" he asked the taxi driver.

"Three shillings, sir," said the driver.

"I have some luggage," said the Scotsman. "How much will you charge for taking that?"

"There is no charge for the luggage. It goes for nothing," replied the driver.

"Right!" said the Scotsman. "Just take the luggage, then. I'll walk."

Ronald Ridout: *Look Alive*, London 1955
By permission of the publishers, Heinemann Educational Books Ltd

VOCABULARY. *Scotsman*: Scotchman; Scot (native of Scotland) — *charge*: ask as a price — *luggage*: trunks and other baggage of a traveller.

8. Another Very Short Story

Jane was a rather greedy girl. One day some jam tarts were missing.

"Have you eaten those jam tarts that I left on the table?" asked her mother.

"I haven't eaten one of them, Mum," said Jane.

"That's very odd," said her mother. "I am sure I left six on the table, and now there is only one there."

"Yes," said Jane. "That's the one I haven't eaten!"

Ronald Ridout: *Look Alive*, London 1955
By permission of the publishers, Heinemann Educational Books Ltd

VOCABULARY. *greedy*: wishing for too much — *tart*: small pie containing fruit or jam — *odd*: unusual, strange.

9. The Cherry Tree

Have you ever heard the story of George Washington and the cherry tree? George became the President of the United States nearly two hundred years ago. It was said that when he was a small boy he chopped down his father's favourite cherry tree. His father was very angry.

"Who chopped down the cherry tree?"

"Father," said George. "I cannot tell a lie. I chopped down your cherry tree."

His father was pleased that he had owned up at once and told the truth.

"Good boy for saying so at once! As you have admitted it, I shan't beat you."

There was another American boy called George Brown. He too chopped down a cherry tree.

"Who chopped down the cherry tree?" demanded his angry father.

"Father," said George, "I will be like George Washington. I will own up straight away. I chopped down your tree."

"In that case, my boy," said his father, "I am going to beat you!"

"But you can't do that!" cried George in alarm. "It's not fair. I owned up at once, just like George Washington. George Washington's father didn't beat him. He was so pleased with him for telling the truth."

"That may be so," said George's father grimly, "but in that story there was one big difference. When George Washington chopped down *his* father's tree *his* father wasn't in it!"

A. Elliott-Cannon: *Good Company, Book Three, Wayfaring*, London 1966
By permission of the publishers, Johnston & Bacon Ltd

VOCABULARY. *chop*: cut by giving blows to — *own up*: confess — *admit*: own the truth of — *straight away*: at once — *grim*: stern; severe.

10. How Does a Dog Lie Down?

If you watch a dog as it is about to lie down, you will notice that it turns round and round before finally coming to rest. Why is this?

Although many dogs today are tame animals, there was a time when all dogs were wild. They did not live in or near the homes of human beings, but stayed as far away from people as they could. It was safer for them to do so.

They liked to live in grass lands. When they wanted to rest they had to turn round and round several times in order to level the grass. Also, when doing this, they made sure that there were no enemies near at hand.

It is strange that dogs, who are so often gentle and friendly, should, in this simple act, do exactly as wild dogs did hundreds of years ago.

Andrew Scotland: *A Junior Panorama—Book One,* London 1966
By permission of the publishers, Odhams Press Ltd

VOCABULARY. *notice*: see — *tame*: not wild or fierce — *level*: make flat or smooth — *at hand*: close by, within reach — *act*: thing done.

11. The Dove and the Ant

The ant is one of the smallest of insects. One day a thirsty ant went down to the river to drink. The river was flowing strongly, and the current snatched at the ant and carried it down-stream.

A dove was resting on the branch of a tree. When the dove saw what had happened to the ant, it quickly dropped a small twig into the water. The ant climbed onto the twig, and in a short time the twig floated to the bank of the river. In this way the ant was saved.

A short time after this a man came into the forest and tried to catch the dove. He very carefully spread a net on the ground near to where the dove was standing. The man worked so quietly that the dove did not see the trap that was being prepared.

But the ant saw what was about to happen, and just as the dove was going to walk into the net, the ant bit the bird on the heel. This frightened the dove, and it flew away to safety.

The dove did a good turn to the ant when it dropped a twig into the river. The ant did a good turn to the dove when it made the dove fly away from the trap.

Andrew Scotland: *A Junior Panorama—Book One,* London 1966
By permission of the publishers, Odhams Press Ltd

VOCABULARY. *dove*: pigeon — *ant*: small, hard-working insect — *thirsty*: having a need to drink — *current*: stream of water — *snatch*: put out the hand suddenly and take — *branch*: arm-like part of tree — *twig*: small branch of a tree — *float*: keep on the surface; move with moving liquid — *spread*: cover a surface — *heel*: back part of the foot — *a good turn*: a good act.

12. The Cat and the Goldfish

"Inky! You naughty pussy! Go away at once!" cried Jim. He chased the big black cat out of the room.

"What was he doing?" asked his sister Alice.

"I found him on the table at the window." said Jim. "He was trying to catch the goldfish. He was about to put his paw into the bowl."

"O dear!" said his sister. "We will need to keep him out of this room. He will eat our two little goldfish."

"I've got a clever idea," replied Jim. "I'm going to teach Inky a lesson."

The boy took the goldfish away. He put the two little fish into a basin of water.

"What are you going to do?" asked his sister.

"Just wait and see!" replied Jim. "Go and bring the little toy fish. You will find them in the big toy-chest."

Alice soon returned with two little toy fish in her hand. Her brother took them and put them into the glass bowl. He then filled the bowl with water from the tap.

"Now we will teach Mr Inky a lesson!" he said.

Jim and Alice returned to the room. The boy placed the bowl with the toy fish on the table. Then they hid behind a big chair to watch the fun. They had not long to wait.

Inky came slowly and quietly into the room. He thought that no one was there. With a quick jump he was up on the table. Jim and Alice saw the cat put his paw into the bowl. He scooped out one of the little toy fish. Crunch! Inky bit it in two. He tried to swallow a part but it nearly choked him. What a horrible taste it had!

"That one must be bad," said Inky. "I'll try the other one."

The cat scooped the other fish out of the bowl. He tried to eat it but soon dropped it. This fish tasted much worse than the first one.

"Strange!" said Inky to himself. "I like fish. These goldfish have a horrible taste. I will never try to catch or eat a goldfish again." Inky walked out of the room in disgust.

When the cat had gone, Jim and Alice came out of hiding. They laughed and joked about poor Inky. Jim took away the bowl and the broken toy fish. He returned soon afterwards with the real goldfish in the bowl.

It is funny to watch Inky. He comes into the room as usual. He looks at the bowl of goldfish in disgust. He never goes near it.

Angus Maciver: *Reader—Book A*, Glasgow 1957
By permission of the publishers, Robert Gibson & Sons Ltd

VOCABULARY. *paw*: animal's foot that has claws or nails — *bowl*: deep, round hollow dish — *tap*: a hole or short pipe which, when opened, allows liquid to run through — *scoop*: get out (with a tool like a shovel) — *crunch*: crush noisily with the teeth when eating — *swallow*: make food or drink pass over the throat into the stomach — *choke*: be unable to breathe because of something in the windpipe — *disgust*: strong dislike, strong feeling of distaste — *hiding*: = hiding-place.

13. A Strange Baby

There was once a poor tabby-cat whose kittens had died. She was very sad and lonely. The master of the house felt very sorry for her. Next day he went to a nearby wood and brought home a baby squirrel. This baby squirrel had lost his mother.

The master of the house had two children who were called Harry and Betty. They were twins and were seven years of age. Harry put the little creature in the box beside the cat. Then he and Betty watched to see what would happen.

At once the mother cat began to lick the baby squirrel. The little animal was so young that his eyes were not yet open. He could not even eat or drink by himself. Then pussy began to feed him just if he was her own baby.

Mother cat took great care of baby squirrel. She nursed him and kept him warm at night. If a dog came near the box, she would get very angry. Pussy would rush at the dog and chase him away.

When the squirrel grew bigger, many strange things began to happen. Mother cat did not know what to do. Her little son had a great big bushy tail. He did not walk in the same way as she did. He hopped about from place to place. Sometimes he would sit up on his hind legs.

That was not all.

They did not speak in the same kind of words. When the cat would say "miau", the squirrel would say "mir-mir." Pussy showed him how to catch mice. He would turn away and not even bother to look at them. Poor Pussy did her best, but it was of no use.

One day the cat and the squirrel went into the garden. At once the quirrel shot up the nearest tree. In a moment he was at the very top.

"Goodness!" said pussy in surprise. She was afraid that her son would hurt himself. "Come down at once!" she cried. The squirrel did not come down. Instead, he began to show off. He darted from branch to branch very quickly. Pussy was sure that he would fall. Then he began to throw nuts at his cat mother. At last poor pussy left him and went back to the house.

The two animals lived very happily together. At night they slept beside each other in the same box. Sometimes the squirrel's bushy tail would rub against the cat's nose. Pussy would say "Stop tickling me!" Squirrel would then turn and say, "Give me more room!" Soon after, the two strange friends would be sound asleep.

Angus Maciver: *Reader—Book A*, Glasgow 1957
By permission of the publishers, Robert Gibson & Sons Ltd

VOCABULARY: *tabby*: cat, esp. of grey or brownish colour with dark stripes — — *kitten*: young cat — *squirrel*: a little animal, usually reddish-brown in colour, with a bushy tail, and living mostly in trees — *twins*: two children born of the same mother at the same birth — *lick*: pass the tongue over — *nurse*: act as a nurse; look after carefully — *bother*: to be a nuisance to; to trouble — *show off*: try to impress people "angeben, großtun" — *dart*: to move suddenly and quickly (dart = pointed, arrow-like weapon) — *tickle*: touch lightly and cause laughter.

14. The Two Woodmen

A woodman was cutting down a tree on the bank of a river. By chance his axe slipped, and fell into the water. The river was deep, and the woodman could not see it. The woodman was very worried, and he sat down on the bank, not knowing what to do.

A river god appeared, and asked the woodman why he was so sad. The woodman told him what had happened to his axe. The river god dived to the bottom of the river and reappeared holding a golden axe in his hand. He asked the woodman if this was the axe.

The woodman answered that it was not.

The river god then dived a second time. He reappeared holding a silver axe in his hand. Again he asked the woodman if this was his axe.

The woodman replied that it was not.

So the river god dived a third time, and reappeared, holding in his hand the axe which the woodman had lost. He asked if this was the axe.

The woodman smiled happily, and said that it was. He thanked the river god for his kindness.

The river god, too, was smiling happily. He was pleased that the woodman had been so honest, and he gave him the gold and silver axes as rewards for his honesty.

On his way home the woodman told his friends what had happened. Another woodman who heard this story went to the riverside, and he let his axe fall into the water. He sat down and began to cry.

The river god again appeared, and asked what was wrong. The man told him how he had lost his axe.

The river god dived, and brought up a golden axe. He asked the man if this was the axe which he had lost.

The man looked at it greedily, and said that it was. With that the river god threw it away, and he would not dive again to bring up the axe which the man had lost.

Andrew Scotland: *A Junior Panorama—Book One,* London 1963
By permission of the publishers, Odhams Press Ltd

VOCABULARY. *woodman*: forester; wood-cutter — *axe*: tool for hewing or chopping — *by chance*: unexpectedly — *slip*: fall by not being held firmly — *god*: being with power over nature — *dive*: dip or plunge into — *honest*: not cheating — *reward*: return or recompense for service or merit — *riverside*: bank of a river, or the land near it — *greedy*: wanting too much.

15. The King and the Figs

One day as a king was walking through his kingdom he saw a man planting a fig tree.

"Why are you doing this?" he asked.

The man answered, "Although I am not very young, I might still live to enjoy figs from this tree. If this does not happen, my son will enjoy them."

"Well," said the king, "if you *do* live to eat the figs from the tree which you are now planting, come and tell me."

Now it happened that the man did live for many years, and the fig tree grew and grew, until one season ripe figs hung from its branches. They were big and fat and juicy.

The man, who was now very old, plucked a basketful of the ripe figs from the tree and took them to the palace of the king. He reminded the king of what had happened many years before. The king remembered speaking to the old man, and he was so pleased that he accepted the figs, and ordered the old man's basket to be filled with gold.

There lived near the old man a very greedy woman. She heard what had happened, and she wondered if perhaps her husband would be as lucky. A fig tree grew in her garden, and she filled a basket with ripe figs and asked her husband to take them to the king.

But the king saw through the trick. He would not accept the gift, and he made the man stand in the courtyard, where he was pelted with his own figs.

He returned home to tell his wife what had happened. She was not in the least sorry for him. All she said was, "It is a good thing they were figs. It would have been much worse if they had been coconuts!"

Andrew Scotland: *A Junior Panorama—Book Two,* London 1963
By permission of the publishers, Odhams Press Ltd

VOCABULARY. *fig*: soft, sweet fruit full of small seeds — *ripe*: ready to be gathered in or eaten — *juicy*: full of juice, succulent — *pluck*: pick — *greedy*: wanting too much — *pelt*: throw things at — *coconut*: fruit of a palm-tree growing in hot countries.

16. The Rich Man and the Foolish Robber

One night a rich merchant and his wife were sitting quietly in a room at their house. The husband heard a noise on the roof, and he knew that a robber was trying to break in.

He was a very wise man. He knew that robbers were in fact very foolish people. So he whispered to his wife, "Ask me in a loud voice how I became rich."

His wife knew that there must be something wrong, so she did what her husband asked. In a loud voice she said to him, "You are a rich man. Tell me, how did you become so rich?"

Her husband replied, "You must not ask me such questions." In a still louder voice she asked again, "Tell me, how did you become so rich?"

The husband seemed to think for a minute, then he said, "It is a great secret, but I shall tell you. I became a rich man because I was a robber."

His wife seemed to be surprised. "Oh dear, I never knew this. How was it that you were never captured?"

The robber, who was on the roof, heard these words and, of course, he was very excited. He was surprised to discover that the rich man had once been a robber. How wonderful it would be if one day he could be as rich as the man in the house beneath him!

The rich man went on speaking very loudly, "I used to climb on the roofs of houses. I always did this when the moon was shining. When I came to a window, I said a magic word. Then I took hold of one of the moonbeams. I slid down the moonbeam using it like a rope. After I had taken all that I wanted, I climbed up the moonbeam and escaped."

"This is wonderful," said his wife. "Tell me the magic word."

"Oh, I cannot tell you," he said, "or we shall lose all our riches."

The robber on the roof listened more closely. If only the merchant would tell the magic word!

"Come," said the rich man's wife, "tell me the magic word. I promise you I shall never repeat it."

"Very well," said the rich man, "since only you are listening I shall tell you. The magic word was FIDDLESTICKS."

The robber on the roof was very excited. Just then the moon shone through a cloud, and the moonbeams seemed to be all around him. If only the rich man and his wife would fall asleep! He listened carefully, and to his delight he heard a noise of snoring. Both the rich man and his wife pretended to be asleep, and they snored loudly.

The robber moved carefully along the roof to a skylight. He could see the moonbeams falling upon the window. He shouted out, "FIDDLE-STICKS," lifted his hands and grasped the moonbeam.

But he did not seem to be able to grasp anything. With a great crash he fell through the skylight and onto the floor below. The rich man captured him easily. The robber groaned, "Your story cannot be true."

The rich man replied, "Of course it is not true. You are indeed a silly man as well as a bad man. Why don't you work hard and live as all good people live?"

Andrew Scotland: *A Junior Panorama Book One*, London 1963
By permission of the publishers, Odhams Press Ltd

VOCABULARY. *foolish*: silly; without sense — *capture*: take by force — *beneath*: below — *magic*: having to do with supernatural forces — *take hold of*: grasp — *moonbeam*: ray of light from the moon — *rope*: thick cord — *escape*: get safe or free — *closely*: in a concentrated way — *fiddlestick*: the bow with which a fiddle is played; *Fiddlesticks!*: nonsense! — *snore*: breathe roughly in sleep — *pretend*: make believe; act falsely — *grasp*: seize firmly with the hands — *skylight*: window in a roof or ceiling — *groan*: utter a moaning sound in trouble.

17. A Tick-Tock Tale

"Tick-tock! tick-tock!" went the old grandfather clock in the hall; "did I ever tell you my tick-tock story?"

"You did not," said the barometer on the wall, "you never tell me anything except the time, and sometimes you are wrong."

"You cannot always be right," said the grandfather clock, rattling his weights with laughter; "I have known you to say 'Very Fair' when there was a thick fog outside."

"It was 'Very Fair' somewhere else," replied the barometer crossly; "but tell me your story."

"Well," went on the grandfather clock, "when I was very young, and even more handsome than I am now, I lived on a farm. I was the only clock for miles around, and so famous was I, that many people called at the farm just to see me. Even the children of the village would visit me and look up at my face and say, 'Oh, yes, it's half past four.' Sometimes I would chuckle to myself because it was nothing of the kind."

"Now living on this farm was a sheep dog named Bob. He was a fine fellow and very good-natured. In fact he was too kindhearted because he would lie dozing in his kennel and allow the mice to come and nibble the food under his very nose."

"One day Bob became sick, and could not do his work. Next day he was worse, and before a week had gone he was so ill that no one expected him to get better. One morning the farmer said to his wife, 'It will almost break my heart but I will need to shoot poor Bob. He ist dying very slowly and very painfully, poor old chap. Call me in from work when the clock strikes one!' There were tears in the eyes of the farmer's wife but she said, 'Oh dear, I suppose it's the best way. Poor Bob has been suffering so much these last few weeks that I cannot bear to see him in such pain.'"

"When the farmer had gone to the fields, his wife came over to me and wound me up. I think she must have been crying, because she forgot to fasten my face, and left it swinging open."

"Just as it was near one o'clock and I was getting ready to strike the hour, a mouse came creeping through the open door, ran along the floor, up my body, and in the cheekiest way in the world, perched himself upon my big hand."

Of course his weight made me stop at once and for the first time in my life I failed to do my duty and did not strike one."

"Because of this, the farmer's wife did not call her husband and he forgot all about his sad task till he came in for his supper in the evening. When he arrived and looked at Bob, he saw to his great surprise that the dog was wagging his tail."

"With a glad shout, the farmer turned to his wife and cried, 'Bless my soul, just look at Bob! He's wagging his tail to welcome me home! He must be getting better!' Better indeed he was, and in a few days the dog was romping about as happy as ever."

"No one ever knew what had made me stop."

"I think it's going to rain," snapped the barometer, "and I must attend to my duties."

Slowly and silently the pointer went round to "Rain."

Angus Maciver: *Reader—Book C*, Glasgow 1962
By permission of the publishers, Robert Gibson & Sons Ltd

VOCABULARY. *rattle*: to give out short, sharp sounds, to clatter — *weight*: heavy body or object — *fair*: good; dry and fine — *cross*: ill-tempered, sulky — *handsome*: good-looking — *chuckle*: laugh in a quiet manner, showing pleasure — *good-natured*: kind — *doze*: to sleep lightly — *kennel*: house for dogs — *nibble*: to take little bites of — *wind*: to tighten the spring of a clock to keep its works in motion — *cheeky*: impudent; saucy — *perch*: to take up position on — *task*: set piece of work to be done — *romp*: play about, esp. running, jumping, and being rather rough — *snap*: to speak quickly or sharply — *pointer*: indicator on a dial.

18. How Did the Black Tracker Know?

One aborigine was leading a search for three lost men. As he walked along, he talked about their actions as they wandered. At one place he said that one of the lost men had put a gun to his left shoulder and killed a wild turkey. The astonished white men could see nothing, and wondered how the black tracker knew.

Can you think out how he knew?

ANSWER:

1. *Footmarks:* when a man shoots from the left shoulder he puts his right foot forward.
2. *Plants:* pellets from the gun-shop had torn scrub and grass.
3. *Feathers:* the tracker could see pieces of feathers from a wild turkey.

Richard Taylor: *Reader's Delight 3*, London 1963
By permission of the publishers, University of London Press Ltd

VOCABULARY. *aborigine* [æbə'ridʒiniː] original or native inhabitant of a country — *action*: deed; movement — *turkey*: large farm-yard bird, whose flesh is eaten mostly at Christmas-time.

19. Boy Detective

It was a very cold day in winter. There was snow on the ground, and the river had frozen over. Peter had made plans the day before to meet his friends and go skating. Now he was on the way to his friend's house.

He soon saw the house. As he came near the front gate, he saw three pairs of footprints in the snow. They were leading away from the house.

"I know those footprints," Peter said to himself. "The biggest ones are John's, the middle-sized ones are Judy's, and smallest ones are little Neil's."

Peter thought again. "It must be late," he said to himself. "My friends must have gone out without me. I'll pretend I am a detective and see how quickly I can find them."

So Peter followed the footprints in she snow. No one else had come this way yet, and the footprints were very clear. He followed them all the way down a lane towards the river. Then suddenly he stared at the snow as if he couldn't believe his own eyes. Instead of three pairs of footprints, there were now only two pairs.

What on earth had happened to the other pair? Peter was very puzzled. No footprints had turned off the lane, and he had not met anyone walking back. Yet it was hardly likely that one of his friends had begun flying!

All at once Peter started laughing. He had solved the mystery. Now he knew how one pair of footprints had disappeared. Do you know?

Ronald Ridout: *Look Alive*, London 1955
By permission of the publishers, Heinemann Educational Books Ltd

VOCABULARY. *detective*: one who tracks criminals — *skate*: go on a pair of sharp-edged steel blades fastened to boots (on ice) — *footprint*: mark of a foot — *pretend*: make believe; claim — *lane*: narrow road (or street) — *puzzled*: perplexed — *turn off*: leave a road and go along another leading from it — *solve*: clear up or explain — *mystery*: sth. strange or secret.

20. The Irish Giant

Do you like stories about giants? Here is a true story about a giant. He was an Irishman called Patrick Cotter, and was born over two hundred years ago. By the time he was eighteen he was nine feet tall! A showman took him to England and put him on show. People had to pay a shilling to see the giant. The cunning showman said that the giant belonged to the royal family of the old Kings of Ireland, who were said to be a race of giants. Poor Patrick was in fact a bricklayer until he met the showman.

We call him "poor Patrick" because we cannot help feeling sorry for him. He was a very shy and modest man. He did not at all like being put on show. But he made a great deal of money in this way. He had a fine house and servants and was able to keep a carriage. He could not go out in the streets without a crowd gathering, so he used to go for a walk all by himself between two and three in the morning. At that time the streets were quiet. If he wished to smoke his pipe during his walk he used to take off the top of a street lamp in order to get a light.

A. Elliott-Cannon: *Good Company, Book Two, Venture Fair,* London 1966
By permission of the publishers, Johnston & Bacon Ltd

VOCABULARY. *Ireland (Irish — Irishman)*: republic — *showman*: person who arranges circuses etc. — *show*: performance — *cunning*: skilful — *race*: living beings of the same kind — *bricklayer*: workman who builds with bricks — *carriage*: vehicle for carrying people — *by oneself*: alone.

21. Old Apple-Seed John

Once there was an old man who lived alone in a little hut. He worked at odd jobs for the people who lived near him. Everyone liked him because he was so kind and happy.

One day the old man was sitting on the doorstep of his little home. He was eating a big red apple and enjoying the warm sunshine. As he sat there he thought and thought and thought.

"What can I do to make others happy?" he asked himself. "I am old and not very clever. There must be some way in which I can help people."

All at once, a smile came over his face. "I know what I will do," he said. "Why did I not think of it before?" Then a very strange thing happened.

Everywhere he worked, the old man asked for part of his pay in apples.

He took the apples home and ate them. He saved all the cores and put them into a bag.

The people of the village thought that he was queer. Some said that he was crazy. The boys and girls did not believe this.

"He is not crazy," they said. "He is a wise old man and we are very fond of him. We know that he puts all his apple-cores into a bag. That is why we call him Old Apple-Seed John."

One day Old John locked the door of his little home and tramped away. In one hand he had a walking-stick. On his back he carried a big bag of apple-cores.

Old Apple-Seed John walked far into the country. Now and again he stopped by the side of the road. The old man made a hole in the ground with his stick. Then he dropped an apple-core into the hole and covered it with earth.

All summer he wandered from place to place. Everywhere he went, Old Apple-Seed John planted his cores by the sides of the roads. When his bag was empty, he went back to work. Always he asked for part of his pay in apples.

When his bag was full of apple-cores, Old John would set off again. Sometimes a farmer would say to him, "Stay here. I will give you a good job and pay you well." The old man would shake his head and say, "Old Apple-Seed John has work to do."

In this way the kind old man spent the rest of his life. Fine trees grew from the cores which he planted. Every autumn they were covered with apples.

Passers-by often stopped to eat some of the fruit. "How nice it is to see such lovely apple trees," they said. "Who planted them here?"

The people who lived in those parts knew the answer. They told the strangers the wonderful story of Old Apple-Seed John.

Angus Maciver: *Reader—Book A*, Glasgow 1957
By permission of the publishers, Robert Gibson & Sons Ltd

VOCABULARY. *seed*: the grain or nut from which a new plant may be grown — *odd jobs*: occasional, not regular work — *pay*: money given or received for work, wages — *core*: hard, central part of certain fruits — *queer*: odd, strange — *crazy*: mad — *tramp*: walk with heavy steps — *passer-by*: one who happens to walk that way.

22. The Talking Dog

A few years ago a man walked into a restaurant with a dog trotting at his heels. He sat down at a table, and the dog sat on his knee.

The man ordered sausages and potatoes. When the meal had been brought to him, the other people in the restaurant were surprised to hear a conversation begin between the man and the dog.

The dog was the first to speak. He said, "I am very hungry. Please, can I have some sausage?"

"Certainly not," was the answer. "You have already eaten something this morning."

"Please," repeated the dog, "I am so hungry."

"Very well," said the man, "here is a piece of skin."

The other people in the restaurant looked around in amazement at this wonderful dog. All through the meal the conversation continued.

"That was a good sausage skin," said the dog. "I enjoyed it."

"I am very glad," said the man.

"Please can I have a piece of the sausage itself?" asked the dog.

"What a greedy dog you are," answered the man. "All the same, I will give you a little bit."

"This is good," said the dog.

The amazement of the people in the restaurant grew. Just then, a man rose from another table and approached the owner of the dog.

"That is a most remarkable dog you have. I am willing to give you £ 50 for it."

Another man said, "I am willing to give you £ 100."

The owner of the dog waved them both aside. "Not enough," was the reply.

The dog now entered the conversation. "Would you sell me? What a cruel thing to do! All these years I have been your friend, and now you would sell me for money."

A third man then came up to the owner, and said, "I will give you £ 500 for the dog."

"Done," said the man. "I will accept your offer."

As the money was being handed over the dog spoke, "Because of what you have done, I will never speak again."

This incident actually happened. Of course, the dog never spoke again because, as you have possibly guessed, the man who took the dog into the restaurant was a ventriloquist.

Andrew Scotland: *A Junior Panorama—Book Three*, London 1963
By permission of the publishers, Odhams Press Ltd

VOCABULARY. *trot*: run slowly — *at one's heels*: close behind one — *conversation*: talk — *skin*: outer covering of the body of a person or animal — *amazement*: great surprise — *greedy*: wishing for too much — *all the same*: in spite of that — *approach*: come near — *wave*: make a sign with the hand — *incident*: happening — *actually*: really; in truth — *ventriloquist*: one who can speak without showing that he is doing it; his voice seems to come from some other person or place.

23. THE UMBRELLA MAN

The first man to carry an umbrella in London was Jonas Hanway, and he did so in the year 1750.

Jonas Hanway, who was born in 1712, became a merchant. His travels took him as far as Persia, and while on these journeys he carried an umbrella to protect him from the rain and the sun.

When he returned to England he saw no reason why he should not carry an umbrella in England, but everyone laughed at him. Up to that time only ladies had carried umbrellas in England. It was not considered manly for men to carry them.

So when Jonas Hanway walked through the streets of London on a rainy day, with an umbrella over his head, people laughed at him. Worse than that, some boys pelted him with vegetables and rotten eggs.

Then the owners of coaches began to complain about him. They said that if everyone went about carrying umbrellas their trade would be ruined.

Jonas Hanway, however, did not allow himself to be put off by these insults and fears, and he used to say, "My umbrella will soon be popular."

But he was wrong. It was a long time before the umbrella became popular.

At first shopkeepers kept an umbrella in their shops so that in the event of rain they could shelter their customers, particularly the ladies, on their journey from the shop to the carriage. But as the years went on, more and more people, men and women alike, began to carry umbrellas, and today there must be very few homes without one.

The umbrella is an everyday object, but it has an interesting story.

Andrew Scotland: *A Junior Panorama—Book Two*, London 1963
By permission of the publishers, Odhams Press Ltd

VOCABULARY. *umbrella*: folding shelter against rain, carried in the hand — *Persia*: country in SW Asia, now called *Iran* — *manly*: having the good qualities of a man — *pelt*: throw things at — *rotten*: having gone bad — *owner*: one who possesses — *coach*: four-wheeled carriage pulled by four or more horses — *complain*: grumble — *trade*: one's job — *put off*: hinder; discourage — *insult*: rude acts or words — *popular*: pleasing to most people — *shelter*: give protection — *particularly*: especially — *alike*: in the same way.

24. Florence Nightingale and the Sheep-Dog

When quite a child Florence Nightingale was kind and helpful to all in distress and she was very fond of the little creatures of the woods. The following story shows her kind nature.

Living near the village was a fine old shepherd named Roger, who had a splendid sheep-dog called Cap. Every day they could be seen out on the hills from early morning till dusk; the shepherd carrying his long crook, and the dog following faithfully at his master's heels.

One day, as Florence and another girl were out walking, they noticed that the sheep were running in all directions and that old Roger was having a hard time trying to keep them together. By the look of things he wasn't managing very well and the two girls stopped to ask him what had become of his dog.

"Oh!" replied the shepherd, "I really don't know what to do! Cap will never be able to help me any more. I am sorry that the poor fellow will have to be destroyed."

"Destroyed!" said Florence. "Do you mean that you must put an end to him? How could you be so cruel? Where is he now and what has he done?"

"He has harmed nobody," replied Roger; "but yesterday a cruel stupid boy threw a big stone at him and broke his right foreleg."

The old man spoke in a very sad voice and Florence was quite sure that she noticed a tear in his eye.

"Poor Cap!" said the shepherd. "He is as wise as a human being and such a true and faithful friend. He knew my every wish and was so obedient to my orders."

"Would you mind if we called to see him?" asked Florence. "We might be able to do something for him."

"It is very kind of you," replied the shepherd. "He'll welcome you,

I'm sure. He must be feeling rather lonely just now, as I have been out on the hills all day."

Florence and her friend went on to the shepherd's cottage and called in to see the poor dog. When the girls talked to him, he began to wag his tail. Then he crawled from under the table, and lay down at their feet. Florence took hold of one of his paws and patted his rough head while her friend looked at the injured leg.

It was badly swollen and it hurt him to have it touched; but he licked her hands for he knew she was trying to help him.

"It's only a bad bruise. I'm glad to say there are no bones broken," said Florence's friend. "If Cap rests for a few days he could be well again."

Florence lit the fire, made ready some hot water, and began to bathe the poor dog's leg. It was not long before he tried to show his thanks by wagging his tail.

On their way back they met the old shepherd coming slowly homewards.

"Oh Roger!" cried Florence. "You will not lose poor old Cap after all. We have found that his leg is badly bruised but not broken."

"I am delighted to hear it," said the old man. "Many thanks for going to see him."

The next morning Florence rose early and went to bathe Cap's leg. The following day she bathed it again, and in two or three days the dog was as fit as ever and able to look after the sheep for his master.

Angus Maciver: *Reader—Book C*, Glasgow 1957
By permission of the publishers, Robert Gibson & Sons Ltd

VOCABULARY. *distress*: pain, trouble — *shepherd*: a man who looks after sheep — *crook*: stick with rounded hook at one end — *heel*: back part of the foot — *harm*: to do a wrong to — *obedient*: willing to do what one is told to do — *cottage*: small dwelling-house — *wag*: move from side to side or to and fro — *crawl*: move slowly along the ground — *injure*: to harm, damage — *bruise*: injury to the body so that the skin is discoloured — *delighted*: greatly pleased.

25. Man's Best Friend

Before the invention of motor cars, farmers often rode to market on horseback. Mr. Trelaw always went to market in this way. He had a farm on the moors in Cornwall. The nearest market town was many miles across lonely moors.

One day in the middle of winter the farmer got on his horse to ride to market as usual. Carlo, the sheep-dog, was there, ready to trot along beside the horse as he always did. It was a cold day. The wind was blowing hard, and the sky was dark.

It had already started to snow when they reached the market. The farmer did his business there as quickly as he could. But it was snowing hard.

He got on his horse and set off across the moors for home. Through the snow trotted the horse, and close beside him ran Carlo, the sheep-dog.

It grew dark very early that night, and the snow was getting deeper and deeper. The farmer could no longer see the way. But the horse had done the journey so many times, that he could almost find his way blind-folded. So Mr. Trelaw left it to his horse to take him home safely.

The snow blew into the farmer's eyes and nearly blinded him. But still the horse trotted on through the deep snow, and still Carlo ran close beside him.

All of a sudden, the horse stumbled. The farmer fell off into the snow. He tried to move, but found that he couldn't. He had broken his leg. It was hurting him. He gave a loud cry of pain.

The horse was so frightened by the sudden noise, he set off at a gallop for home, leaving the farmer alone in the snow. Carlo did not gallop away. He stayed beside his master. He licked his face, waiting for him to get up.

Again the farmer tried to move. The pain was too much. He sank back in the snow.

Mr. Trelaw was very worried. What could he do? It was a very lonely spot. No one would come near it that night, he was almost sure. It was three or four miles to the farm. Yet if he stayed there all night in the cold wind and snow, he would probably be dead before the morning.

Once more he tried to move. He tried to crawl on his hands and knees this time. Then the pain in his leg became so great, he fell flat in the snow. He had fainted.

Carlo was upset. He did not know what to make of it. He ran round and round his master's body, as if trying to find out what he could do to help. He let out a sad little howl, and once more licked his master's face.

Meanwhile, the horse had galloped straight back to the farm. When Mrs. Trelaw saw him without his rider, she was almost beside herself with worry. What could have happened to her husband?

She lost no time in getting help. At once she went to friends at the next farm and told them what had happened. Men quickly set off with dogs and lanterns to look for the lost farmer. But the moors stretch for miles and miles. Mr. Trelaw had not ridden along a road or even a track. He had come straight across country. It is always hard to find anyone on those moors at night.

All night long they looked for Mr. Trelaw, but not a trace of him could they find. They were still looking when morning came. It had stopped snowing by now.

"We shall find him now it is light," said one of the men. "But I am afraid it will be too late."

They put out their lanterns and went on looking. At last they found him. He was lying in the deep snow, unconscious, but not dead. Stretched out along his body, was his best friend, Carlo the sheep-dog.

All through that cold dark night, Carlo had acted as a blanket to keep his master warm. He had saved his master's life.

Ronald Ridout: *Look Alive,* London 1955
By permission of the publishers, Heinemann Educational Books Ltd

VOCABULARY. *invention*: create sth. not existing before — *uncultivated*: land, often covered with heather or marsh — *trot*: go at a pace faster than a walk but not so fast as a gallop — *blow, blew, blown*: (of air) be moving — *blindfold:* cover a person's eyes (with a band of cloth etc.) — *blind*: make unable to see — *stumble*: trip in walking — *gallop*: move by leaps — *lick*: pass the tongue over — *crawl*: move slowly along the ground — *knee*: joint at the bend of the leg — *faint*: fall down senseless — *howl*: make a long, loud cry (e.g. a wolf) — *meanwhile*: in the time between — *to be beside oneself*: to be out of one's senses — *stretch*: an unbroken space — *track*: path — *trace*: mark left — *unconscious*: senseless — *act*: have an effect — *blanket*: woollen bed; covering.

26. The Lost Valley of Diamonds

One story that backed up the legend of the lost valley of diamonds came from an English explorer. It was at the time when Cecil Rhodes was making his strength felt in Kimberley that this man was hunting in the wild country of the North-west Cape and suddenly spotted a leopard poised to spring on his African assistant.

The Englishman shot the leopard in the air and it was dead when it landed on the African, but its weight and its claws injured him severely. He nursed the boy back to health and in gratitude the boy offered to take him to the valley of diamonds. But the Englishman did not believe in the legend and turned down the offer. Besides, he did not relish such a trip in such difficult country.

The African boy then deserted his job and the Englishman thought he had seen the last of him, but the boy turned up several days later and handed over a big diamond. This promptly changed the Englishman's plans and he let the boy lead him to the valley, where he found that he could pick up diamonds from the ground by the handful.

He filled a canvas bag with crystals and eventually sold them in London for £70,000. He tried to find the valley again without success. The boy had taken him such a complicated route that it was impossible to memorize.

Those who do not believe the story say the Englishman invented it because the diamonds were smuggled from the mines. They may have been right! Smuggling diamonds is big business. Many millions of pounds' worth are smuggled every year, into America, into Russia, into almost any country you can name.

The start of the smuggling is at the mines. Diamond workers stealing stones hide them in their hair, beards, ear-holes, between their toes, or swallow them, and all suspected thieves are searched. In their earlier days, De Beers caught one diamond worker who had swallowed ten big stones weighing 348 carats and worth a fortune.

De Beers have stopped most of the leakages from their mines by X-raying and other methods. One of the snags with X-raying is that you cannot X-ray a man every time he leaves the mines, twice a day, otherwise his health would be so badly damaged he would die.

Stealing a diamond is only the first part of the job. The next is to sell it. However, there have always been plenty of illicit diamond buyers, or "I. D. B. s", ever since the first Indian mines were discovered thousands of years ago.

Eric Bruton: *The True Book About Diamonds*, London 1961
By permission of the publishers, Frederick Muller Ltd

VOCABULARY. *back*: help or support — *legend*: wonderful story handed down from olden time — *Cape*: Cape Colony, the name (until 1910) of part of what is now called the Union of South Africa — *spot*: catch sight of — *leopard* ['lepəd] animal of the cat kind, with a spotted skin — *poise*: hold in a particular way — *claw*: hooked nail of a beast or bird — *gratitude*: thankfulness — *relish*: enjoy — *desert*: leave — *canvas*: coarse cloth used for tents etc. — *memorize*: learn by heart — *smuggle*: send secretly — *swallow*: make food or drink pass over the throat into the stomach — *carat*: unit of weight for jewels; *metric carat*: 0.2 grams — *De Beers*: famous diamond concern — *leakage*: sth. that passes out — *X-rays*: short-wave rays that penetrate solids and enable doctors to see into the body — *snag*: difficulty — *damage*: harm — *illicit*: not allowed by law.

27. The Most Fabulous Diamond Mine Story

Perhaps the most fabulous of all diamond mine stories is the most recent one in South Africa. A shy young Canadian mining engineer, Dr John Thoburn Williamson, was sent to a gold mine in South Africa.

He became interested in diamonds. After scientific study he decided that there must be a pipe of diamonds in East Africa. Now here was a young idiot saying there were diamonds thousands of miles away from Kimberley!

Williamson threw up his job and set off with a few native "boys" to help him. For five years, in a semi-desert area of Tanganyika, he prospected, suffering from the effects of fever and the hot sun.

Then, one day in 1940, resting in the shade of a baobab tree, he spotted a diamond, and that led him to the diamond pipe he had been looking for so long. His claims were already staked. Soon the world knew of his find and he was offered £ 5,000,000 for it. He refused.

Barbed wire fences were erected round the mine and red-roofed bungalows put up in rows for the staff. An ex-Scotland Yard man was given the job of security officer.

The pipe was worked from the top, like all the others, and the ground broken up and "washed" which produced a concentrate of heavy gravel containing any diamonds that happened to be in the rock. This concentrate was sorted by Askari workers wearing overalls with one sleeve sewn up at the cuff, so that only one hand could be used to pick out the diamonds. The object, of course, was to stop diamonds from being stolen.

As each diamond was found, the Askari who picked it out gave it to an Askari guard wearing a red fez who had a desk in the sorting shed. In exchange the guard handed over a metal disc that could be turned into money.

Williamson's find was a mine ten times bigger than the Premier Mine. No wonder he was soon one of the richest men in the world. "The Doctor", as the staff called him, remained shy and unassuming. He used to keep his daily takings of diamonds in six old tobacco and roll film tins.

He was not interested in money for its own sake, yet he was not an Empire builder like Rhodes. Most of the profit was turned back into the mine which soon had a fine little community around it with a modern hospital and African living conditions reckoned to be the finest in East Africa.

Although the Doctor shut himself away from most visitors, he always answered letters from schoolboys and schoolgirls who wrote to ask about his amazing diamond mine at Mwadui. He died in 1958, only 51 years old and still a bachelor. De Beers and the Tanganyika government took over the mine.

De Beers have carried on what Dr Williamson started at a fast rate. The fleet of fifteen lorries that used to carry the diamond ore from the mine to the washing plant is gone and in its place is the biggest conveyor belt in Africa. This belt is two miles long and carries 300 tons of rock an hour.

Eric Bruton: *The True Book About Diamonds*, London 1961
By permission of the publishers, Frederick Muller Ltd

VOCABULARY. *recent*: fresh, new — *mining engineer*: one who makes and looks after a place from which metals are dug — *pipe*: cylindrical crack in a rock filled with ore etc. — *prospect*: search for — *semidesert area*: stretch of country resembling the Sahara desert — *baobab*: African tree called also monkey-bread "Affenbrotbaum" — *spot*: catch sight of — *claim*: piece of land allotted to a miner — *stake*: mark out or off — *staff*: group of persons working together — *concentrate*: concentrated form of sth. — *gravel*: small stones or pebbles — *sort*: separate into sorts — *Askari*: European-trained African native — *overalls*: garment worn over ordinary clothes to protect them — *sleeve*: part of a garment that covers the arm — *sew* [səu]: join together with needle and thread — *cuff*: end of the sleeve near the wrist — *fez*: red felt head-dress worn by some Muslim men — *disc*: flat, round shape — *Premier Mine*: situated in the Transvaal — *unassuming*: modest — *takings*: receipts — *reckon*: count; believe — *conveyor belt*: endless belt or chain for moving goods etc.

28. The Black Tracker

A young girl wandered away from her home in New South Wales, Australia. It was in wild and lonely country. Men from nearby farms were told, and soon they were searching everywhere for the girl. Some were on horseback, some on foot. They searched all night without success.

The father telephoned to the police-station, forty miles away. He asked that the black tracker should be sent. The tracker was an aborigine.

When he arrived, just before dawn, there didn't seem to be anything for him to follow. It was summer, and the ground was baked hard. He walked round the house in ever-wider circles, and then suddenly set off in a straight line. The white men followed him.

For hours he followed a track which no one else could see. Perhaps he saw a bruised leaf here, a broken twig there, or a pebble kicked aside. Sometimes he ran. Sometimes he dropped to his hands and knees. Twice he lost the trail and found it. In the late afternoon he led the white men to a log. There, beside it, lay the young girl, fast asleep, exhausted.

There are no better trackers in the world than the Australian aborigines. They are descended from Stone Age wanderers, and they owned Australia before the white men came in 1788. They are one of the most ancient races on earth.

There are about 80 000 of them. Many of them live in settlements, working for the white man. But in the wilder parts of Australia, about 30 000 aborigines live half-wild, almost as their ancestors did.

They know how to keep alive in deserts where white men would die. And they can track down animals in the bush, following tracks which no white man can see. They are often used by the police to track down criminals or find people lost in the thick bush country.

The reason for their skill ist that they cannot keep food fresh in their hot country. Therefore they have to kill animals almost every day, and they have learned how through thousands of years. They use spears, and can kill only when they are within fifty yards of their prey. So they must get close to it.

When hunting the fast-moving kangaroo, for instance, they must be able to tell, from its tracks alone, its speed, age, state of health, size, and anything else which will help them in the chase.

Richard Taylor: *Reader's Delight 3*, London 1963
By permission of the publishers, University of London Press Ltd

VOCABULARY. *tracker*: man tracking out wild animals etc. — *aborigine* [æbə'ridʒiniː]: original or native inhabitant of a country — *bake*: cook by the heat of the sun — *bruise*: cause injury to sth. — *twig*: small branch — *pebble*: small stone — *kick*: hit with the foot — *trail*: track — *log*: bulky piece of wood — *exhausted*: used up; worn out — *Stone Age*: the period, thousands of years ago, when stone was used for tools, weapons etc. — *ancient*: old — *race*: living beings of the same kind — *settlement*: group of colonists — *ancestor*: forefather — *desert*: stretch of barren country, usually hot, dry, and sandy — *criminal*: person who commits a serious offence against the law — *skill*: cleverness at doing a thing — *spear*: long weapon with an iron point — *prey*: booty; plunder — *kangaroo*: large Australian animal with great power of leaping.

29. The Pony Express

The first settlers who went to America lived along the coast and did not go far from the sea.

It was not long before many families made up their minds to go together to this wonderful land that lay on the other side of the mountains. In this way, little villages and towns sprang up all over the country.

As people were eager to hear news of their friends, men were hired to carry letters from one place to another.

A company bought five hundred swift strong ponies, and built a chain of offices and stables between the East and the West. They also hired eighty of the best horsemen in the country.

These pony riders had to be brave, clever, and cool in times of danger. Each rider had his own run and had to cover the distance between two stations which were usually about fifty miles apart. They changed their horses every fifteen miles and they made no stop to eat or rest until they reached the end of their journey.

These brave riders faced many hardships and dangers. No matter how cold or stormy the weather, they had to be ready to leap into the saddle and dash forward to the next station. They had to find their way over lonely and dangerous trails. Often bands of Red Indians or robbers would attack them and they would narrowly escape with their lives.

The best known of the Pony Express riders was William F. Cody, who became the famous "Buffalo Bill." He had to seek work when he was fourteen years of age because of his father's death. One day young Cody met a man who was helping to start the Pony Express Company.

"Cody," said the man, "we are looking for only the best and most fearless riders. Will you take the job?"

As the pay was very good and he had his mother and young brothers and sisters to support, Cody answered at once, "Thanks. I'll be glad to start work right away."

It was not long until Cody made the longest Pony Express ride on record. After a trip of more than a hundred miles he reached the station only to find that the next rider had been killed by Red Indians. There was no one to go on with the mail and this brave lad felt that it was his duty to do so. He changed ponies and was off on another long dangerous ride.

Cody nearly lost his life on this part of the journey. Shortly after leaving the station he was ambushed by a band of Redskins on the warpath. They surrounded him but he escaped by suddenly lying flat on his horse and charging through them. There was a long exciting chase but he managed to avoid capture.

When he arrived at the next station, Cody discovered that he must return at once with a very important message. Off he went again by the same way he had come and, although he was very tired and weary, the mail was delivered on time. In all, he had ridden about three hundred miles with stops only to change to fresh ponies.

With the coming of the railway and the telegraph, the Pony Express stopped, as it was no longer needed. William Cody soon found a job with the railway company. He hunted and killed buffaloes in order to supply meat to the men who were building the railway. That was how he came to be called "Buffalo Bill."

Angus Maciver: *Reader—Book C*, Glasgow 1957
By permission of the publishers, Robert Gibson & Sons Ltd

VOCABULARY. *eager*: anxious to do or get; very much wanting — *chain*: number of connected things — *office*: rooms used as a place of business — *stable*: building for horses — *hire*: employ a person for wages — *hardship*: severe suffering — *saddle*: a seat (usually of leather) on the back of a horse or on a bicycle — *dash*: to rush with speed — *trail*: track — *narrowly*: only just; with little to spare — *support*: to help a person by giving money etc. — *on record*: recorded; put down in writing — *mail*: letters carried by post — *lad*: boy, youth — *ambush*: lie in wait for an enemy and attack him by surprise — *charge*: attack — *avoid*: keep away from — *supply*: give or provide what is wanted.

30. A Parachute Jump

(What does it feel like to make a parachute descent for the first time? Here is a first-hand account written from experience of this adventure.)

I shall never forget my first jump from an aeroplane. There were ten of us and I was the first to step out.

"Don't worry," said the trainer, "the parachute always opens." We did not feel quite so sure.

We climbed into the plane, a bar was swung across the doorway, and soon we were in the air. We looked round and grinned at each other, and that silent sympathy made us feel a little better.

I was the first to be called. "Stand in the doorway," said the trainer. He tapped my shoulder, and then said "Go!" I went.

I had no sensation of falling, possibly because I was passing nothing on the way down. After a moment my feet jerked up in front of me. I looked up, and there above me was billowing white nylon. The parachute had opened.

Suddenly the ground seemed to be rushing at me, and a voice called out "Keep your feet together."

A thump – and I was down.

W. R. Lee: *English at Home*, London 1966
By permission of the publishers, Oxford University Press Ltd

VOCABULARY. *parachute*: apparatus that opens out like an umbrella used for descending from an aeroplane — *descent*: going down — *aeroplane*: flying-machine, aircraft — *swing* (swung): whirl round — *doorway*: the doorway was an open one, and an iron bar across it would be needed to prevent the men from falling out by accident — *grin*: give a broad smile — *sympathy*: fellow-feeling; affectionate understanding — *tap*: knock gently — *sensation*: bodily feeling — *jerk up*: move up suddenly and violently — *billow*: roll like great waves — *nylon*: material made of artificial threads — *billowing white nylon*: the parachute opens and is blown about in big waves (billows) by the wind — *thump*: dull heavy sound (and here also the sensation that goes with it).

31. A Holiday in Cornwall

The family, who had never been to North Cornwall before, were surprised to see such enormous waves.

One day the children wandered farther along the beach to explore some rock pools. Above them rose the great cliffs of the Cornish coast. These cliffs looked very tempting to climb, and there seemed to be a path.

The twins set off, and at first they made good progress. It did not seem far to the top. Then they came to a part where a jutting rock prevented them from going any further. They made up their minds to come down. But when they looked down at the beach they had left, they found that it had been covered by the tide. They had made a bad mistake. They had forgotten that the tide was coming in.

John and Mary shouted for help. They could see people on the beach just round the corner of the headland. They could even see their parents, but they could not make their voices heard against the roaring of the sea.

Again they shouted, "Help! Help!", but nobody seemed to hear them. For a long time they stood on a narrow ledge shouting and waving their arms. Above them was the overhanging cliff; below them large waves broke angrily on the rocks.

Just when they were beginning to think that help would never reach them, they saw a group of people standing on the beach and pointing in their direction. They wondered how they would be rescued. By now the sea was dashing up over the rocks, so that it would be impossible to take them off by boat.

All of a sudden they heard a scraping on the rocks above them. Then a man let himself down on a stout rope. He quickly took Mary in his arms and, in next to no time, they were pulled to the top of the cliff.

The man returned for John and, like his sister, he was pulled to the top of the cliff. How glad they were to be safe at last! Soon they were taken by car to the beach, and to their parents.

Luckily for John and Mary, people in this part of Cornwall are ready for such accidents. Special rescue teams are always ready to help those who are trapped on the cliffs. Although the twins did not know it, as soon as they had been noticed a telephone message had been sent to one of the rescue teams.

Andrew Scotland: *A Junior Panorama—Book One*, London 1963
By permission of the publishers, Odhams Press Ltd

VOCABULARY. *enormous*: immense — *explore*: make a journey of discovery — *cliff*: high steep rock — *tempt*: attract to do sth. — *path*: track — *twin*: either of two children born together of the same mother — *progress*: advance — *jut*: stand out — *prevent*: hinder — *headland*: cape — *roar*: shout out — *narrow*: of small extent from side to side — *ledge*: shelf — *dash*: rush with speed — *scrape*: make a harsh noise — *stout*: strong — *rope*: cord — *message*: piece of news sent to sb.

32. The Mounties

In Canada, one of the largest countries in the world, the North-West Mounted Police was formed in 1873. This was the beginning of the Royal Canadian Mounted Police, "the Mounties," one of the most famous police forces in the world.

In 1897, gold was discovered in the Yukon, in the far north-west of Canada. At once, thousands of people rushed into the Yukon, quarrelling, brawling and hoping that they would become rich. The Mounties kept order. One man who murdered a gold miner thought he was safe when he escaped from the Yukon. But the Mounties tracked him down and caught him thousands of miles away in America.

Still farther to the north, two Roman Catholic priests were murdered by two Eskimos. The Eskimos stole all the furs, blankets, rifles and food belonging to the priests, and made off into the icy wilderness. There they hoped to live on what they had stolen from the murdered men.

Two years after the murder, it was reported to the Mounties that nothing had been heard of the two priests for some time. A young policeman, who already knew the Arctic well, suspected that harm might have come to the priests. There was only one thing to do. He would go and find out for himself.

For another two years he travelled through the Arctic, following every clue no matter where it led. He was nearly drowned in a river; on Great Bear Lake his tiny boat was almost crushed in the ice. Strange to say, he actually discovered a shelter which the two missionaries had used. He came upon Bibles and rosaries in the shelter.

The Mountie was now sure that the missionaries had been murdered. One might disappear, but not two. He continued on his journey, always asking questions. At length he came to an Eskimo village where the inhabitants remembered the missionaries who had helped them many years before.

These Eskimos told him that the murderers were living in a sealskin hut some miles away. The Mountie set out, and in a sudden rush, he attacked the hut and captured the murderers. The Mountie had spent more than two years on the search and had travelled more than 6000 miles in the ice and snow of the Arctic.

Andrew Sotland: *A Junior Panorama—Book Three*, London 1963
By permission of the publishers, Odhams Press Ltd

VOCABULARY. *Mounties*: Royal Canadian Mounted Police; patrol many hundreds of thousands of miles of territory between Hudson Bay and the Rocky Mountains — *Yukon*: great river of Alaska — *quarrel*: disagree; fight — *brawl*: take part in a noisy quarrel — *track*: follow along its marks left — *priest*: clergyman — *fur*: animal skin with soft thick hair on it — *Arctic*: region near the North Pole — *clue*: sth. that helps to solve a problem — *shelter*: refuge — *missionary*: person sent to preach his religion — *rosary*: string of beads used in counting prayers.

33. The Fire Brigade

Mary and her mother were passing the Fire Station. They looked through the doors at the great red fire-engines that stood there bright and clean, and ready for action. Suddenly, a bell rang inside the station. Mary and her mother quickly stepped out of the way, as all at once there was movement.

The doors swung open. In seconds, men had put on their helmets, rushed to the engines, and driven them out of the station. Mary and her mother were amazed at the speed with which the engines raced out. Fire can spread very quickly, so every second counts.

As soon as the men of the fire brigade reach a fire, they unwind the hoses and join them to water-pipes. The hoses are very long, and when they are filled with water they are heavy. The firemen direct the water from their hoses on to the blazing building.

Sometimes the building on fire is a high one. Then long ladders, often more then a hundred feet in length, are raised into the sky. The firemen climb these ladders and direct the water onto the blaze from above.

When people are still in the blazing building, the firemen have the difficult job of saving them from being burnt to death. Ladders are quickly raised as near the building as possible, and the firemen rescue those who are trapped, and bring them down. Sometimes firemen are killed in their attempts to save people who are trapped in burning buildings. Firemen are brave. Only brave men would risk their lives to save the lives of others.

When fires break out in ships that are in port, the firemen often fight them from fire-floats. These are boats with fire-engines mounted on them. All great ports have their own fire-floats. They are important for the safety of the port.

Airports also have their own fire brigades because aircraft use petrol, which easily bursts into flame. Water ist useless for putting out petrol fires, so a special kind of foam is used. When a plane is on fire, firemen pour foam on the flames.

The fire brigade does not deal only with fires. When flooding takes place the brigade is called out, because its pumps can pump water from flooded buildings. Sometimes cats climb very high trees, and go so high that they are afraid to come down. Again, firemen are called to the rescue.

Many fires happen because people are careless. A match carelessly thrown in a wood can destroy thousands of trees. A cinder falling from an open fire-place can set fire to a house.

If we are careful, we can save ourselves—and the firemen—much trouble.

Andrew Scotland: *A Junior Panorama—Book One,* London 1963
By permission of the publishers, Odhams Press Ltd

VOCABULARY. *fire brigade*: company of men for putting out fires — *fire-engine*. machine for throwing water on fires — *swing*: whirl round — *helmet*: protective head-covering worn by soldiers — *amaze*: surprise greatly — *speed*: quickness of moving — *unwind*: draw out at length — *hose*: rubber tubing for carrying water —

pipe: a tube which carries water — *blaze*: burn with a flame — *attempt*: trial or effort — *float*: raft — *mount*: put and fix in position — *airport*: large field where flying machines start and land — *aircraft*: any kind of flying machine — *petrol*: refined petroleum used in motor-car engines — *foam*: froth or bubbles on liquids — *flood*: cover or fill with water — *cinder*: small piece of coal or wood partly burned, not yet ash.

34. A Secret Code Saved His Life

You will know that secret messages are often written in code. Codes have been used for hundreds of years, and some are more difficult to break down than others. Some codes used by governments nowadays are so difficult that teams of experts may spend weeks trying to discover the secret.

Here is the true story of a hidden message written more than three hundred years ago.

The letter

In the English Civil War, Sir John Trevanion was locked up by his enemies in the castle at Colchester. He was kept there under strict guard, awaiting execution by being beheaded. One day a letter was brought to the castle for him. The soldiers who guarded Sir John read the letter very carefully, because their duty was to keep from him any message which might help him to escape. However, they felt sure that this letter was just a kind message from a sorrowful friend, and so a guard took it to Sir John. Here is the letter. Glance through it, but do not trouble to study it as carefully as the guards did.

Worthy Sir John,

Hope, that is the best comfort of the afflicted, cannot much, I fear me, help you now. That I would say to you, is this only, if ever I can repay what I do owe you, stand not upon asking me. 'Tis not much I can do, but what I can do, bee you very sure I will. I know that, if death comes, if ordinary man fears it, it frightens not you, accounting it honour, to have such reward. Pray yet you will be spared this so bitter, cup. I fear not that you will grudge any sufferings. Only if by submission you can turn them away, 'tis the part of a wise man. Tell me, as if you can, to do for you anything you wish. The general goes back on Wednesday.

Resting your servant to command, *R. T.*

A secret code was used in this letter, and when Sir John finished reading it he asked to be taken to the prison chapel. There the guards locked him in, and stood outside the only door, leaving him alone to pray.

But his jailers never saw him again. When a little later on they entered the chapel, Sir John had disappeared.

The message

The code had been arranged months before, and Sir John knew it. It is very simple. Look at every comma and every full stop. Write down the third letter after each comma and full stop. The third letter after the first comma is 'p'. The third letter after the first full stop is 'a', and so on.

You will find that the secret message was this: "Panel at east end of chapel slides." Alone in the chapel, Sir John walked quietly to the east end and found the sliding panel. He opened it. There was a hidden passage.

He bent down and entered. It was dark and narrow. He went slowly along, feeling his way by the damp walls, and suddenly saw sunlight at the other end. He came out into the fresh air among some bushes outside the castle, and hid in the bushes till dusk. Then he got away to join his friends, thanks to the secret code.

Richard Taylor: *Reader's Delight 3*, London 1963
By permission of the publishers, University of London Press Ltd

VOCABULARY. *code*: system of secret writing — *message*: piece of news sent — *break down*: solve; decode, decipher — *expert*: one who is highly skilled — *guard*: watch; (vb) keep safe — *execution*: legal putting to death — *behead*: cut off the head — *sorrowful*: full of grief or sadness — *comfort*: help, relief — *afflicted*: suffering — *account*: consider — *reward*: recompense — *grudge*: feel ill will against — *submission*: surrender — *chapel*: little church — *jailer*: one who has charge of prisoners — *panel*: flat piece of wood let into a wall "Täfelung" — *slide*: slip, move — *bend (bent)*: stoop — *passage*: long and narrow way — *damp*: moist, not thoroughly dry.

35. The Modern Wooden Horse

During the Second World War, some British officers in a prisoner-of-war camp in Germany decided to borrow the idea of the Trojan Horse. They wanted to escape, and this is how they did it.

They made a vaulting horse such as you see in a gymnasium. The top was padded and the framework was strong enough to allow men to vault over it; but the sides were plywood, which made the horse lighter to carry. Every day four men carried the horse out into the open air, and prisoners would line up and exercise themselves by vaulting over it. The German guards thought these British soldiers must be mad to use up their energy in this way. The prison camp food did not exactly build up their strength for gymnastics.

This went on for several days. Once or twice, as if by accident, the horse was knocked over on its side. The guards saw that it was hollow—and empty. The Germans lost interest in the whole business. During the weeks that followed they hardly bothered to watch as the officers vaulted for hours on end.

What the Germans did not know was that they had been tricked. The officers had managed to make them think that the whole affair was harmless, and that the horse was hollow. In fact, after the first few days, when the horse was carried outside *there were men inside it*! When the horse was put down on the ground the men scraped away the top layer of earth from a sheet of plywood which hid a hole they had dug. Then they went down and tunnelled for some hours. When it was time to take the horse indoors again they put back the plywood, and covered it over with earth. Inside the horse they hung bags full of earth they had dug. Then the men, and the bags of earth, were carried back inside a prison hut. Here they got rid of the earth from the tunnel.

In this way they dug a tunnel for about two hundred yards, right under the high barbed-wire fence around the camp. At last they decided the time had come to break through to the surface at the far end of the tunnel. Three men were hidden in the tunnel and the horse taken back indoors. When night came the three brave men broke out of the tunnel into the open air.

They were free! At least, they were free of the prison camp, but many dangers and difficulties lay between them and complete freedom. First of all they had to make their way across Germany, then they had to try to get back to England. But after many adventures they managed to do this. All three men at last got back to their own country. Later one of them, called Eric Williams, wrote about their adventures in a book called *The Wooden Horse.*

A. Elliott-Cannon: *Good Company, Book Three, Wayfaring,* London 1966
By permission of the publishers, Johnston & Bacon Ltd

VOCABULARY. *prisoner-of-war*: captured enemy soldier — *Trojan*: (inhabitant) of Troy — *vaulting horse*: a wooden contrivance for practice in vaulting (*vault*: jump in a single movement, esp. with the aid of the hands) — *pad*: stuff with anything soft — *framework*: part of a structure giving shape and support — *plywood*: a board made up of thin sheets of wood glued together "Sperrholz" — *hollow*: having empty space inside — *on end*: consecutively, without an interval — *scrape*: rub with sth. sharp — *layer*: thickness or covering — *tunnel*: make a tunnel — *hut*: small wooden building — *barbed wire* wire with sharp points — *surface*: outside or top of anything.

36. What do You Think?

A long time ago, three men were travelling in the desert. Each man was making a journey on his own and, as evening was falling, each made his way to an oasis where they met. The three men discovered that they were the only people at the oasis, and they decided to have a meal together.

One traveller had five loaves and another had three loaves. The third traveller said that he had no food at all with him, but he had in his pocket eight pennies. He agreed that if the other two would allow him to share the loaves, he would give them the eight pennies.

This was done and the loaves were shared equally among the three travellers. The man who had five loaves was given five pennies and the man who had three loaves was given three pennies.

Next morning the three travellers made their way to a neighbouring village. As they journeyed along, a quarrel broke out regarding the way in which the money had been divided. The man who had five loaves, and who had received five pennies, said he had not received enough. The man who had three loaves, and wo had received three pennies, said that the division was fair and just.

They could not agree, and the traveller who had given the money said that when they reached the village they should go before a wise man and ask his opinion.

In due course they reached the village and they set out to find the wise man. He considered the problem for a few moments. Then he took the eight pennies and he gave seven pennies to the man who had had the five loaves, and the other penny he gave to the man who had had three loaves.

Do you know why he did this? Try to give the reason before you read the answer.

This is what the wise man said:

"Eight loaves had to be divided equally among three people. Each loaf, therefore, had to be divided into three parts. This meant that there were twenty-four parts altogether.

This meant that each of you had eight parts to eat. The man with five loaves provided fifteen parts altogether. He, himself, had eight parts to eat. Therefore, he gave seven parts to the traveller who had no food. The other man who had three loaves or nine parts, also had eight parts to eat. Therefore he gave one part to the traveller who had no food.

Now, you see how I have divided the money. The seven pennies go to the man who gave seven parts and the one penny to the man who gave one part."

Andrew Scotland: *A Junior Panorama—Book Three*, London 1963
By permission of the publishers, Odhams Press Ltd

VOCABULARY. *desert*: large area of dry waste land, esp. sand-covered — *on one's own*: without a companion — *oasis* (pl. oases): fertile place. with water and trees, in a desert — *loaf*: shaped mass of bread — *share*: divide and distribute — *equal*: of the same size or number — *journey*: travel — *quarrel*: angry dispute — *in due course*: at the right and proper time — *altogether*: completely; wholly — *provide*: give, supply.

37. The Four Ministers

There was once a king who had four wise ministers. He wanted to put a heavy tax on his people, but the ministers advised against it. The king was so angry that he dismissed these wise men and sent them out of the kingdom.

As they were walking away from the city they noticed on the road the tracks of a camel. They were discussing this when a merchant approached them and said he had lost a camel. He asked the ministers if they had seen onc.

One of the ministers then said, "Was your camel lame in one of its hind legs?"

The second minister said, "Was it blind in the right eye?"

The third asked, "Had it a very short tail?"

The fourth asked, "Did it have a pain in its stomach?"

The merchant looked at the ministers in astonishment, and said, "Yes, my camel is just like that. Where did you see it?"

"We have never seen it," they replied, "but we can see its track on the road."

"But you must have seen it," said the merchant. "Indeed, I believe you have found it and sold it. I am going into the city to complain to the king."

This he did and the king recalled his four ministers to punish them for stealing his camel.

"But we never saw this camel," they declared.

"Well," answered the king, "how could you describe it in the way you did?"

The first minister answered. "I noticed there were only three footprints on the track; therefore I guessed the camel was lame in one leg."

The second minister then spoke, "I noticed that the leaves of trees on the left side of the road had been eaten, but leaves on the right side were untouched. It seemed to me that the camel must be blind in the right eye."

Then the third minister spoke, "I noticed faint specks of blood on the track. These seemed to me to come from mosquito bites, so the camel must have a very short tail, otherwise it would have brushed away the mosquitoes."

The fourth minister then spoke. "I noticed," he said, "that the forefeet of the camel were pressed strongly into the ground, but the hind feet scarcely touched it. It seemed to me, therefore, that the camel had a pain in its stomach, and that is why it drew in its hind leg."

Both the merchant and the king listened with astonishment to these explanations. They could not help admiring the wisdom of the four men.

The king decided that he could not do without the advice of such wise men, so he recalled them to his service.

Andrew Scotland: *A Junior Panorama—Book Three,* London 1963
By permission of the publishers, Odhams Press Ltd

VOCABULARY. *tax*: money paid by persons to the government of their country — *advise*: tell a person what you think he ought to do — *dismiss*: send a person from his job — *track*:mark left (e.g. footprints) — *camel*: long-necked animal, with either one or two humps on its back — *lame*: unable to walk normally — *stomach*: part of the body into which the food passes when swallowed — *complain*: say that sth. is wrong — *footprint*: mark of a foot — *untouched*: not the slightest effect being produced on — *faint*: indistinct; not clear — *speck*: small spot — *mosquito*: small flying blood-sucking insect — *bite:* a grasp by the teeth — *brush*: remove by sweeping — *press*: push on; squeeze.

38. A Little Story About a Great Man

In a room in London over two hundred years ago, a famous singer was rehearsing for a concert. The musician who played the harpsichord for his songs was young and unknown. The singer was very conceited and complained of the way the young man played for him. "If you don't play as I tell you," he said, "I will jump on your harpsichord and dance on the pieces."

"Oh," said the musician, "if you decide to do that please let me know. I will advertise it. I am sure people would far sooner see you dance than hear you sing!"

The young accompanist was George Frederick Handel, a German living in London. In time he became a famous composer.

Perhaps you have heard his wonderful *Messiah*, which tells the story of Jesus on the Cross. The words are taken from the Bible. The music is some of the finest in the world, and Handel took only three weeks to write it! You may also have heard his magnificent *Water Music*. This was first played by special command of the King on the River Thames. The King sailed in his Royal Barge. Fifty musicians sailed alongside in another barge, and the rest of the court followed in other barges.

Handel never married, but he loved young people. He gave very large sums of money to care for homeless children.

A. Elliott-Cannon: *Good Company Book Two, Venture Fair*, London 1966
By permission of the publishers, Johnston & Bacon Ltd

VOCABULARY. *rehearse*: practise sth. for public performance — *harpsichord*: piano-like instrument, used from the 16th to the 18th centuries "Clavicembalo, Spinett" — *conceited*: having a high idea of one's self, vain — *complain*: grumble — *advertise*: make known to the public — *accompanist*: one who plays an accompaniment — *Handel*: (1685—1759), German composer; he spent much of his life in England — *barge*: flat-bottomed boat — *alongside*: close to a ship's side.

39. The Bed

Roy loved to buy and better still to pay very little for things. "The best buys," said Roy, "are to be found in the Sale Rooms." Near Roy's school were the Sale Rooms. He often looked in during the dinner hour and at holiday time. The bidding was fun; a shout, a nod of the head, the raising of an arm and somebody came away with a good buy or bargain.

One day he made up his mind that he would buy a bargain. He had a shilling, but what could he get for that? Things to be sold are called 'lots', and lot after lot came up for sale.

Every time Roy started the bidding with his shilling, but every time somebody bid more. The people in the sale room smiled at him. Then a four-poster bed was brought in. It was a big bed with four tall posts of dark oak, a red velvet top and red curtains. There was a hush.

"Now," said the Auctioneer, "what am I bid for this lovely four-poster bed?"

"One shilling," said Roy.

There was silence.

"One shilling I am bid," said the Auctioneer. "Going! Going! Gone! Gone to the lad there in the school cap."

Roy's eyes lit up with pride. That lovely big bed was his. His for a shilling. What a bargain!

When the bed was delivered, his mother was rather cross. It was so big! After a week of having the huge, red bed filling the house, Mother said it must go.

Roy tried to sell it through the local paper, but no one, it seemed, wanted a four-poster-bed. There were no replies. Dad took an axe and chopped it up.

Then the letters began to come. About twenty people wanted the bed, and one person even offered £ 10 for it. Roy said, "There, I told you so," and Dad said, "How was I to know there were so many silly people wanting a four-poster-bed?"

Roy still goes to the sale rooms, but "Please, Roy," says Mother, "not another bed."

Meade Charlton & Zimmerman: *Panorama Book 1*, Edinburgh 1966
By permission of the publishers, Holmes McDougall Ltd

VOCABULARY. *buy*: a purchase — *sale*: occasion when goods are offered for sale by auction — *bidding*: offering a price at a sale — *bargain*: sth. bought cheaply — *bid*: (past tense and p. p. always *bid*) make an offer of money — *four-poster bed*: old-fashioned bed with four posts supporting curtains "Himmelbett" — *oak*: well-known forest-tree, with hard wood — *velvet*: cloth made from silk, with a thick, soft surface — *hush:* silence — *Going! Going Gone!*: (used at an auction to announce that the bidding is almost closed, and that it is closed) — *pride*: feeling of satisfaction, self-respect — *deliver*: hand over — *cross*: sulky — *chop*: cut by giving blows to.

40. Greyfriars Bobby

A little way up the hill from the Grassmarket in Edinburgh is the churchyard of Greyfriars. On a visit to Edinburgh the Baroness Burdett-Coutts heard of a little dog who lived in Greyfriars churchyard. Off she went to have a look at him.

On a grave in the churchyard sat a little Skye terrier. He wagged his tail when she went up to him. This was Greyfriars Bobby, and he was always pleased to see visitors. The story the Baroness had heard about him was a sad one.

Bobby had belonged to an old farmer. When the old man died and was buried at Greyfriars, Bobby had refused to leave his grave. He just made his home there, in the green turf that covered the best friend he had ever had.

The old farmer had been used to going into a nearby inn every day at one o'clock for a drink and something to eat. When this happened Bobby was always given a bun to eat all by himself. After the old man's death Bobby only left the grave once every day. At one o'clock exactly, as the city clocks were striking, the little dog walked into the inn. He stood there wagging his tail and looking at the innkeeper.

"Bless my soul!" declared the innkeeper the first time this happened. "The old farmer's dog has come in for his bun, just as if the old man was still alive."

The old man fed Bobby that day, and every other day after that. Other people fed him too. The children made a special pet of him and visited him in the churchyard to play with him and feed him. He had other friends too. Sergeant Scott, a soldier from Edinburgh Castle, used to buy him a steak once a week.

Now there was a rule in the city that homeless dogs had to be put to death. Bobby was caught and taken away. The children were heart-broken. They went in a body to the City Chambers and demanded to see the Lord Mayor, who in Edinburgh is called a Provost. When he heard their tale the Provost felt he must do something to save Bobby.

"Well, children," he said. "The rule is that homeless dogs must be put to death. Bobby is homeless. But it seems to me that he is something in the nature of a very special citizen! I'll tell you what I'll do. I'll ask the City Council to give him the freedom of the city. Then he will belong to all the people of Edinburgh."

So it was arranged. That is why, when the Baroness went to make friends with Bobby in the churchyard, she found him with a brass plate on his collar, reading,

GREYFRIARS BOBBY
FROM THE LORD PROVOST

A. Elliott-Cannon: *Good Company, Book Two, Venture Fair*, London 1966
By permission of the publishers, Johnston & Bacon Ltd

VOCABULARY. *churchyard*: burial-ground round a church — *baroness*: wife of a baron — *Burdett-Coutts*: Rt. Hon. Angela Georgina, Baroness, inherited the wealth of her grandfather, a banker (Thomas Coutts), which she devoted to all manner of philanthropic as well as patriotic objects — *Skye (terrier)*: small long-bodied short-legged long-haired variety of Scotch terrier — *wag*: move from side to side — *bury*: place a dead body in the ground — *turf*: short grass and the soil below it — *bun*: kind of cake — *bless my soul*: (colloq.) exclamation expressing surprise — *sergeant:* rank in the army above corporal "Feldwebel" — *provost*: (in Scotland) leading magistrate of a town, the mayor — *City Council*: body of persons who govern a city — *freedom*: honour giving certain rights connected with a city — *arrange*: put in order, settle — *brass*: metal made by mixing copper and zinc — *plate*: flat piece of metal — *collar*: band of leather put round the neck of a dog.

41. The Wise Horse

Through the intense tropical heat of midday the horseman made his way down a deep wooded valley. This was South America, and the traveller had not seen a white man for days. He had two horses with him. He rode the first one, and the second horse carried his baggage. The three of them had already covered some thousands of miles on their journey. They had set off from the extreme south of South America and were riding northwards all the way to the United States. It was a dangerous journey no one had ever attempted before.

At the moment the horses were picking their way carefully through deep mud. There were no proper roads, and often the valleys they passed through were just like rivers of mud. They had to go very carefully indeed. They had to be on the look-out for mud holes. These were of course deep and dangerous. Once a horse and rider went into a mud hole they seldom came out again. It was like riding into quicksand. It was a trap from which there was no escape. The mud sucked both horse and rider down into the depths.

The rider was dozing a little. He was tired and he was hot. Suddenly his horse came to a stop. The rider woke up and urged him to go on. The horse refused. The man could see no danger ahead. There were no mud holes as far as he could see. He decided that the horse was just being awkward. So he began to use his spurs to make it go forward.

At that moment another man appeared on the scene. He was an old Indian, and he forced his way through the trees shouting something. When he came up to the horseman, breathlessly he told him in Spanish that he stood on the edge of a very deep mud hole. His horse had known it was there, although no eye could see it. He had saved his own life, and his owner's, by refusing to go forward.

As the horseman said later, "How did the horse sense the danger? There were none of these mud holes in the country where he had been brought up."

The horseman was called Tschiffely. After teaching in England for some time he went to live in South America. He wrote an exciting book about his famous journey on horseback.

A. Elliott-Cannon: *Good Company, Book Two, Venture Fair,* London 1966
By permission of the publishers, Johnston & Bacon Ltd

VOCABULARY. *intense*: high in degree; strong — *baggage*: luggage — *cover*: travel (a distance) — *attempt*: try — *mud*: wet soft earth — *hole*: opening; hollow or empty place — *quicksand*: loose, wet sand sinking under the feet "Treibsand" — *suck:* draw in — *depth*: deepness, deep place — *urge*: drive on — *awkward*: difficult to deal with — *spur*: instrument fitted to the heel of a rider's boot to make a horse go on — *sense*: feel — *bring up*: rear, train — *excite*: stir up the feelings.

42. Pete and His Pal

"I won't be long, Mum," Pete called to his mother. "I am just going down to the river to see if the ice is thick enough for skating."

"Be careful, son," Mrs. Moore replied from the kitchen. "It will not be strong enough to bear you yet."

"All right, Mum, don't worry," answered Pete as he took Spot's collar from the hook by the door. Spot jumped with delight and barked wildly. "Keep still, silly, let me fasten it on you," said Pete.

Together the two friends ran down the street. When they reached the lane that led to the river, Pete slipped off the lead and Spot, barking with delight, raced across the field.

Pete joined his friends on the river bank. They were looking at the ice, wondering if it would bear them. "Another night's frost like last night's," said Bill, "and it will be safe."

Spot ran here and there, scrambling up the bank and back again. Two swans skimmed down the river and landed in an open patch of water in the middle. Spot barked excitedly at them and then rushed across the ice.

"Spot, Spot, come here you fool!" shouted Pete. "You'll fall in." But Spot was deaf to his master's warning; he wanted to chase the swans. He tried to stop, but he started to slide. There was a yelp and he shot into the water. His face appeared over the edge of the ice and he looked a sad sight with his paws on the ice and his black and white head just over the edge. Time after time he tried to scramble onto the ice, but his paws slipped or the ice broke. Under he went again and again.

Pete stripped off his heavy clothes and carefully walked onto the ice; slowly he made his way across. There was a crack like a pistol shot, a long black line appeared on the ice and splash, Pete was in the icy water. He came up and began to smash a way through the crack he had made in the ice towards his dog.

He had gone about twenty yards towards the struggling dog when Spot managed to get a grip on the ice and to pull himself onto it. With a quick shake he ran towards the bank, where Bill held him firmly by the collar.

A crowd collected and watched Pete swim back. Shivering, and with arms and hands bleeding where the ice had gashed them, he slowly made his way to the bank, the crowd cheering as he did so. Many hands helped him out of the water and up the bank. Spot jerked himself out of Bill's grasp and jumped up at his master, licking his face and barking wildly. Quickly Pete dressed and together they ran home.

A hot bath and a rub down for both of them and the friends were no worse for their unwanted dip.

"You stupid boy," grumbled his mother, "you might have been drowned."

"But, Mum, how could I have gone rowing on the river again knowing that Spot had been drowned there?" said Pete, as he hugged his pal.

Meade Charlton & Zimmerman: *Panorama Book 1*, Edinburgh 1966

VOCABULARY. *the Great Ouse (or: Ouze)* [u:z]: river (Norfolk) — *skate*: moving on a pair of sharp-edged steel blades fastened to boots (over ice) — *collar*: sth. worn round the neck — *lane*: narrow road — *slip off*: pull off quickly — *lead*: strap (for leading a dog) — *scramble*: wriggle along, crawl — *skim*: move swiftly along the surface of sth. — *patch*: small area — *slide*: move smoothly over — *yelp*: sharp bark of a dog — *paw*: foot of an animal having claws — *crack*: sudden sharp noise

— *splash*: noise made by sth. falling into a liquid — *smash*: break into pieces; force a way — *crack*: slight break — *grip*: firm hold — *shake*: moving quickly and violently — *shiver*: tremble — *gash*: make a long, deep cut or wound — *jerk*: throw quickly — *grasp*: hand-grip — *dip*: short bathe — *grumble*: utter complaint or protest — *hug*: put the arms round tightly — *pal*: (colloq.) comrade; friend.

43. A Wonderful Dolphin

The dolphin is one of the most interesting creatures that swim in the oceans of the world. It is a large animal, and varies from six to twelve feet in length. It not only swims through the water, but it leaps above the surface, often to a height of twenty to thirty feet.

Through the ages, people have been interested in dolphins. Some believed that they were fond of music. In recent times scientists have studied the dolphin and have shown that it is a very intelligent creature. It can be trained to perform unusual tricks.

For many years a dolphin called Pelorus Jack swam in the waters of Pelorus Sound, in New Zealand. He used to leap out from a place near the shore whenever he saw a steamship. He would swim ahead of the ship and guide it through the narrow passage of the sound. This dolphin became world famous. He seemed to enjoy acting as a pilot in these dangerous waters. He rolled and leaped through the water, and as soon as the ship neared safety, he swam back to his hiding-place.

Once he swam so near the prow of a ship that he was struck by it. For nine months he was not seen. Then, when his wound had healed, he appeared again and continued to guide the ships in the sound. After this incident, he was very careful not to swim too close to any ship that he was guiding.

This wonderful dolphin carried on his work between 1890 and 1914. It is hard to believe, but it is true, that certain people tried to shoot Pelorus Jack. One wonders what kind of people could do this to so interesting and friendly a creature. The New Zealand Government had to pass a law to protect him. This must be the only time that a single animal has ever had a law all to himself!

It is not known what happened to him after 1914. The First World War broke out in that year and lasted until 1918. During that time people very naturally were concerned with what was happening on the battlefields rather than with the fate of a dolphin in Pelorus Sound. Perhaps he died from old age. Perhaps he was run down by a ship.

Although he is no more, the memory of the remarkable dolphin lives on. He was friendly and intelligent, and in a sense he spent his life in the service of mankind. He made the dangerous waters of Pelorus Sound safer for the sailors who passed through it.

Andrew Scotland: *A Junior Panorama—Book Three,* London 1963
By permission of the publishers, Odhams Press Ltd

VOCABULARY. *dolphin*: sea animal like a small whale — *vary*: be different — *scientist*: one who studies in a branch of knowledge — *sound*: narrow strip of water joining two larger areas of water "Sund, Meerenge" — *passage*: long and narrow way — *hiding-place*: place where sb. is hidden — *prow* [prau]: fore-part of a ship — *heal*: become healthy — *concerned with*: interested in — *memory*: recollection — *mankind*: the human race.

44. The Bear Who Stayed at Home

In the far north there was once an old lady who lived in a farmhouse which was sheltered by a forest. One day when she was walking in the forest she came across a baby bear, half dead with cold and hunger. She took him home and nursed him back to health and strength.

The bear grew up to be a friend of the family. A kennel was made for him, and he used to live in it, just as a dog does. He ate the same food as the farm dogs, and often they would eat from the same plate. Bears are very fond of fruit and this little bear liked to eat apples.

Whenever he did anything naughty his mistress usually punished him by giving him a tap on the nose and chaining him up. After the punishment he was usually given an apple, and sometimes a lump of honey. He was so lovable that it was impossible to be angry with him for any length of time.

Every Sunday the old lady went for a walk in the forest. She never took the bear with her because she was afraid that he might attack other animals. She always chained him up before she set off for her walk. When she returned, she took the chain off and, if he had been good, she gave him an apple.

One Sunday afternoon the lady prepared to go for her usual walk. She chained up the bear, told him to be good while she was away, and promised him an apple when she returned. She said goodbye to him and set off on her walk. When she was half-way through the forest she heard the crackle of a branch. Se turned round, and found that a bear was ambling along behind her.

She was very angry. She thought her bear must have broken loose and followed her into the forest. In her hand she had a walking stick, so she thumped the bear severely on the nose. "Go home, you bad bear." But the bear stayed where he was and growled loudly.

Then the old lady saw something which made her even more angry. She noticed that he had no collar round his neck. She had recently bought the bear a new collar, and he must have lost it already. Once again, she hit him on the nose with her walking stick, and this time she hit so hard that the stick broke in half. The bear shook his head angrily, and opened his large mouth, as though he wanted to say something.

"Get back home. Get back home, you naughty bear," the old lady exclaimed.

At this, the bear turned round and ambled away, looking back from time to time at the old lady.

When she returned home that afternoon she found the bear sitting in his usual place outside his kennel. She was very angry, and she went up to him and said, "You will not have an apple for your supper tonight."

One of the servants who heard this came rushing out of the kitchen. "Why are you angry with him," she said. "He has sat here outside his kennel, waiting patiently for you to come back."

The old lady looked at the servant in astonishment. "But I thought. . . ." She never finished the sentence. She suddenly realised that the bear which she had met in the forest, and which she had hit with her stick, must have been another bear!

Andrew Scotland: *A Junior Panorama—Book Two,* London 1963
By permission of the publishers, Odhams Press Ltd

VOCABULARY. *shelter*: give protection to — *kennel*: house for dogs — *tap*: quick light blow — *chain*: fasten with a chain (*chain* = number of rings or links going through one another to make a line — *lump*: shapeless mass — *crackle*: make sharp sudden sounds — *loose*: free, unbound — *thump*: beat heavily — *growl*: make a low threatening sound — *collar*: band of leather put round the neck — *exclaim*: shout out — *realise*: understand completely.

45. Gulls to the Rescue

This story is about something that really happened many years ago.

A brave little company of people crossed the plains of North America in big covered waggons with many horses, and finally managed to climb to the top of the Rocky Mountains, and down again on the other side into a green valley.

The people decided to settle there and so built themselves huts and cabins for the winter.

It had taken them several months to make the terrible journey. Many had died of weariness and illness on the way. The food they had brought in their waggons was nearly finished, and by the time spring had come, they were forced to live on roots dug from the ground.

Their lives now depended on the crops of corn and vegetables which they had sown in the valley.

In good time the seeds sprouted, and the dry brown earth was covered with a carpet of green, growing crops.

Then a terrible thing happened. One day, the men who were watering the crops saw a great army of insects swarming over the ground at the edge of the fields nearest the mountains. These insects were crickets, and they were hopping from the stony places into the fields. Worst of all, it was seen that crickets were eating the young green shoots and leaves. More came, and more, and even more, and as they came, they spread out till they covered a large part of the corn field.

The men rushed forward and tried to kill the crickets by stamping on them and beating them with sticks, but the numbers were so great that it was useless.

Tired and weary, the men went to tell the terrible news and all the village came out to help. They made fires; they dug trenches and filled them with water; but it was all in vain. When the people fought the crickets in one place, new armies of insects attacked the fields in other places.

The people cried in despair. A few knelt to pray. They saw that it would mean starvation and death. Others gathered round them and joined them, weeping. Soon everyone was kneeling in the fields, and praying to be rid of the crickets.

Suddenly from far off came the sound of flapping wings. It grew louder and louder. Some of the people looked up in surprise. They saw, like a white cloud rising from the lake, a huge flock of seagulls flying towards them. Snow-white in the sun, with great wings beating, they came in hundreds and hundreds.

"Oh! woe! woe!" cried the people. "The gulls are joining the crickets and are eating the crops! The crops will be ruined!" All at once, someone called out, —

"No, no! Look! The gulls are eating the insects! They are *not* eating the crops! They are eating *only* the crickets!"

It was true. The gulls devoured the crickets in dozens, in hundreds, in swarms. They ate until they could eat no more and then flew heavily back to the lake. When at last they finished, they had cleared the fields of the army of insects, and thus the people were saved.

To this day, in the city of Salt Lake, which grew out of that village, children are taught to love the seagulls. When they learn to draw and paint in the schools, their first picture is often that of a cricket and a gull.

Angus Maciver: *Reader Book C*, Glasgow, 1957
By permission of the publishers, Robert Gibson & Sons Ltd

VOCABULARY. *gull*: large sea-bird — *root*: that part of a plant that is normally in the soil — *sow* (sowed, sown): put seed in the ground — *seed*: grain or nut from which a new plant may be grown — *sprout*: to begin to grow — *hop*: to leap on one leg or both — *shoot*: new young growth on a plant or bush — *stamp*: put one's foot down with force — *trench*: ditch dug in the ground — *kneel* (knelt): go down on the knees — *starvation*: suffering or death caused by lack of food — *flap*: move up and down or from side to side — *woe*: bitter grief, distress — *devour*: eat greedily or hungrily.

46. LIVINGSTONE AND THE LION

David Livingstone reached Port Elizabeth (South Africa) on 19th May, 1841, and set out overland for the mission station at Kuruman, on the high plateau of Bechuanaland. It was a journey of 700 miles. Livingstone travelled by ox-cart over rough trails through wild country. The journey took him two and a half months.

For eleven years, Livingstone worked as a medical missionary in the country to the north of Kuruman. It is a hot, dry, monotonous region.

In August 1843, he began to build a new mission station in the village of Mabostc, two hundred miles from Kuruman. The natives there were living in fear of a pride of lions. "If you kill one lion, the rest will go away," said Livingstone. He led a party of natives armed with spears to find the lions. Livingstone was armed with a gun. When they came upon a lion, he fired both barrels of his gun at it. "He is shot! He is shot!" cried the natives.

Livingstone saw that the lion was only wounded. "Stop, till I load again," he called. As he did so, the wounded beast sprang at him. He fell to the ground with its great jaws fastened on his shoulder.

The village schoolmaster, Mebalwe, had an ancient flintlock musket. He ran up and fired two shots at the lion. It turned away from Livingstone to attack this new enemy. It sank its teeth into Mebalwe's leg.

Another native ran forward and flung his spear at the lion. Again it turned to meet the new enemy and seized him by the shoulder. Then suddenly its eyes glazed over and it fell in a heap. The wounds received from Livingstone's shots had finally killed it.

All three men were badly hurt, but all of them recovered in time. Livingstone's left arm was torn and crushed. He had to return to Kuruman for treatment. Five months later he was fit to resume work, but his arm was never completely well again.

Robert J. Hoare: *To the Ends of the Earth,* London 1966
By permission of the publishers, Ginn & Co Ltd

VOCABULARY. *plateau*: broad level stretch of high land — *Bechuanaland*: S. W. Africa; stretches from Orange R. to Zambesi R., and merges westward into the Kalahari desert — *cart*: vehicle drawn by a horse or an ox — *trail*: pathway (e.g. through a jungle) — *missionary*: person sent to preach his religion — *monotonous*: dull, unchanging — *native*: person born in a certain country — *pride*: group of certain animals together — *spear*: long weapon, with an iron point — *barrel*: metal tube of a gun — *load*: charge a gun — *jaws*: mouth, including the jaw-bones and teeth — *fasten*: fix firmly — *flint-lock musket*: old kind of gun, in which the powder was exploded by a spark from a very hard stone — *fling* (flung): throw, cast — *seize*: grasp — *glaze*: become glassy in appearance — *heap*: mass of material, things — *recover*: become well again — *crush*: press together with force so as to injure — *treatment*: way of giving medical care — *resume*: begin again.

47. Is This Man's Deadliest Enemy?

Billy's father worked for an oil company in the Middle East. One day, Billy was standing with his father on the edge of a large field. It was a sunny day, and the field was green with growing grain.

Far off, on the horizon, Billy saw a small cloud, dark, and moving fast. As it came nearer it grew bigger. Soon the sun was blotted out, and the air was filled with the sound of a deep humming. The cloud was a swarm of locusts.

For a few moments it was almost dark, and Billy was frightened. His father said, "There is no need for alarm. They will not attack us. But watch this terrible thing."

Suddenly the whole swarm settled on the field. The sun shone, and it was light again. But now the field was no longer green. It was brown, and the whole of it seemed to be moving, covered with brown locusts.

After a little time, some of the locusts rose into the air. More and more went up, until once more the dark cloud covered the sun. Then the swarm flew on, and it was light again. Billy looked up at the swarm, and watched as it grew smaller and smaller, until it disappeared over the horizon.

"Come," said his father, "let's see what is left." Together they walked on to what had been a lovely field of green grain a short time before. There was nothing left. The locusts had eaten everything, the grain, the leaves, the stalks, right down to the bare earth. It was no longer a field. It was just a piece of desert.

The locust flies like an aircraft. The inner wings vibrate and act like a propeller. The jaws of a locust are tiny, but very powerful. A swarm can do more damage than any other living thing.

The locust is a kind of grasshopper. He is very much like an ordinary English grasshopper, but bigger and stronger. When there is not enough food to support these grasshoppers, they band together and fly off in search of food. Then they are called locusts. For thousands of years locusts have destroyed the food of millions of people. They were one of the ten plagues of Egypt.

In a large swarm there may be 500 million locusts. Swarms are found hundreds of miles from their breeding grounds. One swarm was seen out at sea, 1000 miles from the nearest land. They can cross mountains. One swarm flew over a range of mountains 15 000 feet high. The locusts will destroy every green and growing thing over hundreds of thousands of square miles.

Men are working hard trying to keep the locusts down. They fly aircraft over the breeding grounds, spraying deadly poison. Locusts are killed by the ton. But the rest go on breeding. When spring comes, so do the locusts, man's deadliest enemy.

Richard Taylor: *Reader's Delight 3*, London 1963
By permission of the publishers, University of London Press Ltd

VOCABULARY. *deadly*: causing fatal injury; implacable — *cloud*: mass of water-vapour floating above the earth — *blot out*: wipe away — *hum*: make a buzzing sound like that of bees — *locust*: insect like the grasshopper — *stalk*: stem of a plant — *bare*: naked — *desert*: stretch of barren country, usually hot, dry, and sandy — *aircraft*: flying-machines — *wing*: part of an insect by means of which it flies — *vibrate*: shake, tremble — *jaws*: the mouth, its bones and teeth — *damage*: hurt, injury, loss — *grasshopper*: jumping insect — *support*: provide food — *band*:

join together — *plague*: cause of trouble or disaster — *Egypt*: republic, N. E. Africa; capital: Cairo — *breeding*: producing young — *range*: row — *spray*: scatter liquid on — *poison*: sth. which kills or harms — *ton*: measure of weight, 2240 lbs. in Gt. Britain.

48. Two Clever Birds

It was early spring and the plover, who was just over a year old, was performing like a wonderful acrobat.

One day, a boy named John came into the meadow. The plover, who was keeping a sharp look-out while the hen-bird was sitting on the eggs, rose quickly into the air and began to fly about wildly. His mate knew what this meant and, slipping quietly off her eggs, she ran along the ground away from the nest before she too rose into the air.

John searched all over the meadow, but he did not find her, because the nest was very cleverly hidden and the eggs were almost the same colour as the grass.

With a wave of his hand to the two plovers the boy went off down the road. When they were quite sure that he had gone away, they flew down to the ground. When they reached home, the hen-bird at once sat on her eggs.

About an hour or so afterwards, the plover again rose quickly into the air and flew about wildly. This time the danger was much greater than before, because it was their old enemy, the cat. The hen-bird had no chance to slip quietly off her eggs for pussy was too near and would spy the nest. The plover tried to defend his mate and her eggs by flying this way and that, as close to the cat as he could safely go. Pussy was not afraid, however, and each time the bird came near, she crouched ready to spring.

As the cat approached the nest, the birds tried another trick. The hen-bird suddenly rose from her eggs and fluttered towards a nearby stream. She pretended that she was hurt, and it looked as if one of her wings was broken. Pussy ran after her and expected to catch her quite easily. Suddenly the cat made a wild spring at the bird, but the plover dodged to one side and flew away.

Plop! Poor old Pussy landed right in the middle of the muddy stream. Cats are not fond of water and they hate wet sticky mud. In a terrible rage she struggled to the bank and then ran home as quickly as she could. The two birds followed her for part of the way and shouted "Pee-wee! Pee- wee!" as if they were laughing at her.

Back again went the plovers to their nest and, I'm glad to say, they were left in peace. Then one fine day the eggs broke, and out of the shells came four little fluffy chicks. For the first week or so, the tiny birds ran after their parents, who fed them on little worms, spiders, and flies. When they were about seven weeks old, the young ones flew away because they were then fully grown and able to look after themselves.

Angus Maciver: *Reader—Book C*, Glasgow 1957
By permission of the publishers, Robert Gibson & Sons Ltd

VOCABULARY. *plover*: sorts of bird living on marshy ground "Kiebitz" — *perform*: act, play etc. before an audience — *mate*: one of a pair of birds — *slip*: move quickly, get away — *spy*: to watch secretly — *crouch*: bend close to the ground — *flutter*: move the wings hurriedly and irregularly in short flights only — *pretend*: to give as false reason, to act falsely — *dodge*: to start aside "ausweichen" — *mud*: wet soft earth — *sticky*: clinging closely like glue etc. — *shell*: a hard outer covering — *fluffy*: covered with soft, woolly feathers — *chick, chicken*: the young of fowls — *tiny*: very small — *spider*: a small animal with eight long legs that spins a web — *fly*: small winged insect.

49. The King and I

The steamer from Singapore dropped anchor at Bangkok. A white woman leaned on the ship's rails, her small son beside her, looking at the towering walls of the magnificent palace where the King of Siam lived. The year was 1862, and the woman was Anna Leonowens. She had come to take up a post as governess to the royal family.

"I have sixty-seven children," said the King proudly, when he met her. "You shall teach them."

He was a thin little man clad in cloth of gold. He sat cross-legged on his throne like a golden grasshopper, with his glittering eyes fixed on the slender young Englishwoman who stood before him. He was a tyrant, lord of life and death in Burma. He was evil and cruel, and expected his slightest wish to be obeyed.

Anna was introduced to him in the great audience chamber. A crowd of noblemen and servants crouched on the floor on all fours, their heads down so that they were not looking at the face of the King. Anna curtsied and tried to balance herself in a crouching position to indicate respect.

"How old are you?" demanded the King loudly.

Anna was a woman of spirit. She had no intention of proclaiming her age before so many people. A woman's age was her own business!

"I am one hundred and fifty years old, Sire," she said.

"In what year were you born?" snapped the King.

"In 1712, your majesty," she said boldly.

Instead of being angry, the King was delighted at her reply. In all her dealings with him Anna found it paid to be bold and resolute. She had many battles with him. Some she lost: some she won. She tried to get him to spare the life of a sixteen-year-old princess whom he had condemned to death. He promised to do so, then changed his mind and had the girl tortured and executed outside Anna's window, just to show her that he was all-powerful and could do as he liked.

On another occasion, however, he listened to Anna's pleading. Anna, on foot in the town one day, chanced to take the wrong turning. At length she found herself in a paved courtyard where a woman was sitting chained to the ground. She was nursing a small child. She was filthy, ill, helpless, and hopeless. Talking to her, Anna learned her story.

She was called L'Ore and had been a slave; but a rich Indian merchant had seen her, fallen in love with her, bought her freedom and married her. But her former mistress was an evil woman. She had the young woman kidnapped and brought to her house again. Then she was chained in the courtyard. Her child had been born, but still she was chained. She had been kept there like an animal for four years.

At once Anna went to the King. She found him in a good mood and he took steps to free L'Ore. The former slave was restored to her overjoyed husband. Their son had been called Sorrow, but they now changed his name to Free. Because of this and other similar acts of Christian charity, Anna was called White Angel by the people.

Eventually Mrs. Leonowens returned home to England. The King died soon afterwards. Although she had sometimes made him listen to her he died as he had lived, a cruel and heartless tyrant. But Anna's teachings had had some influence in Siam all the same. The new King was one of her former pupils. He reigned for almost thirty years, wisely and kindly. He built hospitals and schools all over the country. He did his best to abolish slavery. He brought about great reforms. When he visited London he met Anna again, and told her that he based his work on her teaching when he was a small boy.

The famous musical play *The King and I* is about Anna's life in Siam.

A. Elliott-Cannon: *Good Company, Book Four, Old and New,* London 1966
By permission of the publishers, Johnston & Bacon Ltd

VOCABULARY. *drop anchor*: lower the anchor — *rail*: wood or metal bar or number of such bars placed as barrier — *Siam* ['saiæm]: kingdom (capital Bangkok) in S.E. Asia, now officially named Thailand — *clad:* (old p.p. of *clothe*) dressed — *cross-legged*: with one leg over the other when a person sits — *grasshopper*: jumping insect — *slender*: thin — *crouch*: bend close to the ground — *curtsy*: make a movement of respect by bending the knees — *balance*: keep from falling — *Sire*: ['saiə] title of respect used when addressing a king (old use) — *snap*: speak sharply — *bold*: full of courage — *dealings*: (business) relations — *plead*: beg earnestly — *chance*: happen — *chain*: fasten with a chain — *filthy*: disgustingly dirty — *kidnap*: carry off a human being by force — *mood*: state of a person's feeling — *restore*: give back — *overjoyed*: filled with great joy.

50. Buried Treasure

Throughout the world great treasures from past ages have been discovered. The stories of these discoveries are fascinating.

An interesting story concerns buried treasure in the Antarctic. Just over a hundred years ago, a ship named the *Starry Crown* left Melbourne, in Australia, for London. It carried a ton of gold from the Australian gold fields. The ship never reached London, and it seemed that nothing more would ever be heard of her.

Twenty years later, a ship named *Swordfish* sailed into the Antarctic to catch whales. A gale from the north drove her on to the pack ice. The ice froze round the vessel and the *Swordfish* was gripped fast. There was little food on board and one by one the crew died, until only five remained.

One morning the masts of a ship were seen in the distance. The two ships drifted closer together and the five men on the deck of the *Swordfish* could read the name; it was the *Starry Crown.* The second mate, whose name was Last, and another man struggled across the ice to the *Starry Crown.* They found that all her small boats except one had gone. There was no trace of life on board, yet there was plenty of food which, because of the cold, was in good condition. They discovered also chests full of gold. But food was more important than gold, and they transferred as much of the food as possible to the *Swordfish.* Shortly afterwards the ice began to break up and the *Starry Crown* drifted away out of sight.

The five men were very weak; their ship, the *Swordfish*, was leaking.

Just when all seemed lost, they were noticed by another vessel, which took them back to Australia. Four of the five men died in the rescue ship, but Last made a good recovery.

A few years later, Last went back to sea on a ship called the *Black Dog*. He told his Captain about the *Starry Crown*, and a decision was made to try and find the treasure ship. They reached the position where the treasure ship was last seen when disaster struck the *Black Dog*. It was crushed by the weight of the ice. Most of the crew, who tried to struggle on to an ice floe, were drowned. Only the Captain and Last survived.

Now comes the most remarkable happening of all. The two survivors were left alone in this wilderness of ice when suddenly they saw the masts of a ship. It was the *Starry Crown*. They made their way towards it and soon scrambled on board. They began to make themselves comfortable, for there was still plenty of food to eat and fuel for warmth. They realised that they must spend the winter in the treasure ship, locked in the Antarctic ice. How often they must have looked at the gold, which could not buy them safety!

In the white solitude, the Captain's nerves gave away. He went mad and in a quarrel with Last he was shot. Last, who must have been an extremely tough man, now made a sledge, and he set out with all the provisions he could gather to cross the ice. Wonderful to relate, he was picked up by another ship and taken back to Australia.

Such is the story of the *Starry Crown*. In the frozen wastes of the Antarctic there is a ton of gold, but whether the *Starry Crown* is still embedded in the ice, or whether the gold is at the bottom of the sea, no one knows.

But someone might find this treasure one day.

Andrew Scotland: *A Junior Panorama—Book Four*, London 1963
By permission of the publishers, Odhams Press Ltd

VOCABULARY. *fascinating*: charming; delightful — *bury*: hide in the ground — *Antarctic*: land and sea round the South Pole — *ton*: measure of weight (20 cwt) — *whale*: the largest sea-animal — *gale*: strong wind — *pack-ice*: large area of broken, floating ice in the polar seas — *grip*: take and keep a firm hold of — *drift*: to be carried or driven — *mate*: a ship's officer, next in rank to the captain — *transfer*: remove; hand over — *leak*: let fluid pass in or out — *recovery*: return to health — *crush*: squeeze together; ruin — *(ice) floe*: mass of floating ice on the sea — *scramble*: climb or crawl — *lock*: become fixed and unable to move — *solitude*: lonely place or state — *give way*: break; yield — *sledge, sled*: vehicle with runners used on snow — *tough*: not easily beaten — *embed*: fix firmly in a surrounding mass.

51. Imprisoned in a Lighthouse

It was a tall lighthouse. The light was fixed at the top of a steel tower, sixty or seventy feet above the sea.

In the lighthouse lived Ethel with her mother and father. Ethel's father was of course the lighthouse-keeper. He had to look after the lamp. In those days it burnt oil. So every day he had to fill it and clean it and trim it, to make sure that it gave a good clear light. And every day too he had to wind up the weights of the clock, for it was by means of this clock that the light was kept flashing regularly all through the night. Without the light, ships out at sea would get no warning, and they might be wrecked on the dangerous rocks.

There is one year that Ethel will never forget. It was 1926. That year, March was in an ugly mood. It was wild and stormy. The sea thundered against the rocks on which the lighthouse was built. The wind roared and blew the foam of the angry waves high up the lighthouse tower.

A week went by in this way. But still the storm went on. Every day they were disappointed. On Saturday it grew quieter. This was the chance Ethel's father was waiting for. He decided that it was still too rough to take Ethel. So he took his wife to help him, and left Ethel at home.

He launched the little boat, and bravely he rowed across the still rather rough sea to the mainland.

They wasted no time. At any moment the storm might grow worse again. As soon as they reached land, they ran off to the shops to buy food and coal and oil. Then they hurried back to the boat.

When they got back to the boat, the weather was as bad as ever. The lighthouse-keeper and his wife had to spend the night at the coast-guard station. How sorry they were that they had ever left the lighthouse! How they longed to get back. Poor Ethel was out there alone. And what about the light?

Meanwhile, back in the lighthouse, Ethel had been curled up in the best armchair, reading her book. It was an exciting book, and the afternoon passed quickly. She found that the storm had already got worse—much worse. Then Ethel knew that her parents would not be back that night.

She did not mind very much. But, oh, she was hungry! She would have to eat the stale bread after all. She had eaten half of it, when she suddenly stopped. "Suppose the storm doesn't die down tomorrow?" she said to herself. So she put the rest of the bread back in the cupboard. Then she lit a little oil lamp.

A thought came so suddenly, she almost dropped the lamp. "Lamp? Lamp?" she said to herself. "But what about the big lamp? If Daddy is not here to light it, I shall have to light it."

Quickly Ethel put on her mackintosh and her sou'wester and opened the door. As she put her foot on the first rung of the ladder, the wind nearly blew her off. But she held on tight, and started to climb. At last she reached the platform. There she waited a moment to get her breath back.

There was worse to come. The next ladder was fixed to the outside of the tower. There was nothing to protect her. She had to climb it in the teeth of a roaring gale.

It seemed an awful long way to the top. Would she ever get there? Or would the wind sweep her away into the angry waves far below? Up and up she went, till at last she saw the steel door right in front of her. She tugged at the door with one hand. With the other she clung to the ladder. The door did not open. Again and again she tugged at the door. She would never be able to open the door.

As she clung there, she heard a ship hooting out at sea. Perhaps if she did not light the lamp, the ship would be hurled against the rocks and wrecked. She must open the door. She must light the lamp.

She tugged and tugged till at last it came open. Very tired, but very happy, Ethel climbed into the lamp room. Back on the mainland, her mother and father were looking towards the lighthouse, but it was already too dark to see it. Then suddenly a light flashed through the darkness. Ethel had lit the lamp. Ethel's mother and father felt very proud of their daughter that night.

Next morning the gale was worse than ever. But night came and once more the light flashed bravely across the wild sea. Ethel had done it again.

Another day came, and still the gale raged. Another night came, and once more the light flashed out across the sea. Yet another day came, and still the wind roared and the waves thundered against the rocks. Ethel was getting very, very hungry, and she wanted food. Three nights and three days she had been alone now, watching and waiting.

Then suddenly, just before it began to grow dark again, she saw a boat on the water. At last it was able to come right alongside. Some of the crew jumped out and pulled it up on to the rocks. Her mother and father were home again. There was food and oil and coal. Ethel was safe, and the lamp would be able to go on flashing, giving warning to ships at sea.

Ronald Ridout: *Look Alive*, London 1955

VOCABULARY. *lighthouse*: tower-like building to warn or guide ships — *trim*: make neat and tidy — *wind*: turn or twist — *flash*: shine out suddenly — *to be wrecked*: (of ships) to be destroyed by the sea — *ugly*: unpleasant to look at; threatening — *thunder*: make a noise like thunder — *roar*: make loud, deep sounds as of a lion — *foam*: froth — *disappointed*: sad at not getting what was hoped for — *launch*: set a ship afloat — *mainland*: country or continent without its islands — *coast-guard*: one who acts as a guard along the coast — *long*: desire earnestly — *curl*: roll up — *stale*: no longer fresh — *mackintosh*: waterproof overcoat — *sou'wester*: waterproof hat with a broad flap behind — *rung*: step of a ladder — *tug*: pull hard — *cling*, clung: stick close to — *hoot*: call like an owl — *hurl*: throw with force — *rage*: to be wild and furious — *alongside*: against the side of a pier etc.

52. An Irishman Faces the English Assizes

I was the first to be tried. The proceedings were short and sweet like an ass's gallop.

The stuff had been caught with me, and as a soldier of the Irish Republican Army I refused to recognize the court. The judge asked me if I had anything to say. I delivered my speech which I had off by heart.

After I had said, My lord and gentlemen, it is my privilege and honour and all that effect, he very rudely interrupted me to say, as casually as he could, that he and the jury did not wish to listen to a political speech.

I waited on him to finish and went on with my speech, in a louder voice. I have a sense of humour that would nearly cause me to burst out laughing at a funeral, providing it was not my own, and solemn speeches are not easily made by me. I can't keep it up. But when I'm speaking to ignorant people I will use any and every means to needle them as best I can according to their particular brand of insolence.

So as this judge was in a vicious and not very judicial temper, I decided to put him in a worse one.

"... and this to a proud and intelligent people, who had a language, a literature, when the barbarian woad-painted Britain was first learning to walk upright.

"By famine and massacre you have striven to drive the people of Ireland from off the soil of Ireland, but in seven centuries you have not succeeded.

"Many times have you announced that you had stamped out the rebels, that you had settled the 'Irish Question'.

"But there is but the one settlement to the Irish Question, and until the thirty-two-county Republic of Ireland is once more functioning, Ireland unfree shall never be at peace.

"God save Ireland. No surrender."

The two screws looked at me, and the judge had given up his pretence of boredom, and settled himself to sentence me.

He stated that I had taken advantage of the mildness of British law in regard to the punishment of persons under eighteen. He also expressed his regret that he had to give me the benefit of his mildness, and that he could not sentence me to fourteen years' penal servitude, which he would have, if I had been eighteen years of age. He could only sentence me to three years' Borstal Detention.

I shouted "Up the Republic!" across the court and right into his face, and went down the stairs in good humour, because I had needled the ill-mannered judge into admitting that he was nearly cutting his throat that he couldn't give me fourteen years, and also because I had only got three years.

I got down the stairs, well satisfied with myself that I had given the judge as good as I'd got.

Thousands had marched in mourning all over Ireland and in the United States, but I was the only one privileged to stand up for the cause, openly and defiantly in the midst of our enemies—great as they were, with their money, their Army, Navy, and Air Force, their lions, unicorns, and ermine robes to hide their hangman's overalls.

Brendan Behan: *Borstal Boy*, London 1958
By permission of the publishers, Hutchinson & Co Ltd

VOCABULARY. *assizes*: meetings before the High Court judges — *stuff*: gelignite (Gelatindynamit), detonators (Sprengkapseln) etc. — *casual*: without special purpose — *funeral*: burial — *needle*: irritate — *brand*: special mark — *insolence*: quality of being offensive — *vicious*: evil; cruel — *judicial*: able to decide wisely — *woad*: blue dye got from the *woad-plant* "(Färber)Waid" — *famine*: great shortage of food — *stamp out*: put an end to — *screw*: (sl.) warder; jail guard — *pretence*: false show — *boredom*: weariness — *benefit*: favour — *penal servitude*: imprisonment with hard labour — *Borstal system*: imprisonment for young criminals, based on the *indeterminate* sentence — *cut one's throat*: kill oneself — *mourning*: grief — *defiant*: openly disobedient — *unicorn*: (in old stories) horse-like animal with one long horn in the middle of its forehead — *ermine* ['əːmin]: white fur of stoat "Hermelin" — *hangman*: public servant who hangs criminals.

53. Leaving Hospital in a Coffin

Most people would prefer not to leave hospital in a coffin. Yet Second Lieutenant 'Sandy' Thomas willingly chose this way of leaving the hospital near Athens in which he was recovering from a bad wound in the leg.

During the Second World War the Germans occupied Greece. Then they attacked the island of Crete, which lies south of Greece. The island was defended by Greek and British forces, but they fought in vain against the invasion from the air. In the fighting Lieutenant Thomas, a young New Zealander, was wounded and captured.

He was first taken to a hospital at Corinth and then moved to a hospital for prisoners of war just outside Athens.

While he was there he was invited by another officer to escape by means of a trick. This was the plan: He would pretend to be dead and then would be carried out of the hospital in a coffin. After that he would of course have to come back to life again before the burial took place. There was only one coffin at the hospital and it had to be brought back from the cemetery after each funeral, so there was no real danger of being buried alive.

A young New Zealand doctor signed a certificate stating that Thomas had died of pneumonia. He was covered with a sheet and arrangements were made by the German sergeant for the funeral to take place the same afternoon. As the German soldiers always stayed outside the cemetery when a British prisoner was being buried, it would be easy for Thomas to get out of the grave before it was filled with earth and then, after a time, to escape to Turkey.

It was bad luck that caused this clever plan to fail. While Thomas was lying beneath the sheet the German doctor who had first attended to his wound at Corinth paid an unexpected visit to the hospital, and naturally came to see the dead body of the young officer he had once tried to save.

Thomas heard him approaching.

"He was a very nice young man," somebody said to the doctor, "and he was only just twenty-one."

The sheet was pulled gently back. Thomas managed to keep absolutely still. The doctor remained silent.

Then, in spite of his closed eyes, Thomas knew that the doctor's hand was slowly approaching his face.

This was more than he could stand. He started to laugh and opened his eyes.

"Mein Gott!" The doctor took a step backward in surprise.

For a moment there was complete silence in the room while every one wondered what the doctor would do. But he had sense of humour. He was amused by Thomas's sudden return to life and he began to roar with laughter. Soon every one in the room was laughing too. Even the German sergeant joined in.

Neither Thomas nor anybody who had helped him was punished.

G. F. Lamb: "A Wounded Officer Escapes at His Fifth Attempt" in *Thrilling Exploits of Modern Adventure,* London
By permission of the publishers, George Harrap & Co Ltd

VOCABULARY. *coffin*: box for a dead body — *Greece*: kingdom, South part of Balkan peninsula — *Crete*: island, east Mediterranean; 60 miles from Greek mainland — *New Zealander*: inhabitant in New Zealand — *pretend*: make believe — *burial*: act of putting a dead body in the ground — *cemetery*: area of ground for burying the dead — *funeral*: burial — *death certificate*: written statement that death has happened — *pneumonia*: disease of the lungs — *sergeant*: rank in the army above corporal "Feldwebel" — *grave*: pit in which to bury the dead — *approach*: come near.

54. All Done by Kindness

Most of us love animals, or at least we will not tolerate cruelty. The circus people understand this very well, and so they spare no trouble in spreading the rumour that their animals are trained by kindness, and they make a display of kindness by rewarding them with titbits during performances. We know that ordinary people by kindness alone can train pet dogs to perform clever tricks, and we are glad to be assured that all this is well. The whip, they say, is only for giving signals to the animals.

But why, then, should all the animals be so obviously afraid of the big leather-thonged whip? And what about the switch so often seen in the trainer's other hand—a short one for dogs, a long one for horses and lions, and a sharp stake for elephants? The helpless rage of the lions and tigers, horses with frightened eyes, and the wonderful obedience of dogs, bears and monkeys show the fear of savage punishment the animals know so well. And what we see in the ring is nothing compared with what goes on behind the scenes in training and practice.

You may wonder how the R. S. P. C. A. can know, since people in the trade will not give one another away. The proof has been brought to light before an inquiry held by a Select Committee appointed by the House of

Commons, and there is no reason to believe that methods have changed since then. Numerous witnesses brought evidence of cruelty in the training and exhibition of all kinds of performing animals. A Report was drawn up stating cruelty was proved as a means used by the trade for speed and reliability in training and for the control of dangerous animals. It contains eight recommendations intended to minimise the cruelty, but only three of them have passed into law, and of these two have been so modified as almost to lose their value.

The R. S. P. C. A. has just cause to distrust all performing animal turns, at least until the law is strengthened. For instance, one recommendation which was not passed by Parliament provided that R. S. P. C. A. Inspectors should have access to places where performing animals are trained, and the opposition of the trade to this recommendation shows that there is something to hide.

From an *R. S. P. C. A. leaflet*

VOCABULARY. *tolerate*: bear, put up with — *reward*: recompense; repay — *tit-bit*: tasty little bit — *perform*: act, do tricks — *performance*: entertainment — *whip*: lash, with a handle, for punishing — *thong*: lash of a whip, narrow strip of leather; vb. provide with a thong — *switch*: thin stick — *stake*: strong stick pointed at one end — *savage*: wild, fierce and cruel — *R. S. P. C. A.*: Royal Society for the Prevention of Cruelty to Animals — *give away*: betray — *appoint*: place in a job — *witness*: one who looks on — *evidence*: facts giving support for sth. — *exhibition*: public show — *recommendation*: good point — *distrust*: have suspicion about — *provide*: declare to be necessary.

55. The Childhood of a Writer

Louisa M. Alcott, who is widely known as the author of *Little Women*, was an unusual child and had an unusual upbringing. She was born in a small town near Philadelphia in 1832. She was the eldest of four sisters, who were all devoted to each other and to their parents. Louisa's father was a teacher who had a natural gift for teaching; but some of his ideas were so unpopular that he was never able to make a good living.

The girls were educated mainly by their father. They were encouraged at a very early age to keep journals, in which they recorded not only daily happenings but also their thoughts. These journals were taken very seriously both by the girls and by their parents. The girls also spent much time in reading and writing, and found great pleasure in acting little plays that they devised for themselves. They had very little to do with other children, and they had no luxuries except books. Nevertheless they seem to have been a happy family.

Louisa herself was a very earnest child. She did not worry about being poor or never having any sweets, but she was sometimes troubled about her conscience. She was taught to think of her mind as a room that needed cleaning. Every Sunday she made an attempt to get rid of the cobwebs, but often she felt that her efforts were unsuccessful. With the help of her parents, however, she persisted in the struggle to overcome her failings and to fill her mind with noble thoughts.

Louisa's father was what some people would call a 'crank'; that is to say, he had strange notions about how people should live. When Louisa was nearly ten, he formed a community of English settlers in Massachusetts. They bought land for fruit-growing, and the idea was that each member of the community should work for the benefit of all.

The life proved to be very hard, and it was made harder for Mrs. Alcott by another of her husband's ideas. He thought it wrong to use anything that could be obtained only by killing or harming living creatures. This meant, according to Mr. Alcott, that the family must not have meat, fish, milk, butter, or cheese, and that none of their clothes could be made of wool. At first he objected also to the use of lamps because only animal oil was available; so the family had to get up at dawn and go to bed at sunset. Finally, however, Mrs. Alcott protested that she must have one lamp in the evening if she was to get the necessary mending done.

Ultimately the community broke up, and the Alcotts moved to a town again. All through Louisa's childhood, however, they continued to struggle against poverty, enjoying little comfort and few friendships. It was only when Louisa proved to be a successful writer that prosperity came to the family.

J. B. Pendelbury: *Fourth-Year English Practice*, London 1966

VOCABULARY. *upbringing*: training and education during childhood — *journal*: daily record of events, esp. a diary — *record*: set down in writing — *luxury*: thing desirable but not indispensable — *conscience*: inward feeling by which we know right from wrong — *cobweb*: spider's web; musty rubbish — *persist*: persevere — *failing*: fault; weakness — *crank*: person with queer ideas "komischer Kauz" — *notion*: idea, whim — *benefit*: profit — *object*: be opposed to — *dawn*: daybreak — *ultimately*: finally, in the end.

56. The Flying Tea Kettle

Frank Whittle was born at Coventry on 1st June, 1907. His father was an engineer who owned a small business of his own. By the time he was ten years old, Frank was helping his father in the workshop. He knew how to drill holes and how to use a lathe. He also knew how to read blue prints and how to use the instruments for drawing these plans of machines.

Frank Whittle had two great interests. One was engineering, and the other was flying. He had been interested in aeroplanes since he was four years old. It was then that his father had bought him his first model aeroplane.

Frank won a scholarship to Leamington College. He was not an outstanding scholar. He never did his homework well. This was because he spent so much of his time reading about aeroplanes. He read all the books on aircraft engineering in Leamington Public Library. He read so many books on how to fly that he felt as if he could climb into an aeroplane and pilot it.

When he was fifteen, Frank tried to join the Royal Air Force. He passed the written examination and went along for a medical examination. The result was a disappointment for him. "Sorry, young man," the doctors said. "You are too small." Frank was only five feet tall. He went home and did exercises for six months. Then he measured himself again. He was five feet three inches tall. So again he applied for a place in the Royal Air Force. Again he was disappointed.

"No one is considered more than once," he was told. "If you are turned down by the R. A. F., there is no second chance."

Frank thought this over for a time. Then he had a bright idea. He would try a third time to join the Royal Air Force, but he would not mention that he had attempted to do so before. So, he sat for the written examination again. Again he passed it, and this time he passed the medical examination, too. At last he was accepted.

No one realized that the young cadet, Frank Whittle, was to change the history of flying. Yet, seventeen years later, as a result of his ideas, a jet-propelled aircraft flew over England for the first time.

By July 1939, Whittle knew enough to set about building a jet engine for use in an aeroplane. The Gloster Aircraft Company were asked to build a suitable aeroplane. The earliest flights of jet aeroplanes caused people to stare up the sky in wonder. The unusual screeching caused the jets to be nicknamed 'Flying Tea Kettles'.

People who said they had seen an aeroplane without a propeller were not at first believed.

Whittle's jet engine was top secret until January 1944. Then the first details of it were made known to the public. Frank Whittle became famous. He had changed the history of flying.

Since the end of the war in 1945, turbo-jet and prop-jet engines have been built for use in airliners. The days of piston-engined aircraft are coming to an end. You are growing up in the jet age, thanks to Sir Frank Whittle. The inventor was knighted in 1948 when he retired from the Royal Air Force.

Robert J. Hoare: *Men, Medicine and Machines*, London 1962
By permission of the publishers, Ginn & Co Ltd

VOCABULARY. *drill*: make (a hole) with a pointed instrument — *lathe*: machine which shapes articles of wood, metal etc. by turning them against cutting edges "Drehbank" — *blue print*: sketch plan of work to be done — *disappointment*: a thing that prevents a plan from being successful — *turn down*: reject; say no to an offer — *attempt*: try — *cadet*: student in air force college — *jet-propelled aircraft*: one driven forward by strong streams of gas directed backwards from it — *screech*: make a harsh piercing sound — *kettle*: metal pot for heating liquids — *turbo jet engine*: having a turbine-driven compressor for supplying compressed air to the combustion chamber — *prop-jet engine*: having a turbine-driven propeller — *airliner*: aeroplane for carrying passengers and mail — *knight*: confer knighthood on (*Sir* before Christian name and surname.)

57. How the Geese Beat Off a Buzzing Buzzard

Indian summer doesn't last very long, and I was not the only one to be taking full advantage of what was left. I lay in a deckchair on the lawn, my dogs at my feet stretched out fast asleep. And in the middle of the paddock basked the goose flock, secure in the knowledge that the ganders Patty and Blandy would protect them from harm.

As a matter of fact, and in strict confidence, Patty and Bandy rely entirely on bluff. But they look so threatening and are so well backed (vocally, that is) by the geese, that their bluff is seldom called.

I used to call it sometimes. When a gander ran at me I would run at him, making hideous noises and waving my arms. Completely dismayed, Patty (or Bandy) would rush for the shelter of the flock. Fearing that this might undermine their authority, I gave it up.

High over the coppice across the little mountain road that served our farm floated a noble buzzard, and I thought that these birds were not unlike geese, relying rather too much on bluff. They look and act nobly until the bluff is called.

There are tales of buzzards ganging up on a weak ewe and stripping it to the bare bones in no time; but I've never seen it happen and don't believe it does. Of all the predators the buzzard is possibly the most harmless, feeding mainly on carrion nowadays with such mice and frogs he can find.

This one was sailing gracefully around on motionless wings and it occurred to me that he too was enjoying the autumn sun. We call this particular bird 'our buzzard' because we fed him in the hard winter of 1963. He now lives in the coppice.

Suddenly he swooped low and without any warning delivered a dummy dive-bomb attack on the somnolent geese. Immediately they awoke vociferously and ran for shelter. This included the two ganders, noticeably in the centre of the flock. But after derisive comment from the geese, they cautiously emerged and struck heroic poses.

The buzzard then buzzed Bandy and took the poor bird quite by surprise. He collected himself and retired to the flock with an indignant honk.

Patty now strode apprehensively out, but alas, next moment he had been well and truly buzzed, retiring in haste to the shelter of the petticoats. The noise became quite deafening.

Down again on silent wings swooped the noble bird. But this time Gully, our oldest goose, belted out at full speed to meet the attack, bouncing like a ball as she strove to get airborne.

I'm not sure whether she nipped the buzzard, but it looked like it, for he retreated at great speed, the flock in full cry behind. But the two gallant ganders were well in the van, leading the ladies by yards.

Why did the buzzard do it in the first place, when he well knew that he couldn't kill a goose? I've long believed that certain animals have a well developed sense of humour. And I think he did it for—how do they say it nowadays?—for a giggle.

Thurlow Craig: "How the Geese Beat Off a Buzzing Buzzard" in *The Sunday Express*
By permission of the publishers

VOCABULARY. *buzz*: move about person, fly very close to — *Indian summer*: period of warm, dry, calm weather in late autumn — *buzzard*: bird of prey — *deckchair*: long chair, used in gardens — *paddock*: small closed-in field — *gander*: male goose — *back*: help, support — *call*: name; cry out — *hideous*: frightful; horrible — *dismay*: terrify — *undermine*: weaken gradually — *coppice*: wood of low-growing trees — *float*: move about freely — *gang up*: join up — *ewe* [ju:]:

female sheep — *strip*: pull off — *predator* ['predətə] robbing animal — *carrion*: rotting animal flesh — *swoop*: come down on with a rush — *dummy*: sham — *somnolent*: sleepy — *vociferous*: loud, noisy — *derisive*: jeering, mocking — *cautious*: watchful — *emerge*: come into view — *strike a pose*: assume an attitude to impress others — *honk*: cry of the wild goose — *stride (strode)*: walk with long steps — *apprehensive*: feeling afraid — *petticoat*: women's under-garment — *deafen*: make unable to hear — *bounce*: jump back when sent against sth. hard — *strive (strove, striven)*: struggle — *nip*: give a small, quick bite — *airborne*: off the ground — *gallant*: brave — *in the van*: amongst the leaders.

58. Mr Fox

(This is a traditional story that was old in Shakespeare's time.)

Lady Mary was young, and Lady Mary was fair. She had two brothers, and more lovers than she could count. But of them all, the bravest and most gallant, was a Mr Fox, whom she met when she was down at her father's country house. No none knew who Mr Fox was, but he was certainly brave, and surely rich, and of all her lovers, Lady Mary cared for him alone. At last it was agreed upon between them that they should be married. Lady Mary asked Mr Fox where they should live, and he described to her his castle, and where it was; but, strange to say, did not ask her or her brothers to come and see it.

So one day, near the wedding-day, when her brothers were out, and Mr Fox was away for a day or two on business, as he said, Lady Mary set out for Mr Fox's castle. And after many searchings, she came at last to it, and a fine strong house it was, with high walls and a deep moat. And when she came up to the gateway she saw written on it:

Be bold, be bold.

But as the gate was open, she went through it, and found no one there. So she went up to the doorway, and over it she found written:

Be bold, be bold, but not too bold.

Still she went on, till she came into the hall, and went up the broad stairs till she came to a door in the gallery, over which was written:

Be bold, be bold, but not too bold,
Lest that your heart's blood should run cold.

But Lady Mary was a brave one, and she opened the door, and what do you think she saw? Why, bodies and skeletons of beautiful young ladies all stained with blood. So Lady Mary thought it was high time to get out of that horrid place, and she closed the door, went through the gallery, and was just going down the stairs, and out of the hall, when who should she see through the window, but Mr Fox dragging a beautiful lady along the gateway to the door, Lady Mary rushed downstairs, and hid herself behind a cask just in time, as Mr Fox came in with the poor young lady who seemed to have fainted. Just as he got near Lady Mary, Mr Fox saw a diamond ring glittering on the finger of the young lady he was dragging, and he tried to pull it off. But it was tightly fixed, and would not come off, so Mr Fox cursed and swore, raised his sword, and brought it down upon the hand of the poor lady. The sword cut off the hand, which jumped into the air, and fell of all places in the world into Lady Mary's lap. Mr Fox looked about a bit, but did not think of looking behind the cask, so at last he went on dragging the young lady up the stairs into the Bloody Chamber.

As soon as she heard him pass through the gallery, Lady Mary crept out of the door, down through the gateway, and ran home as fast as she could.

Now it happened that the very next day the marriage contract of Lady Mary and Mr Fox was to be signed, and there was a splendid breakfast before that. And when Mr Fox was seated at the table opposite Lady Mary, he looked at her. "How pale you are this morning, my dear." "Yes," she said, "I had a bad night's rest last night. I had horrible dreams." "Dreams go by contraries," said Mr Fox; "but tell us your dream, and your sweet voice will make the time pass till the happy hour comes."

"I dreamed," said Lady Mary, "that I went yestermorn to your castle, and I found it in the woods, with high walls, and a deep moat, and over the gateway was written:

Be bold, be bold."

"But it is not so, nor was it so," said Mr Fox.

"And when I came to the doorway over it was written:

Be bold, be bold, but not too bold."

"It is not so, nor was it so," said Mr Fox.

"And then I went upstairs, and came to a gallery, at the end of which was a door on which was written:

Be bold, be bold, but not too bold,
Lest that your heart's blood should run cold."

"It is not so, nor was it so," said Mr Fox.

"And then—and then I opened the door, and the room was filled with bodies and skeletons of poor dead women, all stained with their blood."

"It is not so, nor was it so. And God forbid it should be so," said Mr Fox.

"I then dreamed that I rushed down the gallery, and just as I was going down the stairs, I saw you, Mr Fox, coming up to the hall door, dragging after you a poor young lady, rich and beautiful."

"It is not so, nor was it so. And God forbid it should be so," said Mr Fox.

"I rushed downstairs, just in time to hide myself behind a cask, when you, Mr Fox, came in dragging the young lady by the arm. And, as you passed me, Mr Fox, I thought I saw you try to get off her diamond ring, and when you could not, Mr Fox, it seemed to me in my dream, that you, with your sword, hacked off the poor lady's hand to get the ring."

"It is not so, nor was it so. And God forbid it should be so," said Mr Fox, and was going to say something else as he rose from his seat, when Lady Mary cried out:

"But it is so, and it was so. Here's hand and ring I have to show," and pulled out the lady's hand from her dress, and pointed it straight at Mr Fox.

At once her brothers and her friends drew their swords and cut Mr Fox into a thousand pieces.

Joseph Jacobs: *English Fairy Tales,* London
By permission of the publishers, Frederick Muller Ltd

VOCABULARY. *gallant*: brave; noble; paying great attention to ladies — *wedding*: marriage — *moat*: deep trench round a castle, sometimes filled with water — *gateway*: way through a gate — *gallery*: raised floor extending from inner wall of a hall — *lest that*: (arch.) = lest; in order that ... not — *skeleton*: bony framework of the human body — *stain*: make coloured patches or dirty marks on — *cask*: little barrel — *faint*: become unconscious — *tightly*: fastened firmly — *fix*: make fast or firm — *lap*: front part of legs from knees to body when a person is sitting — *contract*: agreement — *by contraries*: opposite to what is expected — *yestermorn*: (usu.) = yesterday morning — *hack*: cut roughly; chop.

59. Heaven in Your Hand

(This story also is told as a memory of bygone years; it is a study of the feelings of a small girl.)

My mother had a pretty sister, Emily, who had made a very good marriage and lived in a grand big house about ten minutes' walk from the one we occupied. My father had died young, leaving Mother with six of us, the eldest only twelve; and we were beggarly hard up. But the bond between my mother and my aunt was, in its way, pretty strong, and as a consequence I was frequently cast into the company of my cousin Dorothy and spent a good deal of my ninth and tenth years in bitter envy.

I think that my very soul might have become warped but for something which happened on Dorothy's tenth birthday.

It was a perfect June afternoon. The big house was full of flowers, and full of people—girls from Dorothy's school (which was not mine) and their mothers.

What impressed me most was the number of the presents. Dorothy's playroom, where they were all laid out for inspection, looked like a shop. In my foolishness I had thought that Dorothy already possessed everything possible, but money had triumphed and presents had been found. Her mother had given her a little desk and chair for her room. Her father had contributed a new bicycle. Some far-sighted friend had sent a pair of skates. There was a tennis racket. There was writing-paper with a big blue 'D' at the top of each page; there was a fountain pen, and of course many dolls. In all there were sixty presents. All new, expensive and covetable. Sixty of them!

The party drew to its end; a few fathers came and were taken off to have drinks in the study; mothers began to collect their daughters. Dorothy and I found ourselves alone together in the playroom.

You see, I had once had a doll. Her name was Susan and I had adored her. But at least two years ago my little sister had borrowed and dropped her and smashed her pretty china face. I had cried and Mother, busy and worried, had snapped at me, "Fancy crying about a doll! A great girl of eight! You're too big for dolls anyway." I was looking at Dorothy's dolls and thinking my sour thoughts when Aunt Emily came dancing in carrying an enormous white cardboard box. Her eyes were brighter than anybody's; she looked flushed and lovely. She put the box into my hands and kissed me. She smelt like a flower and the kiss was like a butterfly's passing. I felt better and when she asked, "Have you enjoyed yourself, darling?" I was able to say, quite heartily, "Yes, thank you, it was a lovely party." She smiled at me and went and took one of Dorothy's long glossy curls between her fingers.

"To think," she said, "my little girl is ten years old." Dorothy jerked her head free. I stood and stared. I simply could not avoid comparisons. Two years ago I had been a "great girl of eight"; Dorothy, at ten, was "my little girl". I did understand about circumstances, being poor and always too busy and having six children and no husband. Nevertheless . . .

"I think I must go now," I said.

Aunt Emily turned to me with a smile which changed to a look of dismay.

"But darling," she said, "you're ten too. You had your birthday while I was away and I forgot! Oh, I am so sorry!"

She turned to Dorothy who still stood sulking in the window.

"Darling, you've got such masses of things. Wouldn't you like to give her something now?"

My heart froze. The sick feeling came back, worse than ever. My face went hot and stiff. The savage independence which was going to be such a trouble to me later on in life laid hold of me.

"I don't want anything, Aunt Emily, thank you," I said.

"A doll then," she persisted.

She had found my weakness. I did most dreadfully want a doll. Even pride could not make me deny that.

"I . . . would . . . like . . . a doll," I said dragging out the shameful confession.

"Darling," cried Aunt Emily in a tone of delight, "did you hear that? Ennie would like a doll. Which can you spare?"

Twiddling her sash, not turning her head, Dorothy said:

"Any of them. All of them."

Aunt Emily looked a little disconcerted, but she was used to her daughter.

"There you are then," she said to me, "take your choice."

And with that I must needs go proud again. It was damnable of me. For I looked round and deliberately, poisonously, chose the smallest doll there. It was a tiny china doll, no more than three inches long and looked very humble lying between two large dolls.

"I'd like this one," I said.

"But it's such a scrap, almost nothing," Aunt Emily cried. "Have this one, Ennie, or this."

"I like little things," I said, rather sternly. But I made no move to take it. Aunt Emily had to lift it and put it into my hand.

Immediately something happened inside me. As my fingers closed about the little doll's body I experienced that sense of rightness, of completeness, that comes only once or twice in a lifetime. A great flood of happiness broke over my heart, washing away all self-pity, all envy and malice. I knew in a flash that the choice I had made in blind anger was the right, the only one. Anything bigger would have been an embarrassment; the little doll could be carried in my pocket, go with me to school, be tucked under my pillow. No one need know about her; I need share her with no one. She was my doll, made, destined for me.

Perfectly, almost crazily happy, I walked home through the golden June evening, one hand carrying the box of cake, the other curved about the little doll. I saw Dorothy in a new light. With all she had, she was still hungry for more. I had satisfaction here within my bent fingers. And I knew something which, after all these years, still seems to me as true and important as it did then.

Heaven isn't something "that lies about us in our infancy" and then is lost. Heaven is something that you can hold in your hand.

Norah Lofts: "Heaven in Your Hand" in *Good Stories*, ed. W. M. Smyth, London 1964, Edward Arnold Ltd (publishers)
By permission of the Curtis Brown Ltd

VOCABULARY. *beggarly*: fit for a beggar; poor — *hard up*: short of money — *bond*: anything that keeps together — *envy*: feeling of discontent caused by another's good fortune — *warp*: change from the right or natural shape — *skates*: sharp-edged steel blades fastened to boots for moving on the ice — *covetable*: sth. worth desiring greatly — *adore*: love very much — *smash*: break in pieces — *snap*: speak sharply — *sour*: harsh, morose — *cardboard*: thick, stiff material like paper used in making boxes etc. — *flush*: become red, blush — *butterfly*: winged insect with large and beautiful wings — *glossy*: shiny — *curl*: ringlet, e.g. of hair — *jerk*: give a sudden pull or twist — *dismay*: fright or alarm — *sulk*: keep silent because one is displeased — *independence*: unwillingness to be under obligation to others — *persist*: persevere — *drag*: be slow or reluctant to do sth. — *twiddle*: play with — *sash*: band or ribbon worn as an ornament — *poisonous*: harmful because having poison in it — *stern*: unkind; hard — *malice*: ill-will; spite — *tuck*: put away out of sight — *pillow*: cushion for the head — *infancy*: period when one is a very young child.

60. The Breadwinner

The parents of a boy of fourteen were waiting for him to come home with his first week's wages.

The mother had laid the table and was cutting some slices of bread and butter for tea. She was a little woman with a pinched face and a spare body, dressed in a blue blouse and skirt, the front of the skirt covered with a starched white apron. She looked tired and frequently sighed heavily.

The father, sprawling inelegantly in an old armchair by the fireside, legs outstretched, was little too. He had watery blue eyes and a heavy brown moustache, which he sucked occasionally.

These people were plainly poor, for the room, though clean, was meanly furnished, and the thick pieces of bread and butter were the only food on the table.

As she prepared the meal, the woman from time to time looked contemptuously at her husband. He ignored her, raising his eyebrows, humming, or tapping his teeth now and then with his finger-nails, making a pretence of being profoundly bored.

"You'll keep your hands off the money," said the woman, obviously repeating something that she had already said several times before. "I know what'll happen to you if you get hold of it. He'll give it to me. It'll pay the rent and buy us a bit of food, and not go into the till at the nearest public house."

"You shut your mouth," said the man, quietly.

"I'll not shut my mouth!" cried the woman, in a quick burst of anger. "Why should I shut my mouth? You've been boss here for long enough. I put up with it when you were bringing money into the house, but I'll not put up with it now. You're nobody here. *Nobody. I'm* boss and he'll hand the money to me!"

"We'll see about that," said the man, leisurely poking the fire.

Nothing more was said for about five minutes.

Then the boy came in. He did not look older than ten or eleven years. He looked absurd in long trousers. The whites of his eyes against his black face gave him a startled expression. The father got to his feet.

"Where's the money?" he demanded.

The boy looked from one to the other. He was afraid of his father. He licked his pale lips.

"Come on now," said the man. "Where's the money?"

"Don't give it to him," said the woman. "Don't give it to him, Billy. Give it to me."

The father advanced on the boy, his teeth showing in a snarl under his big moustache.

"Where is that money?" he almost whispered.

The boy looked him straight in the eyes.

"I lost it," he said.

"You—*what?*" cried his father.

"I lost it," the boy repeated.

The man began to shout and wave his hands about.

"Lost it! *Lost* it! What are you talking about? How could you lose it?"

"It was in a packet," said the boy, "a little envelope. I lost it."

"Where did you lose it?"

"I don't know. I must have dropped it in the street."

"Did you go back and look for it?"

The boy nodded. "I couldn't find it," he said.

The man made a noise in his throat, half grunt, half moan—the sort of noise an animal would make.

"So you lost it, did you?" he said. He stepped back a couple of paces and took off his belt—a wide, thick belt with a heavy brass buckle. "Come here," he said.

The boy, biting his lower lip so as to keep back the tears, advanced, and the man raised his arm. The woman, motionless until that moment, leapt forward and seized it. Her husband, finding strength in his blind rage, pushed her aside easily. He brought the belt down on the boy's back. He beat him unmercifully about the body and legs. The boy sank to the floor, but did not cry out. When the man had spent himself, he put on the belt and pulled the boy to his feet.

"Now you'll get off to bed," he said.

"The lad wants some food," said the woman.

"He'll go to bed. Go and wash yourself."

Without a word the boy went into the scullery and washed his hands and face. When he had done this he went straight upstairs.

The man sat down at the table, ate some bread and butter and drank two cups of tea. The woman ate nothing. She sat opposite him, never taking her eyes from his face, looking with hatred at him. Just as before, he took no notice of her, ignored her, behaved as if she were not there at all.

When he had finished the meal he went out. Immediately he had shut the door the woman jumped to her feet and ran upstairs to the boy's room.

He was sobbing bitterly, his face buried in the pillow. She sat on the edge of the bed and put her arms about him, pressed him close to her breast, ran her fingers through his disordered hair, whispered endearments, consoling him. He let her do this, finding comfort in her caresses, relief in his own tears.

After a while his weeping ceased. He raised his head and smiled at her, his wet eyes bright. Then he put his hand under the pillow and withdrew a small dirty envelope.

"Here's the money," he whispered.

She took the envelope and opened it and pulled out a long strip of paper with some figures on it—a ten shilling note and a sixpence.

Leslie Halward: *To Tea on Sunday*
By permission of the Literary Agency Mohrbooks, Zürich

VOCABULARY. *breadwinner*: one who earns a living for a family — *pinch*: cause discomfort or pain — *spare*: thin, lean — *starch*: make stiff with starch (starch—substance used for stiffening clothes) — *sprawl*: sit with arms and legs loosely spread out — *suck*: draw in with the mouth — *mean*: poor in appearance; shabby-looking — *contemptuous*: showing disrespect — *hum*: make a buzzing sound like that of bees — *pretence*: false show — rent: regular payment for the use of rooms etc. — *till:* drawer for money in a shop — *put up with*: endure, bear patiently — *poke*: move the wood, coals etc. with a poker to make it burn up — *startle*: give a fright to — *snarl*: act of showing the teeth and growling — *grunt*: (esp. of pigs) low rough sound — *moan*: sound of grief or pain — *belt:* girdle or band — *buckle*: clip (of metal, etc.) for fastening — *unmerciful*: merciless, cruel — *spend*: use up; exhaust; consume — *lad*: boy; youth — *scullery*: room in which pots, pans, dishes etc. are washed — *sob*: breathe irregularly when crying — *pillow*: cushion for the head — *endearment*: act or word of affection — *caress*: loving touch; kiss — *strip*: long narrow piece.

61. The Man Who Died at Sea

My mother was not quite like most people's mothers. She had what people called the 'Celtic Temperament', up one instant and down the next, and making sure that my father and I were up and down with her. When she was down, it was as though a brown fog hung over the whole house, and when she started going up again, it was as though the sun came out and the birds started singing. Living with her had never a dull moment, but it could be rather unnerving, for she had, unquestionably, a touch of the Second Sight.

She saw our beloved dog lying in his accustomed place before the hall fire, six weeks or so after he died; and she heard things—the same old dog padding around the house, even years later; footsteps and voices that weren't there for other people; and occasionally she knew that certain things were going to happen. They didn't always happen, but they happened often enough for my father and I not to like it very much when she predicted something bad. (It generally seems to be future trouble and not rejoicings, that shows itself to the person with the Second Sight.)

The first time that she became aware of this uncanny gift it frightened her so badly and made such a deep impression on her that when she told me about it, thirty years later, she told it as freshly and in as much detail as though it had happened only the day before. It was indeed an unnerving experience for a young girl.

My mother was seventeen at the time, and she was going out to India to stay with an elder brother in the Indian Civil. It was her first trip away from home, and by herself, and at the beginning she felt a little strange and lonely, but she soon got to know a few people and settled to life on board ship. Among the other passengers was a middle-aged man—I shall call him

Mr X. One can't be a month or more in the same ship without coming to know the faces of all the other passengers, so she came to know this man by sight, and she heard other people speak to him by name. But he remained simply a middle-aged face with a name to it, among all the crowd of passengers that she didn't know.

The weeks went by, and she had a flirtation with one of the ship's officers; they were through the Suez Canal, and the *punkahs* (fans) came into use, and the nights as well as the days began to be very hot. And one night in the Indian Ocean, she woke from an uncomfortably vivid dream to find herself in the gangway outside her cabin on her way to fetch the ship's Doctor because Mr X was dying.

She had never walked in her sleep before, and she was bewildered and startled, but she pulled herself together and crept back into her bunk without waking her cabin mate, telling herself that it was probably the heat.

The next night exactly the same thing happened again. Only this time she was more than half way to the Doctor's cabin when she came to herself, and had quite a long walk back, hoping desperately that she wouldn't meet anybody on the way. She still told herself it was the heat; but she began to be very worried in case it should happen a third time and that she actually got all the way to the Doctor's cabin: and finally she decided that the best thing would be to go and tell him the whole story.

So next morning, that was what she did. "If you wake up in the night and find me flapping around your cabin in my nightie, it's because, I've come to tell you that Mr X is dying. I've never walked in my sleep before, but last night and the night before, I woke up on my way here. I think it must be the heat." The Doctor said, "Well I hope to God nobody *does* die this trip, because I've done the stupidest thing—I've forgotten to bring any death certificate forms with me."

And it was when he said that, that my mother realised for the first time, the full, very frightening implication of this sleep-walking to fetch the Doctor. Whenever she caught sight of Mr X that day, she looked at him rather anxiously, but as far as she could judge, never having really looked at him before, he seemed just as usual.

That night she slept beautifully, no dreams, no sleep-walking: and when she woke in the morning it all seemed so comfortably in the past that she decided she had been rather silly and had made a fuss about nothing. Then, while she was dressing, the stewardess came in with a message from the Doctor. She was to go to him in the Sick Bay at once, and not to speak to anyone on the way.

In the Sick Bay she found the Doctor looking rather white. He said, "I didn't want you to hear it from anyone else and get a shock—Mr X had a heart attack and died in the night."

Rosemary Sutcliff: "The Man Who Died at Sea" in *The House of the Nightmare*, ed. Kathleen Lines, London
By permission of the publishers, The Bodley Head Ltd

VOCABULARY. *Celtic*: of the Celts — *unnerve*: deprive of strength or resolution — *touch*: slight quantity, trace — *Second Sight*: ability to know what will happen in the future — *pad*: trudge along — *predict*: foretell, prophesy — *rejoicings*: celebrations for a happy event — *uncanny:* mysterious — *Civil Service*: all government departments except the Navy, Army, and Air Force — *know by sight*: be familiar with his appearance only — *flirtation*: love-affair that is not serious — *gangway*: passage — *bunk*: sleeping-place — *mate*: companion — *flap*: move lightly up and down — *nightie*: night-shirt — *certificate*: statement that may be used as a proof — *implication*: sth. hinted at or suggested — *make a fuss*: busy oneself with trifles — *Sick Bay*: part of main deck used as hospital — *heart attack*: sudden coming on of pain in the heart, with irregular beating.

62. Life With Summats

(Whatever you may think of his parents, in the article that follows Jimmy must surely have your sympathy. Certainly he was a thief, but he seems to have been made one by the force of circumstances. The role of the social worker is to build Jimmy up into a useful and honest member of society. But for Jimmy this just means, as you will see, LIFE WITH SUMMATS)

I was having a last drink in the City Police canteen when the 'phone rang. The steward answered it: "For you, Bob," he called across the bar, "Children's Department."

"Hello, Bob. They told me you were in the building. The Mechanised have just picked up young Jimmy White. He's been missing from home for a couple of days. Can you hold him for Court next Wednesday?"

A quick telephone call to my wife to warn her that I should not be coming home alone, and I made my way over to the Mechanised Division.

I looked at Jimmy standing beside a very large Police Inspector, and Jimmy looked at me. I had never realised before just how big that Inspector was. Jimmy's large eyes set in the middle of a very dirty freckled face below a mop of ginger hair studied me intently. Obeying a sudden impulse I winked at him. Immediately his face broke into a broad grin and I received in reply one of the wickedest winks I have ever seen. In that moment I knew that Jimmy and I would get along together. The Inspector took me to our side.

"Watch him, Bob. He'll run," he said.

I looked over my shoulder at Jimmy. "He won't," I replied, and I knew that I was telling the truth. I've met quite a number of Jimmies since my home was first approved as a private remand home. An hour later, as I tucked up a very much sweeter smelling Jimmy into his bed the same pair of large eyes looked into mine.

"Thank you, sir," he said.

"Why do you call me 'sir'?"

Jimmy looked surprised. "You are a master, aren't you?" He hesitated. "You take us boys so you must be a master . . ." pause, "or summat."

Jimmy wasn't accustomed to ordinary people taking more than a casual interest in him. If grown-ups tried to help him they must be Probation Officers, Policemen, Psychologists, Schoolmasters or . . . summat; not people. I took Jimmy to the local Juvenile Court the following Wednesday. He stood there facing the bench, a pathetic little figure surrounded by summats. His mother, a large woman, sat on a chair beside him, obviously bored by the whole business. His father hadn't bothered to come at all on the pretext of being unable to afford time off work.

Mr Ritchie leaned over and whispered to me. "If he's remanded for three weeks will you have him back?" I nodded my head.

The clerk of the court read out quite an imposing list of chocolates, sweets, potato crisps and other such boyishly appetising items alleged to have been stolen by Jimmy during his two days of freedom, and asked him if he admitted these offences. Jimmy, looking suitably solemn, nodded his head.

Jimmy came back to us for three weeks. He was still rather puzzled about my status and was only partially reassured when I explained to him that I had been a policeman until I retired with an injured leg. This was better. Although I was not a summat, I was a retired summat.

Jimmy didn't talk very much but he loved to be talked to. He would sit on the rug in the evening facing my chair listening with obvious interest to everything I had to say. During the day he was never very far away. As I walked down the garden to feed the animals, a scurry of feet behind me and a small hand pushed into mine would announce his arrival. As I went up the steps into the house his hand would be under my elbow to prevent me stumbling. As I got into the car to go out he would be sitting silently and expectantly in the passenger seat.

We went back to the Juvenile Court after three weeks. Jimmy's mother was still bored; Jimmy's father was still at work. After due deliberation Jimmy was formally placed on probation for three years by the two summats sitting on the bench.

"Talk about a waste of time. He ought to have been sent away. He'll only do it again," his mother exclaimed as we came out of court. Jimmy looked at his mother but he didn't contradict her.

Five days later, at 5 a. m., my wife and myself were woken by the ringing of the front door bell. I opened the door and there, shivering and without a coat, stood Jimmy. He followed me without a word into the kitchen and sat down by the fire which is always kept in all night during the winter months. Silently he watched me as I filled the kettle and put it on the gas.

"Have you run away?" He nodded.

"Where have you been all night?"

"I slept in your hut," he said plaintively; "I didn't want to wake you till morning."

"Jimmy's now in an approved school. He writes to me nearly every week: "Dear Mr Alldred. . . . I played football on Saturday—I'm all right . . . I can't think of anything else to say . . . Love Jimmy . . . P. S. Write to me soon."

He's not what you would call unhappy; Jimmy's a thoughtful boy. He knows he is not an ordinary boy; he's what they call a juvenile delinquent and juvenile delinquents don't live with ordinary people—they live with summats.

R. C. Alldred: "Life with Summats" in *Times and Seasons*, ed. C. D. Poster, London 1966
By permission of the publishers, Collins (William), Sons & Co Ltd

VOCABULARY. *summat*: ('somewhat') an important person (in the boy's language) — *canteen*: place in factories, offices etc. where food, drink etc. are sold — *Mechanised Division*: Div. using motor transport — *freckle*: become covered with light-brown spots on the skin — *mop*: mass of thick untidy hair — *ginger*: bright red — *intent*: eager; earnest — *wink*: shut and open eyes quickly as a private signal — *run*: = run away — *remand home*: temporary institution for young offenders "Vollzugsanstalt f. Jugendarrest" — *tuck up*: cover warmly — *probation*: the time during which a first offender is allowed to go free and prove that he can lead an honest life "Bewährungsfrist" — *probation officer*: one who watches over the behaviour of such offenders — *bench*: the judges of a court — *pathetic*: sad; pitiful — *pretext*: excuse — *off work*: not occupied by business — *crisp*: thin fried and dried slices of potato (marketed in packets) — *item*: single article or unit — *allege*: declare; say firmly — *offence*: wrongdoing; crime — *solemn*: serious-looking; grave — *status*: rank — *scurry*: running with short, quick steps — *stumble*: trip in walking — *plaintive*: sad; sorrowful — *delinquent*: wrong-doer.

63. Case History I: A More Stable Boy

Tony was a lively, friendly youngster who, at the time of my enquiry, had just left school and was working as a clerk. His father was dead and he lived with his mother and married sister in a new flat. He was very much the family 'baby' in relation to his older brothers and sisters who were all married. He complained that, as a consequence, he was 'always being growled at by somebody'. His mother used to go every night to the pub, where she took part in a regular sweep. She entered his name in it to make up the number. None of the family attended church at that time. Tony had not been since he was seven. Up to that age his sister took him with her to a local mission. He was always fond of practical jokes and at one time he used to throw lighted fireworks on to passing buses. In his younger days he was regarded as 'a bit of a bully in the Dwellings'! One horrifying activity was to catch cats and drop them over the balconies. He and his friends killed and injured several in this way.

He had been an active member of a fairly well-knit gang which was entirely composed of boys living in the same block of flats. Most of their activities were quite harmless. They took over an empty storeroom as their headquarters and ran their own football team which played regular matches with teams from other blocks. Sometimes these games were played in the park but more often they made use of the square in the centre block. After the older members were called up for the Army the gang's activities came to an end.

His pocket money as a young wage earner was seven shillings and sixpence a week, and this had to cover fags, pictures, bets, and club dues but he managed to save half-a-crown towards his summer holiday. He spent about sixpence a week on horses, and the same on pools and the sweep. He also used to make a number of *ad hoc* bets with other boys and at weekends he nearly always played cards for money.

He was convinced that his club membership had greatly assisted him and had prevented him from becoming involved with the lawbreaking gangs in which the area abounded. He said his mother had to stop going out at night because of the danger of having the electric meter robbed and that his Gran had additional locks put on her doors and cupboards. Tony knew who was responsible for such raids in the neighbourhood. It was a boy who lived in the same block and who would almost certainly 'end up in Borstal'. He had produced a very suspicious number of shillings when playing cards. While Tony did not avoid this boy when knocking about in the

Dwellings, coming to the club was, amongst other things, a most useful alibi, as it was very dangerous to be seen in the vicinity of a flat which had been raided. When you were vouched for at the club nobody could 'pin things on you'.

Tony had never appeared in the juvenile court, although he might well have done so if luck had not gone in his favour. He told me how when he was about nine he and his mates used to play in a burned-out warehouse. They liked 'nosing around' and climbing. One day they found money bags containing copper and silver which was divided among the gang members. Young children, he said, like to explore and 'you can't stop them'.

One of his elder brothers was a regular thief and went down town shoplifting almost every day. He had three or four court appearances. Tony himself had a spell of lorry-skipping. They stole sugar, nuts, fruit etc. along the dock roads. At the age of eight or perhaps nine he stole from city shops in the company of other lads. Saturday mornings were the favourite times for shoplifting.

Tony told me that a lot of theft took place at school holiday camps. Country shopkeepers are so unsuspecting! One boy at his school was notorious. He used to load up his mackintosh pockets with loot, and in the dormitory at night he auctioned it. He would make in this way as much as £ 6 a week and would return home rolling in cash. Tony bought two expensive compacts from him to take home as presents for his sisters. He bought several things he knew had been stolen, but the bargains were so good that nobody could resist the temptation. He admitted that he had no qualms in the matter. It was to your advantage, so you just did it!

He gave up shoplifting when he was about thirteen, as he became aware of the dangers. He said he knew that he had been open to many bad influences, but had no father and apparently his mother was not very particular. Not only did she allow him to smoke but she actually encouraged him to gamble. There was also the influence of the elder brother, who was a regular thief. The family was, however, an affectionate one and this may have been Tony's salvation. He was very lucky indeed to survive to early manhood without a conviction being brought against him. It would seem that he never received any direct ethical training yet, being an intelligent boy, he emerged more or less unscathed from his delinquent phase and succeeded in throwing off the more deleterious effects of his environment. His story is, I think, in many ways typical of the better adjusted and more stable boy, coming from a united if not very well-organized home, who is, however, constantly a delinquency risk in a slum district. Not all such boys are as fortunate as

Tony. They may be unwisely handled or merely less lucky and find themselves round about the time of the onset of puberty in fairly serious trouble with the law.

John Barron Mays: *Crime and the Social Structure*, London 1967
By permission of the publishers, Faber and Faber Ltd

VOCABULARY. *growl*: to utter a deep sound like that of a dog — *sweep*: form of gambling, the winner taking all the money staked — *make up*: complete — *fire-works*: squibs, rockets etc. sent up at night for show — *bully*: blusterer, tyrant — *dwelling*: house of residence, house — *fag*: (sl.) cigarette — *bet*: agreement about paying money if a certain event happens — *dues*: sum of money to be paid for membership — *pool*: money played for in a game (e.g. football pools) — *ad hoc*: arranged for this purpose, special — *abound*: be very plentiful, have a great quantity of — *meter*: instrument for measuring electricity — *raid*: short, sudden attack — *Borstal*: system of imprisonment for young criminals, based on the indeterminate sentence "Besserungsanstalt für jugendliche Verbrecher" — *suspicious*: having a feeling of doubt about — *knock about*: wander, lead irregular life — *vouch for*: confirm by satisfactory evidence — *pin sth. on*: charge with — *juvenile court*: court for young offenders — *mate*: companion — *nose around*: pry or search — *shoplifting*: stealing things from a shop while pretending to be a customer — *spell*: period of time — *lorry-skipping*: jumping on lorries and stealing — *lad*: boy; youth — *unsuspecting*: not aware of coming danger — *loot*: plunder — *dormitory*: large sleeping-room — *auction*: sell by public sale — *compact*: small, flat container with face-powder — *bargain*: sth. sold cheaply — *qualm*: scruple — *gamble*: play games of chance for money — *salvation*: saving from evil — *conviction*: passing of a sentence upon a guilty person — *emerge*: rise out of — *unscathed*: unharmed — *deleterious*: harmful — *onset*: vigorous start — *puberty*: age at which reproduction of young becomes possible.

64. Case History II: An Official Delinquent

Edward was an official delinquent, had appeared in court more than once and had been on the brink of being sent to an approved school. He was a powerfully made boy, not more than average in intelligence, and somewhat restive by temperament. Games rather than lessons appealed to him, and when it came to a choice of employment he naturally enough gravitated to manual work.

His family was small and very 'respectable'. His only brother, three years his junior, was almost scholarly—a rather solitary unathletic boy who loved music and the arts—in many ways a complete contrast to Edward. Yet they were good friends and often went off on all-day cycle rides together.

Edward's employment history was very chequered, he changed his job no less than five times in two and a half years. But he could not for this reason be called an unstable or unreliable youth. As a club member, he was intermittent, until the age of sixteen. About this time he seemed to settle down and take a more responsible attitude to life. He was a good athlete, a fine swimmer, and the club gave him every opportunity to develop these interests. His probation officer seemed to be giving him the right kind of support during this period and Edward always praised his and the club's efforts on his behalf. Without their help, he said, he would very likely have developed into 'a complete rogue'.

He had a bad record, in many ways typical of the district. But it is hard to see why he became a delinquent while his brother did not. It may be that he felt a little inferior intellectually. It may also be that his restless energetic personality found little during his early years to engage his interest and loyalty. The fact that he was somewhat adrift and exposed to the temptation of a criminogenic environment may have made all the difference in his case. Had he been more of a scholar and more inward-turning like his brother, he might have kept on the right side of the law. As it was he made his first appearance in court for larceny at the age of thirteen. His father paid the fine. A year later he was charged with the same offence and placed on probation. At sixteen, while still on probation, he committed a further offence. But this time the court appearance seems to have shocked him into a realization of the ultimate consequences of that kind of behaviour. Thereafter he was exceptionally cautious. If out after dark without a light he would walk his cycle home rather than risk any further todo with the police. He threw himself into club activities and made close friends with reliable boys and had no further charges brought against him. He did, however, do some shoplifting while away on holiday. Twice he stole presents to take home. He said that boys think it is easier to steal in strange localities and that it is natural for them to take presents which they cannot really afford to buy.

Looking back on his boyhood, Edward said that what he and his pals between eleven and thirteen wanted was adventure. He remembered when they were in school how they waited for the four o'clock bell as a signal for adventure. They would get a skip on a wagon, stealing sugar, fruit and nuts on the way, and enjoying the thrill and fun of it. The risk of capture and sheer physical danger seemed to supply the stimulus they needed to feel really alive.

Edward neither drank, smoked nor gambled. Yet he nearly embarked on a criminal career. He is probably a good example of the easy-going, good-natured boy who takes a very long time learning to adjust himself to the demands of increasing maturity. In an environment wich lacked delinquent suggestions and illicit rewards, he might have been a somewhat different kind of boy. As it was he was a serious risk. Yet I could never quite see why. He had many admirable qualities and I would have been happy if he had been my own son. There was nothing furtive or dangerous about Edward. But he did break the law quite frequently. His story epitomizes the problem presented by many young delinquents who live in similar kinds of deteriorated neighbourhoods in our big cities.

I think I should end by saying that Edward is now a married man doing well in life. He has settled down in a newer neighbourhood. But one realizes how very fine indeed is the line which at times divides the social failure from the social success.

John Barron Mays: *Crime and the Social Structure*, London 1967
By permission of the publishers, Faber and Faber Ltd

VOCABULARY. *delinquent*: wrong-doer — *brink*: edge — *approved school*: State school for young offenders — *restive*: unable to keep still — *gravitate*: move or be attracted to — *manual*: done with the hands — *junior*: younger than another — *scholarly*: fond of learning — *unathletic*: not strong — *chequered*: of great variety — *unstable*: not steady — *intermittent*: coming and going — *probation officer*: one who watches over the behaviour of young offenders — *on behalf of*: in aid of — *rogue*: rascal, dishonest person — *inferior*: lower in any way — *adrift*: floating hither and thither — *temptation*: sth. which leads into evil — *criminogenic*: producing crime — *larceny*: stealing; theft — *fine*: money to be paid as a punishment — *probation*: time during which a first offender is allowed to go free and prove that he can lead an honest life — *cautious*: careful; watchful — *todo*: bustle, fuss — *shoplifting*: stealing things from a shop while pretending to be a customer — *pal*: comrade; friend — *skip*: light leap — *sheer*: absolute — *stimulus*: anything that rouses to activity — *gamble*: play games for money — *easy-going*: not causing trouble, taking things easy — *adjust*: arrange; adapt — *suggestion*: impulse — *illicit*: unlawful — *reward*: repayment — *furtive*: stealthy, clandestine — *epitomize*: give the main points in a short form — *deteriorate*: make or become worse.

65. Two Probation Officers Deal with a Difficult Case

Barnett was a man of thirty. He was married, with two boys aged ten and six. The couple lived with his parents, who were both invalids; for this reason, it had never been possible for them to obtain their own home. He was employed as a driver. His offence was one of systematically delivering short weight to customers when working as a coalman and selling the balance to another man who was charged with him. Prior to the court hearing, he telephoned the probation office, spoke to Mr Green, a probation officer, and asked if it would be possible to be placed on probation; his intention was to admit the offence. Mr Green had to say that this was a matter for the court but offered to see Barnett on the morning of the court hearing. He obtained brief information about his background and position; apart from financial difficulties, it seemed that there was little need for probation. The court, however, decided upon a probation order, possibly influenced by the number of debts he had accumulated and the fact that he had no previous criminal record.

In the course of the first few weeks of the probation period further information about Barnett was obtained. It appeared that both his boys were backward and were being educated at not inconsiderable expense at a local private school. Barnett, and especially his wife, apparently felt that the children would have a better chance than in a state school. Mrs Barnett was described as a very nervous person, who had been greatly upset by her husband's offences and court appearance; she was said also to be apprehensive about the prospect of a visit from Mr Green, since the whole matter had so far been concealed from his parents and she wished this to continue. Mr Green's car would cause gossip amongst the neighbours if it were to be seen outside her front door. Mr Green agreed not to visit. In the discussion about his wife, Barnett also mentioned that she was not far from being at the end of her tether; she had never taken kindly to looking after his parents, though they had only the two children, while some families were far larger and some women far harder pressed.

Although he had usually been in quite remunerative employment, Barnett seemed to have accumulated a number of debts, which he found difficulty in enumerating. Hire purchase figured largely; a car which had been damaged irreparably when still not paid for; money owing to friends who had lent to him when he was short through temporary periods of unemployment.

At the time when Mr Gray, newly appointed from training, read Mr Green's record, the probation period had been running for some six months. Some limited improvement had taken place but there was yet much to do. Nevertheless, Mr Green felt that the situation was satisfactory and recorded it as such:

"Barnett has coped well with the difficulties arising from his offences. He is a fairly competent and intelligent man who, with the help of advice and encouragement, is able to manage his affairs satisfactorily."

Mr Gray, however, found some reason to hesitate before confirming this assessment. He noted that there had been several changes of employment; that there must be considerable difficulty in paying the school bills; that no attempt had been made to discuss the possibility of seeing the wife, perhaps in the office. He wondered about several aspects of the position. Did the fact that Barnett had asked to be placed on probation mean that he had opted for the least painful way of being dealt with? Why did Barnett, a man of at least average intelligence and ability, change jobs so frequently, having failed in fifteen years to settle to any definite occupation? And why, with his uncertain income, opt to educate his children privately? And how were the bills paid? What was the marital situation? Was the wife ambitious for the children? What significance was to be attached to Barnett's unsympathetic remark about other women having far more to cope with than she? Could there be causal factors relating to the offence other than his pressing debts?

Mr Gray found it easier to ask questions than to find answers. This was because Barnett had presented the financial aspect of his problems almost exclusively and Mr Green had dealt only with this.

Mr Gray felt that Barnett and Mr Green had this in common that both avoided consideration of problems other than the financial. Mr Gray knew Mr Green to be a conscientious officer but one who had more confidence in his ability to deal with "practical" problems than with emotional difficulties. Was it really true, for instance, that Mrs Barnett did not wish to see Mr Green or was this just a smokescreen raised by Barnett? What about the problems of work, marriage, parenthood?

Mark Monger: *Casework in Probation,* London 1964
By permission of the publishers, Butterworths & Co Ltd

VOCABULARY. *probation*: sometimes an offender is not sentenced to punishment, but is released "on probation", that is on the condition that he behaves well and follows the directions given by a probation officer "Bewährungsfrist" — *probation officer*: person who acts as friend and adviser — *invalid*: one who is weak in health — *short weight*: not reaching the required amount, i. e. less than required — *balance*: (colloq.) what is left of anything — *charge*: accuse — *accumulate*:gather; heap up — *record*: written report; past history — *backward*: not very clever — *apprehensive*: feeling afraid — *conceal*: hide, keep secret — *gossip*: idle talk — *at the end of one's tether*: at the end of one's powers — *remunerative*: profitable — *enumerate*: count the number of — *hire purchase*: purchase by instalments — *damage*: make less valuable; harm — *owing*: still to be paid — *cope*: manage successfully — *assessment*: approximate judgment — *bill*: statement of money owing — *opt*: make choice — *marital*: having to do with marriage — *causal*: acting as a cause — *conscientious*: careful and earnest — *emotional*: having to do with strong feelings — *smokescreen*: cloud of smoke intended to hide military operations.

66. The Real Crusoe

On the beach of the tropical island, where deep blue waters lapped the white shore, a lone sailor stood. He was watching a rowing boat draw farther and farther away from him, heading for the tall ship which stood at anchor in the bay. Suddenly the sailor raised his hands.

"Come back; come back!" he cried. "I have changed my mind. I don't want to stay here alone."

A mocking laugh floated across the water. It came from a man standing in the stern of the rowing boat. "You've got what you wanted," he called. "You can stay there now."

After that there was only the sound of oars creaking and the waves whispering over the beach. The sailor watched the rowing boat reach the ship. The sails of the ship were spread. She headed out to sea. Soon the tall ship was only a speck in the far distance on the sun-glazed sea. Alexander Selkirk was marooned on the island of Juan Fernandez, in the Pacific Ocean, 400 miles from South America.

Selkirk had been the sailing master on the privateer, *Cinque Ports*. In February 1703, the ship had sailed from England in company with another privateer, the 26-gun *St George*.

When they reached the South Pacific, the two ships parted company. The *Cinque Ports* put into Cumberland Bay on the island of Juan Fernandez to obtain fresh water and food.

Then Alexander Selkirk quarrelled with Captain Stradling. "I wish to be put ashore," he said in the end. "I will not remain another day under your command."

"Very well," said Captain Stradling. "You shall have your wish, Mr Selkirk."

Selkirk's sea chest was set down on the beach beside him. He had clothes, a Bible, some books on navigation, a gun with ammunition, a cooking pot, a pewter kettle and a number of tools including a hatchet.

There was plenty of food and fresh water on Juan Fernandez. The island was overrun with goats which provided the castaway with fresh meat and milk. He found wild fruit and vegetables. From the sea he obtained crawfish and, from time to time, seals. When Selkirk had used up all his ammunition, he taught himself to run swiftly. Soon he was able to outrun the goats when he went hunting.

At first he was troubled by rats. But there were wild cats on the island. Selkirk trained some of them to be his friends. They slept around him and kept the rats away. For fun, he trained some of his cats to dance. He played to them on a little pipe. When his shoes were worn out, Selkirk went barefoot. When he needed clothes, he made some from goatskins.

For four years and four months Selkirk remained on Juan Fernandez. Every day he scanned the horizon anxiously for the sight of a sail. At last, one day in 1709, two ships put into the bay. Selkirk at once hurried to the beach. For a long time he had had a bonfire ready. Now he set light to it.

Time passed. Then the castaway saw a boat let down from one of the ships. Soon he was telling his story to men who stared at him in astonishment.

It was two years before Alexander Selkirk and his rescuers returned to England. Then he told his story to newspaper reporters in London. One of the reporters was named Daniel De Foe or Defoe. He took the details from the story of Alexander Selkirk and wove them into an exciting book of adventure.

Eight years after Selkirk's return, in 1719, Defoe's book was published in London. At once it made Defoe rich and famous. The title of the book was *The Life and Strange Surprising Adventures of Robinson Crusoe of York, Mariner, Written by Himself.*

Robert J. Hoare: *Sea-Routes*, London 1962
By permission of the publishers, Ginn and Co Ltd

VOCABULARY. *lap*: wash or flow against — *head*: go straight for — *mock*: make fun of; ridicule — *stern*: back part of a ship — *oar*: pole with flat blade used in rowing — *creak*: make a sharp, grating sound — *speck*: small spot — *glaze*: make shiny — *maroon*: put on a desert island and leave him there — *Juan Fernandez*: group of rocky islands off the Chilian coast — *sailing master*: officer navigating — *privateer*: armed private vessel allowed to attack enemy ships and plunder them — *part company*: travel in different directions — *put in*: make a stop at a port — *bay*: part of the sea in a curve on the shore — *pewter*: mixture of tin and lead "Hartzinn" — *hatchet*: small axe — *castaway*: deserted or shipwrecked person — *goat*: animal of the sheep familiy with horns and long-haired coat — *crawfish, crayfish*: eatable shellfish sth. like the lobster "Flußkrebs; Languste" — *scan*: examine carefully — *bonfire*: large fire in the open air — *weave*, wove, woven: put together (story, plan etc.).

67. I Served a Maharaja

I served a Maharaja for two years. Ten years later I had to be responsible for deposing him and sending him into exile. But I did not know that then.

All I knew was that this Maharaja ruled a State a little bigger than Belgium and a little smaller than Holland, and had asked for my services as 'Adviser' for a year.

I had heard that the Maharaja's family was very orthodox and that his father had refused to allow the railway from Bombay to Calcutta to pass through his capital because travellers might be eating beef in the restaurant car, and to have the flesh of the sacred cow eaten so near his home was more than he could stomach.

There had also recently been rumours of disaffection in the State. Serious trouble was brewing. Each had different reasons for discontent, but all were combining against the Maharaja, and the pot was obviously ready to boil over.

On arrival I found a gallant friend and supporter; a retired Indian officer from the Punjab who was the State Inspector General of Police. I will call him Singh for short. Singh had traced the committee which was planning the revolt and had succeeded in planting his agent as a member of it. So we knew their plans well in advance and were presently informed of the date fixed for the uprising. While His Highness made his arrangements to shoot tiger, we completed ours. Then, a day or two in advance of the 'explosion' date, in one concerted swoop, the border was closed, the leaders were arrested and all were whisked off to their allotted forts.

I did not sleep much that night, but all was calm until the date fixed for the uprising. The crowds then began to gather and march on the capital, as planned; but deprived of their leaders they soon started to falter and dwindle. The few who did reach the capital were quickly dispersed without a single casualty on either side.

But do not imagine that life was all work.

The royal game was tiger. This was the only State where the white (albino) tiger existed. His Highness had shot hundreds of tigers in his time. He found the easiest way to bag them was to take with him a book and a monkey on a long string. When seated in the *machan*, he would release the monkey, who immediately climbed into the top branches. He would then give the signal for the beat to start and settle down to read. As soon as the tiger approached, the monkey would spot him and give the cough with which all monkeys warn the jungle folk that Sher Khan the tiger is on the prowl. His Highness would then quickly put down his book, pick up his rifle and get ready to shoot.

He did not, however, like having V. I. P. s (Very Important Persons) sent to his State to 'get a tiger'. One Privy Councillor, who had virtually invited himself, spent four days in the jungle without seeing the hint of a stripe. When I suggested to His Highness that was rather bad luck on such an eminent politician, he replied curtly that he had promised him tiger *beats*, not tiger.

When my appointment to serve a Maharaja came to an end, I was not sorry, as he would produce no money to finance the five-year plan and progress was at a standstill. In due course things went from bad to worse and, as I have said, ten years later he was deposed and ended his life an exile in Bombay.

But we parted friends, and in token of our two years together he wished to present me with a gold cigarette case. I had to point out politely that I was forbidden to accept such a present. He smiled and waited until we had occasion to be staying at Viceregal Lodge together for a conference. At the close of our visit I was summoned to see the Viceroy, Lord Willingdon. After a few opening remarks His Excellency inquired what I thought of the rule forbidding government servants to accept presents. I replied that, if the present was one which placed you under no obligation, I could not see that it mattered. "Just my view," he said, and then with a smile: "Would a gold cigarette case put you under any obligation to your Maharaja?"

"Not a bit," I replied.

"Then here it is!" said His Excellency, and he opened a drawer and handed me a packet. I was just about to put the packet in my pocket when he said: "Let's open it and see if it's a real one!" So we did, and it was! You have to be a Viceroy like Lord Willingdon to break rules with such charm.

What I now remember best during my time with the Maharaja was that on the first of each month my salary was brought round to me by the Finance Minister in an envelope bulging with notes and that they added up to the full amount. There were no deductions on account of income or any other tax. Can you believe that such places used to exist?

Sir Conrad Corfield: "I Served a Maharaja" in
English for Proficiency, ed. D. H. Spencer

VOCABULARY. *maharaja(h)*: title given to a great Indian prince — *depose*: remove from a high office — *exile*: banish; person who is banished — *orthodox*: holding correct opinions, conventional — *stomach*: put up with, endure — *disaffection*: political discontent, disloyalty — *brew*: to be gathering — *trace*: follow, discover — *plant an agent*: find a position for the agent in an enemy organization that one wants to spy on — *uprising*: revolt — *concerted*: prearranged — *swoop*: sudden attack (like that of a bird of prey) — *whisk off*: remove suddenly — *allotted forts*: the forts previously selected for their detention — *deprive*: take sth. away from —

falter: hesitate, lose courage — *dwindle*: decline, lose importance — *disperse*: scatter in all directions — *casualty*: a person who is killed or wounded — *game*: wild animals hunted for sport — *albino*: person or animal with white skin and hair — *bag*: shoot or capture — *string*: thick thread — *machan*: (Indian) raised platform used in tiger-shooting — *release*: set free — *beat*: driving of wild animals in a given direction by shouting or otherwise making noise "Treibjagd" — *spot*: pick out, notice — *give a cough*: cough in order to call attention as a warning — *on the prowl*: wandering about looking for prey — *Privy Councillor*: adviser chosen by the Viceroy — *stripe*: tiger, of course, has a striped skin — *curtly*: so briefly as to be impolite — *standstill*: stop — *part friends*: separate without ill will — *token*: sign or symbol — *Viceregal Lodge*: the Viceroy's house — *under an obligation to sb.*: feeling the need to repay him in some way — *salary*: payment for regular employment — *bulging*: swelling outwards — *deduction*: taking away from — *income tax*: tax levied on earnings or profit.

68. Cooper's Creek

A warm north-easterly breeze stirred the leaves of the trees in Royal Park, Melbourne, Australia, one August afternoon just over a hundred years ago. The Park presented an unusual scene. Most of the shops and business houses of the city had closed for the day, and all the citizens had come to see the departure of an extraordinary caravan of camels and horses and wagons and men. An expedition was about to leave in an attempt to cross the unknown heart of the continent to reach the sea on the other side.

Most eyes were fixed on Mr Burke, the dashing Irish police inspector who had been chosen to lead the expedition. Some people wondered why he had been chosen at all. He was brave and resourceful, but quite inexperienced. In fact, people who knew him loved to tell the story of how he had been lost in the bush on the way from Yackandandah to Beechworth along a well-beaten track! He was careless about his personal appearance, and often very odd in his behaviour. Some people thought he was queer in the head. He would sit for long hours saying nothing. He used to scrawl notes all over the wallpaper in his sitting-room. But he was honest and sincere, and all who knew him fell for his easy-going charm.

At a quarter to four, after a speech by the Mayor of Melbourne, the expedition moved off to the cheers of the crowd. It was all so exciting, with the romantic-looking Mr Burke leading the way on his pony Billy. Few who watched them depart realised that they were watching the beginning, not only of a great adventure, but also of a great tragedy.

Nine months later another procession, 800 miles north of Melbourne: the expedition was on its way back. But this time there were no cheering crowds, no camels, no horses, no gay adventurers. There were only three weary men stumbling along the side of Cooper's Creek. The man in the lead, with the long matted beard, the skin burnt almost black with the sun, and the deep, burning eyes, was Mr Burke himself—returning successful. Successful? Yes, they had crossed the continent, through the burning desert where no white man had been. They had reached the gulf of Carpentaria, running, mad with excitement. But Burke had trouble all the way. There had been quarrels, sickness, death. Now there were only three of them left.

The man following Burke was a young man called Wills. He had gone with the expedition as surveyor. He was a clever, rather bookish man, gentle and retiring. He had proved to be the most able assistant Burke had in the expedition.

The third man was John King, a young Irish soldier. He was only twenty-two, cheerful and willing. He had been taken on the expedition because he was used to handling camels. Staggering, stumbling on bleeding feet, faint with hunger, they slowly edged along the creek. They were silent, except for the noise made as they fought for breath in the parched heat. But each man was saying to himself, "Trapped! We are trapped on Cooper's Creek!"

For the relief party which should have met them had failed them. With no food left, and no means of transport, they knew it would be suicide to try to cross the desert. They had to stay near the creek, where there was water to drink, and native nardoo seed to eat. But each man in his heart knew he was near the end. Three weeks later John King was found by a search party, sent at last; but sent too late. He was the sole survivor. He was a dreadful sight, wasted with starvation, burnt by the sun, half-mad with loneliness and privation. He told the rescuers that Wills had become too weak to walk, and had insisted on Burke and King leaving him behind. Like Captain Oates in the Antarctic expedition fifty years later, he sacrificed himself in the hope that the others would live.

Burke and King had left Wills to die, as he wished them to do; but King had not got far with Burke. The leader was very distressed at leaving faithful Wills behind. At last he sank to the ground and said he could go no further. He gave his watch to King, and his pocket-book, in which he wrote: "I hope we shall be done justice to. We have fulfilled our task, but we have been abandoned. We have not been followed up as we expected, and the depot party abandoned their post. King behaved nobly. I hope that he will be properly cared for. He comes up the creek in accordance with my request. R. O'Hara Burke." Soon afterwards Burke died.

John King was taken back to civilisation, but he never fully recovered from the effects of his ordeal, and died some years later.

A Government inquiry was held, which proved that Burke had indeed been deserted and disobeyed by those on whom he relied to secure his return home. It is a heart-breaking story, but an epic one which is known and treasured by every Australian boy and girl.

A. Elliott-Cannon: *Good Company, Book Four, Old and New,* London 1966
By permission of the publishers, Johnston & Bacon Ltd

VOCABULARY. *creek*: small river — *Melbourne*: seaport, capital, Australia (Victoria) — *dashing*: bold; lively; active — *resourceful*: quick at finding a way of doing things — *Yackandandah* — *Beechworth*: towns in Australia — *track*: path — *easy-going*: taking things easily, not causing trouble — *Mayor*: head of a town corporation — *stumble*: walk in an unsteady way — *lead*: first or front place — *matted*: twisted together; tangled — *surveyor*: one who makes plans or maps of land — *bookish*: fond of books — *stagger*: sway from side to side — *edge*: move little by little — *parch*: dry up; scorch — *relief*: that which brings ending of pain — *suicide*: self-murder(er) — *Nardus*: genus of coarse grasses — *waste*: become thinner or weaker — *starvation*: suffering or death caused by lack of food — *privation*: lack of the necessaries of life — *Oates*: British explorer who joined Scott's Antarctic expedition — *sacrifice*: give up sth. for someone else — *depot*: station where stores are kept — *request*: thing asked for — *ordeal*: hard trial or test — *epic*: lofty; grand.

69. Fear

When my great-grandfather was living with the Maoris the wars against the white people were being fought, and against the tribes friendly with the pakeha. He was living up in the Waikato with his princess when the tribe made a raid on their neighbours who were friendly towards the whites.

My father told me, said my grandfather, how the raiding-party returned proudly with their captives and the air was thick with cries from the great haka of their welcome. With them as captive the raiders had brought Rewi Tamati Atahu, a great warrior famous through the Waikato—he was more feared than ten others and mothers used to frighten children with his name.

The raiders told how they reached and entered the pa in the early morning before dawn. They described the great killing and the capture of Rewi Tamati as he slept.

Never would we have dared, they said, otherwise to have brought him here alive.

It was two days later that Rewi Tamati escaped, and with him went Rangi Ngatane, a young girl. She had helped him to escape and had deserted the tribe to live with an enemy.

She must have been a good-looking girl—my father was always talking about her, how beautiful she was.

Well, he said, they soon had search-parties out after the pair. They were in the wet bush for half a day before they found Rangi Ngatane's body lying across an old fallen trunk. That's what Rewi Tamati was—tough. All he wanted of Rangi was to be guided through a part of the bush—women are fools like that; she kidded herself into thinking he loved her and all he wanted was to get through the bush—so he took her with him and when he was through with her he just stabbed her through the breast and left her. Her eyes, my father told me, were wide open, as though she couldn't believe Rewi Tamati would kill her, and they were full of terror and shame, terror and shame not because Rewi Tamati was stabbing her but because she had kidded herself about him loving her and it was a woman's shame and the terror of it showing in her great wide-open eyes.

After that the search-party had to go on for another day and a night before they found Rewi Tamati. And it was only by accident then.

North of the pa were high cliffs and these were dangerous to climb, but once climbed they offered a short-cut out of the country of my father's tribe. And Rewi Tamati had tried to climb those cliffs and the search-party found him about halfway up on a ledge three feet wide, and he had been there about a day and he couldn't move up or down because of the rock jutting out above him and he was *afraid* to come down. He couldn't move from his little ledge. The cliff had him—you could see that by the way he clung back from the edge and how set and stiff his face was. And the search-party found him there and my father was with them and he said that although Rewi Tamati was trapped not one of them would go after him up the cliff. They stayed at the bottom and shouted at him and he shouted back, because Rewi Tamati was not frightened of any man, but only of this great cliff he had tried to climb.

So the raiding-party held a council at the bottom of the cliff and they decided to leave Rewi Tamati where he was and just to pull away the tree that lay up a smooth part of the cliff so that he wouldn't be able to get down even if his fear went. And the cliff was made tapu. And my father felt this was a terrible thing to do, more terrible than anything else, leaving a brave man alone with his fear. They were frightened to climb the cliff and fight because Rewi Tamati was what he was, and my father was frightened too, but they should have left the tree there so as to give him a chance and to let him come down when his fear left him and fight it out. And you could see the cold frantic fear working in Rewi Tamati's face as he watched them remove the old tree, and his hands clutching the rock desperately and his eyes looking everywhere all the time, and he over fifty feet from the ground and not a chance of getting down.

And when they had done that they left him alone in the coming dark with all his fear, and knowing that he would never be able to get down because he was finished.

And the next day all the village was down to look at the man clinging to the cliff. And they sat around and gossiped, and all the girls were saying how handsome he was, and they wouldn't have minded being Rangi Ngatane except for the ending.

And my father said that some of them went every day to look at Rewi Tamati as he hung there on the cliff dying more quickly with fear and slowly with hunger, and they would come back and tell all the village what they had seen and how Rewi Tamati looked that day, and some of the small boys would throw stones at him until they were stopped because the cliff was tapu. And Rewi Tamati lasted for five days up on the cliff because he was so strong and on the fifth day they said he seemed to go crazy for he began shouting. And they listened but they could not hear much because his voice was so hoarse and weak, and what they did hear didn't seem to make words so they came away, and the next day they found him on the rocks at the bottom of the cliff all broken. And they could never make out whether he had become so weak as to fall or whether he had jumped. Maybe, they said, he had become so crazy he thought he would fly, and the young girls giggled and looked at the young men.

But my father thought it was the cruellest thing ever done to a living creature. Leaving a brave man alone with a fear like that and not giving him his chance. Even if he had been an enemy and murdered the girl he was no worse than us, and his death and manner of it was fit for no man.

And my father would never go near the cliff. He hated the whole business but there was nothing he could do.

G. R. Gilbert: "Fear" in *Forty Short Short Stories*, ed. J. C. Reid, London 1965

Maori words: pakeha: white man — *haka*: a war-dance — *pa*: a fort — *tapu*: sacred, untouchable.

VOCABULARY. *Maori*: a member of the native brown race of New Zealand; their language — *Waikato*: largest river in New Zealand, in the North Island and territory near it — *trunk*: main stem of a tree — *tough*: rough and violent — *kid*: (sl.) deceive, delude, humbug — *stab:* push a weapon into — *short-cut*: a quicker way than usual — *ledge*: shelf — *cliff*: high steep rock — *jut*: stand or stick out — *smooth*: not rough, having an even surface — *frantic*: mad — *clutch*: hold firmly — *gossip*: chatter — *hoarse*: having a harsh, grating voice — *giggle*: laugh in a silly manner.

70. Cameras Under the Water

The first underwater photograph was taken in 1894 by Louis Boutan, a science teacher in Paris. After Boutan, other people carried out experiments in underwater photography from time to time. In 1913, a newspaper in Norfolk, Virginia, published a number of photographs taken under water in Chesapeake Bay. A report beside the pictures stated, "No one else has ever gone beneath the sea with a camera and brought back a successful photograph of life in the depths."

Everyone in the town was soon talking about the young man who had taken the photographs. He was Jack Williamson. Williamson's father, Captain Charles Williamson, was a salvage expert. For his work he had designed an underwater observation sphere. This was attached to a barge by means of a wide tube made of flexible metal. The tube could be made longer or shorter to suit the depth at which the sphere was required to work. The sphere was entered from the barge by way of the tube. To take his pictures, Jack Williamson simply went down in the sphere on a clear, sunny day, armed with a press camera.

For Jack Williamson, these photographs were only a beginning. "I want to make a moving picture under water," he said, and the newspaper printed his words. At this time, the great moving-picture industry of Hollywood, California, was beginning to grow. People everywhere wanted to see moving pictures. Producers were looking out for fresh ideas. Williamson was quickly offered the money required to make his film.

In Februar 1914, he sailed for Nassau, in the Bahamas, with a film-making team. Williamson took with him a device called a photosphere. It was very much like his father's salvage rig, a sphere on the end of a telescopic tube, but there was one important difference. It was equipped with mercury vapour floodlights.

In the clear waters around the Bahamas, Williamson soon obtained some splendid moving pictures of underwater scenery and a wide variety of fishes. He also took pictures of native divers going down for coins. He reported this to the business men who had provided him with money. They wanted to be quite certain that Williamson's film would attract large audiences and earn a lot of money. They wired to him, "What about the shark fight?"

The shark fight was supposed to provide the highlight of the film. "I said I'd do it," said Williamson, "so I'll have to do it."

He called in two of the native divers. He said, "I want some photographs of you killing a shark. I'll pay you extra for it."

The divers hesitated. But they could not resist the prospect of extra pay. Williamson prepared to photograph the scene. He flung overboard a dead horse on the end of a rope. At once, hungry sharks began to gather below the ship.

A diver plunged downwards. At the same time, men aboard dragged in the dead horse leaving the sharks swimming around in circles and snapping at each other. The diver selected one of the sharks and swam towards it, his knife ready. The shark swung away—completely out of range of the camera. A few moments later, the diver returned to the surface smiling. He had killed the shark. "What about my extra money?" he said.

Williamson paid the first diver. Then he turned to the second. Very carefully he explained to him what was required. The diver grinned happily. The horse was cast over the side again, and the diver plunged in. At once, a shark swept towards him. The diver lost his nerve and swam to the far side of the dead horse. There he remained splashing—and out of range of the camera.

Williamson could not find another diver to send down. He said,

"I've got to have this picture. I'll do it myself."

He stripped to the waist and cut off the legs of his trousers.

"You're crazy, Jack," said his companions. "No white man has ever done a stunt like this. You'll be killed for sure."

The local people brought some oil. "Rub this on you," they said. "The sharks don't like it."

Smeared with the evil-smelling liquid, Williamson plunged into the clear blue waters. He could see the grey-white forms of a dozen sharks swimming to and fro beside the photosphere. He trod water in range of the camera and waited. One of the prowling sharks suddenly swished its tail and flashed towards him, its great jaws wide open.

Williamson's lungs seemed to be bursting. He had never been under water for so long before. Yet he remained calm. He moved slightly to one side and clutched at the shark's fin. Once he had it firmly in his hand, he moved under the shark's body and drove upwards with his knife into the gleaming white flesh. He felt the blade strike home and go in deeply. Then the wild threshing of the shark threw him aside. Dazed by the blow and bewildered by the flurry of water, Williamson struck out desperately for the surface. For several moments he lost all sense of what he was doing. Then he came to on the deck of the barge.

"We've got some great pictures, Jack," his companions told him. The first underwater motion picture, *The Williamson Submarine Expedition*, was a popular success in all the countries where it was shown. He followed it with other successful films. Then, in 1915, he produced his masterpiece—a film of Jules Verne's *Twenty Thousand Leagues under the Sea.* One of the most thrilling scenes in this film was a fight between a deep-sea diver and a giant octopus.

Williamson was now one of the most famous of all film producers. One studio provided him with two million dollars. "Make us the biggest film yet. Do it in colour and put in a scene showing two hundred divers under water."

Williamson completed this film and it seemed as if it might be his most successful. But, before the film had its first showing, interest in it was killed. The first talking picture, *The Jazz Singer*, was shown in New York. This meant the end of the silent films.

Robert J. Hoare: *Deep Waters*, London 1966
By permission of the publishers, Ginn and Co Ltd

VOCABULARY. *salvage*: saving of property from a wrecked ship — *design*: construct — *barge*: flat-bottomed boat — *tube*: pipe — *producer*: one who is responsible for production of a film — *telescopic*: consisting of sections which slide one within the other "ineinanderschiebbar" — *mercury*: heavy, silvery liquid metal *(quicksilver)* — *vapour*: moisture in the air (e.g. steam, mist) — *floodlights*: strong lamps — *scenery*: general natural features of a district etc. — *diver*: one who dips or plunges — *shark*: large sea-fish, dangerous to bathers — *highlight*: detail of vivid interest — *drag*: pull roughly — *splash*: cause water to fly about in drops — *strip*: put off one's clothes — *waist*: part of the human body between the ribs and the hips "Taille" — *stunt*: special effort, show performance "Schaunummer, Glanzstück" — *smear*: spread with anything sticky — *tread* (trod, trodden): walk, put the feet down on — *prowl*: move about cautiously in search of food — *swish*: swing through the air so that it can be heard — *jaw*: the bones of the mouth in which the teeth are set — *clutch*: seize or grasp — *blade*: cutting part of a knife — *strike home*: get blow well in — *daze*: make unable to think clearly — *flurry*: sudden rush of water — *league*: (old) measure of distance (about three miles) — *giant*: (attrib.) of great size — *octopus*: sea-creature with eight arms "Krake"

71. Nautilus 90 North

On 21st January, 1954, Mrs Dwight D. Eisenhower, the wife of the President of the United States, smashed a bottle of champagne against the dark green hull of a U.S.Navy submarine and named it *Nautilus*, and the world's first atomic-powered ocean-going vessel slid into the water at Groton, Connecticut.

Nautilus, which had cost more than ten million pounds to build, was a large submarine, 323 feet long and 28 feet in breadth. The fuel she used was enriched uranium which, by special processes, was able to produce millions of time more heat than the same amount of coal or oil. This heat produced steam which, in turn, drove the propellers. She had a cruising speed of about 20 knots and could travel right round the world at the Equator without replenishing the few pounds of uranium in her reactor. She made history the moment she put to sea and, in 1957, she was preparing to make a voyage men had dreamed of for centuries.

The shortest distance from Asia or the west of North America to Europe is a straight line passing over the North Pole. As long ago as 1607, Henry Hudson had tried to reach the Far East from England by this route. He was driven back by the vast ice-pack which encircles the North Pole. But the ice-pack would not prevent the passage of the *Nautilus*. The plan was for her to sail *under* the North Pole.

In the autumn of 1957, *Nautilus* made a voyage from New London to the east of Greenland and proceeded northwards under the ice-pack. At first, she followed the same route that Hudson had taken in the Arctic, and cruised on to 87 degrees North—only 180 miles from the North Pole.

In the early summer of 1958, the *Nautilus* probed the approach to the North Pole under the ice-pack off the coast of Siberia. Her captain, Commander William R. Anderson, and his crew had already learnt a great deal about the dangers of a voyage under the Pole. For one thing, the underside of the ice-pack was far from level. In some places, deep ridges jutted down from the main mass to a depth of 100—120 feet. This meant that the *Nautilus* must cruise at a lower depth than 120 feet to allow her sail (conning-tower) to clear the ice. The waters of the Bering Strait off Siberia are shallow in places. Sometimes the gap between the bottom of the ice and the ocean floor was not wide enough to enable the *Nautilus* to get through with a margin for safety.

To measure the distance between the submarine and the ice above and the ocean bed below, the *Nautilus* used sonar equipment. Sonar works out how far away an object is by sending out a sound and measuring the time it takes for an echo to return from the object.

From the Bering Strait, the *Nautilus* sailed southwards to Pearl Harbour, on the island of Hawaii. She set out from Pearl Harbour again on 22nd July, 1958 and, one week later, was almost 3000 miles to the north, once more looking for a safe passage through the Bering Strait.

Shallow water drove the submarine eastwards towards the Barrow Sea, off Alaska, before it could head northwards again. Then, on 1st August, at Longitude 155 East, Commander Anderson gave the order, "Steer due north". *Nautilus* was under the ice-pack and the North Pole lay 1,094 miles ahead.

Outside the submarine, the temperature of the water sometimes fell more than five degrees below freezing-point. Inside, it was a snug 72 degrees. Life was comfortable for the 10 officers and 94 men aboard. The food was good. In the crew's mess there was an ice-cream machine, a soft-drink machine and a juke-box wired to hi-fi loud speakers. Regular film shows were given.

Operation Sunshine, as the voyage was called, went smoothly. Three-quarters of an hour before midnight (G. M. T.) on 3rd August, 1958, Commander Anderson made an announcement over the loud speakers to all parts of the submarine: "The North Pole". From the crew's mess, three cheers rang out.

Two days later, Commander Anderson saw a break in the ice above and gave the order for *Nautilus* to surface. The submarine came up into blue-green water, bathed in bright sunshine, after travelling 1,830 miles under the ice in 96 hours.

At once a wireless aerial was run up and the wireless operator tapped out a message in Morse code. That message startled the whole world, apart from a handful of people in the United States, for Operation Sunshine had been top secret. It was a simple message of only three words: "Nautilus 90 North".

Robert J. Hoare: *Deep Waters*, London 1966
By permission of the publishers, Ginn and Co Ltd

VOCABULARY. *90 North*: the Poles are 90 °Lat. (= Latitude), the equator being 0 Lat. — *smash*: break in pieces — *submarine*: warship that can travel under water — *fuel*: material for burning — *enrich*: make richer in quality — *uranium*: radioactive element, source of atomic energy — *equator*: imaginary line round the earth, half-way between the North Pole and South Pole — *replenish*: fill up one's supply again — *ice-pack*: wide area of ice covering the sea — *encircle*: close round — *probe*: examine thoroughly — *level*: flat, even, smooth — *ridge*: long narrow stretch — *jut*: stand or stick out — *conning-tower*: place on a submarine from which orders are given — *clear*: get past without touching — *strait*: channel of water connecting two seas — *shallow*: not deep — *margin*: sth. extra, beyond what is needed — *sonar*: sound navigation ranging — *longitude*: distance east or west of the Greenwich meridian — *due*: exactly; directly — *snug*: comfortable — *juke-box*: machine that automatically plays selected gramophone records when coin is inserted — *wire*: send — *hi-fi*: = highfidelity: reproducing sound faithfully "mit höchster Wiedergabetreue" — *smooth*: without any difficulties — *G. M. T.*: Greenwich mean time — *surface*: rise to the surface of the sea — *aerial*: wires for receiving or sending radio waves — *tap*: strike lightly — *Morse code*: system of dots and dashes representing letters of the alphabet — *startle*: surprise; give shock to.

72. Mutiny on the Hermione

(At the end of the eighteenth century and in the first years of the nineteenth century, there were many terrible mutinies in the British fleet. One of the most famous was that on the 32-gun frigate, H. M. S. *Hermione*.)

It was in September 1797, the year of the great mutiny at the *Nore* and of numerous smaller mutinies in different parts of the world. It was as if a wave of mutiny swept over the ocean, affecting ships off Cadiz, at the Cape of Good Hope, and in the West Indies. With this infection about, even trifles might cause it to break out in violence; and on board the *Hermione* there were causes which were very far from trifles.

The captain of the *Hermione*—his name was Pigot—was a young man who had been promoted by family interest to the command of a frigate before he had learnt to command himself. It may be that his natural disposition prevented his learning, for he was not so young as many who did very well. Swelling with a sense of his importance he conceived that everything must go exactly as he wished it, and his one way of enforcing this idea was brutal punishment for every departure from it.

It was afterwards said that the ship had in her crew a great many Irish —then notoriously disaffected; and a great many foreigners, who would naturally feel even more indignant at the severity with which they were treated. It is impossible to say how far these statements were true. They were never substantiated; and the list of the crew does not show any unusual number of Irish or foreign names. Some, of course, there always were. I believe it was merely a story got up afterwards, to lessen the shame of the terrible business.

There had certainly been much dissatisfaction and discontent for some time; but they were brought to a head by a new and disgusting exhibition of brutality. On the evening of the 21st September, when the *Hermione* was cruising off Puerto Rico, the men were exercising aloft; and the captain, furious at their not being as quick as he thought they might have been, roared out that he would flog the last man down.

No one had any doubt that he would keep his word; and in trying to avoid the promised flogging, two young men, particularly smart sailors, missed their hold, fell to the deck and were killed. "Throw the lubbers overboard," was what the captain said, and he went into his cabin.

The men took twenty-four hours or rather more to consider this, and on the night of the 22nd September they knocked down the officer of the watch and threw him overboard; killed the captain in his cabin and threw him out through the stern port; butchered every officer except the master, the gunner, and one mate, and took the ship to La Guayra, where they handed her over to the Spanish Governor.

Morally, it is difficult to condemn the killing of Captain Pigot. His whole conduct for months past had been brutal and tyrannical. He had beyond question caused the death of the two seamen on the evening of the 21st, and if the vengeance of the men had wreaked itself on him alone, morality, at any rate, would have had nothing to object to. But when they took to butchering all the officers, who were equally with themselves the victims of their captain's tyranny, they could only be held to be dangerous madmen, to be hunted down by all honest people.

And this was really done. In one way or another a very large number of the murderers were caught, tried, and hanged. It was said that many more men were hanged than were on board the ship at the time; that in fact, the rage against the criminals was so great that any man or woman having a grudge against any one could bring false witness against him, could swear that he was one of the *Hermione's* crew and have him promptly put out of the way for ever.

These stories have long since died out, but even forty years ago they were still told and believed at Portsmouth and Plymouth. I doubt, however, if there was any real truth in them; and though there is no reason to suppose that justice erred on the side of mercy, I do not think that any man was hanged without reasonable evidence that he had been not only on board the *Hermione*, but actually a party to the murders.

(Two years later, the ship was recaptured by Captain Hamilton.)

John Knox Laughton: "Mutiny and Retribution" in
Fifty Famous Sea Stories, ed. Mainsail, London 1961

VOCABULARY. *mutiny*: refusal to obey commands — *frigate*: swift-sailing warship of earlier times — *mutiny at the Nore*: a mutiny in the fleet stationed at the Nore, an anchorage off Sheerness, in the Thames, which broke out on May 20, 1797, and was not suppressed till June 15 — *West Indies*: they are divided into the Greater Antilles and groups of lesser islands — *infection*: anything that spreads widely — *trifle*: thing of little importance — *disposition*: temper — *swelling with*: hardly able to contain — *conceive:* imagine — *enforce*: compel obedience to — *disaffected*: rebellious — *substantiate*: prove the truth of — *get up*: set on foot — *bring to a head*: bring to a crisis — *exercise aloft*: take exercise among the ropes and masts or high above the decks — *flog*: beat; lash — *lubber*: clumsy fellow — *stern port*: left-hand side of hind part — *mate*: ship's officer below the captain — *vengeance*: revenge — *wreak*: carry out — *victim*: person who suffers — *grudge*: bad feeling — *witness*: one who gives evidence — *err*: be wrong — *mercy*: kindness; pity.

73. Retribution

Of all the recaptures of lost ships, the one that is most celebrated is that of the 32-gun frigate *Hermione*—celebrated not only for the brilliance of the recapture, but almost equally for the appalling tragedy of her previous loss.

On 22nd September, 1797, English mutineers, after killing the captain and the officers, handed the *Hermione* over to the Spanish governor of La Guayra.

The *Hermione* remained a Spanish frigate for a few weeks more than two years. In September 1799, Sir Hyde Parker, the commander-in-chief at Jamaica, had news that she was at Puerto Cabello, and was on the point of sailing for Havana. He accordingly sent Captain Edward Hamilton in the 28-gun frigate *Surprise* to look out for her at Point Gallinas, which she would have to pass.

Hamilton waited there for a month, and then, as his provisions were running short, and he was not absolutely certain that the *Hermione* might not have passed in the night, he resolved to go off Puerto Cabello and see if she was still there.

On the 21st October the *Surprise* came off Puerto Cabello, and there saw the *Hermione* lying ready for sea, but moored, head and stern, between two batteries which commanded the mouth of the harbour, and were said to mount nearly two hundred guns.

The position appeared impregnable, and for three days Hamilton cruised to and fro before the port, possibly hoping that the *Hermione* might come out and try to capture him; for she was a much larger frigate than the

Surprise, had been armed by the Spaniards with forty-four guns, and had on board close on four hundred men. So far as the material force went, she was more than double the strength of the *Surprise.* As, however, the Spaniards were not willing to try the wager of battle, Hamilton gradually made up his mind to attempt cutting her out; and on the evening of the 24th, he ordered the men to come aft and spoke to them. He reminded them of the way the frigate had been lost, of the disgrace to the British navy as long as she remained in the hands of the Spaniards, of the time he had been waiting for her, and of his hopes to have met her at sea. He concluded in some such words as these: "It is useless to wait any longer. We shall soon be obliged to leave the station. Our only prospect of success is by cutting her out this night."

A tremendous cheering here interrupted him, and showed him that the men were eager to be led in. He continued: "I will lead you myself. I have here written out the orders for the boats, with the names of the officers and men for each."

During the next few hours all the preparations were made. To each boat was prescribed, in exact detail, where she was to go and what she was to do. There were six boats in all; they were to board as ordered. Some men were told off to fight, others to cut the cables, others to run aloft and loose the sails, others to remain in the boats, to make fast to the ship and take her in tow. Every man was dressed in blue; no white was to be seen. The password was, "Britannia", the answer, "Ireland". The rendezvous was given, "the *Hermione's* quarterdeck". It was near midnight, before everything was ready and the boats shoved off, Hamilton in the pinnace leading.

He had, of course, hoped to take the enemy by surprise; but about a mile from the mouth of the harbour they were met by two Spanish gunboats, which at once opened fire on them. The men in the pinnace gave three cheers and pushed on for the *Hermione,* but some of the other boats stopped to return the enemy's fire, an act of disobedience which nearly cost the expedition dear.

As it was, the Spaniards on board the *Hermione* were awake and at their quarters, blazing away at some black shadows or imaginary enemy; but they could not or did not see the boats advancing from right ahead; and when Hamilton in the pinnace boarded her on the starboard bow—Hamilton himself being one of the first on board—most of the crew were at their guns on the main deck. They were actually ignorant that the English were on board; and the boats coming up one after the other, reinforced the leading parties, and drove the Spaniards on deck into the cabin, where they were presently forced to surrender, or down below, where they were comparatively harmless.

The cables were cut; the boats took the ship in tow; the sails were let fall, and as they swelled to the breeze, the batteries, which now realised that something untoward had happened, opened fire on the ship as she was gathering way and leaving the harbour behind. Some of the shots struck her and probably killed several of their own men, but do not seem to have done any harm to the English. And in less than two hours from the time the pinnace boarded her, the *Hermione* was clear of the harbour, out of range of the batteries, and safe in English hands.

It was a very curious fight. One hundred men, exposed in boats or on the open deck, attacked four hundred under cover and prepared, and overcame them, after inflicting tremendous loss on the defenders, whilst they themselves suffered very little.

The total English loss was twelve wounded, including Hamilton, whose injuries were very serious. He lived to a ripe old age, but never quite recovered from the injuries to his head and back. The king conferred knighthood on him by letters patent; he received the freedom of the city of London, delivered to him in person at a public dinner on the first anniversary of the fight, 25th October 1800; and many years afterwards he was made a baronet.

Whilst the loss of the English was so small, that of the Spaniards was exceedingly large. It amounted to 119 killed and ninety-seven dangerously wounded—some of whom, it is difficult to say how many, must be attributed to the ill-judged fire of their own batteries. Not to be bothered with the prisoners, they were put on board a captured coasting vessel, and sent back to Puerto Cabello. But the ship was taken to Jamaica, where she was restored to the navy under the name of *Retribution.*

John Knox Laughton: "Mutiny and Retribution" in
Fifty Famous Sea Stories, ed. Mainsail, London 1961

VOCABULARY. *retribution*: punishment; revenge "Vergeltung" — *frigate*: swift-sailing warship of earlier times — *appal*: terrify — *mutineer*: person guilty of open rebellion against lawful authority — *commander-in-chief*: head of all the military forces — *Puerto Cabello*: seaport, Venezuela — *moor*: fasten a ship by ropes or by anchor — *stern*: back part of a ship — *battery*: a number of cannon — *mount*: put and fix in position — *impregnable*: too strong to be captured — *wager of battle*: (hist.) ancient form of combat between parties — *cut out*: attack and seize a ship under the enemy's guns — *disgrace*: public shame — *aloft*: among the ropes and masts — *rendezvous*: meeting at a time agreed upon — *quarterdeck*: part of the upper deck reserved for a warship's officers — *shove*: (colloq.) push — *pinnace*:

ship's boat with (usu.) eight oarsmen — *quarter*: post assumed for duty by sailors on a ship — *reinforce*: support and strengthen — *untoward*: unlucky — *range*: distance to which a gun will shoot — *expose*: lay open to — *injury*: hurt — *knighthood*: rank of a knight — *letters patent* [peitənt]: an open letter granting a title — *the freedom of a city*: given as an honour — *baronet*: person lower in rank than a noble but higher in rank than a knight (called: Sir Edward Hamilton, Bart.).

74. Mutiny on the Vittoria

(Though the mutiny described in this story happened more than 130 years ago, in 1830, it is still one of the best stories of crime at sea.)

A most atrocious act of the basest mutiny and murder took place at the above-mentioned period.

Our merchant vessels do not carry many men, in peace, as they hire labourers when in harbour to do the drudgery, and carry no more to sea than are sufficient to manage the sails and keep a look-out. The *Vittoria* appears to have been very weakly manned, and at Manilla they took on board six Spaniards, we presume, because they were to be had cheap.

Captain Smith cleared out from Manilla to London, and he had not been long at sea before the Spaniards refused their duty; they were, however, brought to reason. They had contemplated their murderous intentions from the hour they first went on board, and had secretly provided themselves with stilettos and short pistols. As to the captain of the vessel and the officers, they had no arms whatever. They rested in perfect safety when this dreadful conspiracy was going on and Mr Andrews, alone, had some suspicion of the Spaniards.

In the dead of night, when all the crew were asleep, except the man at the helm, the Spaniards stole upon deck quietly, and secured the crew as they were asleep, murdering three of them with their long Spanish knives, and wounding several others. They then burst open the captain's cabin-door, and stabbed him in his bed in about thirty places; and to secure their act, they also shot him with their pistols, and threw him on the cabin-floor. The second mate and the carpenter were killed in their sleep, and thrown overboard in their beds. The chief mate, Mr Andrews, they put in irons, and a consultation was held what was to be done with him; some were for instantly murdering him; but others knew that they could not navigate the ship without his assistance, and they therefore released him, and compelled him to enter into all their plan. The steward was also spared: but it was agreed among them, that when they made the coast of California, they should murder Mr Andrews and the rest of the crew, and then dispose of the vessel as well as they could; for there are Spanish merchants who will purchase any vessel and encourage piracy on all sides.

This the Spaniards well knew, and thought to make a good bargain; but Mr Andrews, who had got an inkling of the intentions of the pirates, consulted with the steward, and this they had many opportunities of doing, for the Spaniards got drunk almost every day.

On the eighth day after the murder of Captain Smith, the mate and steward put their plan into execution. They were well aware of their disparity in point of numbers; but it was life against life, and they knew that by remaining quiet, death would be their portion that moment that they came so near to the land that the pirates could carry the ship into harbour, without the aid of navigation. Mr Andrews got possession of a hatchet, and the steward of a knife; and the two principal leaders were struck dead by Mr Andrews, and one of the others by the steward, who had a short struggle with him on deck, but succeeded in stabbing him to the heart, though he was himself desperately wounded: the remainder of the Spaniards were all secured by the crew, who had joined their officers, and the vessel was once more in the possession of her original crew. The mate, Mr Andrews, made immediately for the French coast, where the mutineers were brought to trial before a French tribunal; and after a patient hearing they were all condemned to die. The sentence was soon put in execution, and they were put in chains and hung on gibbets as a warning to others. Mr Andrews made his voyage to London, and arrived in security.

The *Vittoria* was insured for £ 6,000, and they made a handsome present to Mr Andrews, and also to the steward, and all the crew. Mr Andrews has since been made a captain, and is a very young, but an experienced seaman, who must be a valuable servant to those who employ him. A great part of the ship's cargo belonged to the firm of Thornton and West, and was uninsured so that they were indebted to the intrepid conduct of Mr Andrews for the safety of their goods, and awarded him accordingly.

Captain Smith left a wife and five children, and most of them left families. They had a good round sum of money collected for them, and the sailors who were on board all got respectable employment on board of ships out of the port of London, and were much respected.

This ought to be a lesson to ship-owners not to send their ships to sea with so few hands. No blame could be attached to Captain Smith, who acted up to his given instructions, and contrary to his own opinions; for he complained to his mate, Mr Andrews, previous to their leaving Manilla, that he was so restricted by the owners to the sum he was to give for wages, that he could not get Englishmen to enter at so low a rate, and must take Spaniards. The event was lamentable, and cost him his life; and for the saving of a few pounds, the owners were near to losing the whole of their valuable property.

Mainsail (editor): *Fifty Famous Sea Stories*, London 1961
By permission of the publishers, Burke Publishing Co Ltd

VOCABULARY. *mutiny*: refusal to obey commands — *atrocious*: cruel — *base*: low; mean — *hire*: employ a person for wages — *drudgery*: hard, uninteresting work — *man*: supply with the men needed — *presume*: suppose to be true — *stiletto*: small dagger — *conspiracy*: coming together for an evil purpose — *suspicion*: feeling of doubt — *the dead of night*: the darkest and quietest part — *helm*: complete mechanism by which a ship is steered — *secure*: seize and hold fast — *stab*: stick a sharp point into — *mate*: ship's officer below the captain — *instantly*: at once — *release*: set free — *dispose of*: get rid of — *purchase*: buy — *piracy*: robbery on the sea — *inkling*: hint or slight sign — *disparity*: great difference; inequality — *portion*: fate — *hatchet*: small axe — *desperate*: extremely serious — *trial*: judging in a law-court — *tribunal*: place of judgment — *gibbet*: a gallows — *insure*: secure payment of sum of money in event of loss or damage — *cargo*: ship's load — *intrepid*: brave — *previous to*: before — *rate*: amount, proportion.

75. Jules Silber—a German Spy

But it was not all success with M. I. 5. The credit for the most important success the Germans had—and it was a big success—went to the spy himself, and not to the espionage organization he worked for.

He was Jules Silber, Germany's most successful spy during the First World War. He was a German who had lived in South Africa, India and America and had become completely anglicized. Between 1902 and 1914 he was in America and had not given a thought to his German nationality until war broke out, when he immediately offered his services to the German Embassy in New York.

He himself chose to go into espionage, as being the best way in which he could serve his country. He had no training and never had any direct contact with the Intelligence departments in Berlin, which gave him an immediate advantage over all other German spies. An intelligent, resourceful man, he worked everything out for himself.

He arrived in England without even a passport, for he had never had one. They were unnecessary for travel between countries before 1914. He underwent a rigorous examination by the immigration authorities. But he was able to establish that he had worked with the British in both South Africa and India, and though he did not have the requisite papers he had plenty of recommendation from reliable sources. This was an intelligent approach from the start. No doubt if he had had the handicap of the Schragmuller training at the German spy-school at Antwerp he would have made the preliminary mistake of being smuggled into the country, and thus been at an immediate disadvantage.

Silber went about his task in the way he began. He never lost his touch or his nerve. He had been told that the greatest thorn in the side of German espionage was the British postal censorship which worked in close co-operation with M. I. 15. Silber got a job in the postal censorship department without any great difficulty, and the first piece of information he sent to Germany was of enormous value—a copy of M. I. 15's black list of suspected addresses in neutral countries used by agents in Britain. The nature of his job solved the problem of communicating with Germany, for he had only to slip his own message into letters he had passed in his job as censor.

Silber was never suspected and continued his successful career in espionage throughout the war. Among important information he gave the Germans was the first news about the tanks. The Germans seemed to have ignored or refused to believe the news of the tanks. Towards the end of the war attempts were made to conscript Silber, despite the important nature of his work at the censorship department. He took drugs in order to disguise his good health. He succeeded only too well and had a complete breakdown by the time the war ended. He lived on in England until 1925 when he returned to Germany where he wrote a book telling of his experiences as a spy in Britain. Until then no one knew.

Silber's success lay mainly in the fact that he worked alone and developed his own techniques. He was not at any time under orders from Berlin. He volunteered to do what he did, and all the information he sent was of his own choosing. He never did any espionage work in the place where he lived, but hired a room well away from his lodgings, where he wrote up his report and did his photographic work.

Charles Franklin: *Spies of the Twentieth Century*, London 1967
By permission of the publishers, Odhams Books Ltd

VOCABULARY. *M. I. 15*: originally the counter-espionage section of British Military Intelligence "Spionageabwehr" — *espionage*: spywork, spying — *anglicize*: to turn into English — *embassy*: residence of an ambassador — *resourceful*: ready at thinking out the right thing to do — *requisite*: (thing) needed or required — *approach*: path or road leading to a place — *handicap*: hindrance — *Schragmuller, Elsbeth:* also known as Fraulein Doktor, ran Antwerp spy-school, a German espionage establishment — *preliminary*: introductory — *smuggle*: send secretly — *thorn*: sharp, woody prickle on the stem of a plant — *censorship*: office of a censor, an official who examines letters etc. — *slip*: put into quietly or secretly — *conscript*: force a person to serve in the army — *disguise*: change one's appearance or look — *technique*: method used by an expert — *hire*: obtain the use of sth. by paying money.

76. The Spy Who Was Dead

Perhaps the most brilliant and imaginative espionage coup of the Second World War went to Britain. This macabre and inspired undertaking was officially named, somewhat equivocally, Operation Mincemeat. Some years ago a film was made which was called *The Man Who Never Was.*

The operation was conceived in order to mislead the German High Command about the Allied intentions after the reconquest of North Africa. The Allies had decided that the stepping stone from Africa to Europe would be Sicily. This strategy would be obvious to the Italian and German General Staffs, who would dispose their armies accordingly. The object of Operation Mincemeat was to convince them that, for reasons best known to itself, the Allied Command had decided to invade via Southern France, with a diversionary action against Sicily to cover their real intentions.

The problem was to plant this information in the hands of the enemy in a manner which would convince them that it was genuine. Lieut.-Commander Ewan Montagu of the Royal Navy came forward with the idea that the necessary papers should be forged and placed upon a dead staff officer in such circumstances that they would be bound to find their way into the hands of German Intelligence.

The circumstances were not difficult to create. Spain was a nest of German espionage and a body washed ashore on the Spanish coast with such papers in its dead possession would certainly be reported to the British authorities and the papers returned—after German Intelligence had examined them. Franco would see to that.

The problem was the body. Corpses abound in any country, particularly during wartime, but the body would have to be a convincing one. It would have to be the right age and physical standard. It would have to be neither wounded nor diseased. Death would have to appear to have been caused by drowning. Finding such a body was as difficult as convincing the higher authorities that the scheme was workable, even ethical.

A body still had to be found. Robbing a cemetery in the national interest was even considered. Finally a happier—if that is the word—solution was found in the shape of a youngish man who died of pneumonia. He had been medically rejected by all three services, but after death he was found to be perfectly fit to serve his country. His relatives patriotically agreed to the plan on the assurance that there would be no desecration of the body, which would have a Christian burial in Spain and they would later be able to visit the grave.

Pathologists assured the Intelligence team in charge of the operation that as the pneumonia had left water in the lungs the state of the body would not arouse any suspicion in the minds of the Spanish doctors who would be sure to examine it at its appointed destination.

And so the cadaver was prepared for its vital mission. It was dressed in the uniform of a Royal Marines major. The brief-case of an official courier was attached to it by means of the usual chain which went round the waist and then down the coat sleeve. The man's dead fingers were gripped around the brief-case handle. Inside the case in wax-sealed envelopes were various official and semi-official documents, one of which contained information which stated that the Allied Command intended to invade Europe by way of Southern France.

Great care was taken to create a convincing personality for Major William Martin, as he was called. Personal letters were carefully forged, even a fiancée invented.

Packed in ice, the dead hero set out on his mission in April, 1943. He embarked on a submarine which a few nights later surfaced near Huelva in Southern Spain. The body was launched into the sea with an offshore wind behind it.

London anxiously awaited events. Presently the Naval Attaché at Lisbon informed Whitehall that the drowned body of Major William Martin of the Royal Marines had been recovered by Spanish fishermen, and had been given a military funeral. This Lisbon attaché was then instructed to try and recover the Major's brief-case, and to do it as discreetly as possible as it contained important papers. In due course the attaché, who had no idea what was afoot, recovered the brief-case from the authorities in Madrid, and returned it to London, where it was carefully examined by technical experts.

It did not take the experts long to discover that the secret papers had been opened and inspected, and then carefully and skilfully resealed after no doubt having been photographed. This would have been done by any country, Britain included.

The information contained in the brief-case was duly passed on to Berlin, with the result that the German military dispositions in the Mediterranean were regrouped in order to repulse the expected attack on Sardinia and Southern France.

It was Britain's best espionage coup in the Second World War.

Charles Franklin: *Spies of the Twentieth Century*, London 1967
By permission of the publishers, Odhams Books

VOCABULARY. *espionage*: spy-work, spying — *macabre* [məˈkɑːbr]: gruesome; grim — *mincemeat*: meat cut up small "Gehacktes, Hackfleisch" — *diversionary*: turning aside the enemy's attention — *genuine*: real, not sham — *forge*: to imitate for fraud — *corpse*: dead body of a human being — *cemetery*: burying-ground — *pneumonia*: disease of the lungs — *desecration*: making bad use of sth. sacred — *pathologist*: expert in science of diseases — *Intelligence Department*: is engaged in collecting information esp. for military purposes — *Royal Marines*: corps trained for service at sea and on land — *brief-case*: small leather hand-bag — *courier*: messenger — *waist*: part of the body between the ribs and hips — *wax*: soft yellow substance made by bees — *seal*: close up completely — *submarine*: warship which can travel under water — *surface*: rise to the surface of the sea — *launch*: throw — *attaché*: junior ambassador — *Whitehall*: street in London where there are many Government offices; hence = the British Government — *reseal*: seal again — *repulse*: drive back.

77. Hidden Meaning

Every boy and girl at one time or another has used secret writing in sending a message. A message of this kind is written in code. Here the code is easily remembered, and so long as the reader knows the code which the writer has used, the message can be decoded and easily read. A code of this kind is so simple that one might easily guess it.

In time of war, important messages are always sent in code. These are very difficult to understand if one does not know the code, but there are always experts who are able to work it out. This is known as breaking the code.

In the Second World War, many messages were sent in code from the B. B. C. in London to the courageous men and women who were working for the Allies in Europe, which at that time was occupied by the Germans.

The messages seemed to be quite innocent, such as "Charles: The hens are now laying eggs" or "Yvonne: Put the kettle on."

These messages told secret agents whose code names were Charles and Yvonne to do certain things. The Germans were very puzzled by these messages, and they knew that they carried vital information. Sometimes the Germans were able to discover the men and women mentioned, but they could not always understand what the messages meant.

The Allied agents in Occupied Europe used radio for sending messages back to London, but this was dangerous because the Germans could usually discover where the message was being sent from. It was often necessary to use other methods in addition to radio.

Invisible writing was often used. This is one of the oldest methods of conveying information in time of war. A message can be written in lemon juice. When it dries, the writing is invisible.

Messages written in invisible ink are not written with a pen, as it is important not to scratch the paper. They are written with an orange stick round which cotton wool has been wrapped.

Usually an ordinary letter is written in ordinary ink and plenty of space is left between the lines. The secret message is written in the spaces. The person receiving the letter places a hot iron on it. The heat acts on the lemon juice and the secret message appears in a brown colour.

Secret messages are not only written on paper. Sometimes a man has his head shaved and a message is written on the bald head. The hair grows again and covers up the message. The design on a scarf, on a handkerchief or on a lady's dress has also conveyed information.

Even eggs have been used for carrying messages.

Messages written in code are often photographed. The film is then thrown onto a screen, and if the code is known, the message can be read. There is also a very special camera called micro-camera. It can photograph a page of writing onto a small piece of film which is sometimes no larger than a dot. This dot, called a micro-film, can be hidden in a variety of places. Often it is hidden beneath a postage stamp on an ordinary envelope.

All kinds of places are used for hiding messages. A bandage covering a cut finger may conceal a message. A spy may be wearing horn-rimmed spectacles which have been specially constructed to take a message. It might be hidden in a hollow inside the rims.

Clothes provide many hiding-places for messages. The inside lining of a jacket or an overcoat is a good place. A micro-film may be concealed inside a button. Boots and shoes may have hollows inside the heels or the soles.

Messages are even concealed inside bootlaces. No place is too small to be used, and the more unexpected the hiding-place the better.

Messages are often hidden inside books. Colonel Pinto, who was a famous spy-catcher during the Second World War, suspected that a certain Dutchman might be a spy. Among the articles carried by the Dutchman was a Dutch-English dictionary. This looked innocent enough. A Dutchman who could not speak much English would be expected to bring a Dutch-English dictionary with him.

But Colonel Pinto was suspicious and he decided to examine the dictionary. He started at letter A and began to read every word in the dictionary. It was slow work and he read hundreds of pages without noticing anything. Then opposite the letter F he saw a small dot. Some pages further on there was another dot opposite a letter. He read carefully every word in the dictionary, noting the letters which had dots opposite them. These letters made up an important message.

In war a continuous struggle goes on to get information and to prevent information passing from one side to another. Modern discoveries and modern apparatus are used in this struggle; the secret message, with which boys and girls amuse themselves, is then used for serious purposes.

Andrew Scotland: *A Junior Panorama—Book Four*, London 1963
By permission of the publishers, Odhams Press Ltd

VOCABULARY. *message*: piece of news sent from one person to another — *code*: system of signs, secret writing etc. — *decode*: get the meaning of sth. written in code — *ally*: person or country allied to another — *kettle*: metal pot — *arrangements*: plans; preparations — *puzzle*: cause sb. to be perplexed — *convey*: send — *scratch*: mark with sth. pointed — *act on*: have an effect on — *bald*: without hair — *design*: drawing or sketch — *screen*: white surface on to which cinema films are projected — *micro-*: (prefix) small — *dot*: small mark — *conceal*: hide — *rim*: outside edge (e.g. of spectacles) — *lining*: inside covering — *sole*: underside of a boot — *bootlace*: string or leather strip for lacing boots — *colonel* [ˈkəːnl]: officer who has command of a regiment — *suspect*: think likely; conjecture — *suspicious*: distrustful — *apparatus*: tools, instruments etc. for some purpose.

78. The Detective

There is one kind of policeman who has nothing to do with the prevention of crime. His job is to detect the criminal after the crime has been committed. He does not wish to be noticed, therefore he does not wear a uniform. He is the detective.

A detective is chosen from the uniformed branch. He must want to be a detective and he must be good at doing the job. He may have to work long hours when investigating serious cases. He has no beat like the uniformed policeman. While his work is mainly in one district, he may have to go many miles away to trace a clue at a moment's notice.

Large build and height are not so important. A detective has to be observant and shrewd. He is pitting his wits against criminals who are cunning and often desperate.

A detective should be able to read character. He must also know how to frame questions to get the answers that will give a criminal away. Many detectives have specialist knowledge. One will study jewellery. Another will be an expert in the detection of forgery. There are gun experts and fingerprints specialists. Photography is another skill that can help to make a good detective.

There are five Detective Training Centres in the country. Here men are trained to make good detectives. They will have lectures about fingerprints, ballistics (the science of firearms and bullets), foot impressions and bloodstains. These lectures will be much more scientific than those the police recruit normally gets.

Mock incidents will be arranged. In the grounds at the training centre a group of detective-students finds a car with a student pretending to be a dead man lying beside it.

Is this an accident, or manslaughter, or murder?

The detectives have to find the clues. They photograph the whole scene and take separate photographs of fingerprints and boot or shoe impressions. Witnesses may be brought into the incident. They are questioned and their statements are taken.

In fact, the students do all the things they would do if this were a real incident and it were a dead body and not Detective Smith lying beside the car.

Afterwards the incident is discussed and the detectives find out if they missed any vital clues or made any bad mistakes.

Detectives can be attached to the Criminal Investigation Department in city or rural forces. The specialists, such as the photographers and fingerprint experts, are very rarely given cases to investigate individually. Some detectives, attached to Scotland Yard, can be sent to forces in other parts of the country to help the local police with difficult cases.

A detective rarely works alone. He may be in charge of a case and he will follow it through until he has brought the criminal to court. But he can call for help from all the special departments of the Criminal Investigation Department. He will often need experts and scientists to help him to solve the case.

The modern Flying Squad began about forty years ago. Scotland Yard found that criminals were using cars and getting away from the scenes of their crimes too quickly for them to be caught. The Flying Squad was made up of detectives held in reserve who could be sent anywhere at a moment's notice.

These detectives sometimes use Q-cars. These are police cars although they do not look like them. They might be vans or battered-looking limousines. But they have the very best equipment, with radio and powerful engines. Despite their battered appearance, they can roar into pursuit and probably will catch the criminal in his fast car.

Boswell Taylor: *999 ... Police!*, London 1964
By permission of the publishers, University of London Press Ltd

VOCABULARY. *prevention*: the act of guarding against — *detect*: find out; discover — *investigate*: search into with care — *beat*: course over which a person goes regularly "Runde, Revier" — *clue*: sth. that helps to solve a problem — *build*: general shape — *shrewd*: having sound judgment and common sense — *pit*: set up in opposition — *cunning*: sly, deceitful — *frame*: put together — *jewellery*: precious stones — *forgery*: copying or imitating in order to deceive — *fingerprints*: marks made by the finger-tips — *ballistics*: science dealing with projectiles — *bloodstain*: mark of blood — *recruit*: newly enlisted and not yet trained member — *pretend*: profess falsely; make believe — *manslaughter*: criminal but not wilful homicide "Totschlag" — *witness*: one who gives evidence — *Flying Squad*: motor-police "Überfallkommando" — *van*: large covered wagon or car — *batter*: hit hard, bruise — *equipment*: things needed for a purpose — *pursuit*: act of following in order to capture.

79. Training a Policeman

A group of boys, rucksacks on their backs, climb the last rocky slope of a mountain. They study a map and look round at the horizon of mountains and hills. Then they pitch their tents and get their meal. They are police cadets in training.

Police cadets are trained in many ways. They have lectures from experts. They visit factories. They have physical training, swimming and games. They may take part in Outward Bound Courses. Some will win Duke of Edinburgh awards.

Many of the things they do may not seem to have much to do with police work. But a policeman must be self-reliant, courageous and determined. He must be able to discipline himself. Cadets need training in these qualities.

A policeman also needs training for his job. He usually works on his own. He must therefore learn to make decisions at once, and they must be the right decisions. He has to know when he can arrest a man. He may have to rescue a drowning man or help a child burned in a fire.

The law is complicated and the policeman cannot afford to make a mistake. An innocent man might suffer. A street quarrel could turn into a riot.

A policeman's job does not end with taking notes at the scene of the accident or crime. Later he will have to stand in the witness box. He must therefore learn how to take evidence and how to give it in court.

After a recruit is medically examined and sworn in, he spends thirteen weeks on a training course at one of the eight Police Training Centres in England and Wales. (Scotland has a different system.) Then he has a month's training and nine months doing the job. He then returns to the centre for another three months' course.

The policeman in school learns some law. He hears about traffic and safety problems. Firearms are shown to him and discussed. He finds out how fingerprints are taken and how records of criminals are kept. He learns life-saving and first-aid. He takes part in mock trials, mock accidents and mock arrests. The scientist, who works in the forensic (criminal science) laboratories, explains his work.

After this training he goes back to the regular force. He puts into practice some of the things he has learned. He may also spend some time in the Criminal Investigation Department, or with the traffic police. If he likes these special jobs he may be able to transfer to them later. He may have to wait a long time if he wants to become a dog handler or a mounted policeman. Finally, his training complete, he becomes a policeman.

Boswell Taylor: *999 ... Police!*, London 1964

VOCABULARY. *rucksack*: bag carried on the back — *slope*: slanting line; sth. which is higher at one end than at the other (e.g. hill-side) — *pitch*: fix in the ground — *cadet*: student in training college — *self-reliant*: having confidence in one's own powers — *on one's own*: independently — *riot*: noisy disorder among a crowd of people — *witness*: one who gives evidence — *evidence*: testimony, facts, making for a conclusion — *recruit*: new member of a group — *swear in*: (swore, sworn) give the oath of office to — *fingerprints*: marks made by the fingertips — *record*: document preserving evidence or information; *records of criminals*: "Strafregister" — *mock*: not real or genuine — *forensic*: having to do with courts of law — *transfer*: move from one occupation to another — *handler*: person controlling men or animals — *mounted policeman*: p. supplied with a horse.

80. A Justice of the Peace

Many Justices of the Peace were known as *trading justices*. They made money out of crime. One of these corrupt magistrates at the beginning of the eighteenth century was Thomas de Veil. Although he made money out of it, he did his job well.

At that time a magistrate's office was in his own home. In 1729 Colonel de Veil set up his office in his house in Bow Street, on the opposite side of the street from where the famous police court now stands.

Colonel de Veil was shrewd and clever. Sometimes he is called the first detective. As a police-magistrate he had to catch criminals as well as prosecute and judge them. He was unpaid, but made money in other ways. Colonel de Veil was the first magistrate to fight crime successfully.

On one occasion a man was brought before him accused of stealing. A witness said that the prisoner had picked a lock to get into the house. The accused man swore that he was innocent.

Colonel de Veil thought of a way of testing whether he was telling the truth. For a time he broke off the examination. He talked to other people in the room. Suddenly he swung round and asked the thief if he had a knife. Taken by surprise, and almost without thinking, the man gave the magistrate the knife he carried. Colonel de Veil saw at a glance that the tip of the blade was broken off.

A constable was instructed to go to the burgled house and bring back anything, no matter what it was, that he could find in the lock that had been picked. The constable returned with the tip of the knife—he had found it in the lock. When the prisoner saw that the broken pieces exactly matched he confessed to his crime.

Many stories are told of the Colonel's bravery. Once a mob, three hundred strong, attacked the magistrate in his Bow Street house. The three ring-leaders managed to break into the room he used as an office. They told the Colonel they would kill him if he did not agree to their demands. The magistrate kept them talking until a servant came into the room. For a moment they took their eyes off the magistrate. Quick as lightning, he snatched a couple of pistols off the table and covered the three men with them.

By this time the angry crowd had broken into his house. Colonel de Veil locked the ring-leaders in his office, and sent a constable for soldiers. Then, with blunderbuss and pistols, he faced the angry mob from the stairs. For nearly three hours he kept them at bay until at last the soldiers arrived.

Colonel de Veil, corrupt though he was, was the first London magistrate to defy the lawless gangs. He broke up one criminal gang after another. He laughed at threats. One gang even tried to kill him. Day by day they lay in wait for him. But he was too clever for them. Not only did he escape from their traps, but he finally collected enough evidence to bring them all to trial.

The fame of the London magistrate grew until he was being called to other parts of the country to track down rogues. By this time he was the chief magistrate for the whole of London except the City itself. Towards the end of his life he was knighted and became Sir Thomas de Veil.

Colonel de Veil is important because he was the first strong magistrate. He fought crime and brought criminals to justice. He did this without the help of a police force.

Boswell Taylor: *999 ... Police!*, London 1964
By permission of the publishers, University of London Press Ltd

VOCABULARY. *Justice of the Peace*: magistrate — *trade*: buy and sell; make a trade of one's influence — *corrupt*: not honest; taking bribes — *colonel* [kəːnl]: highest regimental officer — *shrewd*: cunning — *prosecute*: bring before a court — *witness*: person who was actually present at an event — *pick*: open (with a tool, not a key) — *swing*: whirl round — *tip*: top or point — *blade*: cutting part — *burgle*: break into a house — *match*: be equal to or corresponding with — *mob*: noisy crowd — *ring-leader*: head of a wicked gang — *snatch*: seize quickly — *couple*: a pair, two of a kind together — *blunderbuss*: short hand-gun with a wide mouth "Donnerbüchse" — *keep at bay*: keep an enemy at his distance — *defy*: resist boldly — *threat*: declaration of intention to hurt; menace — *lie in wait*: remain in hiding, in order to attack — *evidence*: anything that proves — *track down*: find by following — *knight*: make a knight; *knight*: man on whom title of honour (*Sir* before Christian name and surname) has been conferred.

81. Sir Alexander Fleming

The discovery of penicillin has been one of the most important events in the world of medicine in this present century. There are many people living today who owe their lives to this drug.

A large number of diseases are caused by tiny creatures called bacteria, which get into the bloodstream. They are so small that they can be seen only through a microscope. If they can be destroyed, many illnesses can be prevented. Unfortunately, there are some kinds of bacteria that are extremely difficult to kill.

Penicillin has the wonderful quality of being able to kill many dangerous bacteria, yet the drug itself does not harm the human body. In other words, penicillin is able to select the things which are harmful in the human body and to destroy them without damaging the body itself.

Penicillin was discovered in 1928 by a British scientist named Alexander Fleming. He was born in Scotland in 1881. His father was a farmer, and from his earliest days Alexander Fleming was brought into contact with nature and the ways of nature.

He went to school at the age of five. The school was a mile away from the farm, and he walked there and back, summer and winter alike. When he was ten he went to a school which was four miles away from the farm. Once again he walked the long distance—night and morning, summer and winter.

In later life he told how, on these walks, he learned much about nature. He watched the progress of crops through the seasons. He knew how to climb trees, catch trout in the streams and find the nests of birds. When he became a famous scientist he was known for his powers of observation. He declared that these were sharpened by his long walks to and from school.

Alexander Fleming was about twelve years old when he went to Kilmarnock Academy. He remained at this school until he was fourteen, when he went to London to live with his brother who was a doctor.

Two years later he became a junior clerk in a shipping firm. He worked there for four years, but he did not care for the work. He was twenty years of age when he decided to sit for an entrance examination for St. Mary's Hospital Medical School. He passed this examination and so began his study in medicine.

He was a clever and industrious student, and his examinations caused him no trouble. He liked to rise early in the morning and to get on with his work. After he had qualified as a doctor of medicine, he took up the study of bacteria. This was to be his life's work.

In 1914 the First World War broke out. Alexander Fleming joined the army as a doctor and he cared for the wounded. He noticed that many soldiers died because dirt got into their wounds. In the case of slight wounds, carbolic acid could kill the bacteria which came from this dirt. But in the case of deeper wounds, although the carbolic acid killed the bacteria, it seriously damaged the body itself. Fleming realised the great need for an antiseptic that would destroy bacteria without harming the body.

When the First World War ended in 1918, he returned to St. Mary's Hospital to continue his work on bacteria.

Ten years later, in 1928, he was working in his laboratory. Around him were dishes containing different kinds of bacteria which he was cultivating in order to study them. He picked up one dish and he noticed that it was different from the others. His first impulse was to throw it away; but he looked more closely at it, and he noticed that there was a clear space in the dish. This could mean only one thing. It meant that the bacteria in that clear space were dead.

He did not throw away the dish. A lesser man would have done so; a careless man would have done so; but Alexander Fleming decided to find out why the bacteria had been destroyed.

He studied the matter further and discovered that the bacteria had been destroyed because of the presence of a particular substance called penicillium. He did not know much about that substance, but he gave it a name. He called it penicillin.

This was the beginning of the wonderful drug. Thirteen years were to elapse, however, before it was made available to the public. Alexander Fleming realised that penicillin had special powers, but unfortunately it was difficult to make. In a sense, it had been made by accident. Dr. Howard Florey, a professor at Oxford University, was the first man to manufacture penicillin and he found that it was a powder, brown in colour.

This was the position when the Second World War broke out in 1939. Everyone knew there would be a demand for drugs and medicines to help the wounded. Alexander Fleming remembered his experiences in the First World War when he watched soldiers die because there was no drug which would kill bacteria. He knew that penicillin was capable of doing so. In both Great Britain and the United States millions of pounds were spent in building factories to produce penicillin. Many fighting men who were wounded owe their lives to the use of this drug.

In peace-time, also, its use is widespread. Nowadays it is supplied not only as a powder but it comes in ointment and in tablet form. It cures many ailments, but there are certain diseases where penicillin has no effect whatsoever.

In recognition of their valuable work, honours were given to both Alexander Fleming and Professor Florey; each received a knighthood. Sir Alexander Fleming died in 1955 when he was seventy-three years of age. He was buried in St. Paul's Cathedral, and many people mourned him. His place in the history of medicine is a high one. He is among the great men who have done much to benefit mankind.

Andrew Scotland: *A Junior Panorama—Book Four*, London 1963
By permission of the publishers, Odhams Press Ltd

VOCABULARY. *bacteria*: simplest and smallest forms of plant life — *drug*: substance used in making medicine — *damage*: harm — *trout*: riverfish, good for eating — *junior clerk*: office worker of lower position — *qualify*: become entitled to do sth. — *carbolic acid*: acid made from coal-tar used as a disinfectant — *antiseptic*: substance for destroying germs — *clear*: pure; without a stain — *mould*: woolly or furry growth of very tiny fungi "Schimmel" — *elapse*: slip away; pass — *ointment*: greasy substance for healing hurts on the skin — *tablet*: small quantity of compressed medicine — *ailment*: trouble, disease — *recognition*: acknowledgment — *knighthood*: rank of a knight; *knight*: rank with the title *Sir* — *mourn*: feel or show sorrow for — *benefit*: do good to.

82. The Red Cross

1. When Mrs Eleanor MacKinnon formed her Red Cross Circles among the school children of Sydney, Australia, in 1914, she little realised that they were to be the start of the Junior Red Cross movement. About the same time Red Cross groups were formed in Schools in Canada. The idea spread from country to country and today throughout the world over 55 million boys and girls are members of the Junior Red Cross.

2. Before the Junior Red Cross sections had been created, children had played a part in Red Cross relief work on many occasions. An outstanding example in the U. S. A. was when they sent materials to give much needed relief to San Francisco, after the earthquake which destroyed the city in 1906.

3. The three aims of the Junior Red Cross are: The Protection of Life and Health; Service to the Sick and Suffering; and International Friendship and Understanding. Its motto is: "Serve one Another."

4. The British Junior Red Cross was officially recognised in 1924 and now has well over 113 000 members.

5. Boys and girls, aged 5 to school leaving age, who belong to the British Junior Red Cross can learn first aid, nursing, hygiene, mothercraft, accident prevention, fire protection, messenger work and artificial respiration so that they may be trained and ready to help those in need.

6. Service to others is the keynote of the Junior Red Cross movement. In Canada because of the shortage of dentists in Newfoundland, the Juniors raised funds to provide the people with a "floating" dental clinic. In summer, the boat carrying the dentist and his assistant sails the hundred and

ninety miles of rugged coastline and in winter a snowmobile is used to visit the patients.

7. British Juniors help at holiday camps for physically handicapped children, where the young guests are given a real holiday, and, through taking part with Junior Members in all the normal activities of camp life, are able to forget their disabilities so that they often return home able to do more for themselves. British Juniors also knit blankets for refugee children and for people in hospital, both in the United Kingdom and overseas. Junior Red Cross members visit and help the sick and elderly often doing the shopping for them.

8. The Red Cross was originally formed to care for sick and wounded soldiers in time of war, but the fight against epidemics and disease is carried on all the time by National Red Cross Societies. The British Red Cross in its Overseas Branches is particularly concerned with the improvement of health and the prevention of disease. In countries such as Ceylon, Ghana, Malaya and Nigeria, which now have independent Societies of their own, though they were once part of the British Red Cross, Junior Members are actively engaged in teaching their companions how to grow strong and keep healthy. During the famine in 1961 Congo Juniors helped to distribute the milk bought for starving children with money sent by many Red Cross Societies.

9. Blood transfusion is used a great deal by surgeons in operations and is responsible for saving many lives. The Red Cross is proud to help with this work. Some of the National Societies have blood banks, where supplies of the correct types of blood are available for hospitals to use whenever they are required.

10. First aid is closely associated with the Red Cross all over the world. When sporting events are held detachments of volunteers are present to render help to the victims of accidents. In factories, medical rooms are established to deal with casualties among the workers; on the highways first aid posts have been set up. On many beaches in Britain and elsewhere, first aid posts are set up by the Red Cross to help holiday-makers in case of sudden illness or accident or injuries, such as cut feet.

11. The work done by the Red Cross brings comfort and happiness to many people especially the old, the sick and the disabled. Juniors visit and take gifts to them so bringing sunshine into their lives. Many members of the British Junior Red Cross have learnt the deaf-blind manual language, so that they may bring pleasure to those who cannot see or hear by talking to them through the touch language and by reading to them or writing letters for them.

12. The Red Cross spans the world. Today over eighty-five nations have Red Cross Societies, and by May 1961 the total membership had exceeded 140,000,000 people; men, boys and girls of every race and creed, all banded together to help suffering people.

13. The motto of the British Red Cross is "Inter Arma Caritas"—Charity in War.

Angus Maciver: *Reader, Book F,* Glasgow 1962
By permission of the publishers, Robert Gibson & Sons

VOCABULARY. *relief*: lessening of pain or anxiety; help to people in trouble — *earthquake*: a shaking of the earth — *mothercraft*: skill in treatment of children — *float*: to rest on the surface of a liquid — *rugged*: rough; uneven — *snowmobile*: vehicle that can move on snowy roads — *disability*: want of power; hindrance — *knit*: to make an article of clothing by means of needles — *detachment*: number of men etc. sent away on a special duty — *casualty*: a person who is killed or wounded — *deaf*: unable to hear — *manual language*: method of expression by gestures.

83. On Not Answering the Telephone

(When people say to William Plomer "I'll ring you up" he has to reply, to their astonishment, "I'm afraid you can't. You see, I'm not on the telephone. I just haven't got a telephone." In an amusing essay he tells us why he has no telephone, and also no typewriter.)

Why don't I have a telephone? Not because I pretend to be wise or pose as unusual. There are two chief reasons: because I don't really like the telephone, and because I find I can still work and play, eat, breathe, and sleep without it. Why don't I like the telephone? Because I think it is a pest and a time-waster. It may create unnecessary suspense and anxiety, as when you wait for an expected call that doesn't come; or irritating delay, as when you keep ringing a number that is always engaged. As for speaking in a public telephone box, that seems to me really horrible. You would not use it unless you were in a hurry, and because you are in a hurry you will find other people waiting before you. When you do get into the box, you are half asphyxiated by stale unventilated air, flavoured with cheap face-powder and chain-smoking; and by the time you have begun your conversation your back is chilled by the cold looks of somebody who is fidgeting to take your place.

If you have a telephone in your house, you will admit that it tends to ring when you least want it to ring—when you are asleep, or in the middle of a meal or a conversation, or when you are just going out, or when you are in your bath. Are you strong-minded enough to ignore it, to say to yourself, "Ah well, it will all be the same in a hundred years' time"? You are not. You think there may be some important news or message for you. Have you never rushed dripping from the bath, or chewing from the table, or dazed from bed, only to be told that you are a wrong number? You were told the truth. In my opinon all telephone numbers are wrong numbers. If, of course, your telephone rings and you decide not to answer it, then you will have to listen to an idiotic bell ringing and ringing in what is supposed to be the privacy of your home. You might as well buy a bicycle bell and ring it yourself . . .

If, like me, one is without a telephone, somebody is sure to say "Oh, but don't you find you have to write an awful lot of letters?" The answer to that is "Yes, but I should have to write an awful lot of letters anyway." This may bring the remark "Ah well, if you don't have a telephone, at least you must have a typewriter." And the answer to that is "No."

"What, no telephone and no typewriter! Do please explain why." Well I am a professional man of letters, and when I was younger I thought a typewriter would be convenient. I even thought it was necessary, and that editors and publishers would expect anything sent to them to be typewritten. So I bought a typewriter and taught myself to type, and for some years I typed away busily. But I did not enjoy typing. I happen to enjoy the act of writing. I enjoy forming letters or words with a pen, and I never could enjoy tapping the keys of a typewriter. There again, there was a bell—only a little bell that rang at the end of each line—but still, a bell. And the fact is, I am not mechanically minded, and the typewriter is a machine. I have never been really drawn to machines. I don't like oiling, cleaning, or mending them. I do not enjoy making them work. To control them gives me no sense of power—or not of the kind of power that I find interesting. And machines do not like me. When I touch them they tend to break down, get jammed, catch fire, or blow up.

William Plomer: from a B. B. C. General Overseas Service talk
entitled "On Not Answering the Telephone", published in the *Listener*
By permission of the author

VOCABULARY. *typewriter*: machine with which one prints letters on paper, using the fingers on a keyboard — *not because I . . . pose as unusual*: not because I act as if I thought myself unusual — *pest*: troublesome thing; deadly disease — *suspense*: time of anxious waiting — *delay*: postponement, putting off — *the number is engaged*: someone else is using the line — *as for*: (linking expression) 'And now

I add a further point' — *horrible*: (here) disagreeable, unpleasant (a colloquial word which has lost much of the force it once had; it used to mean 'causing horror') — *asphyxiated*: suffocated (humorous exaggeration) — *stale*: not fresh — *unventilated*: not getting rid of foul air — *flavour*: give a smell to — *chain-smoking*: smoking one cigarette after another, without interruption — *fidget*: move about restlessly — *you will admit*: the author is conducting an imaginary argument with someone who has a telephone and has never thought about its disadvantages — *it will all be the same*: it will not matter — *dripping*: wet — *chew*: break up food with the teeth before swallowing — *daze*: knock the senses out; stun — *privacy*: undisturbed quietness — *an awful lot of*: very many ('awful' like 'horrible' has lost much of its force) — *anyway*: i.e. even if I had a phone — *man of letters*: writer — *convenient*: suitable; handy — *editor*: one who prepares matter for printing — *I happen to enjoy*: it so happens that I enjoy ..., it is a fact (however surprising it may seem) that I enjoy ... (everyday conversational idiom) — *mechanically minded*: not good at understanding and looking after machines — *drawn to*: attracted by — *jam*: stop working through the blocking of some part — *blow up*: destroy by explosion.

84. Affair at Bristol

I thought perhaps you might like to hear of the fix poor old Fawcett got into over some cheese down at Bristol the other day. It was the oddest thing he ever remembered in his life, Fawcett said when he told us about it, and he may be right, though it's a big thing for a man to say who's been married to Mrs Fawcett for thirty years. The things that woman does!

The two of them were staying in a biggish hotel at Bristol a week or two ago, and in the middle of the night, round about half past two, Fawcett thinks it was, his wife gave him a poke in the back with the shoehorn she uses to get her night-cap on over her bun with and told him she was desperately hungry! 'I'd give my soul for a hunk of bread and some Stilton, Harry,' she said.

Long ago, when they were first married, Fawcett used to argue with her about things like that. 'You must be reasonable,' he used to say, without any idea that he was simply talking foolishness. Now he just goes and does what she asks. It's inconvenient sometimes, he says, but it works out better that way in the long run. Of course if he'd been in London he'd have rung for a waiter, but they look at these things rather differently in the provinces. They're apt to take offence if they are asked to do anything the slightest bit out of the ordinary. Fawcett thought that a request for bread and cheese at half past two in the morning would probably come under that heading.

It was the night porter's moustaches that started the trouble. One expects a day porter to have moustaches, it's in the nature of things, but night porters should be small and clean-shaven and only just not in their shirt-sleeves—an altogether milder type of man. Fawcett says he took one look at those moustaches and started to go up-stairs again. He had only one shilling in his hand and he has been about enough to know that you can't move a moustachioed porter much under half a crown. He went up the three flights of stairs and along the corridor and round to the right and up the five steps and right again and in through the second door on the left. He was fumbling about on the dressing-table when the light went up and a man with bushy eyebrows asked him what in thunder he thought he was doing? Fawcett said he was looking for some money to give to the night porter who wore moustaches and he thought he must have got into the wrong room by mistake. The man said, Yes, he thought he had, and would he oblige him by getting out quickly? Fawcett went out and into the next room on the left and got his money. Then he went downstairs and asked the night porter for a roll and some Stilton.

"Stilton!" said the night porter, as if he could have understood a man wanting Cheddar in the middle of the night, but that this thing went clean outside his experience.

"Please," said Fawcett, and twiddled his half-crown.

The Porter said he would see what he could do, and went away and a little later came back with a plate. "I couldn't find any Stilton," he said. "Will this do?"

Fawcett thanked him and took the plate. Then he went up the three flights of stairs and along the corridor and round to the right and up the five steps and right again and in through the second door on the left. Looking back at it, Fawcett says, he can't think how he came to make the same mistake again, but he was upset and muddled and his feet were cold. He says it's extraordinary how easy it is to go wrong in a strange hotel. Anyway, in he went, and while he was feeling for the light-switch he called out, "I'm sorry I couldn't get Stilton, dear. Will Gorgonzola do?"

This time the man with the bushy eyebrows was really angry. He damned Gorgonzola. He suggested fates and destinations for Gorgonzola that not even a cheese could listen to unmoved. And whatever he said about Gorgonzola he doubled it when he came to deal with Fawcett himself. Fawcett stood it for a time, trying to get in his explanation, but at last he lost patience. "Tchah!" he said, and took himself off.

It wasn't till he stood in the corridor that he realized the bread and cheese were missing. They must have jumped off the plate, he thinks, when he got such a shock at finding himself in the wrong room again.

Most men would have called it a night at this point and gone back to bed, but not Fawcett. There is a good deal of the bulldog about Fawcett. He thought of that half-crown and he thought of his wife lying there in bed getting hungrier and hungrier and off he went downstairs again. He felt it would be better not to trouble the man with the eyebrows again.

"Brought the plate back?" said the porter kindly. Fawcett asked him very politely whether he could possibly get him another roll and just a little more cheese.

"*More*!" said the porter, with his eyes popping out of his head.

"What is this? A Reunion Dinner?"

Fawcett was just beginning to tell him about his wife's appetite when the phone-bell rang in the porter's little box and the porter excused himself. Fawcett could hear a loud crackling coming from the earpiece and he saw the porter's eyebrows rising higher and higher and his eyes coming further and further out of his head. He caught fragments of talk. "Twice, eh, sir?" said the porter. "*Threw* it, you say . . . *did* he? . . . sounds like it, I must say . . . All right, sir," said the porter, "you leave it to me." Then, in a lower voice, "He's down here now, sir, *asking for more*."

Fawcett says he thinks that was more or less the end of the conversation, but he can't be sure because he left at that point. He was tired and fed up and wanted to be in bed. So he went upstairs again. He may even have run part of the way, he says, to warm his feet. He went up the three flights and along the corridor and round to the right and up the five steps and then—suddenly—he remembered. It was *left* here, not right. A minute later he was in bed beside Mrs Fawcett, who was fast asleep.

"But the odd thing was," concluded Fawcett, while we all crowded round to hear what had struck him as unusual about this very commonplace affair—"the odd thing was that I never found out whose half-crown it was I gave to that infernal night porter."

H. F. Ellis: "Affair at Bristol" in *Punch*
By permission of the publishers

VOCABULARY. *fix*: awkward or difficult situation — *poke*: thrust — *bun*: rounded mass of woman's hair — *hunk*: thick piece of bread — *Stilton*: superior kind of cheese named from Stilton in Huntingdonshire — *argue*: quarrel in words — *apt*: quick; likely to — *moustachioed*: having a moustache (= the hair upon the upper lip of men) — *half a crown*: British coin worth 2s. 6d. — *fumble*: feel about uncertainly with the hands — *Cheddar*: kind of cheese (village in Somerset) — *twiddle*: play with — *upset*: worried — *muddle*: bring into a state of confusion — *Gorgonzola*: rich veined cheese (town in Italy) — *destination*: place to which a thing is going — *pop*: move quickly and unexpectedly — *reunion*: happy meeting of old friends — *crackling*: small cracking sound — *earpiece*: telephone receiver — *fed up*: (colloq.) discontened with, tired of — *infernal*: cursed.

85. The Sack of Emeralds

One bad October night in the high wolds beyond Wiltshire, with a north wind chanting of winter, with the old leaves dropping down to decay, with a mournful sound of owls, and in fearsome loneliness, there trudged in broken boots and in wet and windy rags an old man, stooping low under a sack of emeralds. It was easy to see that the burden of the sack was far too great for the poor old man that bore it. And had you flashed a lantern in his face there was a look there of hopelessness and fatigue that would have told you it was no wish of his that kept him tottering on under that bloated sack.

When the menacing look of the night and its cheerless sounds, and the cold, and the weight of the sack, had all but brought him to the door of death, and he had dropped his sack onto the road and was dragging it on behind him, bumping it very slowly over the stones, just as he felt that his final hour was come, just then he saw the bulk and the black shape of the Sign of the Lost Shepherd loom up by the ragged way. He opened the door and staggered into the light and sank on a bench with his huge sack beside him.

All this you had seen had you been on that lonely road, so late on those bitter wolds, with their outlines vast and mournful in the dark, and their little clumps of trees sad with October. But neither you nor I were out that night. I did not see the poor old man and his sack until he sank down all of a heap in the lighted inn.

And Yon the blacksmith was there; and the carpenter, Willie Losh; and Jackers, the postman's son. And they gave him a glass of beer. And the old man drank it up, still hugging his emeralds. And at last they asked him what he had in his sack, the question he clearly dreaded; and he only clasped yet tighter the sodden sack and mumbled he had potatoes.

"Potatoes," said Yon the blacksmith.

"Potatoes," said Willie Losh.

And when he heard the doubt that was in their voices the old man shivered and moaned.

"Potatoes, did you say?" said the postman's son. And they all three rose and tried to peer at the sack that the rain-soaked wayfarer so zealously sheltered.

And from the old man's fierceness I had said that, had it not been for that foul night on the roads and the weight he had carried so far and the fearful winds of October, he had fought with the blacksmith, the carpenter, and the postman's son, all three, till he beat them away from his sack. And weary and wet as he was he fought them hard.

I should no doubt have interfered; and yet the three men meant no harm to the wayfarer, but resented the reticence that he displayed to them though they had given him beer; it was to them as though a master key had failed to open a cupboard. And, as for me, curiosity held me down to my chair and forbade me to interfere on behalf of the sack; for the old man's furtive ways and the night out of which he came, and the hour of his coming, and the look of his sack, all made me long as much to know what he had as even the blacksmith, the carpenter, and the postman's son.

And then they found the emeralds. They were all bigger than hazelnuts, hundreds and hundreds of them. And the old man screamed.

"Come, come, we're not thieves," said the blacksmith.

"We're not thieves," said the carpenter.

"We're not thieves," said the postman's son. And with awful fear on his face the wayfarer closed his sack, whimpering over his emeralds and furtively glancing round as though the loss of his secret were an utterly deadly thing. And then they asked him to give them just one each, just one huge emerald each, because they had given him a glass of beer. Then to see the wayfarer shrink against his sack and guard it with clutching fingers one would have said that he was a selfish man, were it not for the terror that was freezing in his face. I have seen men look at Death with far less fear.

And they took their emerald all three, one enormous emerald each, while the old man hopelessly struggled till he saw his three emeralds go, and fell to the floor and wept, a pitiable, sodden heap.

And about that time I began to hear far off down the windy road, by which that sack had come, faintly at first and slowly louder and louder, the click-clack-clop of a lame horse coming nearer. Click-clack-clop and a loose shoe rattling, the sound of a horse too weary to be out on such a night, too lame to be out at all.

Click-clack-clop. And all of a sudden the old wayfarer heard it; heard it above the sound of his own sobbing, and at once went white to the lips. Such sudden fear as blanched him in a moment struck right to the hearts of all there. They asked him what was wrong, but seemed scarcely to hope for an answer. Nor did he speak, but sat with a frozen stare, all at once dry-eyes, a monument to terror.

Nearer and nearer came the click-clack-clop. And when I saw the expression of that man's face and how its horror deepened as the ominous sound drew nearer, then I knew that something was wrong. And looking for the last time upon all four, I saw the wayfarer horror-struck by his sack and the other three crowding round it to put their huge emeralds back, then, even on such a night, I slipped away from the inn.

Outside the bitter wind roared in my ears, and close in the darkness the horse went click-clack-clop.

And as soon as my eyes could see at all in the night I saw a man in a huge hat looped up in front, wearing a sword in a scabbard shabby and huge, and looking blacker than the darkness, riding on a lean horse slowly up to the inn. Whether his were the emeralds, or who he was, or why he rode a lame horse on such a night, I did not stop to discover, but went at once from the inn as he strode in his great black riding-coat up to the door.

And that was the last that was ever seen of the wayfarer, the blacksmith, the carpenter, or the postman's son.

Lord Dunsany: *Tales of Three Hemispheres*, London 1919
John W. Luce & Co Ltd (publishers)

VOCABULARY. *emerald*: beautiful green gem — *wold*: open stretch of country — *chant*: sing a tune or song — *owl*: bird of prey, night-flying — *trudge*: walk with heavy steps, as if tired — *rags*: worn-out, shabby clothes — *totter*: stagger — *bloated*: puffed and swollen — *shepherd*: man who looks after sheep — *loom*: appear large or dimly — *ragged*: having rough surfaces — *clump*: cluster of trees or shrubs — *blacksmith*: man who makes articles of iron — *hug*: put the arms round tightly — *clasp*: hold closely — *sodden*: soaked through and through — *mumble*: speak indistinctly — *moan*: make a low sound of grief — *wayfarer*: traveller — *zealous* ['zeləs]: very eager — *foul*: stormy — *reticence*: disposition to say little or nothing — *furtive*: having a wish to escape notice — *scream*: shriek — *whimper*: cry with a low, whining voice — *click-clack-clop*: sound of the horse's hooves — *ominous*: likely to bring trouble — *loop*: keep up in the form of a curve crossing itself — *scabbard:* case for the blade of a sword — *lean*: thin, not fat.

86. Weapon

I suppose they thought they had to have one representative of the Army along; possibly I got the invitation because I was once reported as saying that not all politicians were stupid and corrupt. Anyway there I stood, on a bright spring morning, entirely surrounded by civilians. It was easy to tell the politicians from the scientists. It was a scientists' occasion; the politicians, for once, looked abashed.

Professor Norwood, who had a reputation that even I could be expected to have heard of called us to order.

"Gentlemen," he said, "and"—he smiled towards me—"General Sands, before we go next door I think it may be as well to say a few words. The actual work has been kept very secret because it represents the greatest weapon this—or any other country—has ever had.

Our present research was suggested in rather an odd way. An exhibition of sketches of the inventions of Leonardo da Vinci started it all. Looking round them, I could not help being struck by the quality of anticipation in da Vinci's work. The future is not necessarily a closed book. A group of experimenters established, mainly through dreams, a kind of fore-knowledge of what was to happen.

What if the clue to da Vinci's technical genius was simply this—prevision? If a da Vinci could get hold of inventions that still lay four hundred years in the future, it might be possible to do the same thing today.

Nowadays, of course, we are more interested in weapons than in any other branch of technology. Just now we are clinging to what we know is no more than five or ten years' lead in atomic weapons. Multiply that by a factor of ten or twenty. It represents absolute safety."

The professor took a sip of water.

"Well, all that's the theory. The thing to do, of course, was to find those people who had this power of prevision, possibly in a latent form, and then to develop it. The government helped us there. Tests—intelligence tests, character tests, aptitude tests—take place in the school every day. We were allowed to substitute for these a test of our own; a test designed to unearth pupils with what became known as the prevision or 'P' factor.

We found quite a few; the factor differed widely in intensity. We found a number of different ways in which the factor could be brought out—variations in diet, living conditions, and so on. We concentrated particularly, of course, on coaching our star pupils. We got plenty of material, but it wasn't the kind of thing we were looking for. A boy naturally musical came up with interesting fragments from unwritten sonatas and symphonies, but gave us nothing on the technological side. We had to find someone who would have the 'P' factor plus a natural scientific bent."

One of the politicians that I did not recognise interrupted: "How could you be sure the results were really prophetic, and not just the sort of queer dreams that children have?"

"I have a manuscript here," the professor said, "that was produced in our first year—seven years ago. That's the sort of proof we've had.

But to get back to our troubles. We had to find the right blend of 'P' and scientific talent. We got it only two years ago. The aim we had set ourselves was of bringing back a blueprint of the greatest weapon in the world a hundred years from now. That meant the boy had to be taught the essentials of draughtsmanship. We found that he could be put in a hypnotic trance with the command to filch a particular idea from a particular future, and he would deliver the goods every time."

The professor paused and let his gaze roam round our little gathering.

"Gentlemen," he said, "an hour ago the boy, Rudolf Leyton, was left in the adjoining room under the hypnotic instruction that he was to draw in full detail the weapon that will dominate the world in 2064. We shall now go in and inspect the result." Someone muttered something about "Security". The professor held his hand up.

"You need not worry about security. Remember what we are seeking. It will take trained minds possibly months to comprehend fully what you are going to see now."

Professor Norwood nodded amiably as he came abreast of me.

"I hope this is going to put you and your colleagues finally out of business, General. You don't mind me saying that, do you?" I followed him to the door, turning over in my mind visions of an old age spent in directing traffic. I got edged out in the genteel rush for the door and was last in to the adjoining room. There was a large table, well supplied with sheets of drawing-paper; on the other side a boy of about ten—it had not occurred to me before that he would be so young—was slumped forward, asleep.

Professor Norwood went forward and stood beside him.

"Wake up," he said. "Wake up, Rudolf."

The boy woke up, raising his head and looking with bewilderment at the press of people on the other side of the table.

There was a drawing there, all right. A good clear drawing. They were all looking at it, and not one of them had the faintest idea what it was.

Professor Norwood bent over the drawing for perhaps half a minute. He straightened up again.

"It will have to be worked on," he said. "Of course, as I said, we could not expect to grasp the principle on sight. We'll get our best people on it."

The politician who had interrupted him in the other room said: "I wonder . . . It seems to me that this whole business may have been a waste of money. I'm not a scientist, but that drawing doesn't look to me like the best weapon of 2064."

The professor began to protest. I said:

"To me it does."

They turned round to look at me. Even the sceptical politician smiled.

The professor said: "Surely, General, you don't mean to tell us that you know what it is?"

"Yes," I said. "It's the greatest weapon of the world of a hundred years from now."

I began to draw on my gloves, because there was no point in remaining.

"It's a very good drawing—of a crossbow."

Edmund Crispin (editor): *Best Science Fiction Stories 6*, London 1966
By permission of the publishers, Faber and Faber Ltd

VOCABULARY. *abash*: to make ashamed — *anticipation*: action of expecting, of realizing beforehand — *fore-knowledge*: knowledge in advance — *clue*: something that helps to solve a problem — *technology*: science of industrial arts — *sip*: very small mouthful of a liquid — *latent* [ˈleitənt]: lying hidden — *aptitude*: readiness; cleverness — *coach*: teach, train — *bent*: natural liking — *blend*: mixture — *blueprint*: sketch plan of work to be done — *draftsman, draughtsman*: one who makes drawings or designs — *trance*: deep sleep that is not natural — *filch*: steal — *roam*: wander about — *abreast of*: moving side by side in the same direction — *edge*: move little by little — *genteel*: well-bred — *slump*: fall or sink suddenly — *on sight*: at once; without delay — *crossbow*: weapon for shooting arrows, made by placing a bow crossways on a stock or stand.

87. The Virtuous One and the Chinese Riot

(*The Small Woman* by Alan Burgess recounts the true story of Gladys Aylward, the London parlourmaid, who overcame all obstacles to become a missionary in China. After many hardships, she met Mrs. Jeannie Lawson, a Scots missionary, and together they started a Christian settlement which they called *The Inn of Eight Happinesses*)

Gladys was standing in the courtyard when a messenger from the Mandarin rushed in waving a piece of scarlet paper.

"A riot has broken out in the men's prison. You must come at once," said the messenger urgently. "It is most important!"

They hurried up the road and in through the East Gate. From the other side came screams, shouts, yells, the most horrible noises.

"My goodness!" said Gladys. "It certainly is a riot, isn't it?"

The Governor of the prison, small, pale-faced, his mouth set in a worried line, met her at the entrance. Behind were grouped half a dozen of his staff.

"We are glad you have come," he said quickly. "There is a riot in the prison; the convicts are killing each other."

"So I can hear," she said. "But what am I here for! I'm only the missionary woman. Why don't you send the soldiers in to stop it?"

"The convicts are murderers, bandits, thieves," said the Governor, his voice trembling. "The soldiers are frightened. There are not enough of them."

"I'm sorry to hear that," said Gladys. "But what do you expect me to do about it? I don't even know why you asked me to come . . ."

The Governor stepped forward. "You must go in and stop the fighting."

"I must go in . . .!" Gladys' mouth dropped open; her eyes rounded in utter amazement. "Me! Me go in there! Are you mad? If I went in they'd kill me!"

The Governor's eyes were fixed on her. "But how can they kill you? You tell everybody that you have come here because you have the living God inside you . . ."

"*The living God?*" she stammered.

"You preach it everywhere—in the streets and villages. If you preach the truth, if your God protects you from harm, then you can stop this riot."

Gladys stared at him. It was a desperate challenge. But how could she go into the prison? "I must try," she said to herself. "I must try. O God give me strength."

She looked up at the Governor's pale face, knowing that now hers was the same colour. "All right," she said. "Open the door. I'll go in to them." She did not trust her voice to say any more.

"The key!" snapped the Governor. "The key, quickly." One of his orderlies came forward with a huge iron key; soon the immense iron-barred door swung open. The door closed behind her. She heard the great key turn. She was locked in the prison with a horde of raving criminals, who sounded by their din as if they had all gone completely insane. With faltering footsteps she walked forward and came to an abrupt standstill, rooted in horror.

The courtyard was about sixty feet square, with queer cage-like structures round all four sides. Within its confines a writhing, fiendish battle was going on. Several bodies were stretched out on the flagstones. One man, obviously dead, lay only a few feet away from her. The main group of men, however, were watching one convict who brandished a large, blood-stained chopper. As she stared, he suddenly rushed at them and they scattered wildly to every part of the square. No one took any notice whatsoever of Gladys as she stood motionless. The madman with the axe halted only a few feet from her. Without any instinctive plan, hardly realising what she was doing, she took two angry steps towards him.

"Give me that chopper," she said furiously. "Give it to me at once!"

The man turned to look at her. For three long seconds the wild dark pupils staring from bloodshot eyes glared at her. He took two paces forward. Suddenly, meekly, he held out the axe. Gladys snatched the weapon from his hand and held it rigidly down by her side. The other convicts—there must have been fifty or sixty cowering there—stared from every corner of the courtyard. All action was frozen and Gladys knew she must clinch her advantage.

"All of you!" she shouted. "Come over here. Come on, form into line! You, over there! Come on, form up in front of me!"

Obediently the convicts shambled across, forming into a ragged group before her. She regarded them stormily. There was silence. Then suddenly her fear had gone. They were so wretched. They were so hopeless. She could have wept openly that human creatures could be so wretched. With an effort, she tightened her lips and took command again. The fear had gone, yes; but she knew that she must cow them with her authority.

"You should be ashamed of yourselves," she said. "The governor sent me in here to find out what it was all about. Now, what is your grievance? Why did you start fighting like this?" There was no answer. Several hung their heads in shame. A few moments later, one of the taller men of slightly better physique approached. Like the others, he was dressed in rags.

"My name is Feng," he said. "I am their spokesman."

He explained that no one really knew why, or how, the riot had started. They were allowed the chopper for an hour each day to cut up their food. Someone had quarrelled over its possession and someone else had joined in. He could not explain this strange occurrence. Perhaps it was that many of the men had been there for many years, he said. As she knew, unless their friends or relatives sent in food, they starved. It was hard to sit up against a wall and starve to death while other men ate.

"What do you do all day in here?" asked Gladys seriously.

"Do? There is nothing to do."

"No occupation of any sort?"

"None!"

"But a man must have work, something to do. I shall see the governor about it."

It was at this moment she became conscious that the Governor and his retinue were behind her. The noise of the riot had died, and they had now thought it safe to enter and take an official part in the peace treaty.

The Governor bowed to Gladys. "You have done well. We must thank you," he said gratefully.

"It's disgraceful," she said bitterly. "These men are locked up here week after week, year after year, with nothing to do. Of course you have riots if they've nothing to occupy their time. They must have work to do. We must find them all sorts of jobs so that they can earn a little money and buy food, and get a little self-respect."

The Governor nodded. Whether he agreed or not she could not tell.

"We will discuss it later," he said amiably.

"I have promised them there will be no reprisals," she said.

The Governor nodded again. A few corpses were rarely the subject of an official inquiry in the Chinese penal system. "As long as there is no recurrence," he said, "we shall forget all about it."

Gladys saw upon her the dark eyes of the spokesman. "Thank you," he said. "Thank you, Ai-weh-deh." She did not know at the time that the word "Ai-weh-deh" meant *the virtuous one.*

She was known as Ai-weh-deh for all her remaining years in China.

Angust Maciver: *Reader—Book F,* Glasgow 1962
By permission of the publishers, Robert Gibson & Sons Ltd

VOCABULARY. *mandarin:* a Chinese official — *scarlet*: bright-red colour — *riot*: a noisy disorder among a crowd of people; violent outbreak of lawlessness — *scream*: shrill, piercing cry — *convict*: one who has been sent to prison for a number of years — *amazement*: great surprise or astonishment — *stammer*: repeat the same sound several times before completing a word — *orderly*: a soldier who carries the orders and messages of an officer — *rave*: to be mad; to talk wildly — *din*: a loud, lasting noise — *cage*: box closed in with wire or bars — *confine*: limit, border, boundary — *writhe*: to twist or roll about in pain — *fiendish*: savage and cruel — *flag* (or: *flagstone*): flat pavingstone — *brandish*: to wave — *chopper*: sharp tool for cutting meat — *bloodshot:* (of the whites of the eyes) red — *meek*: mild and gentle — *cower*: to lower the body; crouch — *clinch*: settle finally — *shamble*: walk unsteadily without lifting the feet enough — *ragged*: badly torn (rags = old and torn clothes) — *cow*: frighten — *grievance*: wrong; cause for complaining — *physique*: the build of one's body; bodily strength — *retinue*: number of persons who accompany a person of rank — *reprisal*: action taken in revenge — *penal*: having to do with punishment — *recurrence*: repetition; the act of happening again.

88. The Bravest Action of My Life

"You won a D. S. O. in South Africa, General, didn't you?"

"I don't think I was in the least brave on that occasion. It was just an obvious duty. In fact, I don't know that I could have avoided it."

"What do you seriously think is the bravest thing you have ever done in your life? Is there nothing you can pick out?"

"Yes, perhaps there is. I believe there is one thing that I really can call my bravest action. It has nothing to do with the Army. It was when I was a child in fact. Well, I suppose I was six years old at the time; not more. My father was rector of a parish in North Oxford. We lived in a big family house, where everything was spacious and untidy. It was very homely and delightful and all rather ramshackle.

"My father used from time to time to make remarks about the house falling down for lack of paint, and I never knew how seriously to take him. Sometimes I thought he meant it as a kind of obscure grown-up joke, and at other times I thought he was really worried by it. Then I felt very sorry for him and anxious about the whole family; I used to worry and worry because father hadn't got enough money to repair the house.

"One summer afternoon I was playing in the garden. Like the house the garden was large and untidy. It was looked after very little and its overgrown shrubberies and bushes and unused sheds made a happy hunting ground for us.

"At this particular moment I was the only child present, and there were several strange grown-ups. They had come to lunch, I think, and father had brought them out for a stroll round the garden. I went on with my own little affairs, but I was half listening, at the same time, to what the grown-ups had to say to each other.

"Suddenly I heard my father say, 'Look at that! Look at that crack over the back door. Good heavens, we shall have the house about our ears any day.'

"I looked. I saw the crack. There was a large stone which went right across the top of the back door. The crack was in this stone. Fear and horror seized me. I can remember a kind of hot stab of pain that made me gasp, and the summer day suddenly became a nightmare. The grown-ups went indoors, and I was left staring at the crack. It looked to me a terrible crack. At any moment the house might come tumbling down, all because of this crack, and my father and mother and my two sisters, and my new baby brother, would all lie killed or terribly hurt among the ruins of our home.

"Yet the days went by and my father did nothing about it. I went about in a kind of dull agony—the fear of it always with me. I couldn't talk about it. Presently I decided that my father did not know what to do. He, like me, was just waiting for the crash, and he couldn't talk about it any more than I could.

"So, at length, I decided that I must act. It would not matter if I was killed in the attempt. This was my plan. I would arise one morning very early when everybody was asleep, and I would get my modelling wax, and I could fill that crack up with modelling wax.

"Of course it would be desperately dangerous. To go near the crack at all, even to look at it, was frightening: to stand on a chair face to face with the crack—to touch it and fill it up—that was an act which made me quake even to imagine.

"For days I went about trying to screw myself up. Plainly, it must be done one morning, done before the rest of the family were awake. No one must know about it. They would never allow me to risk my life. When I had done it the family would be saved—the whole district would know of my brave action—and I should appear in story books.

"Morning after morning, when the house was hushed, I lay awake trembling with fear, trying in cold blood to force myself to do it. And at last one morning in the chill of dawn, with teeth chattering, I found myself actually creeping downstairs, my heart beating, and a large piece of modelling wax in my hand.

"On the kitchen stairs I met our old tabby cat. He rose and purred and rubbed himself against my legs. In the semi-darkness, I felt for his head; I can recall that he almost broke my resolution and as I stroked him I felt that this might well be the last familiar, homely action I should ever perform.

"Then as gently as I could, I unbolted the back door, and pushed a chair into position. I know that I have never felt so frightened in all my life. I can't understand what infantile will-power it was that drove me on. My heart thumped and thumped and I felt almost certain that when I touched the frightful crack I should at once be crushed to death.

"However, by this time I had been heard. My father, expecting to find a tramp in the garden, came running along the passage in his shirt and trousers.

"For a moment we stared at each other.

" 'You,' he said, 'go back to bed this minute. What on earth are you doing?'

" 'Daddy,' I said, 'the crack. I'm mending the crack.'

" 'What crack?'

" 'The awful crack, that's going to make the house fall down. I'm mending it. I'm saving us all.'

"After some more explanation, he began to understand.

" 'But it was only a joke,' he said. 'Just one of my jokes. The crack's nothing. Have you been worrying about it?'

"Very kindly he led me back to bed.

"Go off to sleep and don't worry about it any more,' he said. 'It was very good of you to try and mend it, but it's quite all right.'

"I lay in my bed wide-eyed and watchful.

"Later in the morning my mother said to me:

" 'Daddy asked me to tell you all about the crack. Let me explain. You see it was quite all right really. Just a joke.'

" 'Oh!' I said. 'Don't! *Don't*!' and I began to sob. All the pent-up emotion poured out of me. I was utterly disgraced. There had been no danger —just a grown-up joke. And I, idiotic little fool, had taken it seriously. I hadn't been brave. I had just been babyish. Now all the uncles and aunts would tell the story of how I had tried to save the house.

" 'What is it, my darling?' said my mother. 'Tell me all about it.'

"But I would sooner have died than revealed myself any further. So I simply sobbed and pushed her away.

" 'You are a funny little boy,' she said. 'If only you'd tell me what it is—'

"But I have never told anybody till this minute. It's funny how your mind goes back to these childish memories when you're getting old. You've got time to think again when you're old.

"I'm sure now, that was the bravest action of my life, and the only one that really came up to my own childish hopes and ambitions of being heroic."

T. O. Beachcroft: "The General Remembers" in *The Collected Short Stories of T. O. Beachcroft*, London
By permission of the publishers, The Bodley Head Ltd

VOCABULARY. *D. S. O.*: Distinguished Service Order — *rector*: (Church of England) clergyman in charge of a parish — *parish*: district of a county with its own church and clergyman — *ramshackle*: falling to pieces — *shrubbery*: place where many tree-like bushes grow — *stroll*: quiet, unhurried walk — *crack*: incomplete break — *stab*: blow with a sharp weapon — *nightmare*: frightening dream — *tumble*: fall — *agony*: great pain — *model*: fashion or shape — *wax*: any substance like that of which bees make their cells — *quake*: shake with fear — *screw up one's courage*: make a special effort to be brave — *hush*: make quiet — *with teeth chattering*: trembling from fear — *tabby*: brown or grey cat that has dark stripes — *thump*: beat heavily — *pent*: shut (up) in — *emotion*: deep feeling — *disgrace*: bring shame upon — *reveal*: make known.

89. With a Prisoner in Canada

(The author of the following passage was an officer of the Metropolitan Police Force who was sent to Vancouver to bring an accused man back to London as a prisoner.)

Then came the question of conveying the man in custody across Canada. In England, a few hours in the train is the limit of one's journey, but in this case the journey would occupy five days and nights, and all the time the prisoner would have to be closely guarded. I think I am right in saying that in Canada and the United States, at least two officers are considered necessary to convey a prisoner across the continent. The chief constable of Vancouver was greatly concerned about my welfare. He was astounded when I told him that I intended to escort the prisoner across to Montreal alone and unaided. He pointed out that in those circumstances the man might easily escape form custody, and suggested that I should at least place leg-irons and handcuffs on him, travel by day only, and get off the train at night and lodge him in a local police station, as was the custom of the Canadian police when conveying prisoners on long journeys. I said I preferred to run what risk there was and go straight through, as I was anxious to get back to England as quickly as possible. "Well, it's your own funeral," smilingly commented the chief constable, who probably thought I was too young to know better.

When the day of our departure from Vancouver arrived, the chief constable and other officers came to the station to bid us good-bye. He brought with him a formidable set of leg-irons and a pair of handcuffs. Honestly, I had never seen leg-irons before, and the sight of them frightened me as much as they did the prisoner. "For heaven's sake," he pleaded, "don't put those awful things on me." I assured him that I had no such intention, nor did I make use of the handcuffs. We just took our seat like other passengers, bade farewell to the chief constable and the other officers, and, after the engine had given a comical shriek and tolled its bell, we began our homeward journey.

I first had a straight talk with my prisoner. He was a professional man, and although he had committed a grave offence, for which he was liable to be sent to penal servitude, I thought I would rely on his good sense to play the game. "We've got a long journey before us," I said, "and it is up to you to decide whether it is going to be a pleasant one for you or not. As far as I am concerned, nobody will know you are my prisoner, or that I am a police officer. You will not be handcuffed, and you will have complete freedom. All I want you to do is to look after me, and I will look after you." He appreciated the position, thanked me for my consideration, and gave me his word of honour that he would never give me the slightest trouble or cause for anxiety.

We got on splendidly together. He had no money with which he could buy extra necessaries, and as he had no change of linen, I lent him my collars, shirts, and socks. He certainly did "look after me." Wherever I went he followed me, and of course we took all our meals together. The other passengers, who had not the faintest suspicion of our identity, used to say what good pals we were—absolutely inseparable. If they had been told that one of us was a prisoner and the other a detective, in all probability I should have been pointed out as the prisoner.

In truth, however, I had a very anxious time. My friend the prisoner did nothing and said nothing that led me to suppose for a moment that he would not justify the confidence I had placed in him. He was an intelligent man, a good conversationalist, and an amusing companion, and he seemed to go out of his way to reassure me of his good faith. But I knew perfectly well that if I did lose him, my career as a police officer would be wrecked. I hope I did not betray my natural fears to him. I tried not to, at any rate, but obviously I had to be always vigilant. At night time, when the seats were converted into sleeping bunks, I told him to take the upper berth, and I occupied the lower. When he undressed, he handed me all his clothes, and as a precautionary measure I put them under my pillow. He slept soundly throughout each night. I, on the other hand, had very little sleep. I used to have visions of my prisoner climbing out of his bunk, stealing somebody else's clothes, and bolting, leaving me alone and helpless with massive iron chains on my paralysed legs. Every time the train stopped, I put my hand up to his bunk to make sure that he was still there, and sometimes I would sit up and listen, but always he was there sleeping as peacefully as a child.

We arrived at Montreal in the early afternoon, and found that the steamer on which our berths had been booked was not due to leave until midnight. Should I put my companion in the local police station for the few hours we had at our disposal, or should I take him for a pleasure tour round Montreal? He had been such an excellent fellow that I decided not to break the continuity of our good relations. We therefore kept together, and enjoyed the sights of Montreal until it was time to go on board. We were dog-tired when we entered our two-berth cabin in the steamer, which was to take no fewer than ten days to get to Liverpool.

Percy Savage: *Savage of Scotland Yard*, London
By permission of the publishers, Hutchinson & Co, Ltd

VOCABULARY. *The Metropolitan Police Force*: It covers a 15-miles radius from Charing Cross (London) — *convey*: take from one place to another — *in custody*: in the hands of the police — *escort*: go with as a guard — *handcuffs*: steel bands, joined by a short chain, put round the wrists of prisoners — *lodge*: put in safe place — *funeral*: burial — *plead*: beg earnestly — *shriek*: to utter a scream — *toll*: ring a bell sadly — *offence*: wrongdoing — *penal servitude*: imprisonment with hard labour — *play the game*: keep the rules — *appreciate*: value highly — *necessaries*: things necessary for living — "*look after*": (pun) = look like — *faint*: weak — *point out*: indicate — *go out of one's way*: make a special effort — *wreck*: destroy — *betray*: give a sign of, show — *vigilant*: watchful — *convert*: change from ... into — *bunk*: spleeping-place, esp. in a ship's cabin — *berth*: sleeping-place in a train or ship — *bolt*: rush away — *massive*: heavy and solid — *paralyse*: make helpless.

90. The U-2

The C. I. A. created perhaps its greatest sensation by the overflights of the U-2 spy-plane. This was an aircraft designed specially to make long-range flights at heights over 90,000 feet—seventeen miles above the earth—and was especially equipped to record military installations on the ground.

The U-2 was developed by the C. I. A. and was used by them for several years in great secrecy. It made many flights over Russia and brought back important information relating to Soviet aircraft activity, missile sites, atomic production and submarine deployment. It made its first flight in 1956, and while Russia was aware of the flights it said little about them, because they had no missiles capable of shooting down the U-2 at the height it was flying.

This went on until the May of 1960 when two things combined to explode one of the biggest international rows of the decade. This was the development of the SA-2 missile by Russia and the date of the Summit Conference between Eisenhower, Kruschev, Macmillan and de Gaulle, due to take place on 16 May, 1960, at Paris. The U-2 flights were approved by Eisenhower in principle, and though he did not suspend the flights when the date for the Summit Conference approached, it was obvious that the White House were not aware that one was about to take place. What happened was that the C. I. A. feared that the conference between East and West might result in a relaxation of tension in which their spy-planes would be indefinitely grounded. So they decided to get one more flight in before the expected *détente,* feared by them, but ardently desired by the rest of the world.

And so on Sunday morning, 1 May, Francis Gary Powers, a C. I. A. pilot, prepared for his eight-hour flight in the stratosphere by means of an hour and a half's relaxation while breathing pure oxygen. His air-tight helmet was sealed to his body with a cork ring before he took off from Peshawar in Pakistan on a 3,300 miles flight which was to take him over the Aral Sea, Sverdlovsk, Kirov and Murmansk, to Bodo in Norway.

Apart from the equipment for photographing specially selected areas of the Soviet Union as he flew over them, Powers was also provided with Soviet money in case he was forced down, and a poison capsule in the event of capture. There was a device for blowing up the U-2 if he had a forced landing. His survival gear included a pneumatic boat, maps of the Soviet Union, compasses, camping equiment and food concentrates. In his pocket he carried rings and wrist watches to curry favour with Russian citizens, in the same way as the nineteenth-century explorers took the trinkets of civilization as currency in their dealings with the savages of darkest Africa, a contemptuous parallel which was duly noted in Moscow.

At 60,000 feet Powers flew over the peaks of the Hindu Kush, crossed the Soviet border and turned on his recording and filming equipment which apparently was able to detect and record the sites of ammunition depôts, oil storage and aircraft installations, as well as the numbers and types of aircraft on the ground.

The intruder was soon spotted on Soviet radar screens and relays of supersonic fighters were sent up to shoot it down, but it was apparently flying too high. When he was over Sverdlovsk in the Urals, Powers radioed back to his base that he had a flame-out in his jet engine and was descending to restart the engine. That was all his base heard from him until the report of his capture.

It seems that what really happened was that the Russians were firing SA-2 missiles at him and that the U-2 was simply knocked out of the sky by the blast wave of one of these rockets. A direct hit would obviously have destroyed it. Powers said that at 68,000 he saw an orange flash and then his aircraft went into a dive. During the long descent he lost consciousness several times, but was able to parachute out of the falling U-2. When he landed he was semi-conscious and did not put up any resistance. The U-2 crashed in a field outside Sverdlovsk. Fourteen missiles were fired at Powers's plane, and one of them shot down a Soviet MIG-19, which was pursuing the U-2, and killed the pilot.

In Moscow Kruschev stormed angrily and self-righteously and cancelled the Summit meeting. Washington at first referred to the U-2 as a "weather plane", then was forced to admit that the U-2 was a spy-plane, but said the flight had not been authorized by Washington. The news that Powers had not been able to destroy his tell-tale plane made Eisenhower realize that denial was useless. He then took full presidential responsibility for the U-2 flight.

Eisenhower's admission was the act of a soldier rather than a statesman. Allen Dulles had offered to accept the responsibility himself and resign. Eisenhower later said that the main reason he made the statement was to protect Powers and impress upon Russia that Powers was acting under orders, and was not to be shot out of hand as a spy.

It is one of the rules of the ignoble game of espionage that spies are disowned when caught, but it was impossible to disown a spy with a U-2 strapped to his back. Eisenhower no doubt believed he was doing the decent thing.

Senator William Fulbright, a strong critic of the C. I. A., said that the President should have taken a position of silence in the matter. "If anyone had to take the responsibility, it should have been the head of Intelligence. It should not have been the President, who embodies the whole sovereignty and dignity of the whole American people."

Powers was sentenced to ten years' imprisonment, but served only twenty months. In February, 1962, the Americans were glad to exchange him for Colonel Abel who was serving thirty years in America for spying. It was a very fair exchange, despite what some Americans said.

The U-2 affair did no good to the C. I. A.'s image, for it was blamed for wrecking the Summit Conference.

Charles Franklin: *Spies of the Twentieth Century*, London 1967
By permission of the publishers, Odhams Books

VOCABULARY. *record*: register facts for future use — *missile* ['misail]: anything that is thrown or fired — *site*: position; place — *deployment*: act of spreading or opening out — *row*: noisy quarrel — *summit*: top; highest point — *air-tight*: made so that air cannot pass in or out — *capsule*: gelatine case for dose of medicine etc. — *forced landing*: compulsory landing of aircraft owing to damage — *gear* [giə]: equipment for a special purpose — *pneumatic*: filled with compressed air —

concentrate: concentrated form of something — *curry favour*: to seek eagerly for favour — *trinket*: small ornament of little value — *peak*: pointed top of a mountain — *depôt*: storehouse — *spot*: catch sight of — *relay*: a number of men to take the place of others; *relays*: "rollender Einsatz" — *flame-out*: bursting out — *blast*: blowing of wind; explosion; *blast wave*: "Druckwelle" — *dive*: act of going quickly to a lower level — *parachute*: jump from an aircraft — *self-righteous*: thinking a lot of one's goodness — *cancel* [ˈkænsəl]: put off — *tell-tale*: revealing secrets — *disown*: say that one does not know.

91. The Problem Solver and the Spy

Richard Verner leaned back in his office chair with the alert look of a big cat, as across the desk, Nathan Bancroft, a quietly dressed men of average height, spoke earnestly.

"Last Saturday, Mr Verner, a technician at one of our most highly classified research laboratories got away with the plans for a new and secret type of laser device. The scientist who invented the device evidently tried to stop him, and was stabbed to death." Verner nodded intently.

Bancroft went on. "To understand the situation that's come about, you have to know that the region round this laboratory has a great many caverns. These are connected in a gigantic system of natural tunnels, rooms, and underground streams that have never been thoroughly mapped or explored.

"The technologist who stole the plans is an ardent speleologist—cave explorer. Possibly one reason for his hobby is that he suffers from hay fever, and cavern air is pure. In any case, over a period of years he's spent entire days in an underground complex of branching tunnels known as the Maze of Minos. A number of cave explorers have been lost in there, and the local people shun it. The only known expert on this underground maze is the murderer himself.

"Now there's no question, Mr Verner, but that this spy expected to be far away before the theft of the plan was discovered. But, by sheer good luck, the director of the laboratory discovered what had happened. The technician, taking the plans with him, escaped into this cavern—this Maze of Minos. We have a great many men on the spot, doing nothing but watching the known exits. But there's always the chance that he'll find some new way out, or knows of one, and get away."

"Is he starving?"

"Not likely. He probably has caches of food for his longer explorations. And there's water in the caverns, if you know where to look."

"You want to get him alive, and by surprise?"

"Exactly. We could put our whole organization in there and get nothing out of a grand-scale search but sore feet, chills, and a dozen men lost in the winding passages. The thing is a stalemate, and he knows it."

Verner laughed, "I can usually solve any problem—though sometimes there's an unavoidable element of luck and uncertainty. We'd better lose no time getting there."

Many cars and several big lorries were parked outside the main cavern entrance. There was a steady throb of engines as Verner and Bancroft walked in.

They were in a brightly lighted chamber in the rock, about forty feet long by ten high, and twelve to fourteen feet wide. Here their voices and footsteps echoed as Bancroft led the way towards the far end, where a faint breeze of cool air blew in their faces. Wherever Verner looked, the stalactites and stalagmites rose and dipped endlessly, with new chambers opening out in different directions.

For a long time they walked in silence except for the echoes of their own footsteps. Then suddenly it was dark ahead.

"Here," said Bancroft, "we come to the end of our string. These tunnels branch, then open out into rooms, and the rooms have galleries leading off from them, and out of these galleries there are still more tunnels. They twist, wind, and occasionally they even rejoin. This whole place is honeycombed, filled with diverging and connecting tunnels.

"There's a superabundance of clues. Dogs have followed one track through the dark right over the edge of a sudden drop, and been killed. We can find signs that he's been just about anywhere we look."

Bancroft shook his head. "Let's go out. There are some people you want to meet."

Outside in the warm autumn night, a group of men quickly gathered round Verner and Bancroft.

The laboratory director sneezed and blew his nose again. "One reason he spent so much time there, especially in the autumn, was the pure air of the caverns. He was, if anything, even more allergic than I am. He once told me that the only place an active man could find recreation out of doors in the autumn, if he suffered from hay fever, was inside a cave."

Verner glanced at Bancroft. "There seems to be a slight, steady current of air in there. It seems to flow into the Minotaur, and then branch out through the maze. It's always fresh and cool."

Bancroft looked at Verner tensely. "Do you have *any suggestion, any* ideas at all?"

Verner nodded. 'If we're lucky, and if what we've been told is true, we *may* have him out of there in a few hours."

"If you can do that, you're a miracle worker."

"No miracle at all—just common sense. But this is a case where we'll need a little luck. And we'll have to work from the upper end—from the Minotaur."

The passages of the Minotaur were larger and looked less complicated than those in the Maze. Here the gentle current of cool air seemed stronger, steadier, and could sometimes be felt even in comparatively wide passages.

Verner and Bancroft waited tensely, and then down the passage ahead came a small group, carrying a struggling man who was swearing violently.

"*Find* him?" said one of his captors, grinning. "All we had to do was follow the sounds he was making. He was sitting by a cache of food that would have lasted a week, with the plans still in his pocket."

Bancroft was looking at Verner, but he didn't speak. An awful choking and strangling from the prisoner made Bancroft turn in amazement. The choking and strangling noises were interspersed with violent sneezing.

Down the passage the men had stopped thrashing the stacks of ragwort ordered by Verner, which had sent thick clouds of pollen drifting through the passage and into the Maze. The pollen had unerringly found its target—the murder-thief who suffered from hay fever.

(Abridged) Christopher Anvil

VOCABULARY. *alert*: watchful — *technician*: person expert in the technique of a particular art — *laser*: light amplification by stimulated emission of radiation — *stab*: stick a sharp point into — *cavern*: deep hollow place in the earth — *map*: draw in the form of a map — *speleologist*: cave explorer — *hay fever*: illness that affects some people in summer "Heuschnupfen" — *maze*: labyrinth — *shun*: keep clear of — *spy*: person who tries to get secret information — *exit*: way out — *starve*: die for want of food — *cache* [kæʃ]: hiding-place — *sore*: causing pain — *stalemate*: (in chess) position in which no new move can be made — *throb*: beat — *faint*: weak — *stalactite*: stalk of lime hanging from the roof of a cave — *stalagmite*: similar deposit, but rising from the floor of a cave — *dip*: lower — *honeycomb*: fill with holes, tunnels etc. — *diverge*: go different ways — *clue*: sth. that helps to solve a problem — *drop*: abrupt fall in level of surface — *sneeze*: make a sudden, cough-like noise through the nose — *allergic*: sensitive to the action of foods, pollens etc. — *current*: stream of air — *tense*: showing concentration or mental strain — *choke*: be unable to breathe — *strangle*: hinder the breathing of — *intersperse*: diversify — *thrash*: beat soundly — *stack*: large pile — *ragwort*: yellow-flowered plant — *pollen*: fertilising dust of flowers "Blütenstaub" — *target*: object aimed at.

92. The Strange Drug of Dr Caber

We had got on to a rather commonplace topic one day at the Billiards Club. We were discussing murder, and how to do it successfully. Some argued that it was easy, and some hard, but I need not go over the arguments.

"I think I may have mentioned to you some time or other," a friend of mine said, "a man I once knew called Dr Caber. He's no longer practising now, poor fellow, and perhaps there is no harm in mentioning that he did a very successful murder. Of course that kind of thing was in his line. I don't mean that he was a murderer, I wouldn't say that of him; but he was a good deal in with people who were, and some of them often came to him for help. Getting them out of their trouble after they had got into it was his line. But on this occasion they wanted something new.

"There was a fellow with a perfect English accent, correct papers, and a good reason for being in England. One of the dangerous sort. One man said he was a German. Norman Smith was his name. Well, this man Smith had a motor-bicycle, and travelled about the roads a good deal, especially where there were aerodromes, and got to know a good deal without leaving the road or doing anything really suspicious; and one day he got to know a secret about aeroplanes in a certain district, which was about the most dangerous secret he could have got hold of. It was sometime in the year 1938."

"What planes were those?" asked a man.

"There weren't any," said my friend. "That was the deadly secret. We didn't even know it ourselves, bar a very few. Over a large area in the East of England there were no planes at all, and only a very few available to be sent there. If he had got that secret home to where he really came from, they would have known that they had us at their mercy. Well, the Government were informed, but they were busy with several other things; so the people who were watching Norman Smith decided to go to Caber; and Caber refused to help them, but in the end they talked him round. Well, first of all Caber asked for all the facts; and then he sat silent a long time, smoking some kind of a pipe carved out of an Indian tree; and then he told them his wonderful plan, or as much of it as he thought it necessary for them to know.

"We weren't entirely blind or deaf in those days, and Smith was watched all right, and his letters were watched; but what they couldn't guard against was his going back to Germany and telling them by word of mouth where we had no defences. Unfortunately he took no interest in the defences we had; he could have been arrested if he had pried into them. But Norman Smith knew how to keep inside our law. His principal precaution was a huge Alsatian, a good savage dog.

"Well, Norman Smith had a house in Hertfordshire, and there he kept his Alsatian, just in case any lawless people should try to get in at night. Caber asked so many questions about this savage dog that my friends got the idea that he meant to poison it, and one of them even hinted that so simple a plan was hardly worth the money. But it was foolish of them to suppose that one of the greatest masters of the underworld would hold his position there by making plans so simple that any little dog-stealer could have competed with him. Nor was it easy to poison the dog, for Norman Smith had him guarded by two or three cur dogs. The dog was the crux of the whole situation, and there seemed no way of getting by him. Among the facts my friends told Caber was that Norman Smith used every now and then to go to the seaside and stay in a large hotel. It is strange how fond spies always are of the sea.

"'You'll have to do it there,' said Caber at last. 'He won't be able to have the dog in the hotel. Two or three men to follow him, a little fracas, and a jab with a small needle.'

"'I don't like poison,' said one of the audience. 'It can always be traced.'

"'But I am not going to give you any poison,' said Caber.

"'Well, what's the use of the needle?' they asked.

"'The slightest jab,' said Caber, 'a little harmless fluid put in with a syringe, then your two men get away; better have three. And after that, he brings a charge of assault, and the police look for the men. But so long as no harm comes to Norman Smith, and the police have only his word that he was pricked by a needle, it is only a local affair, not Scotland Yard and the police of the countryside, as it would be in the case of murder.'

"'Not murder, of course, exactly', said one of my friends. 'But, then, what is going to be the effect of your needle and syringe?'

"'Merely,' said Caber, 'that when he goes home, or very soon after, he will accidentally die.'

"'They'll trace a thing like that,' said the man who didn't like poison.

"'If things I did had ever been traced,' said Caber, 'I shouldn't be here.'

"And somehow that seemed to silence them. And then one said, 'You told us it was innocuous.'

"'Entirely,' said Caber.

"And that in the end was what they did. Well, Norman Smith went to the sea sure enough in a week-or-so's time, and stayed at the large hotel, and left a man in Hertfordshire to feed his dangerous dog, and the three little yapping dogs that were to look after it. And the first morning after he arrived at the sea Norman Smith went for a walk, and he got into a bit of a row with three men near some golf-links, and he went to the police complaining he had been assaulted and alleging he had been impregnated or inoculated with some deadly disease or poison. He had a pin-prick to show on his arm, and he asserted that near it he had seen a drop of some liquid that had a sweaty smell. And the police sent for two doctors, who made tests and examinations, all of which proved that Smith was perfectly fit. By the end of a week the whole thing had blown over, so far as the police were concerned, and nothing was traced to anybody. You see, poisons can always be traced, and bacterial things even easier, because they are rarer, and the police would soon get on to it."

"And what happened?" we asked.

"Norman Smith went home to Hertfordshire," replied my friend, "invigorated by his stay by the sea, and cheered by whatever information spies get when they go to the seaside. And that night his Alsatian killed him."

"Yes, a successful murder," said one of the men, "if you can call a dog a murderer."

And one of us said rather diffidently that he didn't quite see how Caber came into it.

"It was a very subtle drug," said my friend. "Perfectly harmless, as Caber said. But it changed his smell. It gave him an entirely new scent. Of course no Alsatian dog would put up with a thing like that."

Lord Dunsany: *The Fourth Book of Jorkens*, London 1948
By permission of the publishers, Hutchinson & Co Ltd

VOCABULARY. *drug*: substance used for medical purpose — *topic*: subject for discussion — *suspicious*: not deserving to be trusted — *bar*: except — *at the mercy of*: in the power of — *carve*: make or shape by cutting — *pry*: look closely into — *Alsatian*: large, wolf-like dog — *savage*: wild; fierce and cruel — *compete*: take part in a contest — *cur*: dog of poor breed — *crux*: difficult part of a problem — *fracas* ['frækɑː]: uproar; noisy quarrel — *jab*: sharp thrust — *fluid*: liquid — *syringe*: device for injecting liquids into the body — *assault*: violent attack — *prick*: pierce slightly — *innocuous*: causing no harm — *yap*: bark — *row* [rau]: noisy quarrel — *golf-links*: the ground on which golf is played — *impregnate*: penetrate, permeate — *inoculate*: introduce disease germs into — *invigorate*: strengthen — *diffident*: shy, bashful — *subtle*: difficult to describe; mysterious — *scent:* smell.

93. Going on Safari

My profession is one of the smallest in the world. Few people know much about it. In fact, I was once asked if I hunted white men! The technical term for White Hunter is really Professional Hunter. In the early days in East Africa the original White Hunters were the men who hunted by themselves and solely for profit. They killed most elephants and rhinos, but other animals too, and sold the ivory, horns, and skins to traders. With the spread of civilization and the increase of immigration, a game department had to be formed for the protection of wild life. The game laws, from time to time, have been altered and restricted and hunting for profit has now become, quite rightly, a practical impossibility.

The White Hunter of to-day earns his living in a different way. He is now, if not working on his own, engaged by a safari firm which arranges and outfits shooting, photographic, or scientific expeditions. He is in charge and is solely responsible for the success and safety of the safari. He must organize and look after the boys (as all the servants are called), the cars, the stores, guns and ammunition, and every detail of the equipment. He is doctor, mechanic, chef, butler, entertainer, sometimes even script-writer and actor, all rolled into one.

Early in the century, when time was of little consequence, safaris were made on foot with a great number of African porters and ox-wagons or with horses and mules. Those romantic days were over with the coming of motor transport, though the actual hunting and stalking is, of course, still done on foot.

Thirty years ago a successful foot safari could go for one month no farther than thirty or forty miles from Nairobi. Today, in that month, you must travel hundreds of miles by motor-car in search of game. So the Hunter's task is now more difficult with limited time, fewer good shots and less game.

Before the last war, a safari sometimes lasted for six months, or even a year. In our more hectic days, three months is unusual, and one or two months is the normal time for an expedition.

I became a Professional Hunter in 1948 and have, since then, been working for one of the biggest safari firms in Nairobi. Clients are of all professions and come from many nations, though the majority are from the United States. But there is one thing which they all have in common—wealth.

An expedition to the interior of the African wilds requires a large staff. For one visitor alone, a total of eleven people is the minimum:

One lorry-driver,
One cook and his assistant,
Two trackers,
Two personal boys,
One skinner (taxidermist),
Three camp assistants.

The cost of the safari will be no less than a thousand pounds, which will cover all expenses except personal outfits, ammunition, spirits, and tobacco. The presence of a second client will add, perhaps, two hundred pounds to the initial cost, but three or more require a second White Hunter, extra vehicles and boys, and so will be a heavy additional expense.

The Hunter has his own attendants, a personal boy and one or two trackers who go with him on all safaris. All the camp workers are Africans, men of skill, preferring the free and exciting life of the bush to any other.

The interests of visitors vary from shooting and collecting trophies to merely observing and photographing animals. A few people reveal themselves indiscriminate killers who try to shoot every animal allowed on their licence, whether a good trophy or not. They are unpopular with the Professional Hunter who, naturally, tries to stop all senseless slaughter.

Many go on safari for the fun and novelty alone, accepting anything Nature offers in the way of adventure. Others, too, wish to study the rapidly disappearing religions and customs of the aborigines. For a number of people, it is an escape from their battle with noise, speed, telephones, and newspapers, or their bad livers and pills. A few make the bush an excuse for emptying more bottles than they would be allowed to do at home.

Women often come on safari, either accompanying their husbands or independently, to shoot and take photographs. I dare not write this as a general rule, but I have found them easier clients than men. They are intelligent listeners, earnestly interested, and quick to learn. They have patience, endurance, and determination. In my opinion they are less excitable and therefore become more reliable shots than most men. I remember one safari some years ago. Of the five clients one was a woman who had never fired a shot in her life. It took very little time to teach her how to handle and to use a rifle. At the end of the safari, her average shooting was better than any of the men's.

It is a curious fact that in the bush, away from civilization and his familiar surroundings, a man's true character invariably and unmercifully comes to the surface. I have seen a twenty-year friendship turn into hatred with a few weeks. I knew two men who became so childish that they refused to meet or even speak to each other. Their only communication was by notes carried by a servant from one tent to another. There are the brilliant shots who can hit nothing; the foolhardy with a false sense of bravery, who endanger their own and the lives of others trying to create an effect. There are the armchair heroes, braver at home than when only tent-canvas is between them and a lion's roar. There are the timid, bashful, and apologetic, who turn out to be expert shots, tough and courageous.

In his role of entertainer, the White Hunter should be a card player. Once a royal client flew a bridge team to the camp. As soon as the day's hunting was over, the card-table went up and the play continued until the early hours of the morning. At last, I had to make midnight "closing time", much to the relief of some of His Highness's guests, who were losing heavily.

In Africa, mention of the Big Five means the dangerous game: the elephant, rhinoceros, buffalo, the lion, and the leopard. Opinions differ about which one of them is the most dangerous. Personally, I make no distinctions, but the buffalo is responsible for more fatal accidents. He has sharp eyesight, an acute ear, and a keen sense of smell. When angered or wounded, he is a formidable and cunning foe, intent on destroying you.

Our motto is *Nec timor nec temeritas.* In other words, a true hunter should avoid taking unnecessary risks but must show courage and presence of mind when the occasion demands.

I have hunted in East Africa for over thirty years. As a young man I discovered its charm and fascination. I love the free life, the hardships and the wanderings; the velvet nights filled with mysterious sounds; the camp fires and the laughter of the Africans. A personal collection of trophies does not interest me and I have shot comparatively few animals.

Returning home to my farm near Nairobi is always a joy. But it isn't long before I set off again into the bush. Clients and hunter alike get Africa under their skin. Whether the safari was successful or not, they always want to return.

Christer Ashan: "I Am a White Hunter" in
The Book of Leisure, ed. John Putney, London
By permission of the publishers, Odhams Press Ltd

VOCABULARY. *safari*: hunting journey in East Africa — *ivory*: hard, white substance which forms the tusks of the elephant, walrus etc. — *game*: wild animals hunted for sport — *outfit*: complete equipment — *entertainer*: person who gives amusement — *script*: typescript of film-play "Drehbuch" — *stalk*: steal up to game under cover — *hectic*: feverish; wild — *tracker*: hunter who follows wild animals — *skinner*: sb. who withdraws skin from — *taxidermist*: person who prepares and mounts the skins of animals — *trophy*: anything kept as a reminder of successes — *aborigine* [æbəˈridʒiniː]: native inhabitant of a country — *unmerciful*: cruel — *foolhardy*: foolishly bold — *canvas*: coarse cloth used for tents — *bashful*: shy — *apologetic*: saying that one is sorry — *acute*: keen — *foe*: enemy — *velvet*: soft — *get under one's skin*: take strong hold on one.

94. The Crossing of Antarctica

Dr Vivian Fuchs, a geologist from England, had drawn up plans for a Commonwealth Trans-Antarctic Expedition.

His plan for the journey across the frozen continent was almost the same as Sir Ernest Shackleton's, made forty years before. He intended to lead a party into the interior from the shores of the Weddell Sea. Another party was to travel from the opposite of the continent. Their job was to lay depots for the end of the trans-continental journey.

The man chosen by Fuchs to lead this second party was Sir Edmund Hillary, the famous mountaineer from New Zealand who, in 1953, had become the first man to climb Mount Everest.

Mechanical vehicles were to play an important part in the trans-Antarctic expedition. The Sno-cat is a large vehicle like a heavy motor truck. In place of wheels, however, it has four pontoons fitted with linked tracks. The Weasel is a smaller vehicle with a single track on each side of it like the track of a tank.

Aircraft also were to play an important part in the expedition. They had two main jobs. The first was the carrying of supplies to advance depots. The second was flying over an area to be crossed and looking for the best route.

The base that was set up on the Filchner Ice Shelf close to the shores of the Weddell Sea was named Shackleton. Dr Fuchs returned there in January 1957 in a newly-built Danish ice-breaker, the *Magga Dan*.

In the meantime, on the other side of the continent, Sir Edmund Hillary and seventeen companions from New Zealand had been setting up another base, named Scott, on Ross Island.

Midway through August, the sun rose above the horizon for the first time since April. At once the men at Shackleton and Scott began to prepare for the long journey ahead. The aircraft and the vehicles were taken out of their winter shelters and made ready for use again. The dogs were led out and exercised. Equipment was checked and tested.

They were ready by 24th November. That morning Dr Fuchs led the main party south from Shackleton in a Sno-cat named *Rock 'n Roll*. Ahead of the lumbering orange vehicles lay a journey of 2158 miles across the loneliest part of the Earth. It took them four weeks to reach South Ice.

On the opposite side of the continent, Sir Edmund Hillary set out from Scott base on 14th October. On 15th December, he arrived at a point 700 miles from Scott base and 500 miles from the Pole. Soon Depot 700 was completed. Snow cairns, six feet high and marked with flags, were set out at intervals of half a mile for five miles on either side of the depot.

On 4th January, Hillary reached the South Pole. He and his companions had covered the 500 miles from Depot 700 in less than fifteen days. They received a stirring welcome from the men of the United States Amundsen-Scott Base at the Pole. They were the first persons to reach the South Pole overland since Captain Scott and his ill-fated party.

On this date, Fuchs was still 357 miles from the Pole. He was running over rugged fields of sastrugi. Sometimes in a day of thirteen to fifteen hours he was covering only twenty miles.

Every two hundred miles, Fuchs's party camped for a whole day while the vehicles were overhauled. They carried with them welding equipment. It was frequently needed to weld together parts of the vehicles that had been wrenched apart by the repeated jarring as they tumbled over the sastrugi. Two Weasels had to be abandoned as they were beyond repair.

From the Pole, Hillary sent an urgent message by radio to Dr Fuchs. It began, "Dear Bunny. I am very concerned about the serious delay in your plans." Fuchs replied, "There can be no question of abandoning journey."

In the morning of 19th January, Fuchs and his men decked their vehicles with flags. In bright sunshine they ran southwards over a soft, smooth surface. Twelve pairs of eyes scanned the horizon eargerly for markers. In the U. S. Base at the South Pole, Sir Edmund Hillary was looking expectantly to the north. At eight o'clock he saw a convoy of vehicles in the distance.

Four Sno-cats and one Weasel chugged towards the South Pole, with two dog teams made up of seventeen dogs loping beside them. The flags on the vehicles fluttered in the icy breeze—the White Ensign, the flags of Australia and New Zealand, a flag for the county of Kent and another for the city of Bristol.

A group of Weasels drove out from the U. S. base to meet them. The first men out when the vehicles stopped close together were Dr Fuchs and Sir Edmund Hillary. Cameras snapped as they shook hands.

Then Fuchs was greeted by Rear-Admiral George J. Dufek, the commander of the United States's operations in Antarctica.

"How about a hot bath and a hot meal?" he asked.

"We could use that," replied Dr Fuchs.

So there, at the South Pole, Fuchs and his companions had their first bath for several weeks. Afterwards, as they drank hot coffee, they read through mail that was waiting for them in what had once been the most desolate spot on the globe.

Fuchs and his men stayed at the Pole until 24th January. They overhauled and refuelled their vehicles, and for that brief time they enjoyed the luxury of a change of food.

Hillary had flown back to Scott with the dog teams. They were no longer needed as the trail was already marked.

In the first two days from the Pole, Fuchs and his party covered 75 miles. Then the Weasel broke down. They abandoned it and drove on. They reached Depot 700 on 7th February. There Hillary joined them.

The weather remained good. On 24th February they reached the top of the Skelton Glacier and began the difficult trip down to the ice shelf. Next day snow and sky merged in the condition known as a white-out. It was impossible to see the way ahead. Hillary went forward roped to the leading Sno-cat and marked the trail.

On Sunday, 2nd March, Fuchs and Hillary and their eleven companions, their Sno-cats once more bedecked with flags, roared over the ice towards Scott Base. A few miles from their journey's end they were met by a motley collection of vehicles and sledges from Scott Base and the American base, McMurdo.

It had been estimated that the Commonwealth Trans-Antarctic Expedition would cover the 2158 miles across the continent in 100 days at an average rate of 21.58 miles per day. The journey was actually completed in 98 days.

The expedition set sail from Scott Base on 5th March in H. M. N. Z. S. *Endeavour*. Before its departure, messages of congratulations had poured in over the base radio. Among them was one from Queen Elizabeth II. It contained the news that Dr Fuchs was to be knighted.

Robert J. Hoare: *Southwards,* London 1966
By permission of the publishers, Ginn & Co Ltd

VOCABULARY. *geologist*: expert in the science of the earth's history — *Weddell Sea*: arm of S. Atl. Oc., Antarctica — *depot*: place where stores are kept — *mountaineer*: person who is clever at climbing mountains — *Sno-cat* and *Weasel*: tracked vehicles, snow tractors — *truck*: strong vehicle for carrying large or heavy loads — *pontoon*: floating metal structure or support — *track*: set of rails — *single track*: one pair of rails — *aircraft*: any kind of flying machine — *supplies*: stores —

shelter: place of safety — *equipment*: outfit, things needed for a purpose — *lumber*: move heavily — *cairn* [kɛən]: pile of rough stones etc. as a landmark — *ill-fated*: destined to misfortune — *rugged*: rough; uneven — *sastrugi*: ridges of frozen snow — *overhaul*: examine carefully and carry out repairs — *weld*: join pieces of metal etc., usu. heated by hammering "schweißen" — *wrench*: twist or pull violently — *jar*: hurt by shaking — *tumble*: do jumping tricks — *delay*: postponement — *deck*: adorn — *scan*: examine carefully — *marker*: thing used for making a mark — *convoy*: number of vehicles etc. — *chug*: make sound of an engine — *lope*: run with a long stride — *White Ensign*: flag used by the Royal Navy — *Rear-Admiral*: officer who commands the rear division of the fleet "Konteradmiral" — *desolate*: unlived in — *refuel*: supply with material for burning — *brief*: short — *merge*: join together — *white-out*: condition marked by dense snow-cloud and total obscuration of physical features (after *black-out*)—*motley*: of different colours — *H. M. N. Z. S.*: Her (or: His) Majesty's New Zealand Ship — *knight*: confer knighthood on.

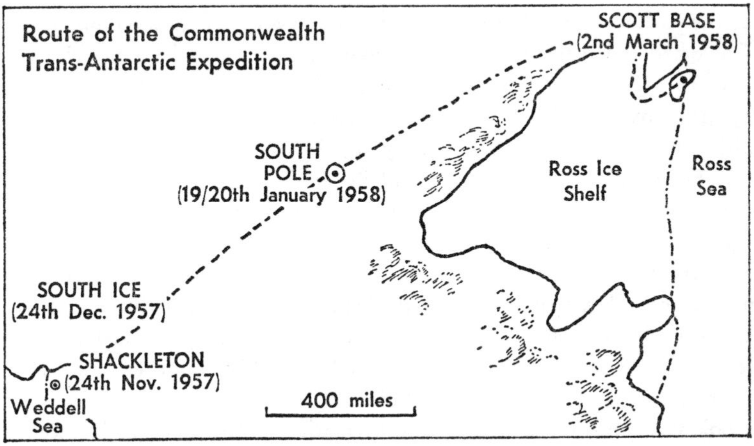

95. The Strange Story of Doctor Cook

On 2nd September, 1909, a message was sent out by wireless from Lerwick, in the Shetland Isles, which startled everyone who heard it. Soon the message was being passed on round the world. It said: "I reached the North Pole on 21st April, 1908. Frederick Cook."

"He has done a wonderful thing," said people everywhere.

"His name will go down in history. He is the first man to reach the North Pole."

"He has done a wonderful thing," said others. "But who is he? We have never heard of him before."

Dr Frederick Cook was not at all famous. Yet his record, when it became known, was one to be proud of. He was a surgeon from New York. In 1891, at the age of twenty-six, he had travelled to Greenland with the famous polar explorer, Robert Peary. Six years later, he had spent fifteen months in the Antarctic with an expedition from Belgium. Then, in 1906, he had claimed to have climbed the highest mountain in North America—Mount McKinley, which is 21 000 feet high.

Dr Cook had landed at Lerwick on his way to Denmark. When he arrived at Copenhagen, he was greeted by the King and Queen of Denmark. Newspaper reporters flocked round him. They wanted to learn more about his journey to the North Pole. Many learned societies invited him to give lectures.

Dr Cook had an amazing story to tell. He said he had made his final journey over the pack ice to the North Pole with only two Eskimos as companions.

Cook had sailed to the Arctic in August 1907 in a yacht owned by a rich friend. In a Eskimo village at Annotok in Greenland he had prepared for his journey over the ice. The Eskimos were his friends and they did all they could to help him. On 19th February, 1908, he was ready. He set out with eleven Eskimos, one hundred dogs and eleven sledges.

Cook and his companions travelled northwards through land where they knew there was game to be hunted. They obtained all the fresh meat they needed from musk-oxen, polar bears and hares. They did not need to use the supplies which they had brought with them from the Eskimo village.

On 18th March, only a month after setting out, they reached the tip of Axel Heiberg Land, which is 82 degrees North. Five hundred miles ahead, over the frozen sea, was the North Pole.

Cook was sure he would be able to reach the North Pole. He went on another thirty miles and then he sent back all the Eskimos save two. They were strong young men named Etukishook and Ahwela.

According to Dr Cook, he and Etukishook and Ahwela reached the North Pole one month later.

His story of the return journey is one of ill luck and hardship. The drifting of the ice carried them to the southwest. They were unable to reach Axel Heiberg Land where they had left a store of food. For fifty-three days they struggled over the ice. Then they reached an island in the far north of Canada. From there they turned eastwards, as they wanted to get back to Greenland.

By this time, they were short of food and they hunted whatever game they came upon. At first, they used rifles, but when they had no ammunition left, the Eskimos made spears from the runners of sledges. No food could be spared for the dogs, so they were turned loose. Then, as winter closed in, Cook and the Eskimos dug a hole in the ice to form a rough shelter. There they lived until the following spring.

In the spring of 1909, Dr Cook and his two companions arrived back in Greenland. The doctor joined a ship which was sailing to Copenhagen and, soon, he was telling his story to the world.

For five days, Dr Cook was treated as a hero. It is true that there were some people who wanted to ask him awkward questions. Some of them even asked, "What proof can you give us that you really reached the North Pole?"

Dr Cook paid little attention to these people. "Don't worry," he said. "Proofs of what I say are on their way. They are coming from the Arctic in another ship."

Before the other ship arrived, startling news came from America. Robert Peary had reached the North Pole. "That is good," said Dr Cook. "Peary's report will show you that everything I have told you is true."

But Peary's report did not help Dr Cook. Peary himself did not believe Dr Cook. He said, "The two Eskimos who went with Cook said he went no distance to the north."

Dr Cook said he had found land near the North Pole. Peary said the Pole was in the centre of the frozen sea. There was no land near it at all.

For a time, people argued about Dr Cook. All great men have their enemies and there were some people who said Cook was right and Peary was wrong. But, in 1910, Etukishook and Ahwela told their story. Cook had been no nearer than five hundred miles from the North Pole!

Yet Dr Cook still said he had reached the North Pole. He wrote a book, "How I attained the Pole", which you may find in public libraries today. He went on writing about his adventures and giving lectures about them. He even appeared on the music-hall stage as the "First Man to Reach the North Pole". Then, as time passed, people began to forget him.

Dr Cook came back into the news again in 1922. He had been arrested. His crime was fraud in selling some shares in a company, and he was sent to prison for fourteen years.

In 1937, Dr Cook's name was in the newspapers again. He had taken the publishers of the *Encyclopaedia Britannica* to court. The *Encyclopaedia Britannica* is a famous reference book. It contains information on almost every subject. It mentioned Cook's claim to have reached the North Pole and it said his claim had been "universally rejected", meaning that no one believed it.

"That is an insult to me," said Dr Cook. "It makes people think very badly of me." He went to court and asked for £ 5,000 to make up for the harm done to his good name. But the judge did not agree with Dr Cook, and he lost the case.

Dr Cook died three years later. By then people had forgotten about him. Even his claim to have been the first man to climb Mount McKinley is not believed today. Men who have climbed the mountain say he went only about half-way up it.

Robert J. Hoare: *Northwards*, London 1962
By permission of the publishers, Ginn & Co Ltd

VOCABULARY. *message*: piece of news sent — *startle*: give a fright to — *record*: past history — *surgeon*: doctor who performs operations — *pack ice*: large area of broken, floating ice in the polar seas — *yacht* [jɔt]: vessel, fitted up for pleasure or racing — *musk-ox*: ruminant found in North America, with strong musky smell — *tip*: pointed or thin end — *store*: place where goods are kept — *runner*: part on which sth. slides — *awkward*: likely to cause difficulty — *attain*: reach — *music-hall*: variety entertainment — *fraud*: criminal (act of) deception — *share*: one of the equal parts into which the capital of a business company is divided — *reject*: refuse to accept — *insult*: affront.

96. Lord Oxhead's Secret

It was finished. Rain had come. Lord Oxhead sat gazing fixedly at the library fire. Without the wind soughed around the turrets of Oxhead Towers, the seat of the Oxhead family. But the old earl heeded not the soughing of the wind around his seat. He was too absorbed.

Before him lay a pile of blue papers with printed headings. From time to time he turned them over in his hands and replaced them on the table with a groan. To the earl they meant ruin—absolute, irretrievable ruin, and with it the loss of his stately home that had been the pride of the Oxheads for generations. More than that—the world would now know the awful secret of his life.

The earl bowed his head in the bitterness of his sorrow, for he came of a proud stock. About him hung the portraits of his ancestors. Here on the right an Oxhead who had broken his lance at Crécy, or immediately before it. Then to the right again the portrait of Sir Ponsonby Oxhead who had fought with Wellington in Spain, and been dismissed for it.

Immediately before the earl as he sat was the family escutcheon emblazoned above the mantelpiece, with the motto, *Hic, haec, hoc, hujus, hujus, hujus.*

"Father!" The girl's voice rang clear through the half light of the wainscoted library. Gwendoline Oxhead had thrown herself about the earl's neck. The girl was radiant with happiness. Gwendoline was a beautiful girl of thirty-three, typically English in the freshness of her girlish innocence. She was the pride of her father's heart, for he saw reflected in her the qualities of his race.

"Father!" she said, a blush mantling her face. "I am so happy; Edwin has asked me to be his wife, and we plighted our troth—at least if you consent."

Then as she gazed into the old earl's stricken face, the girl's mood changed at once. "Father," she cried, "Father, are you ill? What is it? Shall I ring?"

"I hope, Gwendoline," said Lord Oxhead, "that your choice has been worthy of an Oxhead, and that he to whom you have plighted your troth will be worthy to bear our motto with his own." And, raising his eyes to the escutcheon before him, the earl murmured half unconsciously, "*Hic, haec, hoc, hujus, hujus, hujus.*"

"Father," continued Gwendoline, half timidly, "Edwin is an American."

"You surprise me indeed," answered Lord Oxhead; "and yet," he continued, turning to his daughter with the courtly grace that marked the nobleman of the old school, "why should we not respect and admire the Americans? Surely there have been great names among them! But tell me, Gwendoline, this Edwin of yours—where is his family seat?"

"It is at Oshkosh, Wisconsin, Father."

"Ah! say you so?" rejoined the earl, with rising interest. "Oshkosh is, indeed, a grand old name. The Oshkosh are a Russian family. And Wisconsin too; the Wisconsins, or better, the Guisconsins, are of old blood."

"Nay, Father," said Gwendoline, gently interrupting. "Wisconsin is not Edwin's own name: that, I believe, is the name of his estate. My lover's name is Edwin Einstein."

"Einstein," repeated the earl dubiously; "an Indian name perhaps; yet the Indians are many of them of excellent family. An ancestor of mine . . ."

"Father," said Gwendoline, again interrupting, "here is a portrait of Edwin. Judge for yourself if he be noble." The picture represented a typical specimen of American manhood of that Anglo-Semitic type so often seen in persons of mixed English and Jewish extraction. The figure was well over five feet two inches in height and broad in proportion. The pallor of the features was relieved by a drooping black moustache.

Such was Edwin Einstein to whom Gwendoline's heart, if not her hand, was already affianced. It seemed to Gwendoline that it was but a thing of yesterday, and yet in reality they had met three weeks ago. Love had drawn them irresistibly together. To Edwin the fair English girl with her old name and wide estates possessed a charm that he scarcely dared confess to himself. He determined to woo her. To Gwendoline there was that in Edwin's bearing, the rich jewels that he wore, the vast fortune that rumour ascribed to him, that appealed to something romantic and chivalrous in her nature. She loved to hear him speak of stocks and bonds, and his father's colossal business. It all seemed so noble and so far above the sordid lives of the people about her. Edwin, too, loved to hear the girl talk of her father's estates, of the diamond-hilted sword that the Saladin had given, or had lent, to her ancestor hundreds of years ago. He was never tired of asking how old her father was, was he robust, did a shock, a sudden shock, affect him much? and so on.

It had all seemed like a dream: and now Edwin Einstein had come in person to ask her hand from the earl, her father. Gwendoline summoned her courage for a great effort. "Papa," she said, "there is one other thing that it is fair to tell you. Edwin's father is in business."

The earl started from his seat in blank amazement. "In business!" he repeated. "The father of the suitor of the daughter of an Oxhead in business. Are you mad, girl? It is too much, too much!"

"But, Father", pleaded the girl in anguish," hear me. It is Edwin's father—Sarcophagus Einstein, senior—not Edwin himself. Edwin does nothing. He has never earned a penny. He is quite unable to support himself. You have only to see him to believe it. Indeed, dear Father, he is just like you. He is here now, in this house, waiting to see you. If it were not for his great wealth . . ."

"Girl!" said the earl sternly, "I care not for the man's riches. How much has he?"

"Fifteen million two hundred and fifty thousand dollars," answered Gwendoline. Lord Oxhead leaned his head against the mantelpiece. His mind was in a whirl. He was trying to calculate the yearly interest on fifteen and a quarter million dollars at four and a half per cent. It was bootless. His brain, trained by long years of high living and plain thinking, had become too subtle, too refined an instrument for arithmetic. . . .

At this moment the door opened and Edwin Einstein stood before the earl. Gwendoline never forgot what happened.

"You! You!" her father gasped. For a moment he stood to his full height, swaying and groping in the air, then fell prostrate his full length upon the floor. The lovers rushed to his aid. Edwin tore open his neckcloth and plucked aside his diamond pin to give him air. But it was too late. Earl Oxhead had breathed his last. Life had fled. The earl was extinct. That it to say, he was dead.

The reason of his death was never known. Had the sight of Edwin killed him? It might have. The old family doctor hurriedly summoned declared his utter ignorance. This, too, was likely. Edwin himself could explain nothing. But it was observed that after the earl's death and his marriage with Gwendoline he was a changed man; he dressed better, talked much better English.

The wedding itself was quiet, almost sad. At Gwendoline's request there was no wedding breakfast, no bridesmaids, and no reception, while Edwin, respecting his bride's bereavement, insisted that there should be no best man, no presents, and no honeymoon. Thus Lord Oxhead's secret died with him. It was probably too complicated to be interesting anyway.

Stephen Leacock: *Lord Oxhead's Secret*, London

VOCABULARY. *sough* [sau]: to make a sighing sound (of the wind) — *turret*: small tower on the top of a castle — *irretrievable*: that cannot be remedied — *stock*: one's forefathers — *Crécy*: French village, where Edward III defeated the French in 1346 — *escutcheon*: shield on which a coat of arms is seen "Wappenschild" — *emblazon*: adorn (shield) with heraldic devices "mit Wappenbild bemalen" — *mantelpiece*: shelf above a fireplace — *wainscoted*: lined with a wooden panelling — *mantle*: form a covering; spread over — *plight one's troth*: promise to marry — *stricken*: hurt, sorrowful — *Wisconsin*: state (USA) — *estate*: place of property — *extraction*: one's descent — *pallor*: paleness — *affianced*: engaged to be married — *woo*: try to win in marriage — *bearing*: behaviour — *stocks*: shares in a business — *bond*: documentary promise to pay borrowed money "Schuldverschreibung, Obligation" — *sordid*: dirty; mean — *hilt*: furnish with the handle of a sword — *Saladin*: (1137—93) the great Sultan of Egypt and Syria who led the Moslems against the Christians in the Third Crusade; a wise and cultured man, renowned for his chivalry — *amazement*: great surprise — *support*: maintain; provide for — *whirl*: great stir, confusion — *bootless*: useless — *gasp*: breathe with difficulty — *sway*: move unsteadily from side to side — *prostrate*: lying face down on the ground — *summon*: order a person to come — *bereavement*: great loss (esp. by death) — *honeymoon*: holiday taken by a newly married couple.

97. Last Day of Spring

Even though her eyes were still closed, Martha Briggs knew that the sun was shining. The warmth was creeping slowly, gloriously across the blankets, and any minute now it would reach her face, bathe her in lovely, lovely heat. And after that it would creep across the pillow to Thomas's side of the bed, and wake him too. Now that he couldn't get out of bed any more, it was a shame that the sun didn't go to his side first. But she wouldn't open her eyes yet. No, this was the loveliest bit of the whole day, lying here with Thomas, waiting for the sun to reach her face. Strange how the sun seemed to shine every morning now that she was nearly ninety years old. Such lovely sun, too—it must be spring, day after day. If only she could get Thomas into his chair by the window; but he was too heavy, she couldn't lift him any more.

Thomas .... Then she remembered. Of course! It was Thursday. This was the day when the Welfare woman with the clumping shoes was going to come and take Thomas away.

Take Thomas away, indeed! Martha had never heard such nonsense. As if she couldn't look after Thomas herself while he was ill!

She tried her hardest to remember what the creature had said. For a little while she could only remember the great shoes, and the snorting, breathing sort of voice that was so difficult to hear. Then slowly the woman's words came back to her:

"It isn't that we're criticising you, Mrs Briggs, not for one moment. We know you're doing your very, very best—you've done wonders for your age, I know you have. But you see—well, I'm sure you'll agree with me really—it isn't right, is it, that he should be lying like this at past midday, not been attended to, not even had his breakfast yet! And the room! ... You *do* see, don't you. Mrs Briggs? It simply is too much for you. And he'll be quite happy, I promise you, he'll have every attention ..."

On and on went the voice in Martha's mind, and she almost smiled at the absurdity of it all. As if she and Thomas couldn't have their breakfast when it suited them! If they liked to lie like this in the sun for a little while first, whose business was it but their own?

Still, perhaps it would be a good idea, this morning, to teach that creature a lesson. She'd get up early and cook breakfast. Now, what would they have? An egg. Of course. She would fry an egg for Thomas. He would love that, with a bit of fried bread. She knew there was an egg somewhere, and he should have it. Then she would scrub the floor until the boards shone white in the sunlight; she would wash the curtains. She would polish the chest of drawers, and rub the window till it shone. Too much for me, indeed! thought Martha: *I'll* show her.

But the sun was right on her face now, in all its glory. It would be a shame to get up just at this minute, just while it was like this. She would lie and enjoy it for a minute or two longer.... Martha woke with a start. How tiresome! She must have dozed off, and now she would have to hurry to get everything done before that woman arrived.

She climbed stiffly out of bed and fumbled about for her dress. Where *could* it have got to?

Her head was dropped a little forwards, and she could see lots and lots of floor. It was quite true; it *was* dirty. And what was worse, now that she was up all her enthusiasm for scrubbing it had drained away. The vision of sun-lit, white-scrubbed boards was gone, and she could think only of the backbreaking weight of the pail, and the ever more perilous feat of getting down onto one's knees and then, somehow, getting back up again . . .

But as least she had found her dress. At least that woman would find her up and dressed this time, and Thomas with a good breakfast in front of him. She made her way into the kitchen and set about preparing the meal.

But how had the fat in the frying-pan managed to burn black and smoking in just that moment or two it had taken her to find the egg? How tiresome things were! She poured the blackened mess away and started again, and this time it was wonderful. The egg was fried plump and golden, just the way Thomas liked it, and the fried bread was delicately brown. *That's* what he needed to build up his strength, a good breakfast like this every morning. It would be quite a job to buy an egg every day out of her tiny pension, but she'd managed it this time, and she'd manage it again. Oh yes, it would be worth it, to watch her Thomas strong and well again with good food inside him.

Now to get it into the bedroom. Slowly—oh, so slowly, because the boards had grown so uneven of late—she carried it across the landing and into the bedroom. But when she tried to put it down on the chest of drawers she found to her annoyance that there was no room there. It was all cluttered up with stuff—what *was* all that rubbish? She looked more carefully—and a dull bewilderment gripped her. For on the chest of drawers already was a plate with a fried egg on it—ice cold and congealed. And another, and another, and another. Something, half a memory, half a fear, made her turn slowly, slowly, to look at the bed. Yet it was empty. Thomas was gone. She knew she must sit down on the edge of the bed and think this out.

Of course! That was it! It was the wrong Thursday! That woman had already come on some other Thursday—last Thursday?—the Thursday before?—and had taken Thomas away!

Taken Thomas away! The import of the words slowly sank into her. How *could* she have let it happen? She, who had defended her family against all comers—how *could* she have let this flat-footed woman take her Thomas away?

She must think, think. When did they take him? Where would they have taken him to? Where *did* that woman say?

The hospital. Of course, Thomas was ill; it must have been the hospital. She would go there right now and fetch him, fetch him home herself through the spring-sunshine.

Such a long, long way to the hospital, and when she got there and sat down at last on the hard bench, how they did talk! One after another of them, snapping out questions like firecrackers. "No record of it." "No such admission"—the senseless words kept tossing about among them like paper balls....

Sister spoke a little louder, still patiently:

"Do you understand? You must go to the Enquiry desk, and they'll give you a form. You must fill in the patient's name and address, the date of admission ..."

But Martha Briggs was no longer listening to her. Because right now at the end of the shadowy stone corridor she could see Thomas. How well he looked! and—why—he was *running*, actually running towards her, with his dear, grey hair all rumpled and his arms outstretched!

"Thomas!" she cried, in joy and anxiety, "Thomas, my darling, you mustn't run!—your heart ...!"

She drew one breath of sweet, cool air, and then somehow seemed not to need another; for now she too was running lightly, lightly, like a young girl, like a bird, her feet skimming over the stone floor. How wonderful it was to run, and run, and run to meet your love.

"Will you *please* go to the Enquiry desk" ... Sister's voice broke off suddenly. A less expert eye than hers would scarcely have noticed the slight change as the old woman's head dropped a little further towards her chest and the faint breathing stopped.

Celia Fremlin: "The Last Day of Spring"
By permission of Anthony Sheil Associates Ltd

VOCABULARY. *pillow*: cushion for the head — *clump*: tread heavily — *snort*: throw out words with forcing air violently out through the nose — *scrub*: clean by rubbing hard — *chest of drawers*: large wooden box for storing clothes — *doze*: sleep lightly — *fumble*: feel about uncertainly with the hands — *pail*: bucket — *feat*: deed difficult to do — *plump*: rounded; in good condition — *tiny*: very small — *clutter*: crowd together — *rubbish*: waste matter — *bewilderment*: confusion — *firecracker*: firework which explodes with a cracking sound — *record*: written report — *admission*: person that is allowed to come in — *rumple*: crease; crumple — *skim*: pass over lightly — *faint*: weak.

98. A Boy in a Box

He was only a small boy and it was a big box.

The workmen had used it to put their tools in and now they never used it and the boy could get in the box and shut the lid to keep the cold out and he would sleep until morning with nothing to disturb him and nobody would ever find him in the box, or so the boy thought.

It was autumn and the nights were closing in and getting the first cold in them and at night, as he opened the lid and got in, he was glad to have the box to sleep in.

He curled up on his mattress of old rags and dirty clothing and the cat, who was his sleeping companion in the box, curled up with him. For a while the cat's purring kept him awake but that was not as bad as the noise the freight trains made. And sometimes when they stopped and were shunting and the trucks hit up, their shattering noise woke him and kept him awake and they kept hitting, all the trucks, then he could not sleep.

But now it was quiet in the yard and it was dark and only the cat purring, and nothing disturbed him in the box. He thought it must be like being dead, resting in this box.

Soon the boy was asleep and he dreamed he was in a home and nobody wanted him and there was nowhere else to go and suddenly he found this box. And the boy was grateful to find himself warm and comfortable in the box and to hear it raining outside, and he dropped back into a deep sleep.

When his sleep was over he reached down to where the cat was sleeping and picked it up and pushed it out.

He opened the lid quickly and he stood up and the daylight blinded him. He got out and shut the lid of the box quickly and he smoothed his clothes and ran his hand over his hair. He walked through the gateway in the iron fence and into the city.

The day has been beautiful, the boy thought, as he sat on the river bank and looked at the water. The leaves are blowing from the trees into the water and the leaves are yellow. The leaves, too, are no longer wanted, he was thinking.

An old man was sitting under a concrete bridge not far away. He had long grey hair, matted and thick around his ears, and he was dressed in a worn and faded raincoat that probably someone had given him, the boy thought, and he was a frail old man with no socks and broken boots, and noticing all this the boy went over and sat beside him.

"What do you want, boy?" the old man asked, looking curiously at the boy from the cool dark under the bridge. "Is my privacy nothing, that can be invaded by everyone?"

"I am looking for my father," the boy answered.

"I am an old man and I am not your father. And I don't want to be bothered."

"I won't bother you. I thought I might be able to help," said the boy.

"Why don't you go home to your mother, boy?"

"I haven't got a mother."

The old man looked at the boy. "Nonsense," he said. "Everyone has a mother. Somewhere you have a mother waiting for you, boy. All of us have a mother."

"I don't know where she is," the boy said. "She is not waiting for me."

"Do you mean you are an orphan?"

"I think so. I think it must be. I have never seen my mother, only Our Lady. The nuns at the orphanage told me, before I ran away."

"You ran away?"

"Yes."

"Why did you run away, boy?"

"I told you; I am looking for my father. And I did not like it there."

"Then you are truly an orphan. I believe you, boy," the old man said. "And we have a fellowship. I am an orphan since a long time ago."

The boy did not answer and, seeing the puzzled look, the old man continued. "Yes, boy, I am an orphan, too. An orphan of many things in this man's world."

The boy was not listening closely, and then the old man said, "Do you want to share a man's burden before you find your manhood? Go, now, boy, and try in your time to make a good mark in the world, and remember our meeting. Remember that in our time we shared a moment together.

"I cannot go much further unless I find my father," the boy told the old man.

"Did you father leave home, boy? Was he a soldier? Would you like me to be your father, boy?" the old man asked, smiling at the boy.

"No. Our Father is my father now."

The old man looked at the boy and felt sorry for him, and he wanted to be patient and not put the boy off.

"Yes. I am an old man. And together, or not together, we have not done very well in the world, have we? But you still have time," the old man said. "And if you will not have me for a father, then perhaps we can be brothers?"

The boy looked at the old man and didn't answer, and the old man spoke to him again, and the shade from the bridge made it cool around them, and there was a solemnness on the river, the old man thought.

"Our Father is your father and Our Lady is your mother. That is very beautiful, my son. I am an old man, but that is very beautiful."

"It is what the nuns told me at the orphanage."

"It is getting late, now. Soon it will be dark. Do you get enough to eat, boy?"

"Yes, thank you. I manage. The workmen give me some of their food," said the boy, and he prepared to leave.

"Will you be here tomorrow?" he asked the old man, as he stood up.

"Yes," the old man answered, "if I live through the night."

"Where do you sleep?"

"In the railway carriage. Unless the watchman shuts the gate, and then I sleep here, under the bridge. It is a good enough place. And what about you? Do you have some place to sleep?"

"Yes, thank you," said the boy. "I am all right. I have somewhere to go. It is a good place."

"Does the cold trouble you?"

"I do not like it," the boy answered. "But it does not trouble me. Nothing does. Except that I cannot find my father."

"That is good for you, boy. Only a fool allows himself to be troubled by little things," the old man said. "Yes, for all that, I am a lucky old man."

"Why?"

"Because I have my old age. And that is something, in my time. Also I have a place to sleep. And your are lucky, too, boy. You have your youth. So you see, each of us has something," said the old man.

"I see," said the boy. "Well, goodnight, old man."

"Goodnight, boy."

"God be with you, my son," the old man called after the boy, and he watched him walk away.

My son and brother, the old man thought, and he felt a wetness around his eyes, and a tear rolled down his cheek, and it was a long time since he had cried, the old man remembered.

That night it rained, and the boy was walking down the wet street with the dark night stretching out ahead of him and he pulled his leather jacket tight around him and he thrust his hands deep in the warm of his pockets.

It's going to be cold, the boy thought, as he pushed open the gate and walked into the yard.

He stood in the dark yard and the noise of the trains running filled his ears, and there was no better place than this box he knew of, the boy kept thinking as he looked about in the dark. And it was gone.

Edward Mulhall: "A Boy in a Box" in *Summer's Tales* 3, ed. John Iggulden, London 1966
By permission of the publishers, Macmillan & Co Ltd

VOCABULARY. *lid*: cover for a box, pot etc. — *mattress*: large, flat bag, stuffed with wool or horse-hair, forming part of a bed — *rags*: old or torn clothes — *pur(r)*: (of cat) make a low murmuring sound as a sign of pleasure — *freight*: load, cargo — *shunt*: (of railway engines) move to and fro at a station — *truck*: wagon for carrying goods — *concrete*: mixture of sand, cement, etc. used in building — *matted*: twisted together; thick or tangled — *fade*: lose colour or freshness — *pants*: (colloq.) trousers — *nun*: holy woman who lives in a convent — *fellowship*: friendly association; companionship — *orphan*: child who has lost one or both parents — *orphanage:* home for orphans.

99. After the Fair

The Fair was over, the lights in the cocoanut stalls were put out, and the wooden horses stood still in the darkness, waiting for the music and the hum of the machines that would set them trotting forward. One by one, in every booth, the naphtha jets were turned down and the canvases pulled over the little gambling tables. The crowd went home, and there were lights in the windows of the caravans.

Nobody had noticed the girl. In her black clothes she stood against the side of the roundabouts, hearing the last feet tread upon the sawdust and the last voices die into the distance. Then, all alone on the deserted ground, surrounded by the shapes of wooden horses and cheap fairy boats, she looked for a place to sleep. Now here and now there, she raised the canvas that shrouded the cocoanut stalls and peered into the warm darkness. She was frightened to step inside, and as a mouse scampered across the littered shavings on the floor, or as the canvas creaked and a rush of wind set it dancing, she ran away and hid again near the roundabouts. Once she stepped on the boards; the bells round a horse's throat jingled and were still; she did not dare breathe until all was quiet again and the darkness had forgotten the noise of the bells. Then here and there she went peeping for a bed, into each gondola, under each tent. But there was nowhere, nowhere in all the fair for her to sleep. One place was too silent, and in another was the noise of mice. There was straw in the corner of the Astrologer's tent, but it moved as she touched it; she knelt by its side and put out her hand; she felt a baby's hand upon her own.

Now there was nowhere; so slowly she turned towards the caravans, and reaching them where they stood on the outskirts of the field, found all but two to be unlit. She stood, clutching her empty bag, and wondering which caravan she should disturb. At last she decided to knock upon the window of the little, shabby one near her, and standing on tiptoes, she looked in: The fattest man she had ever seen was sitting in front of the stove, toasting a piece of bread. She tapped three times on the glass, then hid in the shadows. She heard him come to the top of the steps and call out Who? Who? but she dared not answer. Who? Who? he called again; she laughed at his voice which was as thin as he was fat. He heard her laughter and turned to where the darkness concealed her. First you tap, he said. Then you hide, then, by jingo, you laugh. She stepped into the circle of light, knowing she need no longer hide herself. A girl, he said, Come in and wipe your feet. He did not wait but retreated into his caravan, and she could do nothing but follow him up the steps and into the crowded room. He was seated again, and toasting the same piece of bread. Have you come in? he said, for his back was towards her. Shall I close the door? she asked, and closed it before he replied.

She sat on the bed and watched him toasting the bread until it burnt. I can toast better than you, she said. I don't doubt it, said the Fat Man. She watched him put down the charred toast upon a plate by his side, take another round of bread and hold that, too, in front of the stove. It burnt very quickly. Let me toast it for you, she said. Ungraciously he handed her the fork and the loaf. Cut it, he said. Toast it, and eat it, by jingo. She sat on the chair. See the dent you've made on my bed, said the Fat Man. Who are you to come in and dent my bed? My name is Annie, she told him. Soon all the bread was toasted and buttered, so she put it in the centre of the table and arranged two chairs. I'll have mine on the bed, said the Fat Man. You'll have it here.

When they had finished their supper, he pushed back his chair and stared at her across the table. I am the Fat Man, he said. My home is Treorchy; the Fortune Teller next door is Aberdare. I've nothing to do with the fair — I am Cardiff, she said. There's a town, agreed the Fat Man. He asked her why she had come away. Money, said Annie. I have one and three, said the Fat Man. I have nothing, said Annie.

Then he told her about the fair and the places he had been to and the people he had met. He told her his age and his weight and the names of his brothers and what he would call his son. He showed her a picture of Boston Harbour and the photograph of his mother who lifted weights. He told her how summer looked in Ireland. I've always been a fat man, he said, And now I'm *the* Fat Man; there's nobody to touch me for fatness. He told her of a heat wave in Sicily and the Mediterranean Sea and of the wonders of the South stars. She told him of the baby in the Astrologer's tent.

That's the stars again, by jingo; looking at the stars doesn't do anybody good.

The baby'll die, said Annie. He opened the door and walked out into the darkness. She looked about her but did not move, wondering if he had gone to fetch a policeman. It would never do to be caught by the policeman again. She stared through the open door into the inhospitable night and drew her chair closer to the stove. Better to be caught in the warmth, she said. But she trembled at the sound of the Fat Man approaching, and pressed her hands upon her thin breast, as he climbed up the steps like a walking mountain. She could see him smile in the darkness. See what the stars have done, he said, and brought in the Astrologer's baby in his arms.

After she had nursed it against her and it had cried on the bosom of her dress, she told him how she had feared his going. What should I be doing with a policeman? She told him that the policeman wanted her. What have you done for a policeman to be wanting you? She did not answer but took the child nearer again to her wasted breast. If it was money, I could have given you one and three, he said. Then he understood her and begged her pardon. I'm not quick, he told her. I'm just fat; sometimes I think I'm almost too fat. She was feeding the child; he saw her thinness. You must eat, Cardiff, he said.

Then the child began to cry. From a little wail its crying rose into a tempest of despair. The girl rocked it to and fro on her lap, but nothing soothed it. All the woe of a child's world flooded its tiny voice. Stop it, stop it, said the Fat Man, and the tears increased. Annie smothered it in kisses, but its wild cry broke on her lips like water upon rocks. We must do something, she said. Sing it a lullabee. She sang, but the child did not like her singing.

There's only one thing, said Annie, we must take it on the roundabouts. With the child's arm around her neck, she stumbled down the steps and ran towards the deserted fair, the Fat Man panting behind her. She found her way through the tents and stalls into the centre of the ground where the wooden horses stood waiting, and clambered up on to a saddle. Start the engine, she called out. In the distance the Fat Man could be heard cranking up the antique machine that drove the horses all the day into a wooden gallop. She heard the sudden spasmodic humming of the engine; the boards rattled under the horses' feet. She saw the Fat Man clamber up by her side, pull the central lever and climb on to the saddle of the smallest horse of all. As the roundabout started, slowly at first and slowly gaining speed, the child at the girl's breast stopped crying, clutched its hands together, and crowed with joy. The night wind tore through its hair, the music jangled in its ears. Round and round the wooden horses sped, drowning the cries of the wind with the beating of their wooden hooves.

And so the men from the caravans found them, the Fat Man and the girl in black with a baby in her arms, racing round and round on their mechanical steeds to the ever-increasing music of the organ.

Dylan Thomas: "Adventures in the Skin Trade" in *Prospect of the Sea,* London

VOCABULARY. *fair*: large market held at fixed times, often with merry-making — *stall*: small, open-fronted shop; table used by a trader in a market — *naphtha*: liquid used for burning or cleaning — *canvas*: strong coarse cloth — *roundabout*: merry-go-round — *sawdust*: tiny bits of wood falling off when wood is sawn — *shroud*: wrap or cover — *peer*: look closely — *scamper*: run quickly — *litter*: scatter carelessly about — *shavings*: very thin slices shaved off wood — *creak*: make a sharp, grating sound — *throat*: front part of the neck — *jingle*: make slight ringing sound — *peep*: look carefully — *Astrologer*: one who foretells good or bad fortune from the stars — *outskirts*: the outer border of a city — *clutch*: hold firmly — *on tiptoes*: walking on the tips of one's toes — *conceal*: hide — *by jingo*: exclamation giving emphasis to a remark — *retreat*: move backwards — *char*: to burn until black — *dent*: hollow made by a pressure — *fortune teller*: person who tells what will happen — *touch*: reach — *Sicily*: largest island in the Mediterranean — *inhospitable*: not giving shelter or safety — *bosom*: the breast — *wail*: mournful cry — *rock*: move from side to side — *lap*: front part (from waist to knees) of a person seated — *woe*: grief; misery — *flood*: fill sth. so that it overflows — *smother*: spread thickly upon — *lullabee* (or: *lullaby*): song for lulling a baby to sleep — *stumble*: trip in walking — *pant*: take short, quick breaths — *clamber*: climb — *saddle*: seat on the back of a horse — *crank*: move by turning a handle — *spasmodic*: taking place at irregular intervals — *rattle*: make short, sharp sounds quickly — *lever*: bar of iron used to raise up sth. heavy — *crow*: make sounds showing happiness — *jangle*: give out a metallic noise — *hoof*: horny part of the foot of a horse — *steed*: (liter.) horse — *organ*: musical instrument.

100. Fear

As soon as the boy got into the compartment he felt there was something queer in it. The only other occupant was a slight, dusky man who sat in a corner. There was also a faint sickly scent. For years afterwards, whenever he smelled that musk odour again, the terror of this afternoon came back to him.

He went to the other end of the compartment, sat in the opposite corner. There were no corridors in these local trains. The man looked at him and smiled friendlily. The boy returned the smile briefly, only aware of a deep, vague unease. But it would look so silly to jump out of the compartment now. The train gave a jerk and began to move.

Then, immediately with the jerk, the man began to utter a low humming chant, slow but with a definite rhythm. His lips did not open or even move, yet the hum penetrated above the noise of the train's wheels. It was in a sort of dreamy rhythm, enticing, lonely and antique. It went on and on.

Startled, and very alive to this proof of there being something odd in the compartment, the boy turned from staring out of the window and forced himself to glance at the man.

The man was looking at him. They faced each other across the compartment's length. The man's brown lips became stretched in a mysterious smile, though that humming chant continued, wordlessly swaying out of his mouth. His eyes, dark and unfathomable, never moved from the boy. The musk scent was stronger.

Yet this was not all. The boy could not imagine what other fearful thing lurked in the compartment. But he seemed to sense a secret power of something evilly antipathetic. Did it come from the man's long tribal hands like claws? And the man continued to smile. Something had flickered in and out of those shadowy eyes, like a dancing malice.

The boy sat stiffly. Somehow he could not return to his staring out of the window. But he tried not to look at the man again. The humming did not stop. And suddenly it took a higher note, like an unhurried wail. The noise of the train, the flying fields and woods, even the walls of the compartment, had vanished. There was only this chant, the man who was uttering it, and himself. He did not know that now he could not move his eyes from those of the man.

Abruptly the train was plunged into blackness. There was a shrieking rush of air. The train had entered a tunnel. With a sudden jerk the boy crouched down. He coiled into the seat's corner, shuddering, yet with every sense electrically alive now.

Then, above the roar of the air and the hurling grind of the train, that hum rose. It called, it unhurriedly exhorted obedience, it soothed. Again it seemed to obliterate the louder, harsher noises. Spent and defeated, the boy crouched. What was this strange presence of evil in the air, stronger now in the dark?

Suddenly crashing into the comparment, the hard blue and white daylight was like a blow. Still he seemed to hear the humming, though actually it had ceased. He saw the man's lips part in a full enticing smile, he saw teeth dazzlingly white between the dusky lips.

"You not like dark tunnel?" the smile continued seductively; once more the flecks of light danced wickedly in his eyes. "Come!" He beckoned with a long wrinkled finger.

The boy did not move.

"You like pomegranates?" He rose and took from the luggage-rack a brown wicker basket. It was the kind of basket in which a large cat would be sent on a journey. "Come!" he smiled friendlily and, as the boy still did not move, he crossed over and sat down beside him, but leaving a polite distance.

The staring boy did not flinch.

"Pomegranates from the East! English boy like, eh?" He smiled with good-humour. There was also something stupid in his manner, a fatuous mysteriousness.

The basket lay on his knees. He began to hum again. The boy watched, still without movement. But he was aware of the sickly perfume beside him and, more pronounced than ever, of an insidious presence that was utterly alien. That evil power lay in his immediate vicinity. The man looked at him again and, still humming, drew a rod and lifted the basket's lid.

There was no glow of magically gleaming fruit. But from the basket's depth rose the head of a snake. It rose slowly to the enchantment of the hum. The snake's eyes seemed to look blindly at nothing. It was a cobra.

Something happened to the boy. He leapt and flung himself headlong across the compartment. He was not aware that he gave a sharp shriek. He curled against the opposite seat's back, his knees pressing into the cushion. But, half turning, his eyes could not turn themselves from that reared head.

And it was with other senses that he knew most deeply he had evoked rage. The cobra was shooting its head in his direction. More fearful was the dilation of the throat, its skin swelling evilly into a hood. In some cell of his being he knew that the hood was swelling in destructive fury. He became very still.

The man did not stop humming. But now his narrowed eyes were focused in glittering concentration on the snake. It was a pitting of subtle power against the snake's wishes and it was also an appeasement. A man was addressing a snake. He was offering a snake tribute and acknowledgment of its right to anger; he was honeyed and soothing. At the same time he did not relax an announcement of being master. There was courtesy, but also there was the ancient pride of man's supremacy.

And the snake was pacified. Its head ceased to lunge towards the boy. The humming slackened into dreamy lullaby. Narrowly intent now, the man's eyes did not move. The length of the tawny body slowly sank back. Unhurriedly the man closed the basked and slipped the rod secure.

He turned angrily to the boy; he made a contemptuous sound, like a hiss. "I show you cobra and you jump and shout, heh! Make him angry! I give you free performance with cobra, and you jump and scream like little girl." The indignation died out of his eyes. "I sing to keep cobra quiet in train," he explained. "Cobra not like train."

The boy had not stirred. "You not like cobra?" the man asked in injured surprise. "Nice snake now, no poison! But not liking you jump and shout."

There was no reply or movement; centuries and continents lay between him and the boy. The man gazed at him in silence and added worriedly: "You going to fair in Newport! You see me? Ali the Snake Charmer. You come in free and see me make cobra dance—"

But the train was drawing into the station. It was not the boy's station. He made a sudden blind leap away from the man, opened the door, saw it was not on the platform side, but jumped. There was a shout from someone. He ran up the track, he dived under some wire railings. He ran with amazingly quick short leaps up a field—like a hare.

Rhys Davies: *The Collected Stories*, London
By permission of the publishers, William Heinemann Ltd

VOCABULARY. *queer*: odd, strange — *musk*: strong perfume — *jerk*: short, sudden movement — *hum*: make a buzzing sound like that of bees — *entice*: tempt or persuade — *lurk*: lie in wait — *antipathetic*: of contrary character — *malice*: ill-will; spite — *wail*: mournful cry — *crouch*: bend close to the ground — *hurl*: move rapidly — *soothe*: make quiet or calm — *spent*: exhausted — *dazzle*: confuse with a strong light — *seductive*: attractive — *pomegranate*: large fruit with many seeds "Granatapfel" — *flinch*: move back in fear — *fatuous*: foolish — *insidious*: doing harm secretly, unseen — *rod*: long, slender stick — *enchantment*: spell; wonder — *headlong*: head first; rashly — *evoke*: draw out; bring forth — *dilation*: becoming wider, expanding — *throat*: back part of the mouth — *hood*: bag-like swelling — *destructive*: likely to destroy — *focus*: direct to one point — *pit*: set against each other (in a fight) — *appeasement*: making calm, satisfying — *honeyed*: sweet — *lunge*: make a sudden forward push — *lullaby*: cradle-song — *fair*: large market, often with entertainments — *snake charmer*: one who tames poisonous snakes, usu. with music — *railings*: fence made of rails — *hare*: timid animal, like a large rabbit.

101. The Virgin Cave

(An unusual story ... If you are a speleologist, you will have a special interest in this story. Cave exploration—in one lesson ...)

Professor Ernst Albracht fussed with the winch motor over the cave opening while his favorite graduate student, Gerard Middleton, finished unloading the jeep.

Nylon sleeping bags. Flashlights. Butane stove kits. Portable ladders. Hammers. Acetylene lamps. K-rations. . . .

Gerard frowned. He wished Ellen wouldn't sit over there in the shade that way, watching and singing. Albracht must not, of course, suspect anything, so they had to act natural. But Ellen shouldn't sing. She shouldn't act happy about what would soon happen to Albracht. She must have had some love or respect for him; she had married him.

Albracht had said he'd seen a small hole in the rocks. He'd stuck his walking stick in, and the hole crumbled away to reveal a virgin cave. Now the opening was four feet wide. A winch had been built over the hillside hole, for they had to make a six-hundred-foot drop by cable.

Albracht clipped webbed shoulder harness to the cable hook, slid down, and watched the lever controlling the cable spool. Gerard and Ellen smiled down at the professor. The professor, pink-faced with boyish excitement, his graying hair fluttering slightly smiled up at them, then suddenly sank out of sight into the earth.

As they explored along, Gerard had another thing to keep in mind. It must happen in such a way that rescue would be impossible. He remembered the cozy secret meetings with Ellen, the exciting, dangerous whispering and planning.

A person could be crushed by a falling rock; fall down a rocky shelf; fall into a bottomless pit; freeze, drown, or get lost.

But all these possibilities shared a common virtue—they appeared accidental. Ellen had taken out two double-indemnity policies on Albracht.

So he must stay alert, ready to seize exactly the right moment and select exactly the right place—and then act with pan-flash decision. Albracht moved on without comment He managed skillfully to find his way through boulders and stalagmites.

Ellen smiled at Gerard, then squirmed out of sight. He shivered. Whatever she said, the way she stood or walked or sat was an invitation and a promise. . . .

He had been grateful for her smile. At first he had been grateful only to Albracht. The professor taught botany and speleology, and the latter was also his hobby. When not lecturing or writing on caves, he explored them. Every summer he favored one graduate student with an invitation to share the Albrachts' vacation in their cabin.

Albracht had first invited Gerard to his house near the campus to share a faculty tea. Gerard had been deeply grateful for Albracht's recognition. He met Ellen that afternoon and she smiled at him. Few women had ever smiled at Gerard, and none had ever smiled at him quite that way. In all his life no woman like Ellen had ever really looked at him. Attractive, sophisticated, much younger than Albracht who was fifty, Ellen had a genuinely hypnotic charm.

Gerard's gratitude was measureless. Too many of his twenty-five years had been fevered away during lonely nights with books, ambitions, and dreams. Gerard had been hungry all his life.

They stood on a dangerously narrow ledge about twelve feet long. And Albracht studied the rent in Ellen's rubberized suit made by a rock. Albracht kept insisting that Ellen turn back at once because of the torn suit. But Ellen insisted on continuing what she called "this most fabulous exploration of the century".

Gerard was more concerned with the sound of the river gurgling below. It can happen here, he thought. Albracht could fall into the river—but only when it was certain he would drown.

Ellen stepped back in disgust and would have fallen from the ledge if Albracht hadn't caught hold of her. But she let out a high sharp yell. Then she toppled end over end, as rigid as a display-window-mannequin.

Gerard saw, only thirty feet downstream, the river boiling. He finally managed to get the nylon line hooked to her webbed belt, and then Albracht helped him reel her into a large eroded pocket.

Albracht evidently wanted to keep on exploring if he found a way, but Gerard was finished.

Albracht yelled for the end of the nylon line. Gerard tossed it out. Albracht hooked it underwater to his belt. "If I don't come back, haul me in," he said.

Then he waved, and his head dissolved in foam. Then darkness. . . .

"We have to know what's happened to him," said Ellen. "He may be hurt. We have to make sure."

"You mean I have to make sure," Gerard rubbed his hands together.

He hooked a nylon line to his belt, tied the other end around a stalagmite, and waded into the river.

A black mouth sucked and swallowed him. His belt shot free. Helmet and head lamp ripped away.

He lay on corrugated rock, somewhere near the river. The river had spewed him up again, but there was no way of knowing where. There was no way out from wherever he was—no way but the river. He didn't want to make that terrible drop again.

He merely existed in the dark. A worm, he thought.

Things seemed to break loose inside him. He began to yell—a monotonous, low yelling as he beat the rocks with his fists . . .

He kept grinning up at the light. He smiled at it. He prayed. The light stayed, and, yes, that was the professor—dear old Albracht!

"Let's go now, Gerard. I'll help you."

Yes, sir, yes, sir—

Albracht led the way without hesitation. He seemed to know exactly where he was and where he was going. But Gerard knew that he would never have the vaguest idea how they got through . . .

And there was the cave opening six hundred feet above his head. Gerard stood quivering below that bar of familiar light.

He stumbled up like a drunken mole in strong light. It was such a short way from where he had lain, where he had died over and over in the darkness. He hadn't known the way. But Albracht knew. He seemed to have known all the time.

Gerard felt a cold charge of fear. Albracht's eyes were close to him now, fixed and unblinking.

"This isn't a virgin cave," Gerard said, "You've been here before. You knew where we were going. You knew exactly where I was all the time."

"I've known about you and Ellen, too, for some time," Albracht said gently. "And I knew what you had planned for me," he took a slow drag at his pipe. "But let's go on up now, Gerard. We've got to break the news of the tragic accident to our friends."

"Accident?"

"Oh, yes, she fell into the river, remember? A search party will be down here inside an hour. We'll all do our best to find Ellen, of course, but no one ever will. No one knows where the river goes."

"We could—" Gerard's voice broke.

"You think you could find her?" Albracht asked. "No, believe me, you can't. No one can ever find her now."

"Why?" Gerard whispered. "Why have you saved me?"

"You're a fine scholar, Gerard, with a great potential to do good. I have always felt responsible to correct in what little ways I can the faults of miseducation."

Albracht smiled around his pipestem. "I left you there for seven hours, my boy, hoping it would bring about a vital change in you—for the better. As an experience, you know—a learning experience ... a lesson for the future."

Bryce Walton: "The Virgin Cave", in:
Ellery Queen's Crime Carousel, London 1966
By permission of the publishers, Victor Gollancz Ltd

VOCABULARY. *speleologist*: explorer of caves "Höhlenforscher" — *winch*: hoisting-machine — *jeep*: small utility motor vehicle — *butane*: hydrocarbon "Butangas" — *acetylene*: colourless gas "Acetylen" — *crumble*: break into small pieces — *clip*: fasten with a clip (clip = small fastener) — *webbed*: having web between the toes (web = skin joining the toes of waterbirds — *harness*: working equipment — *lever* [ˈliːvə]: bar used to lift or move a heavy object — *cozy* (= cosy): warm and comfortable — *shelf*: projecting slab of stone — *pit*: deep hole in the earth — *double-indemnity policy*: "Doppelversicherungspolice" — *boulder*: large stone — *stalagmite*: stalk of lime rising from the floor of a cave — *squirm*: twist the body, wriggle — *campus*: (U. S. A.) grounds of a college — *sophisticated*: worldly-wise; — *ledge*: shelf — *rent*: tear — *rubberized*: (U. S. A.) coated or treated with rubber — *gurgle*: make bubbling sounds — *topple*: to be unsteady and fall — *reel*: wind — *foam*: froth or bubbles on liquid — *suck*: draw in — *rip*: tear; strip off — *corrugate*: make into folds or wrinkles — *spew* (or: *spue*): throw up (food etc.) — *mole*: small animal living in tunnels it makes in the ground — *charge*: (figurative) load — *unblinking*: steady — *stem*: tubular part of tobacco-pipe.

102. The Case of the Drunken Socrates

On four separate occasions had Dr Czissar been able to prove politely but irrefutably, that Scotland Yard in general and Assistant Commissioner

Mercer in particular were not infallible; and, though a simple soul might expect Mercer to be grateful, he was not.

And then Dr Czissar was announced again on a December afternoon. The Doctor walked into the room: "I bring a matter for your advice, if you will be so kind."

Advice! Dr Czissar was asking *him* for advice! Mercer could scarcely believe his ears.

"This case begins," said Dr Czissar solemnly, "with a death. On June 20 of this year my landlady's brother, Captain Pewsey, died suddenly at his house in Meresham, which is a town twenty miles from London. It was a very distressing thing for my landlady, who was very fond of her brother, in spite of his faults. He drank too much whisky. About five years ago he married a woman much younger than he was. Mrs Falcon thinks that this Mrs Pewsey did not make him happy.

"I have said that the Captain drank a lot. About a week before his death he went to a doctor in Meresham and complained of his heart. The doctor examined him and found a little cardiac weakness. He advised the Captain to drink less whisky and to live carefully. There was not great danger, he said, but it would be as well if the Captain avoided excesses.

"For several days after that visit to the doctor the Captain drank less whisky; but on the night of June 20 he spent the evening with a friend—Mr Stenson.

"The Captain was in the business of selling life insurance policies, and he had met Mr Stenson through selling him a policy. The friendship continued through the game of golf. There was, perhaps, a financial reason for the Captain's liking for Mr Stenson: Mr Stenson works in the City of London and he has made much money and knows important persons. The Captain would have found him useful.

"The first part of that evening of the 20th the Captain spent with Mr Stenson and other men at the golf club; but at about ten o'clock the Captain and Mr Stenson left the club together and walked towards their houses. Mr Stenson's house was reached first and the Captain went in with him to drink more whisky. Soon after eleven o'clock the Captain left and went to his own house. It seems that he was then a little drunk. His wife had already gone to bed, and she said afterwards that she heard him stumble along the passage to his room. Then she went to sleep. In the morning, when she went into his room, she found him sitting in an armchair still dressed. He was very blue in the face and seemed dead.

"She called the doctor immediately. He came and found that the Captain was indeed dead. The doctor was a little puzzled. He had examined the Captain a week before, but he had not thought that his heart was in so bad a state that a little too much whisky would kill him. He told these things to Mrs Pewsey and said that before signing the death certificate he would ask her permisson to make a post-mortem examination. She was reluctant, but as he insisted, she agreed. He made the examination, found that the death had been due to a respiratory failure, and, concluding that the cause of it had been the weakness of the heart, issued a certificate to that effect.

"A month ago Mr Stenson married Mrs Pewsey.

Mrs Falcon thought it unpleasant that his widow should have shown so little respect for his memory. It was also a surprise to her, for she had heard nothing of any friendship between the two at the funeral. She wished me to go down to Meresham and make a scandal with questions."

"But why? The suggestion is, I suppose, that Stenson killed Pewsey. From the facts you have given me, that's obviously absurd. Pewsey was a heavy drinker with a weak heart. He got drunk, had a heart attack and died. The cause of death is confirmed by an autopsy."

"No, Assistant Commissioner, it is not Mrs Falcon but I who make the accusation. I will begin by giving you the facts. Three months after the Captain's death, Mrs Pewsey marries Mr Stenson. So soon! Strange, is it not? It seems to me as if the idea of the marriage had been in the minds of Mrs Pewsey and Mr Stenson *before* the Captain died.

"I have interviewed Mrs Pewsey's maid. She heard the Captain return home to die. She says that she had never known him so drunk before. He fell up the stairs and stumbled along the passage to his bedroom. And he was talking to himself. He had never done that before. As he passed the door of her room, she heard one sentence clearly. He was mumbling and then he said: "Socrates! What does he mean, Socrates? My name's not Socrates." She heard no more. But she heard enough, I think.

"In the first place we have the marriage of Mrs Pewsey and Mr Stenson. There is no doubt that they have been having an affair together for many months. I think that they must have made up their minds to murder the Captain very early on. Mrs Falcon says that her brother wrote to her nearly a year ago saying that his wife had asked for a divorce and that he had refused. So stupid of them to get married so soon after the murder.

"Next let us consider the manner of the Captain's death. According to the maid, he behaved in an unusual manner. He stumbled and staggered. Now, Assistant Commissioner, I, too, find that unusual. The Captain was a habitual drinker. In my experience, I have found that such men do *not* usually stumble and stagger from the effects of drink. The Captain was stumbling and staggering. The cause of death was respiratory failure. What is the link between those two facts? I will tell you. It is the word 'Socrates'."

"What?"

"You have heard of Socrates? Ah, yes. Then you may remember the description of his death. For a time he walks about, then his steps become difficult. Paralysis begins to creep up his legs. He is forced to lie down. The paralysis creeps higher to his chest. And then he dies—of a respiratory failure—paralysis of the lungs. There is only one poison which has that effect. It is the poison which was given to Socrates."

"You mean hemlock! But . . ."

"Hemlock is the name of the plant from which it is obtained. The actual poison is coniine. If the coniine is pure and concentrated, a few drops kill very quickly. An ordinary infusion of hemlock leaves would kill, unless treatment were given, in from two to three hours. There are, I find, quantities of hemlock growing in Mr Stenson's garden. There is no doubt, I think, that when the Captain went into Mr Stenson's house that night, he was given with his whisky an infusion of hemlock leaves. He had been drinking all the evening. He would not notice the taste. But Mr Stenson made the first mistake. He has a sense of humour. He was nervous and worried. He was not used to murder. He turned to his sense of humour for comfort. He tried to make a joke of the situation. He called the Captain 'Socrates'."

"But, good heavens, man!" exploded Mercer, "even if this story is true, how on earth are we going to prove it?"

Dr Czissar got to his feet with dignity. "I am sure that you will find a way. Coniine remains detectable in the body for many months. An exhumation and an autopsy by an experienced pathologist with no preconceived ideas about cardiac weakness should help you. Now I understand the English sense of humour. I did not think that it would be so macabre. Socrates!"

(Abridged) Eric Ambler

VOCABULARY. *irrefutable*: that cannot be proved false — *infallible*: never making an error — *cardiac*: having to do with the heart — *insurance*: safeguard against loss, death etc. in return for regular payments — *insurance policy*: agreement made about insurance — *stumble*: almost fall in walking — *post-mortem examination*: examination after death — *reluctant*: unwilling — *respiratory*: relating to breathing — *autopsy*: examination of a dead body by cutting it open to find the cause of death — *divorce*: order for the break-up of a marriage — *stagger*: to sway from side to side — *link*: anything connecting — *paralysis*: loss of the power to move and feel — *hemlock*: poisonous plant "Schierling" — *coniine*: alkaloid, the poisonous principle of hemlock — *infusion*: a liquid formed by pouring water on something — *pathologist*: expert in science of diseases — *preconceive*: form an idea beforehand — *macabre*: gruesome; grim.

103. The Case of the Pinchbeck Locket

Dr Czissar, a distinguished member of the Czech police organisation, had emigrated to England in September 1938. On a winter afternoon he put a newspaper cutting under Mercer's nose, Mercer being an Assistant Commissioner of Scotland Yard.

The cutting was from a Wessex newspaper dated a fortnight previously, and was the report of an inquest. The body of a woman of sixty had been washed up in Shingles Bay and had been identified as that of Mrs Sarah Fallon, of Seahurst, a village five miles from the seaside resort of Seabourne. Her husband had died fifteen years earlier, leaving her a large fortune and Seahurst Grange, with its twenty-acre park. Soon after his death she had assumed the guardianship of his niece, Helen Fallon, who had married, eleven years later, Arthur Barrington, a Searbourne coal and builders' merchant. The Barringtons had lived since their marriage with Mrs Fellon at the Grange.

On the evening of Nov.4 Barrington had reported to the police that Mrs Fallon had disappeared. That afternoon Mrs Barrington had, at her aunt's request, driven her into Seabourne to do some shopping. As Mrs Fallon had said that she might call on a friend for tea, her niece had left her at South Square at a quarter to three, put the car in the municipal car park, and spent the afternoon in a cinema. They had arranged to meet at South Square at six o'clock. Mrs Fallon had not kept the appointment, and later, when attempts to trace her movements through her friends had failed, the police had been informed.

She had not been seen again until eight days later, when her body was found by a coastguard.

Evidence of identification was given by her doctor and her dentist. The post-mortem had revealed the cause of death as being shock following a fracture of the skull. The fracture could have been caused by violent contact with any blunt, hard surface. It would have been consistent with a fall from a high cliff. She had not entered the water until several hours after death. The state of decomposition suggested that she had probably died on the date of her disappearance. Her doctor added that she had suffered from a cardiac disturbance and was liable to spells of dizziness.

A child had given evidence of the finding, on the seventh of the month, of a heart-shaped pinchbeck locket at the foot of Sea Head Cliff, a local beauty spot within a few minutes' walk of South Square.

Mrs Barrington had idenified the locket as having belonged to her aunt. Her aunt, who had attached great sentimental value to the locket, had always worn it. Her aunt had been in the habit of sitting on the seat on the cliff during the afternoon.

The coroner, summing up, had said that there seemed very little doubt that the deceased had, after she had left her niece on the afternoon of the fourth, changed her mind about visiting her friends and walked up the hill to the cliff. Then, fatigued by the walk after her recent illnes, she had had an attack of giddiness and fallen to her death on the beach below. High tide had been at six o'clock. Her body must have lain on the beach until ultimately it had been carried out to sea.

A verdict of 'Accidental Death' had been returned, the jury adding a rider to the effect that the cliff should be fenced.

"Mrs Fallon," said Dr Czissar decisively, "was, I think, murdered." Mercer sighed and leaned back in his chair.

"Sergeant," he said, "get me the file on the Fallon case, will you?" He smiled wearily at the Doctor. "You see, Doctor, we are not so stupid. A rich woman meets with an accident. Her niece, who lives in her house, inherits. The niece's husband, who also lives in the house, happens to be in financial difficulties in his business.

"The niece spent the afternoon as she says she did. Car-park and cinema-attendants both confirm that she spent the afternoon in Seabourne. She arrived home at seven, having waited for half an hour in South Square and spent ten minutes or so telephoning her aunt's friends. Barrington returned home soon afterwards. He had left at two-thirty to keep a business appointment in Haywick—that's fourteen miles farther west along the coast—at three. He kept the appointment, and several others that he had made in the Haywick district for that afternoon. Anyway, no murderer in his senses would try to push anybody off the cliff. He would be too scared of being seen."

Dr Czissar nodded. "Where the servants at the Grange questioned? Did any of the servants report any trouble with the heating arrrangements on the night of Mrs Fallon's disappearance?"

The Inspector shifted uneasily. "There was some trouble with the heating," he said. "The housekeeper said they had trouble with the furnace that night. It went out. She reckoned that it was a sort of sign that the old lady died."

Dr Czissar smiled serenely. "Attention, please," he said. "I will present the case to you. I have made inquiries in Seabourne. About the currents. There is a very strong current running past the cliff to the Shingles. But does it not occur to you, too, that eight days is a long time for a body to take to get from the cliff to Shingles Bay? The current is, as you said, a strong one.

"Mrs Fallon was murdered for her money by Arthur and Helen Barrington, who, because they did not want to be found out, arranged alibis for themselves. They were not very useful alibis, because nobody knew exactly when Mrs Fallon was killed. In my opinion, she was killed between half-past two and twenty-five minutes to three on the afternoon of her disappearance. She was placed in the sea at Haywick Dunes between six and seven o'clock that evening.

"The murder was carefully thought out. You remember the drive up to the Grange, Inspector? It is long and winding, and most of it is invisible from the house because of trees.

"At half-past two Barrington left to keep his appointment at Haywick. But instead of driving straight there, he stopped his car a little way down the road and walked back to the drive. Five minutes later his wife left to motor Mrs Fallon into Seabourne. As soon as she was out of sight of the house, but in the drive, she stopped. Her husband then killed Mrs Fallon with the weapon he had ready. A coal- or mason's hammer would have been suitable. He was a coal and builders' merchant, I think. He then went back to his car and drove on to his appointment at Haywick. Mrs Barrington also drove on to Seabourne."

"And where, pray, was the body?" inquired Mercer acidly.

"At half-past five, I think, Mrs Barrington left the cinema, returned to her car, and drove to the Haywick Dunes, where she had arranged to meet her husband. High tide was at six o'clock. It must have been about then that they arranged to meet. It would be dusk then, too. And that place is very lonely and deserted. The chances of Barrington's being seen as he carried the body to the water were small, I think."

"I don't see where the furnace comes into it," the Inspector remarked.

"The rug and the car mats would be soaked with blood, Inspector. Mrs Barrington would no doubt put them into the furnace after it had been banked-up for the night. Even such thick materials would be charred and destroyed, but they would put the fire out unless the dampers were also opened. Probably the niece of a rich aunt would not know much about furnaces."

"However," said Mercer sourly, "you have yet to explain the presence of the locket on the beach."

Dr Czissar smiled. "One can buy such a locket almost anywhere if one tries. After all, it was Mrs Barrington, wasn't it, who identified it as the particular locket her aunt wore? Clever criminals are so stupid, are they not?"

Then Dr Czissar was gone, and Mercer was alone. He picked up the telephone.

"I want," he said, "to speak to the Chief Constable of Wessex."

(Abridged) Eric Ambler

VOCABULARY. *pinchbeck*: a yellow metal (a mixture of copper and zinc) "Tombak, Talmi" — *locket:* a small case for a portrait, lock of hair etc. worn hung from the neck — *Czech*: native of Bohemia — *bay*: part of the sea in a curve on the shore — *guardianship*: the office of a person who takes care (e.g. of an orphan) — *municipal*: belonging to a town — *coastguard*: officer on police duty on the coast — *post-mortem*: examination of a dead body — *fracture*: break in a bone of the body — *skull*: the bones which hold the brain — *cardiac*: having to do with the heart — *decomposition*: the state of becoming rotten; decay — *be liable*: be subject — *spell*: short space of time — *dizziness*: state of being giddy, dazed, confused — *cliff*: high steep rock — *coroner*: official who inquires into the causes of sudden death — *giddiness*: state of being unsteady, dizzy — *verdict*: decision given after a test — *rider*: additional observation — *scare*: frighten — *furnace*: closed fireplace for heating building — *current*: stream of water moving in a certain direction — *drive*: avenue or road — *acid*: sour; sharp — *soak*: become wet by absorbing liquid — *bank*: cover up a fire with coal — *char*: make black by burning — *damper*: metal plate which regulates the flow of air into a fire "Ofenklappe; Schieber".

104. The Man Who Read Ellery Queen

(Arthur Mindy whose ambition in life—at least, after the age of forty-five—has always been to solve a mystery in the manner of Ellery Queen—and how splendidly he achieves it!)

To make the transition to institutional living easier, each resident of the Goodwell Senior Citizens' Home was allowed to retain one item of personal property. Some of the old men kept their stamp collections, others preferred to treasure voluminous photograph albums. One senior citizen, Gregory Wyczech, had a 1907 ten-dollar gold piece which was almost as precious to him as life itself. Aside from the single personal item, all the necessities and luxuries—food, clothing, bedding and recreational material—were furnished by the home.

The only thing that Arthur Mindy brought with him when he entered the Goodwell Home was a complete collection of books by Ellery Queen.

Shortly after his admittance, Arthur Mindy sat in his small room, discussing his choice with Roy Carstairs, the first floor-attendant.

At this moment a shout—the thin cracked voice of an old man—issued from the hallway outside the door.

Carstairs sprang from his chair and through the half-open door, followed at a more leisurely pace by Mindy.

In the middle of the thick carpeted hall Gregory Wyczech, dressed only in the light green pyjamas and robe which were almost a uniform at the home, was engaged in a boxing match with another similarly dressed resident.

Arthur Mindy looked at Wyczech's opponent. Eugene Dennison had been admitted to the home some time before Arthur. After a short but unsuccessful attempt on the part of the other men to become friendly, Dennison had been classified as a 'cold fish'. He never had any visitors, and his haughty manner repelled even the most amiable of advances. In the crowded world of the Goodwell home he walked aloof and alone.

Dennison stood stiffly just outside Gregory Wyczech's door while Wyczech circled him, chattering like an angry monkey. "He stole my eagle! My ten-dollar gold coin. He stole it!"

"Mr Carstairs," Dennison spoke for the first time. "I have not stolen his eagle or whatever it is. I was on my way to the dispensary to renew my supply of pills. I took the elevator down since at my age the prospect of three flights of stairs is appalling. I came out of the elevator door which, unfortunately for me, is next to Mr Wyczech's door. Then this idiot came around the corner, entered his room, and burst out again, striking out at me. Naturally I fought back."

"You stole it!" Wyczech said again.

"I didn't."

"Here's what happened," said Wyczech, catching his breath. "I'd just gone down the hall and around the corner to wash my hands. My gold coin was in its envelope on the table, and I wanted to wash before handling it. When I got back, just a minute later, the gold piece was gone, and this—this thief in the night was walking away from the door of my room. So I took a swing at him."

"You must have hit him fairly hard. I see you cut his cheek quite badly."

Arthur pointed to the rather long, deep wound on Dennison's cheek from which fresh blood was now oozing.

"To lapse into the vernacular," said Dennison, "he never laid a glove on me. That's where I cut myself shaving this morning."

"Could anybody else have taken the coin?" asked Carstairs.

"Nobody would have had time," said Wyczech. "I wasn't gone that long. And no one else was around."

Dennison looked at the many pairs of accusing eyes turned in his direction. Then he opened the front of his robe and spread it dramatically. "If I submit to a search, will that satisfy everybody?"

Dennison shrugged off the robe and flung it at Wyczech. He loosened the bottoms, let them fall to the floor, and shuffled out of them. He stood on the green carpet, naked as a jaybird, without losing a particle of his massive dignity.

The clothing was quickly searched—even the seams and button-holes. Nothing. No gold coin.

"He must have swallowed it," sputtered Wyczech.

"Mr Carstairs, I leave it to you," said Dennison in the manner of a parent speaking to a dull-witted child. "You know the condition of what's left of my stomach. Considering that my diet for the past several years has consisted only of oatmeal and milk, could I have swallowed a piece of salami, much less a gold coin?"

"That's true, Mr Wyczech," said Carstairs reluctantly.

Wyczech examined Dennison's hair and the inside of his mouth without results. Then he shrugged. "I still say he stole it. He was the only one who could have."

With a shrug Dennison reclaimed his clothing, and not bothering to put it on, shuffled to the carpeted stairway across from Wyczech's room.

"Just a moment, please!" The men in the hallway looked to see who had spoken, and then Arthur Mindy stepped forward and faced Carstairs and Dennison.

"Now," Arthur continued, "if Mr Dennison did take the coin, what did he do with it? Where did he hide it? Unless we can find that out, he's innocent by default. Let's see if the problem will yield to logic."

"Like Ellery Queen?" asked Carstairs, attempting to humor Arthur.

"Precisely. Now I ask you to consider two pieces of evidence, Mr Carstairs. The first is that long, deep cut on Mr Dennison's cheek."

"So he cut himself shaving, Mr Mindy," said Carstairs. "What about it?"

"And the second is that Mr Dennison is now preparing to climb the stairs to his room," Arthur concluded.

"Mindy!" screamed Wyczech. "Where is my gold eagle?"

"Very well," said Arthur, "let's first consider the cut on Dennison's cheek. He said he cut himself shaving this morning. That would have been at least two hours ago, since lunch was served. But you all noticed the cut was bleeding again. Fresh blood. Why?"

"Because Mr Wyczech hit him?" Carstairs suggested.

"By Dennison's own admission, Wyczech never laid a glove on him. But tell me, Mr Carstairs, what do you do when you cut yourself shaving?"

"Use a styptic pencil."

"But suppose the cut is long and deep?"

"I'd stick a piece of adhesive plaster over it."

"Exactly. Adhesive plaster. And if Dennison had just torn a piece of adhesive tape from his face, it would have reopened a long deep cut. Right?"

"Right," said Carstairs.

"So now we have Dennison provided with a piece of adhesive plaster. Where is that adhesive plaster? Evidence Number Two: what did he just do when he was told to leave? He went to the stairway, in spite of the fact that there is an automatic elevator right here for him. What is so attractive about the stairway?"

"So he wanted some exercise," said Wyczech. "Get to the point."

"The point," said Arthur, "is that the stairs are carpeted, while the floor of the elevator is bare wood. When Dennison left the elevator and noticed the door to Wyczech's room open, he walked in—probably just out of curiosity—and saw the coin. He couldn't resist taking it, but as he went back into the hall, he heard Wyczech returning. So he had to conceal the coin in a place where it could not be found even if he were searched."

"I don't get it," moaned Wyczech. "Why didn't he go back to his room by the elevator?"

"He would have clicked."

"Clicked?"

"Clicked. Logically, the only place the coin could be is the one place on his person that we failed to search."

At the age of eighty Arthur was finally given his golden moment.

"You'll find it taped to the bottom of his foot."

Dennison was quickly forced to sit on the bottom stair, and on the ball of his right foot was found the gold coin, held there by a thin strip of adhesive plaster—just as Arthur Mindy had deduced. Dennison's face was now a mask of hatred. Then the mask came apart.

"I didn't mean to do it!" he cried out. "I just wanted something that belonged to me and not to everybody else, too. You men—you have relatives to come and see you. They bring you gifts and tell you about their families. You don't know what it's like to be really alone. I've got nothing—nobody." His thin body was racked by sobbing.

Gregor Wyczech sat down on the bottom step and put his arm around Dennison's shoulders. "I tell you what," he soothed. "Im giving you a half interest in my gold coin, see. Every other week you get to keep it—all to yourself."

The two old men stood up and crossed the hall.

William Brittain: "The Man Who Read Ellery Queen" in *Ellery Queen's Crime Carousel*, London 1967, Victor Gollancz Ltd (publishers)
By permission of the author and of his agent, Scott Meredith Inc, New York

VOCABULARY. *institutional living*: living in a home for old people — *property*: sth. a person owns; possession — *attendant*: servant; employee — *robe*: outer garment; dressing-gown — *eagle*: a U. S. gold coin value ten dollars — *dispensary*: place where medicines and advice are given out — *ooze*: flow gently — *lapse*: fall — *vernacular*: language or dialect of a country or district — *lay a glove on*: deal a blow at, hit, strike — *shuffle*: move with difficult motion — *jaybird*: gay-coloured bird of the crow kind "Eichelhäher" — *seam*: line formed by the sewing together of two pieces of cloth — *reclaim*: demand the return of — *styptic*: something which stops bleeding — *adhesive*: sticky, gummy — *tape*: narrow band or strip — *click*: to make a slight, sharp, hard, non-ringing sound — *tape*: fasten or bind with tape.

105. The Man Who Read John Dickson Carr

(Edgar Gault found the solution to his personal problem in the detective novels of John Dickson Carr.)

Although he did not realize it at the time, Edgar Gault's life first gained purpose and direction when, at the age of twelve, he idly picked up a copy of John Dickson Carr's *The Problem of the Wire Cage* at his neighborhood lending library.

One day he, Edgar Gault, would commit a locked room murder which would mystify the master himself.

An orphan, Edgar lived with his uncle in a huge rambling house in a remote section of Vermont. The house was not only equipped with a library but the library had barred windows and a two-inch-thick oak door.

The victim, of course, would be Edgar's Uncle Daniel. Not only was he readily available, but he was a believer in Ralph Waldo Emerson's philosophy of self-reliance, and in order to help Edgar achieve that happy condition, Uncle Daniel had decided to cut the youth out of his will in the near future.

Edgar, one bright day in early spring, was standing inside the library fireplace, covered with soot and scrubbing the inside of the chimney until it gleamed.

The chimney, of course, was Edgar's means of escape from his locked room. It was just large enough to accommodate his slim body and had an iron ladder which ran up the inside for the convenience of a chimney sweep. It was the only exit available.

It didn't worry Edgar that he would be immediately suspected of the crime. Nobody saw his preparations—Uncle Daniel was away on business, and the cook and gardener were on vacation. And at the time the crime would actually be committed, Edgar would have two unimpeachable witnesses to testify that neither he—nor, for that matter, any other human being—could possibly have been the murderer.

Finishing his scrubbing, Edgar carried the pail of water to the kitchen and emptied it down the drain. Then, after a thorough shower to rid his body of soot, he went to the linen closet, took out a newly washed bed sheet, and returned to the library. Wrapping the sheet around him, he got back into the fireplace and began to climb the iron ladder. Reaching the top, he came down again, purposely rubbing the sheet against the stones at frequent intervals.

Stepping back into the library, he walked to a window, removed the sheet, and held it up to the sunlight. Although wrinkled, it had remained gleamingly white. Edgar smiled as he put the sheet into a hamper. After that, in his own room, he dressed in clothing chosen especially for the crime—white shirt, white trousers, and white tennis shoes. Finally, he removed a long cavalry saber from the wall, took it to the library, and stood it in a shadowy corner.

His preparations were nearly complete.

Early that evening, from his chair in the music room, Edgar heard his uncle's return. "Edgar? You home?"

"I'm in here, Uncle Daniel—in the music room."

"Ayah," said Daniel, looking in through the door. "That's the trouble with you, young fellow. Business first, boy—that's the only ticket for success."

"Why, Uncle, I've been working on a business arrangement most of the day. I just finished about an hour ago."

"Well, I meant what I said about my will, Edgar," Uncle Daniel continued. "In fact, I'm going to talk to Stoper about it tonight when he comes over for cards."

Even the weekly game of bridge, in which Edgar was usually a reluctant fourth to Uncle Daniel, Lemuel Stoper, and Dr Harold Crowley, was a part of The Plan. Even the perfect crime needs witnesses to its perfection.

Later, as Edgar arranged the last of three armloads of wood in the library fireplace—and added to the kindling a small jar from his pocket—he heard the heavy knocker of the front door bang three times. He took the opportunity to set his watch. Exactly seven o'clock.

"Take the gentlemen to the music room and make them comfortable," said Uncle Daniel. "Give them a drink and get the card table ready. I'll be in presently."

"No need to butter the boy up any more," said Stoper. "Dan'l's changing his will tonight."

"Oh," said Crowley surprised. "That's too bad, boy—uh—Edgar."

"Yes, Uncle has already spoken to me about his decision," said Edgar. "I'm in complete agreement with it." No sense in providing *too* much in the way of a motive.

"Uncle," he called. "Dr Crowley and Mr Stoper are here."

"I know they're here," growled Daniel. "Wait in the music room. I'll be along in a few minutes."

The two men had seen Uncle Daniel alive and well. Everything was now ready. In the music room Edgar poured drinks and set up the card table.

"I must have left the cards upstairs," he said. "I'll go and find them." And before his guests could answer, he left the room.

Once through the door, Edgar's pace quickened. He reached the door of the library eight seconds later. Ignoring his uncle's surprised expression, Edgar took the saber from its corner and strode to the desk where Daniel sat, a newspaper still in his hand.

"Edgar, what in . . .?" Without a word Edgar thrust the sword violently at his uncle. The point entered Daniel's neck just below the chin and penetrated the neck to the back of the chair, pinning the old man to his place.

He held the sword in place for several seconds. Then he felt carefully for a pulse. The murder had been carried off exactly as planned—in seventy seconds.

Hurrying to the fireplace, Edgar picked up the small jar he had placed there earlier. Then, shuffling his feet through the generous supply of paper among the kindling and wood, he began to climb up the chimney. Reaching the top, he glanced at his watch. Two minutes had gone by since he had left Stoper and Crowley.

Standing on the roof beside the chimney, Edgar removed several small pieces of blank paper from the jar. During the war they had been dropped from planes to start fires in fields of enemy grain. He knew they would start a fire in the library fireplace. Dropping the papers down the chimney, he waited a few seconds, and finally was rewarded with a blast of warm air coming up through the opening.

Edgar moved along the slanted roof to a large decorative gable in which was set the storeroom window. He raised the window and scrambled inside, taking care not to get dust or dirt on his clothing. He went to his own room, took a fresh deck of cards he had left there earlier, then trotted loudly down the stairs to the music room. He rejoined the two guests a little less than five minutes after he had left them—again exactly as planned.

Edgar apologized for his short absence, privately gloating over the unsullied whiteness of his clothing. Surely he could not just have climbed up inside the chimney from which smoke was now coming. Soon Stoper became restless. "I wonder what's keeping Daniel?" he grumbled.

As they rose to fetch him, Edgar attempted a yawn while his heart pounded wildly. "I believe I'll wait here," he said, trying to act nonchalant.

"John Dickson would be proud of me," thought Edgar as Stoper and Crowley left the room.

Odd, he thought, that there was no shouting, no crashing sounds as the two old men tried to batter down the heavy library door. But there was no need to worry. The plan was perfect, foolproof. It was.

In the doorway of the music room appeared the figure of Lemuel Stoper, looking tired and beaten. In his hand he held a revolver from Uncle Daniel's desk.

"Did his money mean as much to you, boy?" Stoper asked, his voice trembling with shock and rage. "Is that why you did it?"

For only a moment Edgar wondered how Mr Stoper had got into the library so fast. And then suddenly he knew.

What could anyone think of a locked room murder in which the murderer had forgotten to lock the door?

William Brittain: "The Man Who Read Dickson Carr" in *Ellery Queen's Crime Carousel*, London 1967, Victor Gollancz Ltd (publishers)

VOCABULARY. *wire*: thread of metal — *cage*: box to keep birds or animals — *mystify*: to puzzle greatly; confuse — *orphan*: a child who has lost one or both parents — *rambling*: not compact; irregularly built — *victim*: person suffering death, harm etc. — *self-reliance*: confidence in one's own ability and judgment — *will*: written statement showing what one wishes to be done with one's money and goods after death — *soot*: black powder left by smoke — *scrub*: clean by rubbing hard — *slim*: slender, not stout — *convenience*: suitableness; personal comfort — *exit*: way out — *unimpeachable*: free from fault — *pail*: bucket — *closet*: cupboard — *wrinkle*: get small folds in the surface of — *hamper*: large basket — *saber* (Am.; *sabre*: brit.): cavalry sword — *reluctant*: unwilling — *kindling*: material (e. g. dry sticks) for starting a fire — *jar*: bottle with a wide mouth — *butter up*: (colloq.) flatter — *thrust*: push with force — *shuffle*: walk without raising the feet properly — *schedule* [ˈʃedjuːl]: time-table — *slant*: turn in a sloping direction (like the roof of a house) — *scramble*: climb or crawl — *deck*: pack of cards (now chiefly U. S.) — *gloat*: look at with wicked joy — *unsullied*: not dirty, unstained — *pound*: strike heavily and repeatedly — *batter*: beat heavily — *foolproof*: so simple that even a fool cannot make a mistake.

106. Mr Kowtshook

(In the circus, they were used to freaks. But Mr Kowtshook was the most remarkable of all the freaks the tough owner had ever known. And who was Mr Kowtshook hiding from?)

It happened either in '31 or '32; time gets mixed up when you're in the circus business and one tour is very much like another, but I remember that the depression had been running for a couple of years. We had lost our lion during the winter; the poor old devil was on short rations like the rest of us and a dose of 'flu carried him right off—no strength left.

We all had it at the back of our minds that this was no time for being unemployed, especially in a trade like ours.

I was the clown. Anyway, I was glad of the job. We all were.

In the late summer we put up at a place called Crunn. It's a little town up in Scotland—two trains a day and miles from anywhere. That was the kind of place we'd got down to.

This night was a Sunday. It was a fine evening. The sky was big and red over the hills and going through every shade to purple right overhead. I sat on the grass beside the wagon.

I didn't hear this fellow until he was standing almost over me. He gave me a bit of a shock when I looked up: he was tall, maybe six feet three, and he wore a kind of cloak affair from his shoulders down to his knees. Below that he had ordinary blue serge trousers and black shoes.

"I'd like a job," he said.

"I don't run the show," I told him. "But I can tell you there's nothing doing."

He said: "My name is Kowtshook."

"Glad to know you," I said. "Mike Cinnabon."

"I'm an india-rubber man," he said.

"We haven't got one," I admitted. "But it makes no difference." He took his cloak off. Underneath he was wearing a thin grey shirt. He started bending. I've seen some things, being with a circus, but he surprised me. He bent at the joints all right, but unless he had joints in a lot more places than I've got, he bent at other places as well. When he'd finished twisting and stretching himself he said:

"Well?"

"It's good. But we can't afford it."

"Can I wait and see the proprietor?"

Ted, the boss, came back a bit before the others. He shook his head when he heard what this fellow wanted.

The stranger said: "You haven't asked me what I want yet."

Ted laughed. "Board and lodging and ten bob. All right?"

"All right," Mr Kowtshook said softly.

Ted stared at him. "You're crazy."

Ted thought a moment. "O. K. You're hired. And I can stretch it to a quid. More when we can afford it. We'll have to fit you in somewhere, though."

I said: "There's room in my tent. He can pitch in with me, if he's got no objections."

Mr Kowtshook smiled. He had a wonderful smile, fresh and open like a baby's. "I'd like to," he said, "very much."

I don't know why I said that — about there being room in my tent. I've always been very careful to keep by myself. But this was one thing I never regretted. Mr Kowtshook never seemed to be an intruder. It's a funny thing—right from the start he called me Mike. He was calling every one of us by our Christian names within a couple of days. But no one ever called him anything but Mr Kowtshook. I did once ask him what his other name was, and he told me. I never quite worked out how he managed to pronounce it.

He had a wonderful way with animals. He could make them do things that I would never have thought possible. It was almost as though they were reading his mind and he reading theirs.

There was the time when Sammy slipped from the rope, too. He missed the edge of the net. He ran his leg against a spike as he came to the ground and tore a hole in his thigh that jetted out blood like a fountain.

Mr Kowtshook came up from somewhere.

"Don't bother," he said. He kneeled down beside Sammy and wiped the blood away with a sponge. I stood watching. The blood was still coming out fast. Mr Kowtshook reached into his pocket and took out a kind of canister.

"What's that?" I asked him.

"Ointment," he said. He took the sponge again in his left hand and drew it across the wound. As he did, he followed up with the right hand, smearing the ointment on. I looked at the leg when he had finished. One tiny bead of blood stood out above the ointment at the very edge of the wound. Mr Kowtshook gently wiped it away.

"He'll be all right tomorrow."

I met Sammy in the morning. He was walking around as spry as ever. I went back to my tent and saw Mr Kowtshook.

"Look," I said, I've been wondering. Which country do you come from, Mr Kowtshook?"

"A very distant one."

"In Europe?"

"No. Much further."

I can always tell when someone doesn't want to answer questions, and it's my view that every man has a constitutional right to keep his mouth shut. I didn't know what the facts were in Mr Kowtshook's case, but I knew I was on his side.

Ted and me were talking one day. "I've been inquiring," Ted said. "here and there. No one knows him. He's not been in the circus business before—not in this country."

"What do I think, then?" I said.

"What do you think? I think there's one country no one knows much about—Russia. I think he's a Russian."

I said: "He could be in big-time circus."

Ted looked cunning. "And get his picture in the papers?"

Mr Kowtshook and I were sitting in the tent the night they came for him.

I didn't like the look of them when they stepped through the opening into the tent. They were as tall or taller than Mr Kowtshook, and though they were dressed normally they had a foreign look about them! They spoke to Mr Kowtshook in some foreign language. He answered them in English.

"Yes. I recognize you, and your duty."

One of them looked at me, and then spoke in English himself.

"You are ready to come with us?"

Mr Kowtshook said: "I have no choice."

I broke in.

"Look, Mr Kowtshook," I said, "I don't know who these fellows are, but I know they aren't policemen. This is a free country. You're safe here. Let me get a copper and have these blokes thrown out."

"I've had a good run, Mike," he said. "They've been looking for me for a long time. Just tell the others I was called away on private business. Don't let there be any fuss. And tell them how I've appreciated being with them. I've appreciated your letting me share your tent, too."

"Mr Kowtshook," I said. "If there's anything I can do. Anything at all."

He looked at the two strangers, who stood waiting.

"Thanks, Mike. There's nothing."

"Shan't I see you again?" I asked him.

He smiled. "Watch the sky," he said. "Watch the sky"—he glanced at his watch—"about midnight."

He walked out of the tent, and the two men walked after him.

I read a lot in the magazines about spaceships and travel to the stars nowadays. I don't know what they expect to find there. A better world than this?

Somewhere up there in the sky is a world where a good decent fellow like Mr Kowtshook was so out of place that he had to come here to escape. And they sent hunters after him, and even though he hid as a freak in a one-elephant circus, they found him in the end and took him back for whatever kind of punishment they had thought out for him. It's not the kind of place I want to go to, and I can't help feeling that those who do go have got some nasty surprises coming to them.

I watched at midnight. It was like the biggest, brightest meteor ever seen, a golden-white flame, travelling, vanishing, upwards.

John Christopher: from *The Twenty-Second Century,* London

VOCABULARY. *freak*: person full of absurd ideas — *depression*: time when business is less active — *shade*: degree of colour — *cloak*: loose outer garment without sleeves — *serge*: strong cloth — *bend*: turn in new direction — *joint*: place where two bones are joined — *bob*: (pl. unchanged; slang) a shilling — *quid*: (sl.) sovereign; £ 1 — *hire*: employ for wages — *pitch in*: make his home — *spike*: small pointed rod; large nail — *thigh*: thick, fleshy part of the leg above the knee — *jet*: shoot or spout out — *canister*: box or case, usu. of tin — *ointment*: greasy substance for healing hurts — *bead*: small drop — *spry*: lively; gay — *copper*: (sl.) policeman — *bloke*: (colloq.) man, fellow, chap — *spaceship*: spacecraft-for travelling beyond the earth's atmosphere — *meteor*: bright star-like body seen for a few moments falling in the sky.

107. Letter to a Phoenix

I am not immortal. There is only one immortal being in the universe. Compared to it, I am of no importance, but you will not understand or believe what I say to you unless you understand what I am.

There is little in a name, and that is a fortunate thing—for I do not remember mine. That is less strange than you think, for a hundred and eighty thousand years is a long time and for one reason or another I have changed my name a thousand times or more. And what could matter less than the name my parents gave me a hundred and eighty thousand years ago.

What happened to me happened when I was twenty-three years old, during the first atomic war. The first war, that is, in which both sides used atomic weapons—puny weapons, of course, compared to subsequent ones.

The first atomic war wasn't a bad one—the first one never is. I was lucky for, if it had been a bad one—one which ended a civilization—I'd not have survived it despite the biological accident that happened to me. If it had ended a civilization, I wouldn't have been kept alive during the sixteen-year sleep period I went through about thirty years later. But again I get ahead of the story.

I was, I believe, twenty or twenty-one years old when the war started. They didn't take me for the army right away because I was not physically fit. I was suffering from a rather rare disease of the pituitary gland. It caused obesity, among other things. I was about fifty pounds over-weight for my height and had little stamina. I was rejected without a second thought.

About two years later my disease had progressed slightly, but other things had progressed more than slightly. By that time the army was taking anyone; they'd have taken a one-legged one-armed blind man if he was willing to fight. And I was willing to fight. I'd lost my family. I hated my job in a war plant, and I had been told by doctors that my disease was incurable and I had only a year or two to live in any case. So I went to what was left of the army, what was left of the army took me without a second thought and sent me to the nearest front, which was ten miles away. I was in the fighting one day after I joined.

It happened that the time I joined was the turn of the tide. The other side was out of bombs and getting low on shells and bullets. We were out of bombs, too, but they hadn't knocked out *all* our production facilities and we'd got just about all of theirs. We still had planes to carry them, too, and we still had the semblance of an organization to send the planes to the right places. Nearly the right places, anyway; sometimes we dropped them too close to our own troops by mistake. It was a week after I'd got into the fighting that I got out of it again—knocked out of it by one of our smaller bombs that had been dropped about a mile away.

I came to, about two weeks later, in a base hospital, pretty badly burned. By that time the war was over, except for restoring order and getting the world started up again. You see, that hadn't been what I call a blow-up war. It killed off—I'm just guessing; I don't remember the fraction—about a fourth or a fifth of the world's population. There was enough productive capacity left, and there were enough people left, to keep on going; there were dark ages for a few centuries, but there was no return to savagery, no starting over again.

It's not like a blow-up war, when nine-tenths or more of the population of Earth—or of Earth and the other planets—is killed. Then is when the world reverts to utter savagery and the hundredth generation rediscovers metals to tip their spears.

But again I digress. After I recovered consciousness in the hospital, I was in pain for a long time. There were, by then, no more anaesthetics. I had deep radiation burns, from which I suffered almost intolerably for the first few months until, gradually, they healed. I did not sleep—that was the strange thing. And it was a terrifying thing, then, for I did not understand what had happened to me, and the unknown is always terrifying. The doctors paid little heed—for I was one of millions burned or otherwise injured—and I think they did not believe my statements that I had not slept at all. They thought I had slept but little and that I was either exaggerating or making an honest error. But I had *not* slept at all. I did not sleep until long after I left the hospital, cured. Cured, incidentally, of the disease of my pituitary gland, and with my weight back to normal, my health perfect.

I didn't sleep for thirty years. Then I *did sleep*, and I slept for sixteen years. And at the end of that forty-six year period, I was still, physically, at the apparent age of twenty-three.

Do you begin to see what had happened as I began to see it then? The radiation—or combination of types of radiation—I had gone through had radically changed the functions of my pituitary. And there were other factors involved. If my calculations were correct, what happened to me was one chance in a great many billions.

The factors of decay and aging were not eliminated, of course, but the rate was reduced by about fifteen thousand times. I age at the rate of one day every forty-five years. So I am not immortal. I have aged eleven years in the past hundred and eighty millennia. My physical age is now thirty-four.

I've lived through seven major atomic—and super-atomic wars that have reduced the population on Earth to a few savages around a few camp-fires in a few still habitable areas. And at other times, in other eras, I've been in five galaxies besides our own. The human race is the only immortal organism in the universe. There have been other races, and there are other races throughout the universe, but they have died away or they will die.

That is what I am trying to tell you, so that you will never again be afraid. Only a race that destroys itself and its progress periodically, that goes back to its beginning, can survive more than, say, sixty thousand years of intelligent life.

The phoenix, the bird that periodically immolates itself upon a flaming pyre to rise newborn and live again for another millennium, and again and forever, exists and there is only one of it.

You are the phoenix.

Nothing will ever destroy you, now that—during many high civilizations —your seed has been scattered on the planets of a thousand suns, in a hundred galaxies, there ever to repeat the pattern. The pattern that started a hundred and eighty thousand years ago—I think.

It will help your peace of mind, here in the year 1965 of your current era, to know that—for your minds are disturbed. Perhaps, I do not know, it will help your thought to know that the coming atomic war, the one that will probably happen in our generation, will not be a blow-up war; it will come too soon for that, before you have developed the really destructive weapons man has had so often before. It will set you back, yes. There will be darkish ages for a century or a few centuries.

Man will reach the stars again, to find himself already there. Why, you'll be back on Mars within five hundred years, and I'll go there too, to see again the canals I once helped to dig. I've not been there for eighty thousand years and I'd like to see what time has done to it.

The human race will last everywhere and forever, for it will never be sane and only insanity is divine. Only the mad destroy themselves and all they have wrought.

And only the phoenix lives for ever.

Frederic Brown: "A Letter to a Phoenix", in: *Best Science Fiction Stories 6*, ed. Edmund Crispin, London 1966, Faber and Faber Ltd, publishers

VOCABULARY. *phoenix*: mythical bird which was said to burn itself and to rise afresh from its ashes — *puny*: little and weak — *pituitary gland*: small gland at the base of the brain which has an important influence over the growth of the body "Hypophyse" — *obesity*: corpulence — *stamina*: power of lasting out, strength — *facilities*: means for doing a thing easily — *semblance*: appearance — *blow up*: destroy with an explosion — *tip*: put a pointed end on — *digress*: turn aside from the main subject — *anaesthetic*: substance that produces insensibility — *radiation*: sending out rays or heat — *burn*: hurt caused by fire — *incidentally*: by the way — *decay:* become bad or rotten — *age*: grow old — *millennium*: a thousand years — *galaxy*: Milky Way; irregular band of stars — *pyre*: pile of wood on which a dead body is burnt — *seed*: unit of reproduction or germ; offspring — *sane*: of sound mind — *insanity*: madness.

108. Ghost Hunt

Well, listeners, this is Tony Weldon speaking. Here we are on the third of our series of Ghost Hunts. Let's hope it will be more successful than the other two. All our preparations have been made, and now it is up to the spooks. My colleague tonight is Professor Mignon of Paris. He is the most celebrated investigator of psychic phenomena in the world, and I am proud to be his collaborator.

We are in a medium-size, three-story Georgian house not far from London. We have chosen it for this reason: it has a truly terrible story. Since it was built, there are records of no less than 30 suicides in or from it, and there may well have been more. There have been eight since 1893. Its builder and first occupant was a prosperous city merchant: glutton, wine bibber, and other undesirable things, including a very bad husband. His wife stood his cruelties and infidelities as long as she could and then hanged herself in the powder closet belonging to the biggest bedroom on the second floor.

I used the expression "suicides in and from it," because while some have shot themselves and some hanged themselves, no less than nine have done a very strange thing. They have risen from their beds during the night and flung themselves to death in the river which runs past the bottom of the garden some hundred yards away. The owner tells me people simply will not live in the house and the agents will no longer keep it on their books. He will not live in it himself, for very good reasons, he declares. He will not tell us what those reasons are. And he declares that if the professor's verdict is unfavorable, he will pull down the house and rebuild it. One can understand that, for it seems to merit the label, "Death Trap."

And now to business—imagine me seated at a fine satinwood table, not quite in the middle of a big reception room on the ground floor. The walls are light oak panels. The electric light in the house has been switched off, so all the illumination I have is a not very powerful electric lamp. I shall remain here with a mike while the professor roams the house in search of what he may find. He will not have a mike, as it distracts him and he has a habit, so he says, of talking to himself while he conducts these investigations. He will return to me as soon as he has anything to report. Is that all clear? Well, then, here is the professor to say a few words to you before he sets forth on his tour of discovery. I may say he speaks English far better than I do. Professor Mignon—

Ladies and gentlemen, this is Professor Mignon. This house is without doubt, how shall I say, impregnated with evil. It affects one profoundly. It is bad, bad, bad! It must be pulled down, I assure you. I do not think it affects my friend, Mr Weldon, in the same way. Now shall we see ghosts, spirits? Ah, that I cannot say! but they are here and they are evil; that is sure. I can feel their presence. There is, maybe, danger. I shall soon know. And now I shall start off with just one electric torch to show me the way. Presently I will come back and tell you what I have seen, or if not seen, felt and perhaps suffered. But remember, though we can summon spirits, will they come when we call for them? We shall see.

Well, listeners, I'm sure if anyone can, it's the professor. In fact, he wasn't quite correct when he said this place didn't affect me at all. I don't find it a very cheerful spot, by any means. You can be sure of that. I've certainly got a sort of feeling it doesn't want us here, resents us, and would like to see the back of us. *Or else*! I felt that way as soon as I entered the front door. One sort of had to wade through the hostility.

It's very quiet here, listeners. I'm having a look around the room. This lamp casts some queer shadows. There is an odd one near the wall by the door, but I realize now it must be one cast by a big bookcase. I know that's what it is because I peeped under the dust cover when I first came in. It's a very fine piece. It's queer to think of you all listening to me. I shouldn't really mind if I had some of you for company. The owner of the house told us we should probably hear rats and mice in the wainscoting. Well, I can certainly hear them now. Pretty hefty rats, from the sound of them—even you can almost hear them, I should think.

There's a bat in the room. I think it must be a bat and not a bird. I haven't actually seen it, only its shadow as it flew past the wall just now, and then it fanned past my face. I don't know much about bats, but I thought they went to bed in winter. This one must suffer from insomnia. Ah, there it is again—it actually touched me as it passed.

Now I can hear the professor moving about in the room above.

Hello! Did you hear that? He must have knocked over a chair or something—a heavy chair, from the sound of it. I wonder if he's having any luck. Ah, there's that bat again—it seems to like me. They're smelly things, bats—I don't think they wash often enough. This one smells kind of rotten.

I wonder what the professor knocked over—I can see a small stain forming on the ceiling. Perhaps a flower bowl or something. Hello! Did you hear that sharp crack? Something ran across my foot then—a rat perhaps. I've always loathed rats. Most people do, of course.

That stain on the ceiling has grown quite a lot. I think I'll just go to the door and shout to the professor to make sure he's all right.

Professor!—Professor!—

Well, he didn't answer. I believe he's a little bit deaf. But he's sure to be all right. I'll sit down again for a minute or two. I'm afraid this is rather dull for you, listeners. I'm not finding it so, but then of course—There, I heard him cough. Did you hear that cough, listeners—a sort of very throaty double cough? I tell you, listeners, this place is beginning to get on my nerves just a wee little bit, just a bit. I wouldn't live in it for a pension, a very large pension—Get away, you brute! That bat—it stinks.

Now listen carefully—can you hear those rats? I really shall be quite glad to get out of there. I can quite imagine people doing themselves in in this house. Saying to themselves, after all, it isn't much of a life when you think of it—figure it out, is it? Let's end it all in the river!

I'm not being very cheerful, am I? I wonder what the professor's doing, besides coughing. That bat'll be the death of me! Death of me! Death of me!

I'm glad I've got you to talk to, listeners, but I wish you could answer back. After a time, if you've been talking in a room alone, you get fanciful. Have you ever noticed that?

There you must have heard that! What a crack that paneling makes! Well, you must have heard that, listeners—better than nothing! Ha, ha! Professor! Phew, what an echo!

Did you hear it? I'm not exactly sure what it was. Not sure. I wonder if you heard it? Not exactly, but the house shook a little and the windows rattled. I wonder how long one could endure the atmosphere of this place. It certainly is inclined to get one down.

Gosh, that stain has grown—the one on the ceiling. It's actually started to drip. I mean form bubbles—they'll start dropping soon. Colored bubbles, apparently. I wonder if the professor is okay? Professor! Professor! I shall certainly advise the owner to have this place pulled down. Emphatically. I must go upstairs in a minute or two and see what's happened to the professor.

D'you know, listeners, I really believe I'd go completely crackers if I stayed here much longer—it wears you down. That's exactly it, it wears you down. I'm afraid this is all awfully dull for you, listeners. I should switch it off if I were you—

That stain's started to drip drops, drip drops, drip drops! I'll go and catch one on my hand—

Good God!

Professor! Professor! Professor! Now up those stairs! Which room would it be? Left or right? Left, right, left, right, left has it. In we go—

Well, gentlemen, good evening! What have you done with the professor? I know he's dead—see his blood on my hand? What have you done with him? D'you want me to sing it—tra-la-la—

That can't be him lying there—he hadn't a *red* beard! Don't crowd round me, gentlemen! Don't crowd me, I tell you!

What do you want me to do? You want me to go to the river, don't you? Ha, ha! Now? Will you come with me? Come on, then! To the river! To the river!

(Abridged) H. R. Wakefield
By permission of the author and of his agent, Scott Meredith Inc, New York

VOCABULARY. *ghost*: spirit, usu. of a dead person — *spook*: ghost — *psychic*: of the soul or the mind — *phenomenon*: (pl. phenomena) remarkable or unusual thing — *Georgian*: of the time of the first four Kings George of England — *suicide*: self-murder(er) — *glutton*: one who eats too much — *bibber*: tippler (= one who drinks liquor habitually) — *closet*: private or small room — *verdict*: decision — *panel*: flat piece of wood let into a wall — *satinwood*: smooth wood — *mike*: (colloq.) abbrev. of *microphone* — *impregnate*: fill, saturate (with) — *affect*: act upon — *torch*: light that can be carried in the hand — *summon*: order a person to come — *resent*: be angry at — *wade*: make one's way with effort — *wainscot*: wooden boarding on the wall — *hefty*: (colloq.) big and strong — *bat*: flying animal with a mouselike body — *fan*: send a current of air on to — *insomnia*: sleeplessness — *loathe*: dislike greatly — *throaty*: thick (as when one has a cold) —

do in: (sl.) bring disaster upon, kill — *fanciful*: full of whims or oddness — *phew!*: exclamation of astonishment — *bubble*: ball formed of liquid and containing air — *crackers*: (sl.) crazy, mad.

109. In Search of a Ghost

(Although Eric Roberts has yet to see a ghost for himself, he is convinced that ghosts—and especially poltergeists—really do exist.

He thought his chance had come when he spent an evening in a haunted house on Dartmoor—an experience that he broadcast on the B.B.C. programme *Home This Afternoon.*)

It was when I was in Devonshire on holiday that I was offered the opportunity of making the acquaintance of a ghost, a thing I had long wanted to do as I had always been a firm believer in ghosts, although only through second-hand experience.

Hence my interest when the owner of a large house in the wilds of Dartmoor informed me that, any time from about 10.30 onwards, a little lady in a grey cloak was in the habit of making a nightly perambulation along the corridors and into some of the rooms.

Not that the owner lived in the house herself. In fact, the place was uninhabited except on those occasions when people came down to fish the nearby river, and used the premises more for shelter than for comfort. For the rest of the time it stood empty, a tall gaunt building exuding an inhospitable atmosphere, with its windows so tightly shut that they gave the impression of having been sealed.

I collected the key as night began to fall, and made my way up the weed-strewn narrow path that led to a heavy porch in whose dark recesses stood the front door like a bastion defying entry. It was almost with a sense of guilt at my intrusion that I turned the massive key in the lock and swung the door back on its creaking hinges.

The house was without electric light, but I had been told that I should find candles in the hall, and when I lit one the shape of furniture gradually separated itself from the shadows—a hall-stand, chairs, and a solid mahogany table all looking as if they had been built into the floor, so long had it been since they were last moved.

Before settling down to await the arrival of the ghost, I made as swift an inspection of the house as my flickering candle would allow, first negotiating some stone steps that led to a vast stone-floored kitchen that occupied the whole of the basement. From there I returned to the hall and made my way upstairs to peer cautiously into several bedrooms where old iron bedsteads stood like sentinels against the walls.

At one end of the landing, I found a room that had obviously served as a study, although the only books that were now in evidence were a few paper-backs yellow with age. I found their titles a trifle disturbing—*The Hangman's Noose, Death Under the Stairs,* and *The Creeping Flesh* were typical examples.

But it was time for my vigil to start, so I steered my way to a huge armchair whose upholstery had provided a banquet for the moths, put my candle on the floor, and waited.

Nothing happened. Then, after a time, it occurred to me that as the ghost only visited some of the rooms, she might be giving this one a miss, so I decided to pay another visit to the bedrooms.

It was in the third of these that I saw her—at least, I thought I did. In the feeble light of my candle a figure at the far end of the room moved perceptibly towards me as I approached. My heart thumped with excitement as I rather fatuously bade her good evening, but as I drew nearer I saw that this was no little old lady in a grey cloak but a middle-aged gentleman whose hair was beginning to recede at the temples, and who looked rather in need of a shave.

It was me—staring wide-eyed at myself in the long mirror of a tall wardrobe lurking in the gloom of the bedroom. Bitterly disappointed, I returned to the landing, and was halfway towards the next bedroom when a crash from the kitchen shattered the silence.

So that's where she was! And by the sound of it, the dear old thing had tripped over a bucket. So, with candle held aloft, I clattered helter-skelter down the stairs thinking that the sight of a ghost rubbing its shins and muttering spooky oaths as it dusted itself down would be something worth seeing.

But there was nothing there. I examined every corner of the vast kitchen, but all was exactly as it had been before, giving the impression that nothing had been moved for years.

I stayed a little while longer, and for a time even extinguished the candle so that the dense shadows thrown by the flame vanished into darkness as black as pitch. But the ghost failed to walk that night.

Or did it?

When I finally decided to leave, I locked the door from the outside, and then tried it to make sure it was secure. But the handle turned uselessly in my hand. So I unlocked the door again and tried to go back in, but the handle would not withdraw the catch. The door was held fast, so that any further entry was most effectively barred.

You may say this was just a normal failure of a lock. But was it?

A week or two later I heard from the owner that not even a locksmith had been able to discover what had gone wrong with the lock, and they had been obliged to get into the house through a downstairs window. Which makes me wonder if the ghost was really there all the time, and having seen me off the premises, took care that I didn't return to disturb her privacy again.

After all, *something* must have caused that crash in the kitchen, mustn't it?

Eric Roberts: "In Search of a Ghost"
By permission of the author

VOCABULARY. *poltergeist* ['pɔltəgaist]: noisy mischievous spirit — *haunt*: visit habitually — *second-hand*: not based on personal observation — *cloak*: loose outer garment without sleeves — *perambulation*: walking through or over — *premises*: building, along with its outer buildings, yard etc. — *gaunt*: grim or desolate-looking — *exude*: give off — *seal*: close tightly — *weed-strewn*: overgrown with wild herbs — *porch*: covered-in doorway of a building — *recess*: hidden, secret place — *bastion*: projecting part of fortification — *defy*: resist boldly — *guilt*: culpability — *creak*: make a sharp, grating sound — *hinge*: joint on which a door turns — *candle*: wax stalk, used for giving light — *flicker*: burn unsteadily — *negotiate*: get past or over — *peer*: look closely — *bedstead*: frame which supports the mattress and bed-clothes — *sentinel*: sentry, soldier on guard — *landing*: platform at top of a flight of stairs on to which doors open — *noose*: running loop, tightening when pulled — *creeping flesh*: making sb. shudder with fear or horror — *vigil*: time of watching esp. during the night — *upholstery*: padding and coverings — *banquet*: feast — *moth*: sorts of winged insect flying chiefly at night — *give a miss*: avoid, leave alone — *thump*: beat heavily — *fatuous*: very foolish — *recede*: go back — *temple*: part of the head above the cheek-bone — *lurk*: be out of view — *trip*: stumble — *helter-skelter*: in a great hurry — *shin*: large bone in the leg, below the knee — *spooky*: (colloq.) like a ghost — *dust*: clear of dust — *pitch*: black sticky substance made from coal-tar — *catch*: contrivance for checking motion of door "Schnäpper" — *locksmith*: maker and repairer of locks for doors.

110. "Here I Am Again!"

Copy of a letter dated July 10th, 1917,
from Charles G. S.-Esq., to Lord Halifax.

Dear Lord Halifax,
I send you herewith my plain, unvarnished tale, according to your kind request. I may say in confidence that the house was . . ., Deal, but I would rather that my name and the name of the house should not be mentioned in case you are at any time to give publicity to the story. The only tales dealing with ghostly phenomena which seem to me to be of any value are those relating first-hand experiences.

My experience was *horrible*, so much so that I have vowed never to have anything to do with spiritualism in any shape or form.

The house in question is an old Georgian house in Deal. It was built about 1740 and Nelson addressed many of his letters to Lady Hamilton from there, calling it 'dear . . . House'. My host and I had been yachting together, and on our arrival from the sea unexpectedly found the house full of relations who had come to stay. A bed was arranged for me in a dressing-room. On a previous visit I had heard that the house was haunted and that all the daughters had seen the figure of someone they called their great-grandmother gliding about. The servants had been terrified, and in consequence of what they saw had refused to stay. I had forgotten this. I was in rude health after my Channel cruise and nothing ghostly was discussed before I retired to bed.

In the middle of the night I awoke, feeling that something uncanny was about me. Suddenly, there appeared at my bedside the phantom of either an old man or woman, of dreadful aspect, who was bending over me. That I was wide awake is beyond all question. I at once became cataleptic, unable to move hand or foot. I could only gaze at this monstrosity, vowing mentally that if I ever recovered from this horrible experience I would never dabble in table turning etc., again, for here was a real materialisation and the reality was too terrifying for description.

Next mornig I told my host privately of what had occurred. He said he was not in the least surprised, as everybody living in the house except himself had, at one time or another, seen something of the sort.

Twenty years passed and I had almost forgotten the incident. I had frequently re-visited the house and had seen nothing. Then one day I was again invited and found my host alone. We played billiards together and retired rather late. I was suffering from toothache and on getting into bed was utterly unable to sleep. The room was in a different part of the house from the dressing-room in which I had slept on the occasion of my first visit.

Suddenly, although it was early summer, I began to feel very cold. I seemed literally to freeze from my feet upwards, and although I put on more clothes, the cold rapidly increased until I imagined that my heart must be failing and that this was death.

All at once a voice (unheard physically) appeared to be saying over and over again to me, "Here I am again! Here I am again, after twenty years." Once more, in an exact repetition of my feeling twenty years before, I pulled myself together and said to myself, "This time I will see this thing through and definitely prove whether my former experience was an hallucination and whether there really is such a thing as a ghost. I am wide awake beyond all possibility of doubt and only too conscious of a raging toothache."

The thing again spoke to me mentally: "Look round. Look round."

I now had that unaccountable feeling of horror which all accounts of such manifestations agree in declaring are produced on such occasions. Turning round, I saw in the corner of the room facing me a curious column of light revolving spirally like a whirlwind of dust on a windy day. It was white, and as I gazed, it slowly drew near to me.

"Here I am again!" the thing kept repeating.

I stretched out my hand for the matches at my bedside. As the things got gradually closer and closer to me, it rapidly began to take human shape. Under my eyes and within my grasp it assumed that very figure I had seen twenty years before. There was no doubt whatever about this, and having reached the limit of my endurance, I shouted out, "Who's that?" No answer coming, I hurriedly struck a match and lit a candle.

Next morning I told my host what had befallen me. He was greatly interested, and related two weird occurrences in the house, both of which had taken place during the three weeks previous to my visit.

On the first occasion he was in his dressing-room, when a servant came up to say that a friend had called to see him. He ran hurriedly downstairs and, as he turned on the landing for the next flight, he saw the figure of a man rushing upstairs. My friend, unable to stop himself, put up his hands to avert a collision and went right through the figure.

The second occasion had been when one evening an officer of Marines came to play billiards with him and brought his dog, which lay under the table. Suddenly the dog sprang up and began barking furiously at something invisible in the corner. It went on barking till its mouth foamed and its hair stood on end. They endeavoured in vain to calm it. From under the table it kept making violent rushes at the corner and then retreating again. Neither my friend nor the officer who was visiting saw anything.

Lord Halifax's Ghost Book, London
By permission of the publishers, Geoffrey Bles Ltd

VOCABULARY. *unvarnished*: plain and straightforward — *phenomenon*: thing that appears to the senses — *vow*: make solemn promise — *spiritualism*: belief in the possibility of receiving messages from the spirits of the dead — *Lady Hamilton*: her notorious intimacy with Lord Nelson began in 1793 — *yacht* [jɔt]: travel in a yacht (= small ship for pleasure cruising) — *relations*: = relatives — *haunt*: visit often — *glide*: move smoothly — *cruise*: sea-voyage of any kind — *uncanny*: full of mystery — *phantom*: ghost — *cataleptic*: subject to suspension of consciousness accompanied by rigidity of the body — *dabble*: study in a half-hearted way, but not seriously — *table-turning*: turning of table thought by spiritualists sitting at a table to be done by spirits — *materialisation*: taking material form — *hallucination*: illusion; apparent perception of external object not actually present — *raging*: violent — *unaccountable*: not able to be explained — *revolve*: go round in a circle — *spiral*: winding round and round — *whirlwind*: swift, circling current of air — *endurance*: ability to bear — *befall*: happen to — *weird* [wiəd]: unnatural; unearthly — *avert*: avoid — *collision*: coming together violently — *marine*: soldier serving on a warship — *foam*: emit froth at the mouth — *on end*: upright.

111. Father Sews On a Button

It must have been hard work to keep up with the mending in our house. Four boys had to be kept in repair besides Father, and there was no special person to do it. The baby's nurse did some sewing, and Cousin Julie did a lot when she was around, but the rest of it kept Mother busy and her work-basket was always piled up.

Looking back, I wonder now how she managed it. I remember her regularly going off to her room and sewing on something, right after dinner or at other idle moments, when she might have sat around with the rest of us.

There was more talk about Father's socks and shirts than anything else. Most of this talk was by Father, who didn't like things to disappear for long periods, and who wanted them brought promptly back and put in his bureau drawer where they belonged. This was particularly true of his favourite socks. Not the plain white ones which he wore in the evening, because they were all alike, but the coloured socks that were supplied to him by an English haberdasher in Paris.

In that day of sombre hues for men's suits and quiet tones for men's neckties, most socks were as dark and severe as the rest of one's garments; but Father's, hidden from the public eye by his trousers and his high buttoned shoes, had a really astonishing range of colour and fancy. They were mostly in excellent taste, but in a distinctly French way, and Wilhelmine used to tease him about them. She called them his 'secret joys'.

Father got holes in his socks even oftener than we boys did in our stockings. He had long athletic toes, and when he lay stretched out on his sofa and smoking, or absorbed in talking to anyone, these toes would begin stretching and wiggling in a curious way by themselves, as though they were seizing on this chance to live a life of their own. I often stared in fascination at their leisurely twistings and turnings, when I should have been listening to Father's instructions about far different matters. Soon one and then the other slipper would fall off, always to Father's surprise, but without interrupting his talk, and a little later his busy great toe would peer out at me through a new hole in his sock. Mother felt that it was a woman's duty to mend things and sew, but she hated it. She rather liked to embroider silk lambrequins, but her darning of Father's socks was an impatient and not-too-skilful performance. She said there were so many of them that they made the back of her neck ache.

Father's heavily starched shirts, too, were a problem. When he put one on, he pulled it down over his head, and thrust his arms blindly out right and left in a hunt for the sleeves. A new shirt was strong enough to survive these strains without splitting, but life with Father rapidly weakened it, and the first thing he knew he would hear it beginning to tear. That disgusted him. He hated any evidence of weakness, either in people or things. In his wrath he would strike out harder than ever as he felt around for the sleeve. Then would come a sharp crackling noise as the shirt ripped open, and a loud wail from Mother.

Buttons were Father's worst trial, however, from his point of view. Ripped shirts and socks with holes in them could still be worn but trousers with their buttons off couldn't. The speed with which he dressed seemed to discourage his buttons and make them desert Father's service. Furthermore, they always gave out suddenly and at the wrong moment.

He wanted help and he wanted it promptly at such times, of course. He would appear at Mother's door with a waistcoat in one hand and a disloyal button in the other, demanding that it be sewn at once. If she said she couldn't just then, Father would get as indignant as though he had been drowning and a life-guard had informed him he would save him tomorrow.

When his indignation mounted high enough to sweep aside his good judgment, he would say in a stern voice, "Very well, I'll sew it on myself," and demand a needle and thread. This announcement always caused consternation. Mother knew only too well what it meant. She would beg him to leave his waistcoat in her work-basket and let her do it next day. Father was inflexible. Moreover, his decision would be strengthened if he happened to glance at her basket and see how many of his socks were dismally waiting there in that crowded exile.

"I've been looking for those blue polka-dotted socks for a month," he said angrily one night before dinner. "Not a thing is done for a man in this house. I even have to sew on my buttons. Where is your needle and thread?"

Mother reluctantly gave these implements to him. He marched off, sat on the edge of his sofa in the middle of his bedroom, and got ready to work. The gaslight was better by his bureau, but he couldn't sit on a chair when he sewed. It had no extra room on it. He laid his scissors, the spool of thread, and his waistcoat down on the sofa beside him, wet his fingers, held the needle high up and well out in front, and began poking the thread at the eye.

Like every commander, Father expected instant obedience, and he wished to deal with trained troops. The contrariness of the needle and the limp obstinacy of the thread made him swear. He stuck the needle in the sofa while he wet his fingers and stiffened the thread again. When he came to take up his needle, it had disappeared. He felt around everywhere for it. He got up, holding fast to his thread, and turned around, facing the sofa to see where it was hiding. This jerked the spool off on to the floor, where it rolled away and unwound.

The husbands of two of Mother's friends had had fits of apoplexy and died. It frightened her horribly when this seemed about to happen to Father. At the sound of his roars, she rushed in. There he was on the floor, as she had feared. He was trying to get his head under the sofa and he was yelling at something, and his face was such a dark red and his eyes so bloodshot that Mother was terrified. Pleading with him to stop only made him more apoplectic. He said he'd be damned if he'd stop. He stood up presently, tousled but triumphant, the spool in his hand. Mother ran to get a new needle. She threaded it for him and he at last started sewing.

Father sewed on the button in a violent manner, with vicious haulings and jabs. Mother said she couldn't bear to see him—but she couldn't bear to leave the room either. She stood watching him, hypnotized and appalled, itching to sew it herself, and they talked at each other with vehemence. Then the inevitable accident happened: the needle came forcibly up through the waistcoat, it struck on the button, Father pushed at it harder, and it burst through the hole and stuck Father's finger.

He sprang up with a howl. To be impaled in this way was not only exasperating, it was an affront. He turned to me, as he strode about on the rug, holding on to his finger, and said wrathfully, "It was your mother."

"Why, Clare!" Mother cried.

"Talking every minute," Father shouted at her, "and distracting a man! How the devil can I sew on a button with this gibbering and buzz in my ears? Now see what you made me do!" he added suddenly. "Blood on my good waistcoat! Here! Take the damned thing. Give me a handkerchief to tie up my finger with. Where's the witch-hazel?"

Clarence Day: *Life With Father,* New York 1948

VOCABULARY. *pile*: heap up — *bureau*: writing-table — *haberdasher*: person who sells such things as ribbons, tape etc. — *sombre*: dull, gloomy — *hue*: colour; tint — *range*: extent — *toe*: finger-like joint on the foot — *wiggle*: move with quick, short, side-to-side movements — *fascination*: strong attraction — *slipper*: loose shoe, easily put on — *embroider*: ornament with designs in needlework — *lambrequin*: short piece of drapery — *darn*: mend — *starch*: make stiff — *split*: break open by bursting — *wrath*: violent anger — *rip*: tear — *wail*: mournful cry — *waistcoat* ['weiskəut]: short jacket, without sleeves, worn by men under the jacket — *disloyal*: unfaithful — *consternation*: terror; dismay — *inflexible*: unbending — *dismal*: gloomy — *polka-dotted*: "mit Punktmuster" (special design on textiles) — *reluctant*: unwilling — *implement*: tool or instrument — *poke*: thrust — *contrariness*: being self-willed — *limp*: not stiff or firm — *obstinacy*: stubbornness — *jerk*: throw quickly — *unwind*: become drawn out at length — *apoplexy*: loss of power to move or think "Schlaganfall" — *bloodshot*: marked with blood — *tousled* ['tauzld]: put into disorder — *vicious*: fierce — *haul*: pull with force — *jab*: *sharp* thrust — *hypnotize*: produce hypnosis in — *appal*: terrify — *itch*: desire strongly — *impale*: pierce with sth. sharp — *affront*: insult — *wrathful*: very angry — *jibber*: (= gibber) speak fast and inarticulately, chatter like an ape — *buzz*: sound made by people talking — *witch-hazel*: a lotion for the skin made from the witch-hazel, a shrub with yellow flowers.

112. THE PURPLE CHILDREN

The outrage took place at eleven o'clock on a moonless night. It was the sentry at the rear gate of the Town Hall, an eighteen-year-old new to the town, who was singled out as the weakest spot in the defences. Half-dozing on his walk back and forth across the gate, he heard the most innocent sound in the world, a girl's voice calling softly: "Puss, puss, puss . . ."

A little figure with the light running steps of a child darted towards the gate, and halted with her hands locked upon the bars. He saw how slight she was, and how young, no more than fifteen. "You can't go in there," said the sentry gruffly. "You ought to be in the house at this time of night. Don't you know there's a curfew?"

"I *was* in the house. I only came out because of my cat; she got out when I went to bring in wood, and I couldn't catch her. She's young, she runs away. It's no use telling *her* there's curfew."

The boy felt the small, cold hand laid entreatingly upon his arm. She was only a kid, she hardly came up to his shoulders, and she was beginning to sniff ominously. He couldn't see any harm in it. "I can't! I should get into trouble if anybody found out . . ."

"Well, who's going to find out? All I want is to get my cat."

He hadn't meant to do it, but somehow he had set his hand to the bars beside hers, and thrust the gate open before her. She slipped past him like a shadow.

"There she is!" whispered the girl triumphantly, and darted forward and was lost among the deeper shadows under the wall. It took them ten minutes to run the cat to earth at the foot of the cellar steps, against the closed door. The girl snatched it up and held it struggling in her arms.

"Thank you! Now I'll go home." But she did not move; she stoood looking at him still, her eyes enormous and shy and wary. When she looked at him like that he felt how alien he was in this place, and even her thanks could not compensate him for the quiet, patient hatred of her people.

Then they both heard, clear through the silence, the sudden light impact of feet, as though someone had dropped from the high wall.

The sentry spun round and went up the cellar steps three at a time, just in time to see the figure of a boy disentangle itself from the severed ropes of the flagstaff, and run head-down for the gate.

The shout of rage and alarm was out of him before he knew it. He hurtled after the racing boy, holding the loaded spray-gun round from his shoulder in flight to bring it to bear upon the fugitive. When the girl saw him check for an instant to steady the gun, she ran past him and flung the cat sprawling and clawing in his face.

He threw up his left arm to cover his eyes, and swerved aside, firing the gun blindly. The spray spattered darkly over her cheek and her spread hand, but she had gained the few yards she needed for herself and her partner, and she flew through the gate and pulled it to with a clang. Before the sentry could fling off the cat and wipe his eyes clear of the blood from his scratched forehead, both the fugitives were snatched away into the silence and darkness of the little streets.

People got the major out of bed, and the sentry reported to him with every excuse he could think of. "She was looking for her cat."

The major had been in the country for over a year, and was accustomed to the local style of warfare. "They're always kids of fifteen. Haven't you learned that yet?"

"But there was a cat, sir, that was true, anyhow."

"That skinny tabby," said the major wearily, "belongs to the caretaker. I imagine its appearance was a stroke of luck. Well, you seem to have spent practically a quarter of an hour being civil to her, I take it you can pick her out again?"

The sentry said: "No, sir, I don't think I could. It was pretty dark there under the wall. There's scores of them that same build, thin as a monkey."

"And scores of them with purple hands and faces? At least you had the sense to fire your charge."

"The sentry looked at the long dark stain like blood upon the stones, and was filled with a treasonable but unmistakable regret. "I'm sorry, sir," he lied. "I reckon I missed her."

"Then why," asked the major gently, "did she drip violet dye practically all the way to the gate? A heavier charge, and we might have been able to follow her all the way home. Did you mark the boy, too?"

"No, sir. He was well out of range, only he turned back to catch hold of her hand."

"Whoever it was," the major replied, "he's left about ten feet of the flagstaff coiled round with barbed-wire as he came down. You must have been very absorbed in your cat-hunt. And he must have spent a long time practising the movements involved, before he could produce them at that speed. Yes, I should like to congratulate that boy! But when we've found her we shall have found him, too. We'll try the grammar school first," he said, smiling to himself, beginning to feel the terrifying satisfaction of hate reacting against hate.

In the shed behind a shop Mariposa knelt over a pan of water, scouring with a handful of wet sand at the backs of her hands. "Its no use," she said, letting her hands lie quiet in the wet skirt of her dress and looking up at him with enormous black eyes. The misshapen blotches of purple ate away half her face into shadow. Behind her all the silent, intent partisans drew closer with a long sigh. "It won't come out," she said with the calm of despair. "Now they have only to look for me—I can't be hidden. Teo, what am I to do?"

"If they find you," he said, taking her stained hands in his, "they find me, too."

"That's foolish! You'll be needed again. And besides, they'd beat you; they'll only imprison me." But she was frightened. He felt the small, wet hands, hot with scouring, tremble in his own.

"They'll come straight to the school," said Juanito. "Perhaps if you stay at home and take care not to be seen . . ."

"For how long?" said Teo shortly. "You see the marks will have to wear away gradually. Do you think she can be hidden for months?" "If they do not find me in the school," said Mariposa with authority, "they will want to see the register and find out who is missing."

Teo stood up slowly, still holding the thin, marred hands in his. "Come!" he said, drawing her up by the hands. "I have an idea! Come, all of you! It will be hours yet to daylight, we have a little time. Don't be afraid, they won't find you! They'll never find you!"

The grammar school opened at eight o'clock; at half past eight the major presented himself there with a sergeant and two men. "You must do what you feel to be your duty," agreed the headmaster, "but so must our children. Would you like to begin with the little ones?"

"I am looking for a girl of about fifteen. You may not know that we have recently adopted the use of a spray-gun loaded with one of the local vegetable dyes. The girl will be stained purple. This time I can promise you there will be no collective punishment. This time it will not be necessary."

"Purple!" said the schoolmaster reflectively. "A royal colour. Also the colour of mourning. A nice choice!"

The major strode across the polished lobby, the sergeant and his men keeping step behind him. The headmaster pushed the door wide, and stood back for his visitors to enter.

The major marched over the threshold with the briskness of complete confidence, almost of triumph. Fifty-three young heads were raised to confront him, the challenging light of fifty-three pairs of dark, wide, Byzantine eyes. He had come looking for a marked outcast. He beheld a regiment of embattled children, all their delicate olive faces spattered from forehead to chin with the resplendent purple of royalty and mourning.

Edith Pargeter: *Pick of Today's Short Stories,* London
By permission of the publishers, Putnam & Co Ltd

VOCABULARY. *purple*: dark colour formed by the mixture of blue and red — *outrage*: wicked act of great violence — *sentry*: soldier on guard — *curfew*: time (under martial law) for people to remain indoors — *gruff*: rough in manner — *entreat*: beg earnestly — *alien*: foreign — *impact*: striking on sth. with force — *disentangle*: extricate or free from — *sever*: cut apart — *flagstaff*: pole from which a flag is flown — *spray-gun*: gun for scattering liquid "Spritzpistole" — *sprawl*: spread out — *claw*: scratch — *swerve*: turn quickly to one side — *spatter*: splash in all directions — *tabby*: female cat — *caretaker*: person who takes care of a public building — *stroke of luck*: piece of good fortune — *scores of*: very many — *dye*: substance used for giving colour — *charge*: amount, quantity — *coil*: wind in rings; twist — *barbed wire*: wire with sharp points — *scour*: clean by rubbing with sth. rough — *blotch*: dark spot on the skin — *partisan*: devoted to a cause; guerilla — *register*: written list of attendances — *mar*: spoil; ruin — *mourning*: grief — *senior*: older in age — *challenge*: invite to duel, defy — *Byzantine*: of Eastern Empire — *outcast*: homeless and friendless — *embattle*: set in battle array — *resplendent*: very bright.

113. A Young Irishman and an English Priest

(Brendan Behan, aged 16, arrested for militant participation in Irish Republican Army activities, is kept in Walton Prison.)

There was a small queue for the priest outside the room, and I fell in and waited happily. Every time a boy came out, a screw came out with a list and called a name till at last he called "3501 Behan" and I smiled and willingly hurried to his side. "Go inside and stand to attention, feet to the mat."

I ran in, and came smartly to attention at the mat, looking at the priest.

It was the same man, a stout block of a man, God bless him, that had said Mass. He was a bit bald and wearing glasses. I smiled at him and said, "Good morning, Father."

"When are you going to give up this business?" His two eyes glared at me from behind his glasses, and his accent was that of someone who had got a better chance in life, as they'd call it, than their parents.

I shivered and hadn't been expecting this, but now it happened that this priest, too, was part of Walton Prison, I wasn't surprised.

The priest had a bad name amongst Irish Republican prisoners, even the most pious of them.

"Haven't you any manners, Behan?"

"Answer Father Lane, Behan," said the screw, who had shut the door and was standing beside me.

"I don't know what business you're talking about, Father," said I.

"You know all right—your membership of this murder gang—the I. R. A."

"The I. R. A. is not a murder gang, Father," said I.

"Don't answer Father Lane back, you . . ." With difficulty the screw held back the low expletive, in deference to the man of God. The screw took a step half-towards me, but the priest put up his hand.

"It's all right, Mr Milburn," he sighed, and they nodded to each other sympathetically. "The Hierarchy of England have issued pastorals denouncing the I. R. A., and while you're here I cannot let you come to the altar, unless you tell me once and for all that you're giving up having anything to do with this gang."

His small eyes looked up at me, and his mouth closed tight in authority.

"Why should the Bishops of England be supposed to have the right to dictate about politics to an Irishman, Father?" I asked, as steadily as I could.

Mr Milburn looked angry and indignant towards me, but the priest held up his patient hand. "The Bishops of Ireland have denounced the I. R. A., Behan, time and time again, even early this year. The Church has always been Ireland's best friend, in Ireland, here in England, and all over the world. I must inform you that your own clergy and Hierarchy have excommunicated the I. R. A. Surely you can't set yourself up against the Bishops, an ignorant lad against educated men, who have spent their lifetime studying these matters?"

"I didn't spend a lifetime studying theology, but I know that the Church was always against Ireland and for the British Empire."

Mr Milburn again looked angry, but the priest looked wise and tolerant, and indicated that I might continue.

"With no disrespect to you, Father. The O'Neills in Ulster even after the Reformation had to threaten to the Pope that they would burn the Catholic Archbishop of Armagh out of the Cathedral if he didn't take Queen Elizabeth's soldiers out of it. In 'Ninety-eight weren't the rebels excommunicated and wasn't Father John Murphy, that was burnt alive by the yeomen, excommunicated?"

"Look here, you," said the screw, Mr Milburn, and Father Lane looked angry, through his little eyes, but a bit surprised. But I didn't care now. My blood was up.

"Didn't they condemn the men of 'Forty-eight and tell the people to give up their crops and die of the hunger in the ditches at home . . .!"

"Here, you," began the priest, in a gathering roar.

"Weren't the Fenians excommunicated, and didn't the Catholic chaplains join with the rest of the warders in driving Dr Gallagher mad with torture?"

Mr Milburn glared at me in amazed anger. The priest swallowed his temper and tried to speak, but rage got the better of him and he could only signal to the screw to take me out. But I wasn't done yet. Before Milburn reached for me, I said to the priest right into his seething little eyes: "And excommunication is nothing new to the I. R. A. Didn't you excommunicate De Valera and ten thousand others in 1922? Wasn't my own father excommunicated and wasn't he in Kilmainham Prison in 'Twenty-two?"

"Get out, you swine," said Mr Milburn and threw me out of the priest's office. But I was quiet now. I had said what I wanted to say and would go peacably to my cell. If I was let. But I wasn't.

"Mr Mooney," said Mr Milburn to Mr Mooney, who hurried up the wing from where the rest of the Young Prisoners were sitting in rows sewing their mailbags. In indignation, "This—Irish swine—insulting—the priest . . ." Mr Mooney nodded, shocked, and hit me a blow in the face, "This—Irish—insulted priest—bloody bastard—and especially Father Lane, decent man beloved by all and spending his time working for the prisoners!"

They took me to the cell, and beat me in the face, slaps but not punches. The punches they gave me in the ribs, in the kidneys, and once or twice they hit me across the face with a bunch of keys, but concentrated mostly on the guts, when they sent me sprawling across the room and shouted all the time about killing me. The cell was in disorder with the bedboards and bedclothes scattered all over the place, and then they shouted at me to clear that bloody mess up and went off banging the door locked, and left me alone, thank Jesus, and still breathing, though heavily.

I fumbled around the cell as best as I could. I had left the jug full of water in the cell in the morning and I took the liberty of bathing my face with the cold water, and had a look in the mirror when I was finished. My face was not too bad, nothing noticeable, though my lip was cut on the inside where I got the blow of the bunch of keys, and I could feel the blood going down my throat and sickening me. A cold clammy sweat was coming out on my hands and on my forehead. I wiped it off and then got a kind of sick bilious headache. The door opened and a prisoner and a screw stood in the doorway. They had a parcel of books, and the prisoner handed me two and wrote my name on a card.

It didn't look like there was going to be anything more about this morning, and I could have a read tonight, resting my bruises for a bit before the lights were put out, for all my mouth was raw and bleeding still a bit and painful on the inside, and my kidneys, if that's the thing you have on your sides, were sore.

In any event I should have a read, and a read every week, and a kind of pay-day to look forward to when they changed the books; and, thinking these thoughts, I had the cell, between bedclothes and all, laid out and tidied up, and I gave myself another rub with the cold fresh water and had a look at myself in the mirror and I looked all right, except my mouth was a bit bloody with a thin red line around the edge of it, but I wiped that off too and then let myself have a look at the books.

It's a queer world, God knows, but the best we have to be going on with.

Brendan Behan: *Borstal Boy*, London 1958
By permission of the publishers, Hutchinson & Co Ltd

VOCABULARY. *fall in*: get into line — *screw*: (sl.) warder, gaoler — *stand to attention*: stand straight and still — *Mass*: ((in the Roman Catholic Church) the service of the Lord's supper — *bald*: without hair — *glare*: look angrily — *pious*: religious; godly — *gang*: company of people met together for evil purpose — *expletive*: swear-word — *deference*: respect — *hierarchy*: body of church-rulers in order of rank — *pastoral*: letter from bishop to clergy or people "Hirtenbrief" — *denounce*: speak publicly against — *lad*: boy; youth — *excommunicate*: put out of the Church — *yeoman*: cavalryman — *crop*: yearly produce of grain, fruit etc. — *ditch*: trench dug in the ground — *roar*: cry aloud — *Fenians*: Irish political organisation of the 19th century having for its object the overthrow of English rule in Ireland and the establishment of a republic there — *chaplain*: clergyman — *warder*: jail guard — *get the better of*: beat, conquer — *seethe*: boil — *Kilmainham*: suburb of south-west Dublin — *sew*: [səu] join together with a needle and thread — *mailbag*: bag in which letters are carried — *slap*: blow with the hand — *punch*: blow with the fist — *kidneys*: two bean-shaped organs in the body, separating waste liquid from the blood — *bunch*: number of things tied together — *guts*: bowels — *sprawl*: with the limbs spread out — *scattter*: send in all directions — *bang*: give a violent blow to — *fumble*: feel about uncertainly with the hands — *jug*: deep vessel for liquids, with a rounded handle and lip — *throat*: passage from the back of the mouth to the stomach — *sicken*: become ill — *clammy*: damp, moist — *bilious*: ill with bile; sick — *bruise*: injury to the body, so that the skin changes colour — *sore:* causing pain — *pay-day*: that day on which wages are paid.

114. The Fisherman's Tale

There is a village in Scotland called Gourloch, situated on the shore of a fine bay, and inhabited mostly by fishermen, who let part of their homes in summer months, to people who resort thither for the purpose of bathing.

From the summit of a hill of very precipitous ascent, a little way to the east of the village, the view is particularly fine.

When descending one day, during my visit to the west country, from this commanding spot, I sat down on a huge isolated rock. Presently, an elderly man, of grave aspect, and maritime appearance, winding slowly up the hill, came and sat down near me on the rock. I guessed him to be one of the better class of fishermen from the village. After the usual salutations we fell into discourse together, and he remarked, "Is it not strange, sir, the thoughts that sometimes come into the brain of man, sleeping or waking, leave behind them an impression and a feeling; are as things real and authentic. I was thinking at this moment of something which has sat, for many days past, like a millstone on my mind; and I will tell it to you with pleasure."

Without more preamble the Scottish fisherman began his story, as nearly as I remember, in the following words: "About six months ago, a wedding took place in our village; and a more comely and better looked-on couple never came together. Mr Douglas, though the son of a poor man, had been an officer in the army; and when his regiment was disbanded, he came to live here on his half-pay, and whatever little else he might have. Jeanie Stuart at the time was staying with an uncle, one of our folk, her parents having been taken away from her; and made up for her board as far as she could, by going in the summer season to sew in the families that came out then, like clocks, from the holes and corners of the great towns. So gentle she was, and so fair to look on, that even these nobility thought it no dishonour to have her among them.

"Well, they soon got acquainted, our Jeanie, and Mr Douglas, and the end of it was, they were married. They lived in a house there, just beyond the point that you may see forms the opposite angle of the bay, and Mr Douglas just employed himself like any of the rest of us—in fishing and mending his nets, and such like. Jeanie was now a happy woman, for she had a companion and an equal, and indeed a superior; for Mr Douglas had seen the world, and could while away the time in discoursing of foreign lands, among strange people and unknown tongues. And Jeanie listened and listened, and thought her husband the first of mankind. His pleasure was her pleasure—his sorrow was her sorrow—and his bare word was her law. One day, about two weeks ago, she appeared dull and dispirited, and complained of the headache, on which Mr Douglas advised her to go to bed, and rest herself, which she said she would do; and having some business in the village, he went out. On coming back, however, in the forenoon, he found her just in the same spot, leaning her head on her hand, but she told him she was better, and that it was nothing at all. He then began to get his nets ready, saying he was going out with some lads of the village to the deep-sea fishing, and would be back the next day.

"She looked at him long and strangely, as if wondering at what he was doing, and understanding not anything that was going on. But finally when he came to kiss her, and bid her good-bye, she threw her arms round him, and when he would have gone, she held him fast—but still she said nothing.

"'Stay with me today!' she said at last;—'just this one night—it is not much to ask—and tomorrow I will not be your hindrance a moment.'

"But Mr Douglas was vexed at such folly, and she could answer nothing better to his questions, than that a thought had come into her head, and she could not help it. So he was resolved to go, and he kissed her, and threw his nets on his shoulder and went away. For some minutes after, Jeanie stood just on the spot, looking at the door where he had gone out, and then began to tremble all over like the leaf of a tree; at length, coming to herself with a start, she knelt down on both knees, and throwing back her hair from over her forehead, turned her face up towards heaven, and prayed with a loud voice to the Almighty, 'that she might still have her husband in her arms that night.' For some moments she remained motionless and silent, in the same attitude, till at length a sort of brightness, resembling a calm smile, passed over her countenance. She then went as usual about her household affairs, and appeared as tranquil and happy as if nothing had happened.

"Now the weather was fine and calm in the morning, but towards the afternoon, it came on to blow, the wind increased, till towards night it blew as hard a gale as we have seen in these parts for a long time; the ships out there at the tail of the bank, were driven from their moorings and two of them stranded on their beam-ends, on the other side; and as the night came on, in darkness and thunder, it was a scene that might cow even the hearts that had been brought up on the water. There was a sad lamenting and murmuring then among the womenfolk—especially them that were kith or kin to the lads on the sea; and they went to one another's house in the midst of the storm and rain, as if searching for hope and comfort. But there was one that stirred not from her home, and who felt no terror at the shrieking of the night-storm—and that was the wife of Mr Douglas. She sometimes, indeed, listened to the howling of the sea, and starting, would lay down her work for a moment; but then, she remembered the prayer she had prayed to Him, who says to the roaring water, 'Be still,' and they are still. So her soul was comforted, and she said to herself, 'God is not a man that He can lie,' and she rested on this assurance as on a rock, and laughed to scorn the trembling of her woman's bosom. Then she got up and put the room in order, and placed her husband's shoes to air at the fireside; and stirred up the fuel, and drew in the armchair for her weary and stormbeaten mariner. Then would she listen at the door, and look out into the night for his coming, but could hear no sound, save the voice of the waters. She then went in again, and walked to and fro in the room with a restless step, but an unblanched cheek. At last, the neighbours came to her house, knowing that her husband was one of them that had gone out that day, and told her they were going to walk down to the Clough, to try if they could not hear some news of the boats. So she went with them, and we walked all together along the road, it might be some twenty or thirty of us; but it was remarked that she came forth with her head uncovered, and in her usual raiment of white, like a bride to the altar. And as we passed along, it must have been a strange sight to see so many pale faces, by the red glare of the torches they carried, and to hear so many human wailings, filling up the pauses of the storm; but at the head of our melancholy procession, there was a calm heart and a firm step, and they were Jeanie's. Sometimes, indeed, she would look back, and strange thought would crowd into her mind; and once she was heard to mutter—if her prayer had but saved her husband, to bind some other innocent victim on the mysterious altar of wrath. But now as we drew near the rock where the lighthouse is built, sounds were heard distinctly on the shore, and we waved the torches in the air, and gave a great shout, which was answered by known voices—for they were some of our own people, and our journey was at an end. A number of us then went on before, and groped our way among the rocks, as well as we could for the darkness; but a woeful tale met our ears; for one of the boats had been shattered to pieces, while endeavouring to land there—and when we went down, they were just dragging the body of a comrade, stiff and stark, from the sea. When the women behind heard it, there was a terrible cry of dismay, for no one knew but it might have been her own brother or son. There was one, however, who stood calm, and unmoved by the side of the dead body. She spoke some words of holy comfort to the women, and they were silent at her voice. She then stepped lightly forward, and took a torch from the trembling hand that held it, and bent down with it beside the corpse. As the light fell one moment on her own fair face, it showed no sign of womanish failing. A bright and lovely bloom glowed on her cheek, and a Heavenly lustre burned in her eye; and as she knelt there, her long dark hair floating far on the storm, there was that in her look which drew the gaze even of that terrified group from the object of their doubt and dread. The next moment, the light streamed on the face of the dead—the torch dropped from her hand—and she fell on the dead body of her husband.

"*Her prayer was granted.* She held her husband in her arms that night, and although no struggles of parting life were heard or seen, she died on his breast."

Mainsail (editor): *Fifty Famous Sea Stories*, London 1961
By permission of the publishers, Burke Publishing Co Ltd

VOCABULARY. *bay*: part of the sea in a curve on the shore — *resort*: go to — *thither*: (old use) to that place — *summit*: highest point — *precipitous*: very steep — *discourse*: (old use) talk or conversation — *authentic*: genuine; true — *preamble*: introduction — *disband*: break up and send home — *board*: supply of meals — *dispirited*: discouraged; depressed — *vex*: annoy; trouble — *folly*: stupid conduct — *countenance*: face — *gale*: strong wind — *tail*: end part of anything — *moorings*: cables etc. by which a ship is fastened — *strand on their beam-ends*: run aground, lying on their broadside in a state of complete capsize — *kith and kin*: friends and relations — *shriek*: scream — *scorn*: look down on, despise — *bosom*: breast — *air*: dry — *fuel*: material for burning — *unblanched*: not white or pale — *raiment*: clothing — *glare*: dazzling light — *torch*: piece of wood used as a flaming light — *wail*: cry or moan for sorrow — *victim*: person who suffers — *wrath* [rɔθ]: violent anger — *grope*: search by feeling — *woeful*: sorrowful — *shatter*: break in pieces — *stark*: stiff, rigid — *dismay*: fright or alarm — *corpse*: dead body of a human being — *failing*: weakness — *bloom*: rosy colour — *lustre*: brightness — *parting*: going away.

115. Paving the Way for Pearl Harbour

Ruth Kuehn belonged to a family of spies who lived at Hawaii from 1935 to 1941, and whose signals and information assisted the Japanese in their attack on the American fleet at Pearl Harbour on 7 December, 1941, an act of aggression which brought the Americans into the Second World War. By her own claim Ruth was the master-spy and no doubt she can claim the major credit for what was unquestionably a big espionage success.

Her stepfather was Dr Bernard Julius Otto Kuehn, who had served in the German Navy in the First World War, then went into medicine without any great success. He was an early member of the Nazi Party and became a member of the German Security Service, when he was uprooted and sent to the other side of the world by the Party. There was a wife, Friedel, and two sons, one of whom was a stormtrooper.

This family was sent to Japan ostensibly to learn the language of the country which was to become Germany's most important ally. In Japan, however, the Kuehns suddenly found themselves wealthy. They had had an "inheritance" and in 1935 they arrived in the Hawaiian Islands as substantial citizens who had arrived for a long stay. They bought property and Dr Kuehn claimed to be a professor of anthropology who had come to study the influence of the Japanese people upon Polynesian culture. A cultivated and charming German family they were welcomed in the islands.

Ruth became particularly popular. The American Pacific Fleet was stationed there and its officers found the pretty German girl with her delightful accent a great attraction. The women of the island community liked her too. The Kuehns had a fine home and gave an impression of culture and wealth. In three years $ 70,000 was received into their bank account in Honolulu, and occasionally Mrs Kuehn went to Japan and came back with wads of money. In return for this Kuehn was of course supplying Tokyo (carbon copy for Berlin) with an endless stream of naval information.

When war broke out in Europe, the naval situation in the Pacific became of increasing interest to Tokyo, where the government had already decided in principle to join in on the side of their Axis ally. In 1941 Hitler invaded Russia, and, with the Soviet Union's attention fully occupied in the West, Japan's main target now became South-east Asia, to subdue which they knew that they had to neutralize the American Pacific Fleet. The Pearl Harbour attack was the brain-child of Admiral Yamamoto, C. in C. of the Japanese Navy.

In order to be most effective, the attack upon the American fleet must be made at a time when its main units were in Pearl Harbour. It was for the purpose of obtaining this information that Ruth Kuehn opened her celebrated beauty parlour which catered for the wives of the American fleet, whose chatter provided the ever-listening Ruth and her mother Friedel with much of the information the Japanese needed. It was only natural that these women whose lives revolved around the movement in and out of port of their husbands should supply just those titbits of information which the Japanese experts in Tokyo required to assess American naval intentions, as well as the movement of the individual ships.

It should be remembered that America was not at war at that time, and most Americans did not think that they would enter the war. Nor did they suspect that Japan harboured any evil intentions towards them. There was not therefore a very high standard of security at Pearl Harbour.

Meanwhile Dr Kuehn regularly took his ten-year-old son along the fortified part of Pearl Harbour where the warships were moored, and the boy rapidly made friends with the American sailors, who can never resist children. The boy was soon being shown over the ships and the sailors talked freely about where they were going and what they were doing.

Kuehn bought a house at Kalamar on Lanakai Bay on the windward side of Oahu. The house was called "Kalamar", and in its steeply sloping roof was a prominent dormer window, which could be seen for miles out to sea. From this Ruth made regular reports by signal to Japanese submarines, using a crude but effective code devised by her father. Lights burning in the window at certain hours meant different things, and in the daytime signals were made by pieces of linen lying on the beach.

By November, 1941, Tokyo was fully resolved on war and Yamamoto was at sea with his task force of thirty-one warships waiting for the right moment to strike at Pearl Harbour. On Saturday, 6 December, Tokyo were most insistent about the precise number and types of ships at Pearl Harbour, and Ruth Kuehn was able to give them just the answer they wanted. No less than nine battleships were moored in pairs in the harbour with their crews on week-end leave. These great ships tied up close together, and, as a class of ship notoriously vulnerable to air attack, could not have been placed more conveniently for Tokyo's purpose. After a further assurance of the Kuehns that there were no captive balloons over the fleet, the order was given for the task force to strike at dawn on the seventh.

The attack on Pearl Harbour was a sensational—and for the Americans disastrous—success. Two battleships were sunk, three disabled, three heavily damaged, and there was extensive damage and destruction to cruisers, destroyers and aircraft. Three thousand men, mostly sailors, died in the attack, which was carried out by 350 bombers from carriers steaming 200 miles to the north of Hawaii.

It was said that Ruth Kuehn guided the bombers by means of torch signals from the famous dormer window at Kalamar, but no one can believe that the Japanese pilots were so inefficient that they needed any guidance to an obvious and well-marked target.

The Kuehns were all arrested before they could get away. Dr Kuehn was sentenced to be shot, but the sentence was commuted to fifty years' imprisonment, of which he served only four. He was deported in 1946. Ruth and her mother were not even sent to prison but were merely interned until the end of the war when they were repatriated to Germany.

There has been some interesting speculation in sophisticated American espionage circles about the attack on Pearl Harbour. The effect of this is to belittle the Kuehn espionage, for the somewhat chilling suggestion has been made that the White House deliberately allowed the attack to take place, knowing that it was the only way in which reluctant America could be goaded into the war which the White House knew they would have to enter if the world was to be saved from Nazi-Nippon domination. The attack on Hawaii was the only thing which could unite America against the Axis, and it is thought that the event was a not unwelcome one in Washington. The loss of ships and lives is regarded as a strategic sacrifice made for the object of the final victory of which there was no doubt once America was in the war.

This theory ignores the obvious fact that, if this was the thinking in the White House, the Navy could still have been prepared for the expected attack, which it was not, and even repulsed it, for the attack itself would have been the desired *casus belli.*

On the other hand, considering the enormity of the Pearl Harbour disaster, and the part she played, apparently, in bringing it about, it was surely strange that Ruth Kuehn got off so lightly, when so many spies were executed for accomplishing for less.

Charles Franklin: *Spies of the Twentieth Century,* London 1967
By permission of the publishers, Odhams Books

VOCABULARY. *pave the way for*: prepare the way for — *Pearl Harbour*: seaport, Oahu Island, Hawaiian Islands, U. S. Naval base — *espionage*: spying, spy-work — *stormtrooper*: member of a Nazi semi-military organization — *inheritance*: that which one gets when a relative dies — *substantial*: wealthy — *anthropology*: science of man — *Polynesia*: small islands in Pacific Ocean east of Australia — *wad*: bunch of bank-notes — *carbon copy*: copy made with carbon paper "Durchschlag" — *Axis*: pact between Germany and Italy — *target*: mark to fire at — *C.-in-C.*: Commander-in-Chief — *cater for*: supply what is wanted — *titbit*: choice bit of news — *assess*: fix or decide the amount of — *moor*: fasten a ship by means of cables etc. — *windward*: in the direction from which the wind is blowing — *dormer window*: window built from a sloping roof "Dachfenster" — *task force*: specially organized unit — *captive balloon*: held by rope from ground "Fesselballon" — *disable*: put out of action — *aircraft carrier*: ship that serves as a base for aeroplanes — *torch*: electric hand-light and battery — *commute*: change a punishment for one less severe — *repatriate*: send back to his own country — *sophisticated*: worldly-wise — *goad*: urge on — *casus belli*: act justifying war.

116. 'Kim' Philby—Double Agent

Kim Philby was born on 31 December 1911 in Ambala in the Punjab province of India, where his father was assistant commissioner. In the early 1930s Kim Philby, the shy freshman at Cambridge, soon became a participant in the left-wing circles which dominated political discussions at Trinity. The Depression, the mass unemployment, the hunger marches, seemed overwhelming proof that the capitalist system and democratic society had become rotten at the core.

Philby's small circle of friends was suddenly and greatly enlivened by the arrival of a boy from Eton, Guy Francis de Moncy Burgess, son of a distinguished Royal Navy Officer. The old Etonian proclaimed almost on the day of his arrival, very loudly and firmly, that he was a Marxist; that he hated the rotten capitalist society and every bloody convention it stood for. He radiated unlimited energy and was a conversationalist far beyond his youthful age.

A year after Guy Burgess's spectacular appearance at Trinity, destiny sent the third member of the future spy ring to Cambridge. Donald Maclean is the tragic figure in the conspiracy of the three men who built one of the most effective and fantastic of Moscow's spy rings.

The Unholy Trinity, once formed, grew into the most dangerous conspiracy of post-war history.

By the spring of 1933, there is evidence from various sources that Kim Philby was working for the Communists, but did not, for good reasons, become a card-bearing member of the British Communist party. In 1939 he had gone to Berlin for *The Times*. His reporting from Berlin for *The Times* was brilliant. Probably, too, he gathered valuable information from his German friends for Moscow.

In 1940 Guy Burgess proudly informed Philby that he held a job with a secret service department. A few months later the chiefs of the Secret Intelligence Service welcomed Kim Philby into one of their departments.

It is astonishing that two Communist agents were able to infiltrate the British secret service to such a degree. They remained for more than a decade its trusted officials, and one of them, Kim Philby, rose to a top appointment as chief liaison officer to the United States Central Intelligence Agency. All the time they supplied Soviet espionage with closely guarded secrets. How was this possible? Kim Philby and Guy Burgess had supplied information of extreme value at two critical moments of the war.

In 1940 Burgess had been instrumental in causing the capture by MI 15 of two Nazi agents who had communicated to the Germans messages exchanged between Winston Churchill and President Roosevelt. One was caught inside the United States Embassy in London. Philby had put Secret Intelligence Service in touch with a Russian-run espionage network in Switzerland, which for several years was the most efficient in Europe, and which had succeeded in penetrating Hitler's High Command and German military intelligence.

The exact date of Maclean's betrayal cannot, of course, be ascertained. But it is probable that he had come to an understanding with Philby and Burgess sometime early in 1944. In the Spring of 1944, Donald Maclean began to make inquiries with his superiors at the Foreign Office about an appointment to the embassy in Washington. At the end of 1946, he was appointed British joint-secretary of the Combined Policy Committee on Atomic Energy. Never in the history of espionage had an infiltration succeeded so completely. Not only did Donald Maclean attend their meetings but as a joint secretary he handled the minutes of the Committee and all documents from its discussions. He was able to copy them at will and convey them to his Soviet contacts.

In 1949 Philby was given the rank of First Secretary in the Diplomatic Service and told that he would be posted to the Washington embassy as a link-man to the director of Central Intelligence Agency in the USA.

In July 1950, with Philby's help, Guy Burgess was given the acting rank of Second Secretary and sent to the Washington embassy to fill the post of assistant to Kim Philby.

Thus all members of the Unholy Trinity served in Washington at one time or another—to the greater glory of Soviet espionage and with disastrous effects for the Western world.

In February 1951, when Philby returned to Washington, he learned that the name at the top of the list of the CIA investigations was that of Donald Maclean. Burgess had got himself into trouble in Washington. Philby had little doubt that if Burgess, who had many enemies, were run in, he would talk and talk about him, Kim Philby, too. Maclean would just collapse and confess. There was only one solution: they had to disappear quickly. Philby told Burgess of the looming danger. He was to go to Russia and take Maclean with him.

On Friday, 25 May 1951, ad midnight, they boarded the cross-channel excursion steamer *Falaise* and arrived in St Malo on Saturday at 9 a. m. From the moment they went ashore, the trail of the two men dried up almost completely. On 7 June the *Daily Express* gave the public a sensational scoop:

Two British Diplomats Missing
They are believed to have left London with the intention of getting to Moscow.

There was no evidence which could connect Philby with the missing diplomats, but he had to resign because of his long association with Burgess. Eventually, an amazing secret 'trial' was staged in the summer of 1952 in the conference room at the MI 15 building. However, Philby must have satisfied the assembled spy masters and lawyers, because he soon afterwards left London again for Spain.

In June 1956 the Editor of *The Observer* decided to engage Philby as a regular contributor, and the Editor of *The Economist* agreed to pay Philby £ 200 a year plus expenses for contributing regular reports from Beirut.

The beginning of the end was rapidly approaching. Shortly before Christmas in 1962 two senior SIS officers arrived in Beirut. They had come to interrogate Philby and confront him with the evidence of his prolonged treachery. The evidence came mainly from a Soviet defector, Dolnytsin, who had come over to the Americans in West Berlin in March 1962. Dolnytsin had brought out a file of secret documents from which evidence of Kim Philby's work for Soviet espionage emerged with terrifying clarity.

For several weeks a battle of wits ensued between Philby and the emissaries who, by appealing to his conscience and also by threats that he could be taken by force, were trying to persuade him to go with them to London. But Philby knew that they would not stage a kidnapping, so he refused, saying that he must think carefully about it, not so much for his own sake but for the sake of his wife and children.

On 23 January 1963 Philby and his wife were invited to dinner. When he did not return home by 8 p. m., Mrs Philby decided to go to the party alone hoping that he would arrive there a little later. On that evening of Wednesday, 23 January 1963, in pouring rain, Kim Philby went to the harbour of Beirut and boarded a Polish cargo ship. She sailed at dawn for Odessa.

Kim Philby, the archtraitor of the Unholy Trinity, prospered after his escape. He is also probably the only one of the three who found happiness in Russia.

I wonder whether Philby ever remembers Kipling's description of a boy: "Kim—a poor white of the very poorest."

E. H. Cookridge: *The Third Man,* London 1968,
Arthur Barker Ltd (publishers)
By permission of the author

VOCABULARY. *commissioner*: high official — *Trinity*: Trinity college (date of foundation: 1546); a group of three (e.g. The Father, the Son, and the Holy Ghost) — *depression*: time when business is less active — *radiate*: send out — *spectacular*: making a great show — *liaison-officer*: keeping two allies in touch with each other — *instrumental*: helpful — *embassy*: residence of an ambassador — *betrayal*: the act of giving away or selling to the enemy — *link-man*: go-between; middleman — *loom*: appear in a threatening way — *scoop*: exciting piece of news which one newspaper prints before other papers have heard about it — *stage*: arrange to take place dramatically — *defector*: giving up one's beliefs or faith; apostate "Abtrünniger" — *emissary*: person sent on an underhand mission — *kidnap*: carry off a human being by force — *cargo*: a ship's load — *archtraitor*: chief traitor — "*Kim*": one of Rudyard Kipling's novels. Kipling, author and poet, born in Bombay (1865—1936).

117. The Rosenbergs

The frank and uncomplicated American mind was wounded and outraged to discover in the 1950s that the accommodation which Stalin had made with them during the war was merely a stepping stone in his world-wide conspiracy to destroy everything that America stood for. The Americans discovered, as all the world discovered, that the Communist movement was more of a conspiracy than a political party, and in America the conspiracy was in particular directed against the safety of the state.

Julius Rosenberg was born in New York's East Side in 1918, the son of Polish-Jewish immigrants. Ethel Greenglass was also a product of the New York slums. Julius was more impressed by her labour-rousing record than any physical charms she possessed. She was older than he—twenty-one to his eighteen—and from that moment until the end in Sing Sing death house seventeen years later she was the dominant personality.

Ethel's brother David joined the Young Communist League at the urging of his sister and brother-in-law, though David was never an enthusiastic convert to the cause.

Julius and Ethel's whole life revolved around the Party, and like good Communists they were obedient and subservient to its every wish. They wanted ardently to help the Soviet cause underground and were eager to get into espionage.

Meanwhile David Greenglass had joined the Army, and after training was posted as a machinist to an installation at Los Alamos in New Mexico. David did not know what this project was, except that it was Top Secret. Despite his Communist connexion he was reluctant to spy. But, if he was not devoted to the Party, he was certainly devoted to Julius and Ethel, whom he greatly admired. Both David and his wife Ruth were persuaded to agree to the spying, and during 1945 young Greenglass provided the Russians with a steady stream of vital information from Los Alamos which included details of the early atomic bombs.

In 1945 the U. S. Army Intelligence found out that Julius Rosenberg was a Communist and sacked him from his comfortable job in the Signals Corps.

In 1949, Harry Gold, another spy, admitted his guilt and made a full confession to the F. B. I. which implicated David Greenglass. Now David was in a fearful position. He loved his wife, Ruth, who was ill. He would go to the electric chair and she would get a long term of imprisonment. So he had to choose between his sister and his wife. David made a bargain with the F. B. I.—a bargain which was kept. He would give the vital evidence which would condemn the Rosenbergs providing he escaped with a prison sentence and no charge at all was made against his wife.

David told his questioners that he gave secret information about the inside working of the first atomic bombs to Harry Gold and Julius and Ethel Rosenberg.

The Rosenbergs were accused under the Espionage Act of 1917, and David and Ruth Greenglass were the principal witnesses against them.

Obedient to the Party edict, the Rosenbergs flatly denied everything. To Communism it was a gift more precious than all their espionage had been. Such martyrs are worth their weight in gold—only when dead, of course.

The jury retired on the afternoon of 4 April, 1953. They deliberated all night, and by eleven on the following morning they found the defendants guilty as charged. The following day, 6 April, Judge Kaufman sentenced the Rosenbergs to death, telling them that they had committed a crime worse than murder, for by their action they had given the Russians the atomic bomb years before they could otherwise have developed it.

The Rosenbergs stood side by side as they were sentenced to death, ashen-faced, unable perhaps to believe what was happening.

There were twenty-six actions for appeals and stays of execution, and the affair dragged wretchedly into 1953. Pleas for clemency came from all over the world, from the Pope, the French President, the American Ambassador in Paris. But the American Government was adamant. Eisenhower, the old warrior, turned a deaf ear and did not exercise his supreme power. . . .

At Sing Sing the Rosenbergs took their last agonizing farewell of their children. It was a painful scene, from which the children had to be removed screaming.

With what courage remained to them after their ordeal, the Rosenbergs prepared themselves for the death which they could avoid by a full confession. No one can know the agony of these hours. But they did not waver.

They emerged for the final and dreadful act in the limelight with a blazing courage. Three reporters witnessed their execution on the evening of 19 June, 1953.

Julius was the first to come into the death-chamber—"ashen and numb with terror"—preceded by the Jewish chaplain chanting: "The Lord is my Shepherd, I shall not want."

Julius stumbled into the electric chair, assisted by two guards, who strapped him in and adjusted the electrodes.

As the two-thousand-volt current hit the condemned man, his body leaped and writhed in the containing straps. He was given three seconds at two thousand volts and further shocks at five hundred volts. Then the current was switched off and the prison doctor stepped forward, pulled up his shirt and applied the stethoscope to his chest.

"I pronounce this man dead," he said.

Rosenberg's body was removed from the chair, put on a trolley and wheeled out of the death-house, while an attendant wiped the seat with a dark brown sponge.

They knew all along who was the weaker one. Ethel Rosenberg had the firmest tread in the grim little procession from her cell. As she passed Julius's empty cell she said: "We are the first victims of American fascism."

They gave her the Fifteenth Psalm to send her on her way to whatever awaited her.

As she came into the death-chamber it was observed that her face was frozen into a strange smile.

Ethel bade a quick farewell to the two wardresses who then fled from the death-room, dabbing their eyes. Ethel walked serenely to the chair and sat in it, "as though taking a seat in the bus."

As the guards strapped her in, she looked above the reporters' heads, and they were awed by her composure and the expression of bliss upon her face.

The chaplain was now giving her the Thirty-first Psalm. "Have mercy upon me, O Lord, for I am in trouble . . ."

The hood was shut over her head, and the current was switched on. Again the electricity crackled, the body leaped against the straps and the smoke issued upwards. After three shocks, the doctor went forward with his stethoscope.

There was a terrible pause as he bent over her. Then he said in a ragged voice: "This woman is still alive."

In the death-room there was a horrible silence. Smoke wisped up from the still figure in the chair.

The executioner came out of his cubby-hole, puzzled, disturbed, scratching his head as he looked at his victim who refused to die according to the rules.

"Want another?" he asked the doctor, who nodded dumbly.

They had to give Ethel two more shocks before the doctor finally declared her dead. It took four minutes and thirty seonds to kill her. Julius succumbed in two minutes forty-five seconds.

On that night nearly every United States Embassy in Europe had to be given police protection, but in Nashville, Tennessee, a fiery cross was lit by the Ku Klux Klan outside the house of a lawyer who had defended the Rosenbergs.

The echoes of the case were a long time dying. Perhaps they never will die completely.

Charles Franklin: *World-Famous Trials,* London 1966
By permission of the publishers, Odhams Books

VOCABULARY. *conspiracy*: coming together for an evil purpose — *convert*: one who has changed his opinion — *subservient*: weak-willed; servile — *espionage*: spy-work, spying — *reluctant*: unwilling — *F. B. I.*: Federal Bureau of Investigation — *Signals Corps*: (Am.) "Fernmeldetruppe" — *martyr*: one who undergoes death or suffering for any great cause — *ashen*: pale, like the colour of ashes — *stay*: delay; postponement — *clemency*: readiness to forgive — *adamant*: hard (like a diamond); unwilling to give way — *agony*: great pain; *agonize*: cause great pain — *waver*: to be unsteady — *in the limelight*: receiving great publicity — *numb*: without power to feel or move — *electrode*: conductor through which electricity enters — *writhe*: twist the body in pain — *stethoscope*: instrument used by doctors for listening to sounds in the body — *trolley*: handcart; small truck — *wardress*: woman acting as guard in a prison — *dab*: touch lightly or gently — *ragged*: rough — *cubby-hole*: comfortable place — *dumb*: unable to speak — *succumb*: to yield, die — *Ku Klux Klan*: secret organization in U. S. to combat alien influences.

118. William Joyce

The trial of William Joyce was a remarkable event in the history of English criminal procedure. It seemed that the law was somewhat stretched in order to hang him.

Although a number of traitors broadcast for the enemy during the Second

World War, William Joyce, nicknamed Lord Haw-Haw, whose voice became known to millions of English people who listened to Hamburg radio during the war, was the first, the most famous, and the most effective. His voice, with its curious, rasping and compelling quality, was unforgettable. He was convincing, persuasive, and far more demoralizing than the authorities admitted at the time, or have admitted since. He was perhaps Hitler's most effective weapon of propaganda.

Joyce was of Irish extraction, but his father, Michael Joyce, was a naturalized American, and Joyce was born in New York in 1906. In 1909 the family returned to Ireland. William Joyce did well at school and went to London University where he took a first-class honours degree in English.

His father had written to say that though William was born in the United States, the family were never American citizens. Why Michael Joyce told this lie is not clear, but it seems that when the family returned to the British Isles they found their American status an inconvenience.

When he was seventeen young Joyce joined the British Fascist Party, but he was quick to realize that Mosley, leader of the British Union of Fascists, would never be taken seriously, as Hitler and Mussolini had been, so he founded his own British National Socialist League, a small but vigorous band of pro-Nazis. Joyce himself was regarded by his followers as a great leader and prophet. He was a man of some intellectual activity with a brash charm and an amusing manner. He was also a lover of violence and frequently became involved in brawls.

In 1933 he applied for and obtained a British passport, wrongly describing himself as a British subject by birth, an illegality which was to have fatal consequences for him later. This passport was renewed in 1939.

By 27 August, 1939, Joyce had already decided to throw in his lot with the Nazis in the war which was now inevitable. Britain declared war on Germany on 3 September and Joyce immediately joined the German radio service as an announcer in English.

Joyce's broadcasts to England made an instant impression, and he was widely listened to.

In September, 1940, Joyce had been granted German nationality. In 1942 he became chief English commentator on the German radio and in 1944 Hitler awarded him the War Service Cross, a civilian award, for his services to propaganda. But by the late spring of 1945 the Nazi dream was over. Hitler was dead in the Berlin bunker, his armies collapsed.

Joyce made his last broadcast from Hamburg on 30 April, 1945, during which he bitterly admitted German defeat and prophesied the coming Cold

War. "Britain's victories are barren," he concluded. "They leave her poor; they leave her people hungry; they leave her bereft of the markets and wealth she possessed six years ago. ... I ask you earnestly, can Britain survive? I am profoundly convinced that without Germany she cannot."

Within a few weeks after Joyce's arrest, the Treason Act, 1945, was hurried through the Houses of Parliament, and Joyce was not brought to England until it had become law. The Treason Act, 1945 altered the judicial procedure so that treason committed abroad could be tried in the same manner as any other capital offence, such as murder. Equating treason with murder and exacting the same penalty for it is a practice open to dispute.

But Joyce's solicitors discovered that Joyce was not a British subject and never had been. He was an American who had later become a German citizen.

It would surely be a revolutionary principle of justice to convict an alien for a treason committed against this country when he was living abroad. On that principle surely all our enemies were guilty of treason—a ridiculous proposition.

This was the opinion held by many people in England at the time. It was believed that Joyce was wrongly convicted and hanged. He was an American and therefore could not be guilty of treason against England.

But the core of the English law lies in the following maxim: "Protection draws allegiance, as allegiance draws protection." The point the prosecution made was that, although Michael Joyce's children, including William, were Americans by birth, William had fraudulently obtained a passport and thus, it was claimed, he owed allegiance.

That he had a defence at all was a surprise to William Joyce who was convinced that he was guilty of treason and was quite resigned to being hanged.

The trial began at the Old Bailey on 17 September, 1945. Joyce was charged with high treason between 18 September, 1939, and 29 May, 1945, in the realm of Germany, contrary to the Treason Act of 1951. He pleaded not guilty.

Mr G. O. Slade, Joyce's counsel, submitted that as his client was not a British subject, there was no case against him. A man cannot make himself a British subject by declaring himself to be one. The defence called six witnesses whose evidence incontestably established Joyce's American nationality.

The jury found Joyce guilty after twenty minutes' deliberation and the Judge sentenced him to death.

Whatever might be said of Joyce, there is no doubt as to his sincerity and intellectual honesty.

Joyce elected to become a Nazi. For him it was a simple intellectual choice. He believed in violence and authoritarianism and he believed in it to the end. He never wavered. He never went back, never asked for mercy. He died bravely and with dignity, pausing on the way to the scaffold to look down at his trembling knees with a calm and cynical smile.

There was a widespread feeling among the public that revenge had been taken upon Joyce and that his case had been decided more by emotion than by law. What useful purpose was served by his execution? Can treason in broadcasting be compared with treachery in the field?

Charles Franklin: *World-Famous Trials,* London 1966
By permission of the publishers, Odhams Books

VOCABULARY. *trial*: examination before a judge (and jury) — *rasping*: rough and unpleasant — *extraction*: one's descent — *naturalize*: give rights of citizenship — *inconvenience*: trouble, discomfort — *Fascist*: patriotic movement — *brash*: (colloq.) rash, cheeky — *brawl*: quarrel — *award*: give or grant sth. — *barren*: unfruitful, not giving any profit — *bereft*: robbed of — *accost*: to go up to and speak to — *treason*: treachery to one's own country; disloyalty — *capital offence*: crime punishable by death — *equate*: consider as equal — *penalty*: punishment for breaking a law — *convict*: declare in a law-court that sb. is guilty of a crime — *alien*: foreigner — *proposition*: statement — *core*: heart or centre of a thing — *allegiance*: obedience; loyalty — *fraudulent*: dishonest — *realm* [relm]: kingdom, country — *counsel*: lawyer — *jury*: body of persons who have to decide the truth of a case before a judge — *waver*: become unsteady — *scaffold*: platform on which criminals are executed.

119. The Tomb of Tutankhamen

The modern city of Luxor stands on the eastern bank of the River Nile in the heart of Egypt. In an outcrop of limestone hills, separated from the river by a wall of grey cliffs, is the valley of the kings. It is a desolate place of barren rocks and patches of deep shadow in the bright sunshine. Yet once it probably contained more wealth than any other place on Earth.

Over a period of two hundred years, more than thirty kings were buried in the valley in this way. But in spite of all precautions, their tombs were ransacked.

Late in the nineteenth century, the story of the Valley of the Kings was pieced together by archaeologists. They had explored the inside of certain tombs, and they had found empty coffins and mummies. But they could only guess at the original contents of the tombs. Almost everything of value had gone.

From 1902 to 1914 more archaeologists were at work in the Valley. They also found empty tombs. One of them said, "I fear the Valley of the Kings is now exhausted."

Two men did not agree. One was Lord Carnarvon, whose hobby was Egyptian history, and the other was Howard Carter. Carter was an Englishman employed by the Egyptian Government. His job was to protect the relics in the Valley of the Kings from thieves.

Lord Carnarvon obtained permission to dig in the Valley and provided the money for Carter to equip a party of workmen. Carter made a large-scale map of the area. He divided this into sections and, as each section was inspected, he marked it off on the map.

Five years of digging produced hardly anything of value, and, in the summer of 1922, Carter was back in England to discuss progress with Lord Carnarvon.

"I am thinking of stopping this work," said Lord Carnarvon. "The cost is becoming too high."

"I still believe we shall find something," said Carter. "I believe there is at least one more tomb in the Valley—the tomb of a king named Tutankhamen."

"But where is this tomb?" asked Lord Carnarvon. "Haven't you been right through the Valley by now?"

Carter unrolled his map and spread it on the table before them. His marks showed that the whole Valley had been inspected apart from one small triangle.

"We have not dug there," said Carter. "Until we have dug this part of the Valley, we cannot be certain there is nothing left to find."

"Very well," said Lord Carnarvon. "I will provide the funds for just one more season's digging."

That autumn Carter left England for Egypt. On 28th October, he arrived at Luxor. Nine days later, Lord Carnarvon received a cable. It said: "Have made wonderful discovery in Valley. Magnificent tomb with seals intact. Recovered same for your arrival. Congratulations. Carter."

On 24th November, Lord Carnarvon, his daughter, Lady Evelyn Herbert, and Howard Carter approached the sealed tomb. Carter had found a flight of sixteen stone steps under the sand and rock chippings below the tomb of Rameses VI. They now proceeded down these steps and, at the foot, came to a doorway sealed with the cartouche of Tutankhamen.

Carter broke open the door. Beyond lay a dark passage filled with rubble. The workmen began shovelling this away. It took them two days. Then a second door was revealed, sealed and plastered. Carter made a hole in the top left-hand corner and thrust a metal rod through the hole. He felt nothing. He made the hole larger, thrust in a candle and peered after it.

For a long time, he stared into the hole. Behind him Lord Carnarvon waited anxiously. "Can you see anything?" he asked.

"Yes," replied Carter. "Wonderful things . . ."

By the flickering light of the candle, he could make out the shapes of statues and strange animals, and see everywhere the glint of gold.

Howard Carter had made the greatest single discovery ever made in Egypt. There are more than thirty royal tombs in the Valley of the Kings. This was the only one that had not been robbed. It had been sealed for more than 3000 years—from before the time of Moses.

Carefully and painstakingly, Carter inspected the tomb. He entered on a card the description of every article he found, however small, adding a neat sketch of it. He called expert photographers to the scene to photograph the discoveries. He took great care to see that nothing was lost or damaged. After inspection on the spot, the relics were taken out to the Cairo Museum.

After that first chamber seen by Carter through the hole in the door, others were discovered. The second was crammed with precious objects: caskets of wood plated with gold, ivory and semi-precious stones; rich clothing, jewelled weapons and ornaments of various kinds; ornamental couches; chairs, decorated chariots, and a beautiful throne.

Beyond this chamber was a third. When it was opened, the way was blocked by what seemed to be a wall of solid gold. This was the side of a large wooden shrine, covered with thin gold plate. Within this shrine was a second, smaller shrine of gilded wood; then a third and, finally, a fourth was discovered.

The fourth shrine contained the coffin of Tutankhamen, hidden in a chest of sarcophagus carved out of sandstone. The lid of this chest was raised for the first time in 3,000 years. In it was discovered a coffin of wood plated with gold and inset with red and blue jewels. Inside this coffin was a second—again plated with gold, and this time decorated with a face mask of the dead king. Within the second coffin was a third and last. This was made of solid gold and was so heavy that it took four men to lift it. The coffin was in the shape of a mummy bearing a portrait of Tutankhamen.

Yet another mask of solid gold was found on the mummy itself, inside this final coffin. The body was that of a youth aged seventeen or eighteen.

This was the boy king Tutankhamen, "Lord of Lords, King of the South and North, son of Re (the sun god)". He had been buried about 1,350 years before the birth of Christ.

Howard Carter worked on in the Valley of the Kings until 1928. With infinite care, he removed the treasures from the tomb and sent them to Cairo Museum.

Tutankhamen's body was replaced in the outer coffin. That was replaced in the sarcophagus, and the sarcophagus was returned to its place in the burial chamber. There it remains today and is seen each year by thousands of tourists who, during the cool season, stream across the plain from Luxor in taxis and buses.

Robert J. Hoare: *To the Ends of the Earth*, London 1966
By permission of the publishers, Ginn & Co Ltd

VOCABULARY. *tomb* [tuːm]: grave — *outcrop*: layer of rock which comes to the surface of the ground — *limestone*: kind of rock mainly composed of calcium carbonate "Kalkstein" — *patch*: small piece of ground — *barren*: unfruitful — *ransack*: plunder — *piece*: put together — *archaeologist*: one who studies ancient things, esp. ancient cities, buildings etc. — *coffin*: box for a dead body — *mummy*: dead body preserved by being treated with wax, spices etc. — *relic*: dead body — *scale*: measure; ratio of enlargement and reduction in map — *triangle*: three-cornered figure — *fund*: sum of money — *seal*: design stamped on material so that it cannot be secretly opened — *chip*: cut or break piece off — *Rameses* [ˈræmisiːz]: the name of several kings of Egypt — *cartouche*: oval ring containing hieroglyphic names and titles of Egyptian kings etc. — *rubble*: small, rough stone — *plaster*: cover with a mixture of lime, water and sand — *rod*: long, slender stick or bar — *candle*: wax stalk to give light — *peer*: look closely — *glint*: gleam or flash — *painstaking*: very careful — *damage*: harm — *cram*: press closely — *casket*: small case for holding jewels etc. — *plate*: cover with a coating of metal — *ivory*: hard, white substance which forms the tusks of elephants — *couch*: resting- or sleeping-place — *chariot*: carriage used for fighting — *shrine*: holy altar — *sarcophagus* [sɑːˈkɔfəgəs]: stone coffin — *carve*: make or shape by cutting — *lid*: cover of a container — *inset*: place in; insert — *mask*: cover for the face — *replace*: put sth. back.

120. Colonel Fawcett—The Lost Explorer

In the National Library of Brazil, in Rio de Janeiro, lies a faded manuscript known by the number 512. It bears the title: Historic Account of a large, hidden City of great age, without inhabitants, which was discovered in the year 1753.

In 1920, Lieutenant-Colonel P. H. Fawcett, a British explorer, came upon Manuscript 512. It meant a great deal to him.

Fawcett was thirty-nine years old and stood over six feet tall. For twenty years he had been an officer in the Royal Regiment of Artillery serving in Ceylon, Malta and Hong Kong. In his younger days he had been an all-round sportsman and he was still tremendously fit. He never smoked and he did not take alcoholic drinks.

Fawcett spent six years mapping parts of the Amazon Basin. He believed that, hidden somewhere there, must be traces of an old civilization. "Perhaps even some descendants of unknown races such as the Incas live there," he said.

His idea was not unreasonable. The Amazon Basin covers an area equal to the area of Europe. Of this vast area, only a small fraction had been explored.

Today, aeroplanes fly over the jungles and steamers sail 3000 miles up the Amazon into the heart of the country. But away from the river, the jungle is hard to penetrate. Even now, hundreds of thousands of square miles remain unknown to white men.

Manuscript 512 provided Fawcett with an extra piece of evidence. He called the city it mentioned "Z" and stated that he intended to find it.

In 1920 Fawcett headed into the tropical forests once more. He had only one companion, a young man named Felipe. They set out from Bahia (now Salvador) on the coast of Brazil and travelled westwards. At first, they passed plantations and ranches carved out of the jungle. But beyond the last plantation they entered jungle that was thick, trackless and gloomy.

Fawcett hoped to pick up information from Indians, but he never saw one. Yet all the time the two explorers must have been watched. They saw plenty of signs along the trail. These told them that savages had been there recently.

At one time, rain began to fall in a ceaseless downpour. They plodded on, soaked to the skin.

Much of the time Felipe grumbled. Each day he complained of some new ailment. Unlike Fawcett, he was not used to life in the wild.

It was a life to tax the hardiest of men. They were plagued by a variety of flies and ticks. At night, they sometimes had to pull 60 or 80 ticks from their bodies. Each of these inflicted a slight, irritating wound. These must not be scratched for, in such conditions, the slightest sore may easily become poisoned.

Once Fawcett saw a spider the size of a sparrow sitting in its web. But what he disliked most were the blood-sucking vampire bats. He said, "In the morning we woke to find our hammocks saturated with blood. Any part of our bodies touching the mosquito nets or sticking out of them were attacked."

The expedition did not seem to be successful. Yet Fawcett returned from it undismayed. He said, "I have learned a great deal. I am now sure I can find Z. But I want the right companions and the right organization."

It took Fawcett five years to obtain the right companions and the right organization. The two companions were his eldest son, Jack, who was twenty-two, and Raleigh Rimmell, an old schoolmate of Jack's. The organization depended upon money. Fawcett obtained this from various scientific societies and from a news agency. The story of the lost city of Z had received a great deal of publicity in newspapers in the United States.

Fawcett and the two young men left Cuyaba in April 1925. They set out with two Indian guides, two horses and eight mules. They intended to enter a stretch of unknown jungle between two rivers that flowed from the south into the Amazon—the Xingu and the Araguaya.

On 29th May, the little party were more than 350 miles to the north of Cuyaba. The Indians were afraid to travel any farther. Fawcett sent them back with the horses. The horses would not be able to survive in the jungle. Fawcett also sent back a letter to his wife. It showed that he was sure that he was going to reach the lost city. He wrote, "You need have no fear of failure ..."

Colonel Fawcett and his two companions were never seen again by any civilized person. No further message was received from them. After sending back their guides, they vanished.

In 1928, a newspaper company in the United States sent out an expedition to search for Fawcett. They followed the route he and his party had taken. A native chief told them about an old white man with two companions who had travelled into the jungle. But they found no definite clue as to what had happened to Fawcett.

Two years later, a newspaper reporter set out to follow in Fawcett's footsteps. He himself was never heard of again.

As time went by, contact with the savage tribes in the jungle improved slightly. From time to time stories were heard of an old white man living in the jungle. The legend persisted that somehow Fawcett had survived and was living with primitive Indians. Other expeditions set out in search of him. But they found little conclusive evidence.

In 1932, a Swiss trapper reported to the British Consul in Rio de Janeiro. He said he had met and spoken to a white man who was held prisoner by

Indians. Afterwards, the trapper set out alone to try and rescue the mysterious white prisoner. He, too, was never heard of again.

Up to the beginning of the Second World War, in 1939, the mystery of Colonel Fawcett's disappearance was often referred to in newspapers. When the war ended, the mystery still claimed attention.

In 1950, Colonel Fawcett's younger son, Brian, visited Brazil. In an effort to solve the mystery, he followed his father's trail into the jungle. From an aeroplane, he surveyed the area where his father had vanished. He returned with many problems unsolved. He said, "I believe there is a chance that my brother Jack may still be alive somewhere in the jungle."

In 1962, thirty-seven years after Colonel Fawcett disappeared, a programme on B. B. C. television recalled the mystery. By their own firesides in England, people were able to follow, through the camera, the route Fawcett had probably taken. They also heard the probable solution to the mystery.

In 1950, Señor Orlando Vilas Boas, one of the foremost experts on the Amazon Basin, was at the bedside of a dying Indian chief. This man made a confession. He said that, in a quarrel, he clubbed Fawcett and his two young companions to death.

But Brian Fawcett did not accept this solution to the mystery of his father's last expedition. For him, and for many others, the mystery lives on.

Robert J. Hoare: *To the Ends of the Earth,* London 1966
By permission of the publishers, Ginn & Co Ltd

VOCABULARY. *Brazil*: republic in South America — *fade*: lose colour — *map*: make a map of — *descendant*: one who has a certain person as a forefather — *head*: go straight for — *carve*: make or shape — *trackless*: without a path — *downpour*: heavy fall of rain — *plod*: travel slowly and steadily — *soak*: wet through and through — *grumble*: murmur with discontent — *ailment*: trouble, disease — *tax*: put a strain on — *plague*: annoy — *tick*: small insect that fastens itself on the skin and sucks blood "Zecke, Holzbock" — *sore*: wound — *sparrow*: small, dull-coloured bird — *vampire bat*: one of various kinds of bat found in S. A. which suck the blood of animals and sleeping persons — *hammock*: hanging bed of rope network — *saturate*: make very wet — *stick out*: stand out — *undismayed*: not terrified — *vanish*: go out of sight — *persist*: persevere — *conclusive*: deciding — *survey*: look over; inspect — *club*: beat with a heavy stick.

121. The Strange Story of the Abominable Snowman

In 1887, Colonel W. A. Waddell, an officer of the Indian Army, spent a period of leave climbing in the highest mountain chain in the world, the

Himalayas. He climbed above the snow-line, reaching a height of 16 000 feet, and there he came upon a curious set of footprints. They appeared to be those of a man of giant size with bare feet.

Colonel Waddell was accompanied by a number of Sherpa porters. He asked them about the footprints. "Who made them?"

The Sherpas answered nervously, "They were made by a yeti."

So, for the first time, someone from the western world heard about the yeti. They were strange creatures living high in the mountains. The name "yeti" means "unknown animal that lives in the rocky regions". It is used by the Sherpas of Nepal. But the people of Tibet have another name for the same creature. They call it "Metch Kangmi", which means "Abominable Snowman". This is the name it came to be known by in the western world.

From time to time, after the end of the nineteenth century, vague stories of the Abominable Snowman were told by travellers in the Himalayas. On 22nd September, 1921, another climber, Colonel C. K. Howard-Bury, came upon gigantic footprints in the snow at a height of 23 000 feet. He was a celebrated mountaineer. His story claimed a great deal of attention.

In Tibet, there are many monasteries high in the mountains. Sometimes one of the monks would come in with a warning: "Metch Kangmi are on the slopes close to the monastery." At once, all the doors would be locked. The monks would turn their prayer wheels and blow horns loudly. They believed that noise made the Snowmen go away.

In 1925, a German scientist claimed to have seen an Abominable Snowman in the Himalayas, in Tibet. He said, "He closely resembled a human being. He was walking upright, but stooped every now and again to pick a dwarf rhododendron."

In 1930, Frank Smythe, a famous British mountain climber, found strange tracks in the snow 16 000 feet up Kanchenjunga, the second highest mountain in the world. "Yeti! Yeti!" cried his two Sherpa porters fearfully.

Smythe took photographs of the tracks. In London, he showed the photographs to scientists at the Natural History Museum. The scientists said, "Those are the tracks of a bear."

As red bears are found in the Himalayas, what the scientists said should have put an end to talk about mysterious two-legged creatures. But people pointed out two things. Red bears never walk on their hind legs for more than a few steps. Also, the marks of claws can usually be seen on their footprints.

At this time, perhaps the most famous of all Himalayan mountain climbers, Eric Shipton, came upon strange tracks at 15 750 feet. His porters refused to go any farther. Shipton said, "I believe there is some foundation for these stories of the yeti."

During the Second World War of 1939—45, the mystery of the Abominable Snowman was forgotten. But, after the war, it claimed attention once more.

On 6th December, 1951, *The Times,* which is said to be the most serious newspaper in the world, published photographs showing strange footprints in the snow. The photographs had been taken in the Himalayas by Eric Shipton. The footprints were thought to belong to an Abominable Snowman.

A Sherpa described a yeti he had seen to Shipton. He was sure that the creature he saw was not a bear or a monkey.

In April 1952, members of a Swiss expedition to Mount Everest photographed more strange footprints in the snow.

Footprints made in melting snow soon grow larger. The giant footprints might be ordinary footprints made larger by the sun. In this case, then, who had made the ordinary footprints?

Red bears live in the forests and two kinds of monkeys. The red bear's spoor looks like a man's footprints. But neither bears nor monkeys can walk upright on two feet for more than fifty steps. Could they have made the yeti tracks? Some of these tracks have been followed for miles. Also, both bears and monkeys would be expected to leave in the snow the mark of a tail.

In 1954, the *Daily Mail* sent out an expedition to the Himalayas. Its job was to try to photograph or even capture an Abominable Snowman.

The expedition returned with many photographs of tracks in the snow, including some of footprints measuring 13 inches. But the expedition did not bring back an Abominable Snowman alive or dead, nor did it bring back a photograph of one.

Three years later, an expedition from the United States went out to try and solve the mystery. It brought back more photographs of footprints, but it did not bring back an Abominable Snowman, dead or alive, or even a photograph of one, either. In 1960, the mystery was still claiming much attention. A scientist at the University of London made another careful inspection of the photograph taken over ten years before by Eric Shipton. He said, "The owner of these footprints was a heavily-built two-legged creature, probably like the fossil Gigantopithecus." Gigantopithecus is one of the most mysterious fossils in the world. It is the name given to a creature like a man, eleven to twelve feet high. The only knowledge scientists have of this creature comes from a tooth, which was found by a Dutch scientist in a Hong Kong shop in 1934. No one knows where that tooth came from. No one knows whether the type of creature it came from still exists. Experts thought the creature might live somewhere in Central Asia, so it might still be in existence in the Himalayas, which are in Central Asia.

In 1960, Sir Edmund Hillary led a new expedition to the Himalayas. It, also, attempted to find out more about the Abominable Snowman.

He found the tracks of a fox or wild dog screened from the sun by rocks. He followed these tracks out into the sunshine and watched them grow as they melted. The result was a "perfect yeti track".

In the monastery at Pyngboche, there is preserved a relic. It is supposed to be the hand of a yeti. Scientists with Hillary inspected it, and they said it was probably a man's hand.

Three monasteries possess what are supposed to be yeti scalps. Hillary borrowed one and flew with it to Chicago, where he showed it to scientists. Afterwards it was examined by scientists in London and Paris. These experts all agreed that the relic was not a scalp at all. It had been moulded out of the skin of a kind of goat called a serow.

"The yeti is part of the mythology and tradition of the people who live in the Himalayas," said Sir Edmund. "Undoubtedly, it belongs to the field of mythology."

Robert J. Hoare: *To the Ends of the Earth*, London 1966
By permission of the publishers, Ginn & Co Ltd

VOCABULARY. *abominable*: hateful; disgusting — *footprint*: mark of a foot — *giant*: huge — *Sherpa*: one of a Himalayan people living on the borders of Nepal and Tibet — *yeti*: native (Sherpa) name for the Abominable Snowman — *monastery*: house for monks — *slope*: piece of rising or falling ground — *dwarf*: not growing to full height — *track*: mark left — *hind*: placed behind — *claw*: hooked nail of a beast or bird — *monkey*: animal somewhat resembling man — *melt*: become liquid by heat — *spoor*: footmarks or trail left by an animal — *fossil*: recognizable prehistoric animal or plant changed to rock — *relic*: sth. that has survived from the past — *scalp*: skin and hair of the top of the head — *mould*: give a shape or form to — *goat*: animal of the sheep family with horns and long hair — *mythology*: collection of old-time gods or heroes.

122. The Mate's Story

(The true story of the disaster which befell a sealing ship in March, 1898, as told by one of the survivors.)

The sealing steamer *Greenland*, when berthed in Glasgow harbour, became a vessel of more than usual interest. The terrible disaster which befell her crew in March, 1898 when, of some 150 men who were sent out on the ice to "pan" seals, almost a third lost their lives, excited a great deal of attention.

The *Greenland* was an ideal sealer. There was no new-fangled nonsense about her. A steamer, but with sails enough to make her independent of steam when on the fishing ground.

Ambrose Critch, the second mate, by birth a Newfoundlander, was the ideal of a sealing fisherman, and gave the impression, which is no doubt true, that he was more at home on the deck, or even on ice, than on a city's streets. Bronzed and weather-beaten, yet hardy and earnest, he spoke seriously, but without restraint, of the terrible three weeks spent on and among the ice off the coast of Newfoundland.

"You want to hear about the disaster?" he said to a visitor who boarded the *Greenland*. "I am not sure that I can tell the story very well. It is too terrible a story.

"We left St John's on the 10th of March; a Thursday, it was. There were, I think, 207 of us on board altogether. Steering N. N. E., we made 'The Funks' the following day. About 60 miles, maybe, N. E. of the island, we struck seals—on the 12th, I think—it was the Saturday, anyhow. We kept getting seals from then till the 20th—that was a Sunday, and, as perhaps you may know, we don't seal on Sundays.

"At three o'clock on Monday morning, Captain Barbour sent a watch out on the ice to kill and pan seals. At five he sent two other watches." (A watch generally consisted of from forty to fifty men, and to "pan" seals was to gather them into heaps on the ice floes, so that they could be taken to the ship more conveniently.)

"The men were on the ice all day," the mate continued. "About five o'clock at night the storm came on—snow and drift. We could hardly see across the ship. It was like that from five on Monday till three on Tuesday afternoon, and we knew nothing of the poor men who were blindly wandering —perhaps frozen—among the ice and water. We knew the storm had made an opening that they could not get across. The ship was thrown on her beam ends by the wind, and the coal and provisions and seals had to be shifted to right her.

"At three on Tuesday the weather was better, and at five three men were seen on the ice, trying to make for the ship. Those on board were sent to search for the rest. Boats were provisioned and sent out, and before night we had found about eighty of the men. They were frost-bitten, all of them, and some so badly injured that they had to be led on board. You see it was smooth ice, not the humpy, loose kind, on which the men could have built huts and sheltered themselves. So they could only stand or lie all the time. They were a mile or so from the ship.

"The men were in extremity, and could not have lasted much longer. We got no bodies on the Tuesday. On Wednesday the drift had cleared, and more searchers were sent out, and on that day many of the dead men were found. Captain Barbour had hoisted flags at half-mast and men from the *Diana* and the *Iceland*, two other sealers, were sent to help us. The bodies were found scattered all over the ice, in ones and twos and threes. Many of the men seemed to have been crawling. They would know of the open water that was between them and the ship, and in the blinding drift they would be afraid to walk. One man, who was found alive, was creeping away from the ship. He had lost his mittens, and he had no feeling in his hands.

"The searchers got out the small boats, and hauled them over the ice with ropes. When they found bodies, they put them into the boat and hauled them back to our ship. Our own men did not use boats; they made 'drays'—things like lorries, but without wheels—and hauled them over the ice. We found twenty-four bodies in all."

"Was that the total number lost?"

"Over twenty-four. They must have suffered terribly. I never saw such a storm. It was a wonder how men could have lived at all on the pans. Some of them that the survivors told of actually went mad, and thought the ship was near, and ran into the open water to reach her, and were drowned. There was water all around them, you know.

"There were two boys saved, who had spent fifty-two hours on the ice, in the storm. We found them on the Wednesday, when the storm was over. They had been alone for a while, but they were joined by one of the men, and the three kept together.

"One curious thing there was. It was not the big, hardy-looking men who lived through the storm on the ice. They died, and those who survived were the slight and weak-looking kind.

"The last body we got was found on the Friday, about two miles from the ship. We cruised about for a while, but gave up the search on Saturday, and made for Bay de Verde. The twenty-four bodies were on board here, and I made a pound—a big box, you know—along by this stanchion, and put them all in. I iced them—you have seen salmon iced, a row of fish and a fold of ice—to keep them till we should reach port. We left Bay de Verde on Sunday morning, and after an uneventful voyage, we got to St John's the same afternoon."

"And the bodies?"

"We saw them buried, of course. I had to take them out of the ice. When I put them in I had put tickets on them, so that we would know them again. No one of us knew them all, but among us we managed to find all their names. It was terrible work taking them out of the ice. The pound was one solid mass. I had to cut each body out in a square piece.

"It was an awful day in St John's when we arrived. Not many of the lost and dead men belonged there, but there were other ships out, and the folks were frightened. They knew of the disaster, because our captain had telegraphed from Bay de Verde. The Governor did all he could, and the members of council all took part in the work of providing for the suffering, and disposing of the dead. We buried them in the cemeteries of their different churches.

"A relief fund was started, and the Glasgow owners of the ship, as well as the agent in St John's, contributed handsomely. The crew all belonged to Newfoundland.

"About the seals? The voyage was abandoned when the disaster happened. It lasted three weeks. We had 14 500 seals on board, and we left as many on the ice as would have loaded the ship. We landed the seals on Tuesday at Harbour Grace, after the bodies were buried, and the ship stayed there until we took on board a cargo of oil and skins for Glasgow.

"You don't often have a sealer in your harbour, I daresay. No, I thought not. We had to come here because the vessel needed a new boiler. No, I don't think I can tell you more about the disaster. There is plenty more to tell, but somehow I can't tell it. It was terrible."

Mainsail (editor): *Fifty Famous Sea Stories*, London 1961
By permission of the publishers, Burke Publishing Co Ltd

VOCABULARY. *mate*: ship's officer below the captain — *befall*: happen — *berth*: fasten a ship in a suitable place at anchor — "*pan*": gather into heaps — *seal*: fish-eating animal valued for its fur "Seehund" — *new-fangled*: new and strange, but having no value — *Newfoundland*: large island off the eastern coast of Canada — *bronze*: make the colour of bronze — *hardy:* daring, brave — *without restraint*: freely — *board*: go on board — *St John's*: capital of Newfoundland — *seal*: hunt seals — *drift*: driving mass (snow etc.) — *on her beam ends*: she was lying on her broadside in a state of complete capsize — *shift*: move from one place to another — *right*: put back in the proper position — *humpy*: rounded, bulging out — *extremity*: great distress — *hoist*: lift — *scatter*: put here and there — *mitten*: kind of glove, without fingers — *haul*: pull with force — *dray*: low strong cart — *cruise*: sail to and fro — *pound*: kind of box — *stanchion*: upright post meant to support the beams — *ice*: cover with ice — *salmon* ['sæmən]: large fish — *fold*: part of sth. — *folks*: one's family or relations — *cemetery*: burying-ground — *relief fund*: money subscribed to help people in distress — *Harbour Grace*: town, port, Newfoundland.

123. Escape in Korea

(In June 1950 the people of North Korea invaded South Korea. The Chinese Communists joined in and by April 1951 they had driven the United Nations Forces almost out of North Korea. Captain Anthony Farrar-Hockley, of the Gloucestershire Regiment, was captured by the Chinese Communists.)

The staff of the interrogation centre were the most unpleasant and unscrupulous captors I had encountered up to that time, being either fanatical Communists, sadists, or a combination of both. For instance, the officer who dealt principally with us was an infantry major—referred to by Kim, the civilian interpreter, as the Young Major. He hated us bitterly. Whenever possible, he would find us unpleasant tasks, such as cleaning out the filthy headquarters latrine. What enhanced his pleasure in setting us this duty was that he could refuse us permission to wash afterwards, so that we must return to our quarters filthy with latrine matter. I protested to Kim on my first two initial interrogations about this treatment, without result. He excused himself by saying that is was no affair of his, but betrayed his feeling, by replying to my remarks about the Geneva Convention and its Prisoner-of-War clauses, with a comment that the Convention was an instrument of bourgeois reaction which, anyway, was inapplicable to war-criminals such as ourselves.

We made the final decision to escape while working on the hill one morning.

We had put twelve miles between us and our prison; a broad stretch of the Taedong river, and the fertile Taedong valley lay below us in the morning sun. Our hill-top gave us ample cover in which to rest from the night march. We ate our raw *diacons*, taken from the fields far back, as we discussed the route to the coast.

North of Chinam-po, we knew the seashore was covered with soft mud that often ran out for more than five miles, even at high water. But there were deep-water inlets northwards, and the port of Chinam-po would be about twenty miles south of the point at which we expected to find the sea. Ron and Jack agreed with me that we should turn north on reaching the coast, and seek the deep-water inlets and the fishermen's craft that lay in them rather than risk the sentinels of Chinam-po. Once we got to the sea, we could only hope that wind and tide would not be against us. The problem of water for the journey was one that concerned me most; for I felt that, in our present condition, we should not be able to handle the boat effectively, if we remained at sea for more than a week without water.

After a second careful reconnaissance, we descended from our hill at dusk, with a stream and valley to cross before climbing a range in the far side which led to the sea. The brown and yellow leaves lay everywhere, as we passed through the woods on the lower slopes. There had been plenty of chestnuts here, but the village boys had taken them all, leaving the spiky cases strewn beneath the trees. Reaching the rice-paddy in the valley, we made a detour round the first village that lay on our course. Beyond, the stream flowed past and deep between high banks of soft mud. I was hoping that we should find a crossing-place higher up, for I was anxious that we should not get our clothes wet; the heavy night frost would certainly freeze them, and we could not count on a sunny day to dry them out before another night fell.

A young civilian came suddenly upon us from a tiny side-path, glancing curiously at us as we passed. We continued across the valley without looking back until he was out of sight, when we quickly ran back along the track we had crossed, changed our direction and took the small, disused footpath that led along the river bank. As soon as we reached good cover, I led the way into the bushes to see if we were being followed. Sitting there on the cold earth, we could hear nothing but the river noise below us. Only after ten or fifteen minutes did we hear light footsteps. Looking through the branches, I saw the civilian we had passed earlier coming along the footpath, looking carefully about him as he went. He passed without seeing us and I watched him take a path that led to the main track running to our right. Half an hour went by; he did not return. I decided to go on.

We made another detour to avoid the next village, and were about to descend to the stream again when we were challenged. I heard the action of a rifle-bolt close by, and as the moon emerged at that moment from the clouds, saw a sentry about twenty-five yards away, his rifle covering us. Jack and Ron were behind me. It was foolish of us all to get recaptured; their chance of withdrawal was better than mine. Signalling to them to crawl away along a rice-paddy bank nearby, I walked slowly towards the sentry, speaking in a normal voice, hoping to distract his attention.

Attending to me, he did not spot the other two. He halted me firmly when I was about ten paces from him. Each of us stared at the other: he did not know what to make of me; I wondered how I could slip away from that weapon that covered me.

The guard turned out. I was led into the guard-room in a nearby village, which we had not observed in our daylight reconnaissance because it lay in a re-entrant. By this time I had decided to attempt a bluff and, in the friendliest voice I could raise, I said, *'Tovarich!'* pointing delightedly at a coloured picture of Stalin on the wall.

The soldiers looked at me in puzzlement for a few moments. They regarded my black raincoat and the Chinese Communist cap that Tom had given me for the escape; they indicated my beard and blue eyes to one another as they discussed me amongst themselves. One of them came forward and said a few words to me in what I believed to be elementary Russian, and I replied heartily in gibberish, ending as many words as possible with 'ski', 'shi', 'ish', and 'off'. As their brown eyes grew friendlier, I began to indicate that I must be on my way, pointing to their watches as if asking the time. I really believed that I was going to get away with it; for they were smiling now and two men shook my hand. With luck, they might take me out on to the path and escort me to the edge of the village. I was about to light a cigarette offered to me, when the door opened and a North Korean police captain entered. He stepped towards me, speaking rapidly and apparently fluently in a language that was certainly neither Korean nor Chinese. After a couple more sentences I realized that the game was up: he was evidently a Russian interpreter. I took a good pull on the cigarette and said in English:

"I am afraid there seems to have been some sort of mistake." By the look on his face, I could see that he intended to rectify it. I left the guard-room with my arms bound tightly behind me.

I spent a very unpleasant night, being awakened every half-hour or so by the guard, just to make sure that I had not slipped out of my clothes and crawled through a crack in the floorboards. Two or three hours after sunrise, the door of my cell in the local police-station opened and I looked up to see the commander of the interrogation centre standing above me.

"Ah," he said, greeting me with a friendly kick. "So it is you they have caught. I wondered which one it was."

I was removed from the cell, still bound, and taken into another village, where Kim and a lieutenant-colonel of the police were waiting for me. As I approached, Kim looked up to say:

"You have been very foolish. You must be killed for this, I think." His face was twisted with rage.

The whole party of seven or eight who had come out to fetch me breakfasted in a house while I remained outside. Their meal over, I was brought in for a preliminary examination. In order to infuse the proper spirit into all concerned, the police lieutenant-colonel cocked his pistol, brandished it in my face, and then began to hit me over the head with it. He had made sure that my hands and arms were securely bound before he began.

Eric Williams: *Great Escape Stories,* Harmondsworth 1958
By permission of the publishers, Penguin Books Ltd

VOCABULARY. *invade*: enter a country as an enemy — *encounter*: meet — *sadist*: person who gets pleasure from cruelty — *filthy*: disgustingly dirty; foul — *headquarters*: place from which activities are controlled — *latrine*: pit or trench to receive waste matter from the human body — *enhance*: add to — *Geneva Conventions*: dealing with the treatment of the wounded in time of war etc. — *bourgeois* [bəːˈdʒɔis]: of the middle class of society — *inapplicable*: unsuitable — *diacon*: cross between a turnip and a radish — *mud*: wet soft earth — *inlet*: small bay — *craft*: a small ship — *sentinel, sentry*: soldier on guard — *reconnaissance* [riˈkɔnisəns] scouting-out of a stretch of country-line or row of mountains — *chestnut*: large tree producing reddish-brown nuts — *spiky*: having sharp points — *paddy*: growing rice — *detour*: roundabout way — *challenge*: call to account — *bolt*: metal bar or pin — *emerge*: come out from — *spot*: catch sight of — *re-entrant*: angle pointing inward — *puzzlement*: bewilderment — *gibberish* [ˈdʒibəriʃ]: quick, gabbling talk; words without meaning — *the game was up*: at an end, over — *rectify*: put right — *crack*: split — *cell*: small room for one person — *infuse*: pour upon — *cock*: raise — *brandish*: wave.

124. Jumping for Joy

I have never yet been able to explain to myself how I was ever persuaded to do anything so foolhardy as to jump out of an aeroplane. I had no need of what is described rather sinisterly as 'danger money'; I did not greatly desire sensation; I am not given to bravado; I was not oppressed by unrequited love. But somehow I felt myself propelled to take the chance; some conspiracy of impulses had betrayed me, and for the first time I was about to do it and wondering what it was going to be like.

Now I know that jumping is rather like diving from an immense height into a large pool of cold water without any water in it. All the expected preliminary sensations and shock are present and, in a way, felt. I am sure it reduces my life by years every time I do it, but for some reason I go on doing it.

With jellified knees, sanded mouth, hollow stomach, I edged forward down the plane, making last-minute mental and equipment checks. The roar of engines filled my ears; the door was open; the red light flickered...

Back on the training station preparations had been accompanied by an atmosphere of informality. There the instructors had treated 'jumping' as casually as they would an elementary domestic task. That in itself was both reassuring and exasperating. But now we were airborne things were different. The line of pale, preoccupied faces told how different. Occasionally someone shouted a forced jocularity to sustain his flagging spirits, but responses were polite and perfunctory. Each man had withdrawn into himself, and what was going on inside him was nobody's business.

Seen from below, the rapidity of ejection is surprising. The bodies spill and curve from the door like a squad of circus acrobats. Doing it is less artistic but a great deal more surprising.

As I shuffled forward to the opening I remembered what I had to do: knees drawn up, feet together, head tucked in. I stood at the edge of what seemed an appalling vacuity. The noise of the engines was shattering, but the silence of my mind and myself was more so. The air rushing past seemed almost visible and the earth beyond incredibly distant and immobile. I felt an acute sense of being ludicrous, but at the same time I was paralysed. Laughter was impossible. I should never have started this, I thought. I should have remained at my office desk, safe, comfortable, habitual. It was ridiculous to be jumping out of an aeroplane with only a large piece of silk to support me. Supposing it hadn't been packed properly? Supposing there was a flaw or a tear in it? Supposing it didn't come out? Or, if it did, supposing it didn't open? Or, supposing it opened, what if it shut again?

The possibilities raced through my brain. I had heard macabre details of how high bodies bounced when they struck. Already it seemed to be happening to me. What a fool I had been, I thought. I was no Icarus, no bird man; no land or sea would be named after me; merely another bald, terse note in the middle of the evening paper: "There was an accident . . . his parachute failed to open . . . an inquiry will be made."

If I had been sensible, I thought, I might at this moment be signing memoranda in my office in Mincing Lane and thinking about my lunch at the 'local'. Then I thought of the miraculous escapes: people landing in reservoirs and snowdrifts and haystacks. It was absurd. I knew there weren't any reservoirs; there hadn't been any snow for months and most of the haystacks were consumed by this time of the year. The seconds were ticking by. At any moment we would be over the dropping zone. I went on looking out of the door, hypnotized by my own fear, stiff and yet trembling. I knew I had to go. There was no turning back. Even at that stage my pride came to my rescue. It was any minute now. I ceased to think. My mind and body were paralysed by a total negation.

GO! My stomach seemed to fall out of me as I hit the slipstream and was sucked away. Something rattled in my brain. I was certain it was the end; and, still mesmerized by my complete helplessness, the last vestiges of strength and purpose drained out of me as I began to plummet downwards. In the corner of one eye I saw the world, chequered, extraordinarily neat, roll beneath me. How absurd! How little! How enormous! And, what was more, I was going to hit it very shortly. Then, as I turned, I saw the plane in the corner of my other eye, at what seemed miles away. I was certain my 'chute wasn't going to open. It couldn't open. It hadn't opened. The cold air blasted through me and I was falling at a terrible speed. Then the first jerk went through my body. It was opening. I giggled and looked up. It was open, completely open. Then I looked down and felt sick. I still couldn't do anything. The total abdication of will had allowed no successor.

Then suddenly I felt quite comfortable. The earth was not far away. It was coming up fast. The details on the ground were startlingly clear. I began to remember what I must do when I landed and how to land. For a second or two I felt wonderfully free, exhilarated, almost ecstatic. Then ... down ... rolling over ... being dragged along.

I scrambled to my feet and looked up and about. The others were landing. I trod the ground deliberately and felt ridiculously light-hearted. It had actually happened. How dull, I thought, to be in Mincing Lane signing memoranda, thinking about my lunch. And then I remembered that we had to do another jump the next day. Twenty-four hours to go. Twenty-four hours in which—but I wasn't quite sure what. Perhaps it would be rather dull; but then there was always the chance that tomorrow the parachute wouldn't open.

J. A. B. Cuddon: "*Jumping for Joy*" in *Contemporary Short Stories,* ed. Wood, London, Blackie & Son Ltd (publishers)

VOCABULARY. *foolhardy*: bold and taking foolish risks — *sinister*: unlucky; suggesting misfortune — *bravado* [brəˈvɑːdəu]: show of bravery — *unrequited*: not paid back — *edge*: move slowly along — *casual*: without special purpose — *exasperate*: make very angry — *airborne*: off the ground — *preoccupied*: lost in thought — *jocularity*: humorous behaviour — *flag*: become weak or tired — *perfunctory*: done merely as a duty; superficial — *ejection*: throwing out — *spill*: fall out — *curve*: take the form of a curve — *squad*: small group of persons being trained together — *shuffle*: walk along without raising the feet properly — *tuck in*: draw, push — *vacuity*: emptiness; unoccupied space — *ludicrous*: ridiculous — *paralyse*: cause to be incapable of action — *flaw*: fault — *macabre* [məˈkɑːbr]: gruesome; grim — *bounce*: spring back when thrown down to the ground — *Icarus*: son of Daedalus, who, flying with his father on wax-fastened wings, dropped into the sea, giving name to that part of it — *terse*: brief and to the point — *memorandum*: (in business) informal letter — *Mincing Lane*: street in the City of London — *local:* (colloq.) = the local public house — *reservoir* [ˈrezəvwɑː]: place where water is stored — *snowdrift*: bank of snow heaped up by wind — *haystack*: hay built in a pile — *hypnotize*: fall into a state resembling deep sleep — *slipstream*: turbulent air-current under and behind an aircraft in flight — *mesmerize*: charm; exercise a powerful influence on — *vestige*: trace — *drain*: use up — *plummet*: plunge — *chequered*: marked like a chess-board — *jerk*: short, sudden movement — *giggle*: ['gigl]: laugh in a silly manner — *abdication*: giving up — *successor*: thing that follows another — *exhilarate*: cheer up — *ecstatic*: madly delighted.

125. A Delinquent Child

Cecil Young had been in no fewer than six children's homes and, by his behaviour, had come near to wrecking each one. His aggressive dishonesty and complete inability to accept any generosity without grumbling, tested the patience of the most charitable staff member. He came to us mulish, defiant and depressed. The tests he applied were manifold. An act of generosity would be taken as a right and would soon be followed by a continual grumbling that of all in the school he was treated in the most unfair manner.

His mother was a prostitute and daily he had been inflicted with the company of her men as they would call upon her. One afternoon when he was eleven his mother returned home and, from her almost demented conversation, he discovered that she had gone to the river and drowned a baby she had borne a few weeks previously, and her maniac comments further seemed to suggest that she would soon kill herself. She left the house and the boy followed to discover, by the side of the river about an hour later, some men and policemen standing over her drowned body. She had drowned herself in the same part of the river in which earlier that day she had drowned her baby.

He was now put into care of the local children's committee but his behaviour caused his quick passage from one home to another. If we were to succeed, the path was long, but after five months he had begun to smile; he had taken to asking for, instead of demanding things, and he had even learnt to say thank you.

His first Christmas with us came, and it was clearly undesirable for him to return to the area which was filled with bad memories for him. Casually I asked him if he would like to accept an invitation, if such were offered, from a staff member, and when he agreed I asked him to choose one such, saying that I would then, without involving him, see if such an invitation could be offered. He chose myself and naturally the invitation was offered. Along with my own three children, my wife and myself he had his own pile of presents which, in his case, included a bicycle. He had known that this was likely because I had asked him what major present he wanted, but he had not really believed in the probability. When he had that bicycle on Christmas morning, his real sense of gratitude glowed, and despite the troubles of the first half year of his stay at the school his behaviour as a guest in my house was almost impeccable. There was a ready acceptance of household chores, a willingness to fetch coal, an agreeable attitude to doing odd shopping, and later the traditional outing to the pantomine seemed to seal his acceptance.

After this fortnight, his return to the school was marked by a relapse to his unhappy truculence, and I noticed him wearing a watch. I believed that he had stolen this, but to ask him the obvious question would have been a denial of the trust I showed him. I took off my own watch, and a few hours later met him, apparently by chance, in the corridor. I lifted my wrist as if to look at the time and then said, "Oh, damn! I've left my watch somewhere. Do you know the time, Cecil?" Quite naturally he looked at his own wrist, and because of this I realized that it was perhaps improbable that he had stolen the watch. Later enquiries showed that although it was a type of loan from another boy, it had about it certain qualities of sharp practice. Two days afterwards, on hearing that he had returned the watch to the other boy, I told him sharply, "Come to my house tomorrow morning at a quarter to eight." He replied, "Oh surely you can trust me without a lot of explanation." In the event he came to my house, had breakfast and afterwards accompanied me to a shop in the village where I had previously arranged that the most expensive watch stocked cost three guineas. I had taken him to choose a watch he would like, and when he had done so I said, "Right. That is yours." Immediately he demurred, "Oh, I can't take that, it's too valuable," to which I replied, "Oh, damn it! Can't you even trust me as far as accepting a gift from me." A few seconds later in the car I noticed that he was crying. The whole point of the story is that it anticipated a theft.

After these pieces of drama, the path was much easier until we came to an extraordinary difficulty reported mainly by the English teachers. Without warning, the boy's spelling had deteriorated so that very often a word in his exercise book was completely meaningless. It was demonstrable that if one could only prevent errors in words involving the letters a, e, i, d, and s, then his spelling would be correct. The boy himself brought up the matter with me privately and I pretended to establish with him what in fact I had already discovered. We then took the five significant letters and wrote them on small pieces of card which I asked him to arrange in any way his imagination suggested. After some preliminary hesitation he had arranged them and, looking at his arrangement, he blushed and his eyes filled with tears. I could not see anything in the arrangement as the word SADIE conveyed nothing to me, but in stumbling phrases he said, "That's my mother's name. She was called Sadie." Over and over again he muttered, "That's my mother's name." At that time of this curious impairment of his spelling he had realized that it was the second anniversary of his mother's death. This discussion was later shown to have completely remedied the mis-spelling.

In the Spring after he had been with us for a year and a half he said, "I wish I could come away with you on holiday." While it is a pleasure to be relieved of the company of difficult children from time to time, I did not feel that his company need be an infliction so he came with us on an annual holiday to a far away Irish island in the Atlantic. For the first time he was on an aeroplane and for the first time he was in an hotel and, for that matter, for the first time he was on a Gaelic speaking island.

After that holiday his interest in adults other than myself became very apparent. He wanted his social life to include all adults, men and women, at the school; his relationships with boys became easier and friendly and we were happy in the knowledge that he had found a much better sense of security than had promised when he first arrived.

Very recently he has obtained a degree in mathematics and is shortly to be married. His visits to us and to other staff members are very ordinary and simple, and now that he is in a position to do so he has made contributions to the School Building Fund.

Otto L. Shaw: *Maladjusted Boys*, London 1965
By permission of the publishers, George Allen & Unwin Ltd

VOCABULARY. *delinquent*: doing wrong, guilty — *wreck*: destroy — *grumble*: murmur with discontent — *staff*: group of assistants, under a head — *mulish*: stubborn — *defiant*: bold and impudent — *manifold*: many in number — *prostitute*: woman who sells her body for sexual intercourse — *inflict*: cause sb. to suffer — *demented*: mad — *maniac*: affected by mental disorder — *demand*: call sharply for — *casually*: without special purpose — *involve*: mix sb. up in an affair — *pile*: heap — *major*: more important — *impeccable*: faultless — *chore* [tʃɔː]: ordinary daily task — *outing*: short excursion away from home — *pantomime*: dumb show — *seal*: close up completely — *relapse*: falling back — *truculence* [ˈtrʌkjuləns]: fierceness — *denial*: refusing — *loan*: lending, sth. lent — *practice*: trickery; underhand scheming — *stock*: have a store of goods — *guinea*: twenty one shillings — *demur*: protest; say 'no' to — *anticipate*: do sth. before sb. else does it — *deteriorate:* grow worse — *arrange*: put in order — *preliminary*: introductory — *convey*: make known; give ideas to — *stumble*: speak in a hesitating way — *impairment*:

weakening or damaging — *remedy*: cure — *relieve sb. of sth.*: take it from him — *infliction*: punishment — *Gaelic*: language of Celts — *degree*: rank or grade given by a university — *contribution*: money given to — *Fund*: stock of money.

126. Wanting Adventure?

My own particular research into delinquency developed from my work as a boys' club leader on Merseyside. I found out after a while that an astounding proportion of my club members had broken the law at some time or another or had actually been found guilty of some offence. Many of these good, solid, reliable types were in fact delinquents. Privately they told me of their illegal exploits and exposed a part of their lives which had hitherto been quite unknown to me. This is what we knew as gang life.

Now what amazed me was not so much that many of my club members had broken the law. I had sufficient contact with the local probation service to know that several offenders were numbered among my flock. It was that almost every boy, even those I thought of as my 'best', had taken part in illegal exploits at some time in childhood and early adolescence.

One boy said, telling me about shop-lifting parties which used to operate on Saturday mornings during his schooldays, that they always knew on the night before exactly where they were going. He also told me how he and his mates broke into a grocer's shop. They watched it very carefully for several days to discover the best way of entering and to see whether or not anyone lived above. Then they took advantage of a moonless night to force a back window, having taken the precaution to leave 'sentries' both front and back to give warning of any approaching danger. While the actual raid was on, he said, it was very thrilling, but best of all was "when you knew you'd got clean away and were walking back up the street."

Another boy described to me how one daring youth would incite the others to take greater risks. He once saw a boy coolly remove a whole chemistry set from a shop counter, tuck it under his coat and walk off with it. Such escapades were talked about with relish and admiration.

During most of the discussions I had with these lads it was remarkable how little sense of guilt was expressed and how they talked about delinquency as something which everyone they knew took part in during his youth. "You used to enjoy yourself," one boy said, although like many others he admitted that "at the time it made you sweat." One young man recalled how he and his pals deliberately broke into one shop merely in order to be able to brag in the neighbourhood that they were the first to do it. Once committed to this dare-devil, delinquent life, it was extremely difficult to withdraw without being branded as a coward. They just kept on doing dangerous and criminal things because they did not know how to stop. Everybody did them. It was part and parcel of the life they knew.

John Barron Mays: *Crime and the Social Structure*, London 1967
By permission of the publishers, Faber and Faber Ltd

VOCABULARY. *delinquent*: wrong-doer — *delinquency*: failure in duty; crime — *Merseyside*: large conurbation (= aggregation of urban districts "Gruppe zusammengewachsener Städte"), comprises Birkenhead, Liverpool etc. — *astound*: amaze — *proportion*: part, share — *guilty*: having done wrong — *offence*: hurt; crime — *illegal*: against the law — *exploit*: daring deed; feat — *gang*: band of persons acting together esp. for evil purposes — *probation*: time during which a first offender is allowed to go free and prove that he can lead an honest life — *adolescence*: period of youth — *shop-lifting*: stealing from shops while pretending to be a customer — *mate*: companion — *sentry*: soldier on guard — *raid*: predatory incursion — *thrilling*: very exciting — *clean*: unobstructed — *daring*: bold, fearless — *incite*: urge on — *counter*: long table on which goods are shown — *tuck*: push — *escapade*: daring act — *relish*: pleasure; enjoyment — *admit*: confess — *sweat*: perspire; be in a state of terror — *brag*: boast — *dare-devil*: foolishly bold — *withdraw*: go away — *brand*: make a lasting mark on — *part and parcel of*: an essential part of.

127. The Clapham Common Murder Case

Press publicity itself sharpened the lines of conflict between society and Teddy boys. The cinema riots, which were repeated in a number of forms, were in themselves no profound event. Another incident, however, which illustrated to the public how far these fantasies of spurious youthful gangster life had spread in England, was the so-called Clapham Common murder case of 1954.

This took place on Clapham Common, on a peaceful summer evening, at a spot where a band was playing. The audience sat listening on park chairs while some young people were dancing on the concrete. Lounging on the seats were a seventeen-year-old youth called Beckley and three of his friends, who sat smoking with their feet up on other chairs. Because of this they became involved in an altercation with another boy, only sixteen, but already the leader of a gang with an unpleasant reputation in the neighbourhood. Seeing this whole gang converging on them in force, Beckley and his friends tried to get away, but the gang closed in. The astonished bystanders on

Clapham Common were witnesses of a silent and desperate struggle in which flick-knives were flashed and two boys held Beckley on the ground while a third kicked his head. Next, dirty and bleeding Beckley and one companion were running across the grass for their lives, with their enemies streaming in pursuit. At the edge of the Common, the fugitives jumped on to a bus, but as the bus stopped the gang surged forward. Beckley, his friend and the conductor were dragged off. Before the passengers could intervene, Beckley lay stabbed to death on the pavement, his companion was badly wounded, and the assailants had scattered to the winds.

It was of course not long before they were picked up and the ringleaders stood trial at the Old Bailey. The nineteen-year-old who had wielded the fatal knife, and now stood white-faced in the dock, was sentenced to death, and then reprieved, while four other youths went to prison for common assault.

A fight on the Common—such a spot of trouble could easily occur whenever boys and girls were congregated. However, the new traits illustrated by the incident, and not easy to explain, were the complete disregard of surroundings and bystanders, and the deadly use of knives, all part of the gang-life fantasy in the minds of these youngsters.

T. R. Fyvel: *The Insecure Offenders,* London 1961
By permission of the publishers, Chatto & Windus Ltd

VOCABULARY. *Clapham*: a SW suburb of London, 4 miles from St Paul's, with a large common — *common*: area of grassland for all to use "Gemeindeland" — *Teddy boys*: an 'anti'-group "Halbstarke" — *riot*: outbreak of disorder — *fantasy*: strange dream, vision — *spurious*: false — *concrete*: building substance made by mixing cement with sand etc. "Beton, Steinmörtel" — *lounge*: lie back at one's ease — *involve*: mix up — *altercation*: quarrel — *converge*: come together — *in force*: in large numbers — *witness*: one who looks on — *flick-knife*: knife with blade springing out when button is pressed — *flash*: come suddenly into view — *stream*: flow freely — *in pursuit*: pursuing — *surge*: move like waves — *stab*: wound with a sharp pointed weapon — *assailant*: one who attacks — *ringleader*: head of a wicked gang — *trial*: judging of a prisoner in a law-court — *Old Bailey*: London Central Criminal Court — *wield*: swing or handle — *dock*: box in a lawcourt where the accused person stands — *reprieve*: change punishment into another less severe — *assault*: attack with blows or weapons "tätlicher Angriff" — *congregate*: come together in a crowd.

128. The Shock of Recognition

The real and overwhelming fear is that once a boy is arrested and sitting in a cell, his whole illusion, his whole fantasy of being safe as a member of a gang is suddenly taken from him, and it is this loss which is so terrifying. Each time another hero is arrested, a myth is destroyed. The power of the police represents in fact the flaw in the Teddy boy's dream of secure rebellion. The more intense the fantasy, i. e. the more neurotic a boy's belief that as a member of the gang he can live amorally, do what he likes and disregard the law, the more intense also becomes hatred of the police, who threaten the fantasy.

It is of course not only the authority of the police which exposes the Teddy-boy rebellion. Behind the police stand the Courts, the power of magistrates and judges. As the futile young rebels come up against the real strength of the society they had tried to oppose, the result is usually an overwhelming shock. There are of course a minority who remain hardened, but I have often heard the opposite stories of reckless young Teddy-boy offenders who, when they find themselves in the dock, are at first as dazed as young prisoners of war whose entire familiar universe had collapsed. A social worker from West London who had attended the Court proceedings where some of his boys were up on fairly serious charges gave me this picture:

> The thing which shocked me extremely was my own lack of preparation for seeing the boys in Court look so differently from what I had thought they were like in their normal social setting. They looked even physically smaller—they were really only infants, suddenly finding themselves completely helpless and without even being able to express it. When I asked them about this they didn't know how to put it into words, but what seemed to me the worst was the sudden awareness on their part that all their fantasy strengths were of no use to them. The boys were now surrounded by police, having to answer to a person who had very definite authority—it was not a matter of their giving this man authority—they weren't asked. I think their helplessness was linked with something else as well, that no matter how many do-gooders there were in their outside world, at this point they could not be helped. Where even that failed, everything had failed them.

Of course, this sense of shock—the shock of recognition—does not last. Youth is resilient and adaptable.

T. R. Fyvel: *The Insecure Offenders*, London 1961
By permission of the publishers, Chatto & Windus Ltd

VOCABULARY. *recognition*: act of seeing the truth — *overwhelm*: master; overpower — *cell*: small room in a prison — *fantasy*: whimsical speculation — *myth*: false belief; fable — *neurotic*: one who has bad nerves — *amoral*: non-moral — *threaten*: give warning — *magistrate*: judge in lowest courts — *futile* [ˈfjuːtaɪl]: of no use — *reckless*: without care; rash — *offender*: person who breaks the law — *dock*: box in a lawcourt where the accused person stands — *daze*: make sb. unable to think clearly — *social worker*: "Fürsorger" — *charge*: accusation — *setting*: background — *awareness*: state of being conscious — *resilient*: elastic.

129. Johnnie—a Borstal Boy

Pollington Camp is an experimental open Borstal, housing selected boys. During a visit I could tell from the firm posture and relaxed expressions of the boys that they were not the usual Borstal boys but the pick of them.

This was confirmed by Johnnie, a tall boy picked out at random to show my companion and myself over the institution with explicit freedom to comment. He took us through the dormitories, explaining relative points of spit and polish and neatness that gained or lost marks—Johnnie laughed at this. Six foot two, tousle-haired, he was engagingly frank. In his present institutional situation he had no inhibitions. He had the look, I kept thinking, of a confident young man who back in his home town would go far, who would presently be a solid citizen, perhaps a works foreman, driving his new Austin, with his children perhaps going to grammar school.

As we stood at the edge of the road I suggested that it would not be difficult to get away from Pollington. Johnnie agreed; all one had to do was to thumb a ride on a lorry. But what would that get him? Only back to the punishment Borstal at Reading.

"So you wouldn't do it?" "I'd be silly, wouldn't I?" said Johnnie. "Today I *think*. I'm supposed to be learning self-discipline. That's why I'm here—because I didn't know how to think."

He came from a small town in East Anglia. There was an American air base in the neighbourhood and an R. A. F. depot not far off. The town had coffee bars and pubs with bands; it was a place of many fights; there were rough places, a lot of Teddy boys about. His father kept a small shop there. He himself was the only son.

I asked how he had managed to get himself sent to Borstal. "Just for a laugh. It's a fact." There had been trouble in the family, father and mother at it every evening, then finally mother walked out. For a while his father made him help in the house. Going out nights to get away from home, he had got in with a rough mob. His mate at the café had said to him: "Do you want a laugh tonight?" He found it meant breaking into a television shop, but the way he was feeling about things, it would have been chicken to refuse. And in any case, "I just didn't *think*. It's a fact."

Johnnie had two more months to go before his discharge. On the face of it, if he had learned nothing else, he gave every sign of having learned to think cautiously.

T. R. Fyvel: *The Insecure Offenders*, London 1961
By permission of the publishers, Chatto & Windus Ltd

VOCABULARY. *open Borstal*: the atmosphere is more relaxed and the inmates are given more personal responsibility than in *closed Borstals* — *posture*: position of the body; appearance — *relaxed*: less severe and strict — *pick*: choice; the best — *at random*: without any plan or purpose — *explicit*: outspoken — *dormitory*: large sleeping-room — *mark*: unit for measuring quality or result — *tousel* ['tauzl]: put into disorder (usu. of the hair) — *engaging*: pleasant, charming — *inhibition*: instinctive or induced shrinking from some impulse or action as a thing forbidden "Hemmung" — *foremen*: workman in authority over others — *thumb a ride* (or a lift): try to get a ride from a passing motorist by such sign — *mob*: noisy crowd — *mate*: companion — *discharge*: dismissal — *on the face of it*: judging by appearance.

130. A Day in Feltham Boys' Prison

Our days in Feltham were the same every day except Sunday. We got up at seven, washed, and went to a big hall with tables each seating about twenty where we had breakfast. This was a great and happy surprise to us after Walton. It consisted of any amount of bread, a piece of margarine, and wonder of God! a rissole, and a big bloody rissole at that. There was a big pot of tea to each table, and you could usually get three mugs, if you wanted them.

After that we cleaned up the place. There were orderlies selected for it but most of the others joined in, to pass the time. To tell the truth, I've never had much difficulty passing the time, and I usually stood over looking out of the window.

After that we were brought up to a bag-shop to sew mailbags. So long as you didn't exactly shout the place down, the screw didn't mind you talking. At twelve o'clock we went down to this hall again for dinner and a good dinner it was too.

After dinner we sat around till it was time to go to work again, and sewed more mailbags for a couple of hours. We came down and sat or walked round the hall till tea. This was good and substantial. With plenty of bread, the same-sized piece of margarine each that we got at breakfast and the same big pot of tea for each table and some fried stuff usually made up of what was left over at dinner.

Then after tea, from seven o'clock till eight, we had the famous Borstal 'silent hour'. This meant you had to sit at the table, write a letter home, if you hadn't already written your fortnightly letter, or else read your library book. If you didn't do that you had to sit there, anyway, and just sit, but not talk.

Well, we had a good library and most fellows had got into the habit of reading; anyway it was only for an hour and even if it seemed a bit balmy, they were decent in Feltham with scoff and the screws were decent and the boys were that surprised to get enough to eat and be treated so well, after their remand prison, that they did not mind the silent hour.

After the silent hour we got a supper of cocoa and a couple of slices of dry bread, and went up to bed, to dormitories or cubicles. The only thing we did not get was exercise, except on Sunday morning. We only got one hour's outside exercise in the week. That was because the place was overcrowded and was catering for more prisoners and more sorts of prisoners than it did normally, because of the war.

There was a certain amount of monotony about our days, but you'd get that in any nick, only more of it, and there was always a certain amount of diarrhoea amongst new arrivals, due to getting too much food all of a sudden.

Brendan Behan: *Borstal Boy*, London 1958
By permission of the publishers, Hutchinson & Co Ltd

VOCABULARY. (The author, aged 16, is sentenced to three years' Borstal Detention for unlawful activities in the Irish Republican Army. — Borstal = Besserungsanstalt für jugendliche Verbrecher. — First he ist sent to Feltham Boys' Prison.) *seat*: have seats for — *Walton prison*: it is a remand prison "Untersuchungsgefängnis" — *rissole*: small ball of meat minced and fried — *mug*: thick cup for drinking — *orderly*: attendant — *sew* [səu]: work with a needle and thread — *mailbag*: bag in which letters are carried — *screw*: (sl.) warder; jail-guard — *substantial*: large, considerable — *stuff*: material; food — *balmy*: (sl.) = barmy: cracked, crazy "plemplem" — *scoff*: mocking words — *dormitories*: large sleeping-rooms with many beds — *cubicle*: small separate sleeping-compartment — *exercise*: bodily activity — *cater for*: provide sth. for "sorgen für" — *the war*: the Second World War (1939—1945) — *nick*: (sl.) prison — *diarrhoea*: too frequent emptying of the bowels "Durchfall".

131. A Serious Experience

(The following incident happened in Switzerland)

I record this incident that it may be a warning to others. I went for a row with another boy a little younger than myself. When we were more than a mile from the shore, we decided to have a swim, pulled off our clothes, jumped into the water and swam about in great delight. When we had had enough, the boat was perhaps a hundred yards away. A breeze had begun to stir the waters. The boat had a small red awning over its stern seats. This awning acted as a sail by catching the breeze. As we swam towards the boat, it drifted farther off. After this had happened several times we had perhaps halved the distance. But meanwhile the breeze was freshening and we both, especially my companion, began to be tired. Up to this point no idea of danger had crossed my mind. The sun played upon the sparkling blue waters; the wonderful panorama of mountains and valleys, the gay hotels and villas still smiled. But I now saw Death as near as I believe I have ever seen him. He was swimming in the water at our side, whispering from time to time in the rising wind which continued to carry the boat away from us at about the same speed we could swim. No help was near. Unaided we could never reach the shore. I was not only an easy, but a fast swimmer, having represented my House at Harrow, when our team defeated all comers. I now swam for life. Twice I reached within a yard of the boat and each time a gust carried it just beyond my reach; but by a supreme effort I caught hold of its side in the nick of time before a still stronger gust bulged the red awning again. I scrambled in, and rowed back for my companion who, though tired, had not apparently realised the dull yellow glare of mortal peril that had so suddenly played around us. I said nothing to the tutor about this serious experience; but I have never forgotten it; and perhaps some of my readers will remember it too.

Winston S. Churchill: *My Early Life*, London
By permission of the publishers, Odhams Books

VOCABULARY. *record*: put a matter down in writing so that it may be read afterwards — *breeze*: wind — *awning*: covering to give shelter from the sun's rays — *stern*: back part of a ship — *drift*: be carried along — *halve*: cut in two — *sparkle*: shine in a glittering way — *whisper*: speak very softly — *represent*: stand for — *gust*: sudden blast (e.g. of wind) — *in the nick of time*: only just in time — *bulge*: curve outwards — *scramble*: climb or crawl — *apparent*: seeming; evident — *glare*: dazzling light — *peril*: serious danger — *tutor*: private teacher.

132. A Seaside Incident

(Very many British families take a summer holiday at the seaside in Britain, although nowadays a lot of people go abroad. Abigail Hill, broadcasting in *Woman's Hour,* tells of a holiday misfortune.)

The first morning of our holiday on the Lleyn Peninsula began well. The boys and I took the beach ball out into deep water, leaving my daughter behind with father on the edge. While I was swimming I turned to wave and was astonished to see my husband beckoning urgently. I raced over to him. He told me a particularly large wave had hit him in the back, broken right over his head, and knocked out his new teeth; and they were now somewhere at the bottom. The children thought it was tremendous fun. They dived under the waves and felt with their feet, and soon the churned-up sea-bed looked like a solution of the Sahara Desert. The tide was coming in rapidly, and we soon realized that our task was hopeless. Shivering with cold we sadly abandoned the search, hoping that we should have more luck when the tide turned. In the afternoon we retraced our steps. We searched the sands, the rocks, the breakwaters, but alas there was no trace of the missing teeth. We telephoned our dentist but, of course, he couldn't help until we got home. The prospects for the rest of our stay were gloomy. To make matters worse the weather deteriorated and the rain just poured down.

When our holiday was ten days old, my husband strolled to the harbour, where the local fishermen sold their catch early in the morning. He stopped to admire the baskets full of pink prawns and large orange crabs which decorated the quayside.

"Had your teeth out, I see, governor," said one of the fishermen sympathetically. My husband told him the story. "You come round to my cottage at eleven o'clock when I've finished here," said the fisherman, "and I might be able to help. Here's the address," he added mysteriously, but would say no more.

At eleven o'clock precisely his caller was waiting on the doorstep. He was ushered into the front parlour and there on the mantelpiece he saw a collection of jam-jars, each one holding false teeth. Every jar had a cover and bore a neat label stating the date when the teeth had been found. "Always finding them, governor," said the fisherman. "Some get left on the breakwaters: and some are washed in by the tide." There in the jar right at the end of the row were my husband's lost teeth: somewhat stained and sandy but otherwise undamaged.

Abigail Hill (Mildred Draper): from a B. B. C. "Woman's Hour" talk entitled "Flotsam", published in the *Listener* Sept., 28th 1961
By permission of the author

VOCABULARY. *broadcast*: send out by wireless — *the Lleyn Peninsula*: is in North Wales — *beach ball*: large ball used for games on the beach — *on the edge*: i.e. in the shallow water — *wave*: make a sign with the hand — *beckon*: make a sign to — *wave*: a swell on the surface of a large body of water — *dive*: dip or plunge — *churn*: cause to move up violently — *looked like ... Desert*: lot of sand had been mixed with the water — *task*: piece of work to be done — *shiver*: tremble — *abandon*: give up — *when the tide turned*: when the sea began to go out again — *retraced our steps*: went back over the same ground — *breakwaters*: low walls built into the sea to break the force of the waves — *alas!*: unfortunately — *prospect*: view before the mind — *gloomy*: sad — *deteriorate*: get worse — *stroll*: walk slowly, in a leisurely way — *their catch*: the fish they had caught — *prawn*: shell-fish like the shrimp "Garnele" — *crab*: ten-legged shell-fish "Taschenkrebs" — *quay*: place for landing or unloading goods from ships — *had your teeth out*: (uneducated style of speech) I see you've had your teeth out — *governor*: sir (word used by some working-class people in addressing others, particularly those who appear to be better off) — *you come round*: come round (strong command or request; *you* is stressed) — *mysterious*: puzzling, difficult to understand — *on the doorstep*: at the door of the cottage — *usher into*: lead into — *parlour*: (old-fashioned word) sitting-room of a private house — *mantelpiece*: shelf over the fireplace — *jar*: tall vessel, usu. round, with wide mouth — *neat*: trim, tidy — *label*: small written note fixed on to sth. — *always finding them*: i.e. I am always finding them — *get left*: are left — *stain*: change the colour of — *undamaged*: not harmed.

133. A 'Holiday' at Home

(Mr Jones, who is not bothered by the 'travel bug', lets the family go away while he remains at home, intending to have a complete rest.)

"When are you taking your holiday?" I asked, as I settled down beside an old friend of mine in the train one evening.

"Holiday!" he exclaimed. "My dear fellow, after Friday the office will see me no more for two weeks."

"And where are you off to?" I inquired.

He shook with laughter. "I'm driving my wife and children down to Cornwall, on Saturday, to visit her relations," he said. "But I'm returning. For a whole blessed fortnight I shall have the house to myself. Just think of it! Hours of reading without interruption, and no one to tell me to stop and come in to meals."

I smiled to myself.

Half-way through his holiday, I ran into Jones again.

"Hullo!" I said. "How is the holiday going?"

"Well," he replied, "you know how it is. Meals are becoming a bit of a problem, and the washing-up is certainly mounting. To be quite honest, I shan't be sorry to see them home again."

W. R. Lee: *English at Home*, London 1966
By permission of the publishers, Oxford University Press Ltd

VOCABULARY. *bug*: (colloq.) bacillus, microbe — *settle down*: sit down and make oneself comfortable — *where are you off to?*: (colloq.) where are you going? — *shake with laughter*: laugh heartily — *relations*: relatives and *relations* are both in common use and in this context mean the same thing — *I'm driving ... I'm returning*: notice the use of the present continuous-form here to refer to future events. *I'm returning* = I shall return (in a fortnight's time—not even the *immediate* future) — *blessed* ['blesid]: happy, fortunate — *interruption*: sudden break — *ran into Jones again*: met Jones by chance again — *how is the holiday going?*: how are you enjoying the holiday? — *you know how it is*: you know what usually happens — *mount:* go up, become greater in amount.

134. A Model's Day

Sue is 22, and she has been modelling for three years. She now has as much work as she can manage, and has the enviable reputation of knowing the job thoroughly and being easy to work with. Her income last year was nearly £ 2,000. One week she earned as much as £ 80, and one week it went down to £ 15. She shares a furnished flat with another model. Sue's home is in Surrey, but as soon as she began to get plenty of work she realized that it would be more convenient and much less tiring to live in London during the week. She has a long-suffering boy-friend who works in the City and who spends a lot of time waiting about for her when jobs run late. She prefers to limit her social engagements during the week, as she has to find time at night to keep her clothes and accessories spick and span and attend to hair and manicure, etc. Also, too many late nights would spoil her appearance in the mornings, and photographers soon give up booking a model who arrives looking washed out and listless.

Sue was up at 7.30 a. m.—she has a hairdressing appointment at 9 a. m., a special set for a beauty shot at 10.30. Contrary to the popular notion of the way models live, Sue eats a large breakfast of poached eggs, fruit and coffee. She limits the toast, however. Food must be sustaining, but not fattening—Sue knows that she will be lucky if she has time for lunch today, and the right type of breakfast will help her not to feel too hungry in the middle of the afternoon. After breakfast she dresses in a simple jersey suit and checks the accessories for her day's bookings against the list she has made in her diary. She has been asked to take some cocktail or evening blouses for the first job—she has a good idea of what will be required since this studio has booked her many times before and she knows exactly the sort of work the photographer produces. She thinks that white *broderie anglaise* will be particularly suitable, and includes a blouse in this material along with several others. She also takes some costume jewellery and one or two hair ornaments. This helpful attitude is one of the things people like about Sue—a reputation for always turning up with a good selection of the right accessories can make a great difference to a model's bookings. She uses only a simple make-up as anything more finished would be spoiled by the hair-drier, and leaves with suitcase and make-up box at 8.40.

John and Pamela Dixon: *Fashion Modelling*, London 1963
By permission of the publishers, Robert Hale Ltd

VOCABULARY. *model*: person who poses for artists; mannequin — *enviable*: worth having — *flat*: set of living rooms — *engagement*: arrangement to go somewhere — *accessory*: sth. extra that is added — *spick and span*: bright, clean, tidy — *spoil*: harm — *book*: order beforehand — *washed out*: (colloq.) pale and tired-looking; exhausted — *listless*: having no interest; weary — *shot*: photograph taken with cinematograph camera — *poach*: cook an egg by boiling it without the shell — *sustaining*: giving strength — *suit*: set of clothes — *check*: to see if sth. is correct — *broderie anglaise*: open embroidery on white linen or cambric — *costume jewellery*: artificial jewellery "Modeschmuck" — *finish*: perfect, put final touch to.

135. A Difficult Customer

Dolores works in a shop selling gramophone records. One afternoon a middle-aged woman came in, sat on a stool in front of the counter, and smiled at her brightly.

"I want a record, dear," she began. "One I heard on the radio this morning."

"What was the record called?" Dolores asked, without much hope. The woman shook her head.

"I don't remember. I should know if I heard it, though. Perhaps if you play me a few records, I shall be able to pick it out."

She settled herself more comfortably on her stool.

"We have hundreds of records in stock," Dolores pointed out. "It would take a very long time to play you even a little of each. Could you hum it to me?"

The woman shook her head again. "I can't even sing the National Anthem in tune. We should only get into a complete muddle if I were to start humming." She looked quite depressed, as if this reminder of her own lack of musical ability were the last straw. Then suddenly her face brightened.

"I've just remembered something," she said. "It comes from a play. There's a girl who speaks very badly, if you see what I mean. But after a time she learns to talk well. Something about—what do you call it? Phonetics."

This was enough for Dolores. "If you ask me, it's from *My Fair Lady*," she said.

"That's it, dear. If you'd thought of it sooner, we wouldn't have wasted so much time. I suppose you are new to the job."

W. R. Lee: *English at Home*, London 1966
By permission of the publishers, Oxford University Press Ltd

VOCABULARY. *record*: disk — *stool*: low seat without a back — *counter*: long table on which customers are served — *pick it out*: (here) find it, choose it — *settle*: sit down and make oneself comfortable — *in stock*: in the shop — *hum*: make a buzzing sound like that of a bee — *National Anthem*: national song or hymn of a country — *muddle*: state of disorder and confusion — *depressed*: (here) sad — *reminder*: that which brings a matter back to a person's mind — *the last straw*: the final small addition to a burden which makes it impossible to bear — *Phonetics*: study and science of speech sounds and the symbols used to represent them — *if you ask me*: (colloq.) = my opinion is — *My Fair Lady*: a musical show based on Bernard's Shaw's *Pygmalion*. (The girl is Eliza Doolittle, a flower-seller, who is taught to speak like a fine lady.) — *new to the job*: new to the job of selling records, inexperienced at it.

136. Dog Handler

Rex the alsatian is a police dog. When he was six months old he joined the Dog Training Establishment. There he met P. C. Titley, his handler. His handler helped to teach him to be a good police dog.

At first Rex had to learn to be obedient. He had to come when he was called, or sit, or lie down. He had to obey even a nod. He was taught to guard. He had to wait and wait, but he never betrayed his trust. After this test he was given a good meal by his handler as a reward.

He also had to learn how to attack. He was taught to leap at the right arm. Most people are right-handed, so that is the arm to put out of action. Rex seizes it just above the wrist. Once his teeth have taken hold Rex will not let go.

Rex was taught to follow a scent. A long white tracking lead was fastened to his shoulders. When he was told to go, he raced away, following the scent.

When his training is over, Rex goes to live with his handler. He is taken for long walks by his handler. He is fed by him. He is loyal and obedient. With his handler he is gentle and friendly. To the criminal he can be a barrier to freedom. He is the tracker. He is the hunter. He is a flash of teeth and a grip upon the arm that will not let go.

Rex knows his job as well as any policeman. When he is called to an incident, he knows what to do. P. C. Titley and Rex are a team.

Boswell Taylor: *999 ... Police!*, London 1964
By permission of the publishers, University of London Press Ltd

VOCABULARY. *handler*: sb. who manages or deals with people or animals — *alsatian*: large, wolf-like dog "Schäferhund" — *P. C.*: police constable — *nod*: slight bow — *betray*: be false or unfaithful to — *trust*: responsibility — *wrist*: joint between the hand and arm — *hold*: the act of holding, grip — *scent*: smell; trail of smell — *track*: follow along its marks, scent etc. — *lead*: strap for leading a dog — *tracker*: man tracking out criminals etc. — *flash*: a sudden burst — *grip*: firm hold.

137. The Rocking-Horse Winner

It was about one o'clock when Paul's mother and father drove up to their house. All was still. Paul's mother went to her rooms and slipped off her white fur cloak. She had told her maid not to wait up for her. She heard her husband downstairs mixing a whisky and soda.

And then, because of the strange anxiety at her heart, she stole upstairs to her son's room. Noiselessly she went along the upper corridor. Was there a faint noise? What was it? She stood, with arrested muscles, outside his door, listening. There was a strange, heavy, and yet not loud noise. Her heart stood still. It was a soundless noise, yet rushing and powerful. Something huge in violent, hushed motion. What was it? What in God's name was it? She ought to know. She felt that she knew the noise. She knew what it was.

Yet she could not place it. She couldn't say what it was. And on and on it went like a madness.

Softly, frozen with anxiety and fear, she turned the door-handle. The room was dark. Yet in the space near the window, she heard and saw something plunging to and fro. She gazed in fear and amazement.

Then suddenly she switched on the light, and saw her son, in his green pyjamas, madly urging on the rocking-horse. The blaze of light suddenly lit him up, as he urged the wooden horse, and lit her up, as she stood, blonde, in her dress of pale green and crystal, in the doorway.

"Paul!" she cried, "Whatever are you doing?"

"It's Malabar!" he screamed in a powerful, strange voice. "It's Malabar!"

His eyes blazed at her for one strange and senseless second, as he ceased urging his wooden horse. Then he fell with a crash to the ground, and she, all her tormented motherhood flooding upon her, rushed to gather him up.

But he was unconscious, and unconscious he remained, with some brain fever.

D. H. Lawrence: "The Rocking-Horse Winner" in: *Selected Tales*, London 1963

VOCABULARY. *rocking-horse*: painted, wooden horse fitted with rockers for children to ride on — *slip off*: push off with a quick easy movement — *faint*: weak — *hush*: make quiet; silence — *frozen with*: filled with — *plunge*: dive — *to and fro*: backwards and forwards — *gaze*: stare — *amazement*: great surprise or astonishment — *urge*: drive on — *blaze*: rush of light — *Malabar*: = one of the horses running for the Derby — *senseless*: foolish; unconscious — *crash*: noise made by violent fall — *torment*: torture, cause great pain — *unconscious*: without mental faculties awake — *brain*: centre of feeling and thinking.

138. Ittel and the Rich Man

I can tell you a story.

Once there was a very rich man who took a poor man into his house.

The poor man, whose name was Ittel, ate at the rich man's table, slept in a good warm bed, wore the rich man's clothes. One night the rich man was about to eat when Ittel stopped him.

"Stop," he cried, "don't eat!"

"Don't eat?" repeated the rich man, puzzled.

"Don't eat," cried Ittel, and he jumped up from his place at the table and rushed over to the rich man's seat. "You call that salt?" he scolded, and put more salt on the rich man's food.

"But I don't like so much salt," objected the rich man, "and besides it's bad for my heart."

"Heart!" scoffed Ittel. "Enjoy your food!" And he dumped the silver salt dish on the rich man's meat. "You call that pepper?" he demanded, and dumped on the pepper, too. "You call that garlic?" And he chopped up a whole clove of garlic and put that on, too.

"But I'm not well, Ittel," the rich man complained. "My doctor says . . ."

"Doctor, schmoctor," ordered Ittel, "you paid for this salt, right? You paid for this pepper? *Enjoy* them."

So the rich man ate, and what do you think? he had a heart attack that night and died.

And what did Ittel do? The whole household was wailing and moaning, and Ittel just stood there with a scowl on his face and a lip curled in scorn. The doctor came by and saw him. "Ittel," he accused, "what's with you? This man was your benefactor! Now that he is dead, can't you at least look sorry?"

Ittel gave the doctor a look. "Sorry!" he said. "Sorry! I try to do something nice for him, and look how he pays me back!"

Frederik Pohl: "A Life and a Half" in *The Abominable Earthman*
New York 1963,

VOCABULARY. *scold*: find fault with, blame — *scoff*: make fun of, mock — *dump*: put or throw down carelessly — *garlic*: plant of the onion kind, with a strong smell and burning taste "Knoblauch" — *chop*: cut with a sudden blow — *clove*: one of small bulbs making up compound bulb of garlic "Nebenzwiebel" — *wail*: cry or moan for sorrow — *scorn*: contempt — *curl*: twist into ringlets; twist.

139. 'The Converted Snake'

A snake dwelt in a certain place. No one dared to pass that way; for whoever did so was instantaneously bitten to death. Once a Mahatma (high-souled one) passed by that road, and the serpent ran after the sage in order to bite him. But when the snake approached the holy man he lost all his ferocity and was overpowered by the gentleness of the Yogin. Seeing the snake, the sage said: "Well, friend, thinkest thou to bite me?" The snake was abashed and made no reply. At this the sage said: "Hearken, friend; do not injure anybody in the future." The snake bowed and nodded assent. The sage went his own way, and the snake entered his hole, and thenceforward began to live a life of innocence and purity without even attempting to harm anyone. In a few days all the neighbourhood began to think that the snake had lost all his venom and was no more dangerous, and so everyone began to tease him. Some pelted him; others dragged him mercilessly by the tail, and in this way there was no end to his troubles. Fortunately the sage again passed by that way and, seeing the bruised and battered condition of the good snake, was very much moved, and inquired the cause of his distress. At this the snake replied: "Holy Sir, this is because I do not injure anyone after your advice. But alas! they are so merciless!" The sage smilingly said: "My dear friend, I simply advised you not to bite anyone, but I did not tell you not to frighten others. Although you should not bite any creature, still you should keep everyone at a considerable distance by hissing at him."

Similarly, if thou livest in the world, make thyself feared and respected. Do not injure anyone, but be not at the same time injured by others.

VOCABULARY. *convert*: change from one form into another — *Mahatma*: one of a class of persons with preternatural powers; prefixed to names of exalted personages, esp. Gandhi — *sage*: wise man — *abash*: to make ashamed — *hearken* [ˈhɑːkən]: to hear with attention — *thenceforward*: from that time forward — *venom*: poison — *pelt*: to throw things at — *merciless*: cruel — *bruise*: cause injury so that the skin is discoloured — *batter*: beat heavily — *hiss*: make a sound like that of letter *s*.

Sri Ramakrishna: "The Converted Snake", in: *Best Mystery Stories*, London 1968

140. The Man in the Road

(Miss Pilkington is of Scots and Irish parentage and is very much aware of the supernatural. This is her earliest ghostly experience.)

When I was about eleven, I went out one evening with my mother to take her dog for a walk before bedtime. We were then living in Kingstown, some miles down the coast from Dublin.

There was a bit of road not far from where we lived which was said to be haunted, but none of my family had ever seen anything supernatural there. On this occasion it was dark, the gaslamps were lit, and we were just turning out of our road into this particular stretch, when the dog suddenly ran ahead, and then began barking furiously. My mother called to him to come back, but without success, and this was very unusual, for he was a well-trained and obedient animal. We went up to where the creature stood, growling and barking by turns, just by one of the lamp-posts, and saw, standing directly in the lamplight, a tallish man, wearing a hat with a pointed crown, and a small plume on one side, a dark cloak, and buckled shoes—we were not near enough to see his features clearly.

My mother went forward and gripped the dog's collar, saying as she did so, "I must apologise for my dog's bad behaviour." I was just behind her, and quite suddenly, as I looked at him waiting for him to speak, the man vanished completely. As it was a straight road, with a high wall on that side with no doors, there was no normal explanation for his disappearance.

My mother did not seem perturbed—it was not her first encounter with a ghost—but I must confess that my legs shook, and I was very glad when we got home. The dog was trembling all over, with the hair along his back standing straight up, and it was some while before he would stop growling. I suppose the shock for me was all the greater because I had quite thought the man must be going to a fancy-dress ball, and had not felt in the least frightened until he vanished so strangely.

F. M. Pilkington: "The Man in the Road" in *The House of the Nightmare*, ed. Kathleen Lines, London 1967
By permission of the publishers, The Bodley Head Ltd

VOCABULARY. *Scots*: of Scotland or its inhabitants (adj.) — *parentage*: birth — *ghost*: spirit of a dead person; *ghostly*: adj. — *haunt*: visit often — *stretch*: unbroken space — *obedient*: willing to do what one is told — *growl*: make a low threatening sound — *by turns*: one after the other — *pointed*: having a point; tapering — *crown*: top of a hat — *plume*: feather, esp. one worn as an ornament — *cloak*: loose outer garment — *buckled shoes*: shoes with a clip of metal fastening them over instep — *grip*: take fast hold of — *collar*: band of leather etc. worn round the neck — *apologise*: make excuse — *vanish*: go out of sight — *perturb*: trouble, make anxious — *encounter*: meeting — *shake*: tremble — *fancy-dress ball*: unusual costumes worn at a ball "Kostümfest".

141. Late One Evening

One evening, long after most people had gone to bed, a friend and I were making our way merrily home through the silent and almost deserted streets. We had been to a musical, and were talking about the people we had seen and heard in it.

"That show made him a star overnight," said my friend about one of them. "He was completely unknown before. And now thousands of teen-agers send him chocolates and love-letters by every post."

"I thought him quite good," I said, "but not worth thousands of love-letters daily. As a matter of fact, one of his songs gave me a pain."

"What was that?" my friend asked. "Sing it to me."

I burst into a parody of the song.

"Be quiet, for heaven's sake." My friend had given me an astonished look. "You'll give everybody a fright, and wake people up for miles around. Besides, they'll think you a drunkard, and me too, probably. And then we'll have a policeman after us."

"Never mind," I said, intoxicated more with the sound of my own voice than with the few drinks we had had. "I don't care. What does it matter?" And I went on singing him the latest tunes at the top of my voice.

Presently there came behind us the sound of a heavy tread, and before you could say "Jack Robinson" a policeman was standing in front of me, his notebook open, a determined look on his face.

"Excuse me, sir," he said. "You have a remarkable voice, if I may say so. Who taught you singing? I'd very much like to find someone who can give my daughter singing lessons. Would you be kind enough to tell me your name and address? Then my wife or I would drop you a line and we could discuss the matter."

W. R. Lee: *English at Home*, London 1966

VOCABULARY. *making our way*: (here) going — *desert*: go away from; leave — *musical*: = musical comedy: light dramatic entertainment of songs, dialogue and dancing connected by a slender plot — *overnight*: immediately, very quickly —

teenagers: young people in their teens, i.e. aged thirteen to nineteen — *pain*: suffering — *parody*: bad or mocking imitation — *fright*: sudden fear — *drunkard*: one who drinks too much — *never mind*: (here) don't let that worry you — *intoxicate*: make drunk — *tune*: music of a song — *at the top of my voice*: very loudly — *presently*: after a little — *tread*: step — *line*: short letter.

142. The Six Burglars of Calais

Edward III laid siege to Calais in order to be ready to return to England if necessary, and on the capitulation of the town ordered the six richest citizens to come forth with halters round their necks and wearing only their shorts, and to surrender all the keys in the city. The inhabitants therefore at once appointed the six chief burglars of Calais and Edward agreed with this, romantically commanding that they should be put to death as soon as they came in. His Queen, however, pointed out what a much more romantic thing it would be to pardon them and make them barons in the Exchequer. Edward therefore pardoned them in spite of his private feelings that the original plan was more romantic still.

After this Edward had all the wool in England kept in a stable at Calais instead of in a sack in the House of Commons; this was a Bad Thing, as it was the beginning of Political Economy.

Sellar and Yeatman: *1066 and All That*, London 1936
By permission of the publishers, Methuen & Co Ltd

VOCABULARY. *burglar*: one who breaks into a house by night to steal; *burgher*: citizen (used chiefly of persons in Dutch or German towns) — *halter*: rope for hanging person with — *the Exchequer*: government department in charge of public money "Schatzamt, Finanzministerium"— *sack*: refers to the Woolsack, the seat of the Lord Chancellor in the House of Lords — *political economy*: science dealing with the production and distribution of wealth.

143. Charles I and the Civil War

With the ascension of Charles I to the throne we come at last to the Central Period of English History (not to be confused with the Middle Ages, of course), consisting in the *utterly memorable Struggle between the Cavaliers (Wrong but Wromantic) and the Roundheads (Right but Repulsive)*.

Charles I was a Cavalier King and therefore had a small pointed beard, long flowing curls, a large, flat, flowing hat and *gay attire*. The Roundheads, on the other hand, were clean-shaven and wore tall, conical hats, white ties and *sombre garments*. Under these circumstances a Civil War was inevitable.

The Roundheads, of course, were so called because Cromwell had all their heads made perfectly round, in order that they should present a uniform appearance when drawn up in line. Besides this, if any man lost his head in action, it could be used as a cannon-ball by the artillery (which was done at the Siege of Worcester).

Sellar and Yeatman: *1066 and All That*, London 1936
By permission of the publishers, Methuen & Co Ltd

VOCABULARY. *ascension to the throne*: becoming king — *repulsive*: repelling, causing disgust — *attire*: (liter. & poet.) dress — *curl*: ringlet e.g. of hair — *conical*: cone-shaped (cone = solid body which narrows to a point from a round, flat base) — *draw up*: get into formation — *line*: double row of men standing side by side (contrasted with column).

144. The Great War

King Edward's new policy of peace was very successful and culminated in the Great War to End War. This pacific and inevitable struggle was undertaken in the reign of his Good and memorable Majesty King George V and it was the cause of nowadays and the end of History.

Causes of the Great War

The Great War was between Germany and America and was thus fought in Belgium, one of the chief causes being the murder of the Austrian Duke of Sarajevo by a murderer in Servia. There were many other Causes of the Great War, such as

1. German Governesses, a wave of whom penetrated Kensington in King Edward's reign and openly said that Germany ought to be top nation, and
2. The Kaiser, who sent a telegram consisting entirely of ems to one of the memorable Boerwar leaders.[1]

These are now agreed to have been causes of the War though at the time the newspapers (rather conceitedly)declared that it was caused by a *strip of paper*.

The War

The War lasted three years or the duration, the Americans being 100%

[1]) And, during a subsequent crisis, a panther to Agaçiers (a brutal act and quite contrary to the Haig Convention).

victorious. At the beginning the Russians rendered great assistance to the American cause by lending their memorable steam-roller and by passing silently through England one Sunday morning before breakfast with snow on their boots. The Americans were also assisted by the Australians (AZTECS) and some Canadians, and 51 Highlanders.

The Peace to End Peace

Though there were several battles in the War, none were so terrible or costly as the Peace which was signed afterwards in the ever-memorable Chamber of Horrors at Versailles, and which was caused by the only memorable statesmen, President Wilson and Col. White House, who insisted on a lot of Points, including

1. that England should be allowed to pay for the War; this was a Good Thing because it strengthened British (and even American) credit;
2. that the world should be made safe for democracy, i. e. anyone except pillion-riders, pedestrians, foreigners, natives, capitalists, communists, Jews, riffs, R. A. F. S., gun-men, policemen, peasants, pheasants, Chinese, etc.;
3. that there should be a great many more countries: this was a Bad Thing as it was the cause of increased geography;
4. The Freedom of the Seas: this was a Good Thing as it did not apply to Britain or America (or Switzerland);
5. that the Kaiser should be hanged: this was a Good Thing as it was abandoned, together with Mr Lloyd George, the Irish Question, etc.

Sellar and Yeatman: *1066 and All That*, London 1936
By permission of the publishers, Methuen & Co Ltd

VOCABULARY. *culminate*: reach the highest point; end in — *Sarajevo*: The Great War arose out of the assassination of the Archduke Francis Ferdinand, heir to the throne of Austria, by a Serb at Serajevo on June 28, 1914 — *conceited*: having a high idea of one's self, vain — *Agaciers-Agadir*: in 1911 the German gunboat *Panther* was sent with promises of assistance to the natives in their struggle against France — *Haig Convention*: (pun) The Hague Convention (Haig: famous British general in the Great War, raised to the peerage in 1919) — *steam-roller*: heavy machine driven by steam — *aztec*: the Mexican people dominant till the conquest of Cortes — *pillion*: seat for a passenger on a motor-cycle — *riff:* Riff = a Berber of the Rif district of Morocco; riff-(raff) = disreputable persons.

145. A Rogue

Any morning about two hundred and fifty years ago an elegant gentleman might be seen leaving his fine house at Old Bailey in the city of London. He carried a sword and wore rich laced clothes. He liked to carry a short silver staff with a crown on the head to show that he was an important person. He liked people to think that he worked for the government.

This elegant gentleman was not a government official at all, although he called himself the Thief-Taker General of Great Britain and Ireland. He was a terrible rogue.

Jonathan Wild was the director of most of the thieving gangs in London. One of his gangs burgled houses, another stole from shops. He had gangs of highwaymen and pickpockets.

Goods were stolen by his order and put in one of his warehouses. People who had been robbed went to his Lost Property Office and asked him to find the stolen goods. He had the goods brought from his warehouse, given back to their proper owners, and then claimed the reward.

If the goods were not claimed they were sold. Mechanics altered watches and jewellery, which could then be sold safely. He did not bother to alter some articles. He shipped them in his own sloop to Holland to sell them there.

When thieves threatened to expose him, or proved clumsy or unwilling, Jonathan Wild betrayed them to a Justice of the Peace. He boasted that he had sent sixty-seven men in this way to the gallows.

At last this rogue was himself betrayed. He ended his wicked career on the public gallows at Tyburn in the spring of 1725.

Boswell Taylor: *999 ... Police!*, London 1964
By permission of the publishers, University of London Press Ltd

VOCABULARY. *rogue*: dishonest person; rascal — *sword* [sɔːd]: weapon with a long blade — *lace*: trim with a fine ornamental fabric of threads — *staff*: stick — *thieve*: steal — *burgle*: enter or rob house — *gang*: company of people met together for evil purpose — *highwayman*: robber who attacks people on the public road — *pickpocket*: one who robs people's pockets — *warehouse*: building or room where goods are stored — *claim*: demand as a right — *reward*: sth. given in return for services — *mechanic*: machine-workman — *jewellery*: precious stones — *sloop*: small onemasted sailing-vessel — *expose*: show up sb. — *clumsy*: not skilful — *betray*: give away to the enemy — *Justice of the Peace*: magistrate — *boast*: brag, speak proudly — *gallows*: wooden framework on which criminals are hanged — *Tyburn*: place of execution in London on site of Marble Arch.

146. The Capture of William Joyce

William Joyce, born in New York in 1906, founded his own British National Socialist League in the nineteen-thirties. By August 1939, he had already decided to throw in his lot with the Nazis. He left with his wife for Germany. In September, 1940, Joyce had been granted German nationality. In 1942 he became chief English commentator on the German radio and always began his broadcasts by saying "Jairmany calling". In 1944 Hitler awarded him the War Service Cross for his services to propaganda. But by the late spring of 1945 the Nazi dream was over.

In common with other Nazis who had everything to fear from capture, Joyce and his wife fled and became fugitives. They had been on the run for nearly a month, enduring both hardship and hunger, and were hiding in a wood near Flensburg close to the Danish border, when they encountered two British officers who were looking for firewood. Foolishly, Joyce accosted them, and even more foolishly addressed them in English.

He was instantly recognized by his memorable voice. Captain Lickorish and Lieutenant Perry, in common with everyone else in England, had often heard it. The two officers were aware, too, that William Joyce was wanted for high treason, and Perry said to him: "You wouldn't happen to be William Joyce, would you?" Joyce had on him a German passport in the name of Wilhelm Hauser and he put his hand in his pocket to get it out to show to the officers. But Perry misunderstood the action and thought he was trying to pull a gun on them. Perry drew his own revolver and shot Joyce in the leg. Joyce fell, groaning that his name was Hauser. But he had not taken the impersonation very seriously, for he was carrying a German military passport made out in the name of William Joyce.

When his stretcher was being taken into a military hospital, William Joyce discovered for the first time that his countrymen regarded him neither with awe nor the respect for a fallen enemy, and not even with hatred. He was greeted with jokes and jeers and with a chorus "Jairmany calling".

The only section of the community who showed hatred towards him were his fellow prisoners, who raged against his presence in the prison and even planned to murder him. But criminals do not lack what they imagine to be patriotism.

The trial began at the Old Bailey on 17 September, 1945. The jury found Joyce guilty of treason and the Judge sentenced him to death.

In England many people held the opinion that Joyce was wrongly convicted and hanged. He was an American and therefore could not be guilty of treason against England.

Charles Franklin: *World-Famous Trials*, London 1966
By permission of the publishers, Odhams Books

VOCABULARY. *lot*: fortune, fate — *encounter*: meet — *accost*: to go up to and speak to — *treason*: treachery to one's own country — *groan*: make a deep sound expressing pain — *impersonation*: playing the part of — *stretcher*: framework for carrying a sick or injured person — *awe*: wonder mixed with fear — *trial*: the judging of a prisoner in a law-court — *convict*: declare in a law-court that sb. is guilty of a crime.

147. Using Eggs for Carrying Messages

Secret messages are not only written on paper. Even eggs have been used for carrying messages.

In the First World War, the line of trenches ran through a village so that part of it was within the French lines and the other part within the German lines. One day an old woman came up to the French sentries and asked if she might visit her brother whose farm lay within the French lines. Permission was given, and she crossed over to the French side. That evening she returned with some butter and eggs from her brother's farm in her basket. After this the sentries came to know the old woman well, as she made regular visits to her brother's farm.

One day the sentry put his hand in the old woman's basket and took out an egg. He noticed that it was hard-boiled. He threw it up in the air and caught it in his hand. The woman seemed frightened. Again he threw it in the air and again she showed fear.

The sentry looked at the egg, but he could find nothing wrong with it. "Give it back to me," said the woman. "That egg is for my breakfast in the morning."

Then the sentry cracked the shell and peeled it off. On the white of the egg he saw writing.

He took the woman with her eggs straight to his officer. The egg was examined and the mystery was solved. The Germans had discovered that if a message is written in vinegar on the shell of an egg, the writing will go through to the white without leaving any trace on the shell.

The old woman was a clever German agent who, by her disguise as a

French village woman, was able to wander between the French lines collecting important information for the Germans. She made drawings in vinegar on the egg and these showed the position of guns and men within the French lines.

Andrew Scotland: *A Junior Panorama—Book Four,* London 1963
By permission of the publishers, Odhams Books

VOCABULARY. *message*: piece of news sent to sb. — *trench*: ditch dug in the ground as a protection for soldiers against the enemy's fire — *sentry*: soldier keeping watch or guard — *hard-boiled*: boiled until it is hard — *crack*: split — *shell*: hard outer covering — *peel*: strip the skin, shell etc. from sth. — *vinegar*: sour, acid liquid "Essig" — *disguise*: use of changed dress or appearance in order not to be known.

148. Anti-Sabotage in Gibraltar Harbour

In 1940 Lord Rothschild was head of the anti-sabotage section of MI 15 and absent for long spells from London. During the war Lord Rothschild was promoted to the honorary rank of colonel in the British army and awarded the George Medal and two high United States decorations for risking his life on many occasions when tackling enemy bombs.

He was concerned with the detection of ship sabotage occurring at Gibraltar and neutral Spanish and Portuguese ports. Throughout 1941 British merchantmen, carrying precious foodstuffs and raw materials to Britain, suffered severe damage from time bombs which sometimes exploded days after a ship left an Iberian port. Gibraltar had become a hunting ground for enemy saboteurs, despite precautions taken by Naval Intelligence. A large number of ships were damaged, including vessels in convoy to Malta, which called at the Rock for refuelling. At first it was assumed that the Germans or Italians were using a one-man submarine, then still an untested novelty. Measures taken included the protection of all ships in Gibraltar harbour by deep and tough anti-torpedo nets; but the explosions continued. Lord Rothschild was given the task of detecting the saboteurs and ending the destruction of ships. He was aided by Superintendent Burt. They went to Gibraltar and the menace was eventually quelled. They discovered that German agents in neutral ports and a few Spanish dock workers in Gibraltar, recruited by the Germans, had been regularly smuggling time bombs aboard British ships. Some of the bombs were hidden in small suitcases under layers of clothing, others were small enough to be put into thermos flasks which were then topped with tea or coffee, so that they escaped examination by naval security men.

A large number of these bombs were discovered and made harmless by Lord Rothschild, who invariably ordered his assistants to take cover and insisted on defusing the charges himself. A few of the saboteurs were caught. The most dangerous was José Estella Key. He was a British subject, and so was taken to London, tried at the Old Bailey, sentenced to death and executed by hanging in May 1942.

Lord Rothschild was recognized as one of the world's greatest experts in this branch of Military Intelligence.

E. H. Cookridge: *The Third Man*, London 1968,
Arthur Barker Ltd (publishers)
By permission of the author

VOCABULARY. *anti-sabotage*: fight against wilful destruction — *tackle*: deal with; seize — *merchantman*: a trading ship — *Iberian*: of Spain and Portugal as one country — *convoy*: merchant ships protected by warships — *fuel*: supply with a substance by which a fire is kept going — *tough*: not easily broken — *net*: open-work material of knotted string, rope etc. — *quell*: crush; subdue — *layer*: thickness, covering — *thermos flask*: container in which a liquid changes its temperature very slowly — *top*: put a cover on — *defuse*: take off the device for causing an explosion "Zünder entfernen, entschärfen".

149. The Berlin Tunnel

One of the C. I. A.'s most celebrated coups was the famous "Berlin tunnel". Just outside Berlin in the East Zone was a junction of telephone cables which served the Soviet Military headquarters. C. I. A. agents in the East Zone pinpointed its position, and the United States military authorities erected a building, which they said was an experimental radar station, on their side of the border, and dug a tunnel to the telephone terminus. It was not a difficult operation using modern tunnelling techniques. The important thing was the exact locating of the terminus, which was five feet underground below the village of Alt-Glienicke, six hundred yards from the nearest point to the American Zone.

The tunnel was dug from the basement of the supposed radar station. Many hundreds of tons of clay were dug out, packed in large wooden crates on which were put deceptive labels calculated not to arouse the interest of the Communist spies in the area. As the work had to be done in great secrecy it took longer than such a tunnel would normally take, and it was thus months before the C. I. A. excavators finally broke into the telephone terminus. The tunnel itself was lined with corrugated iron, was air-conditioned and properly drained.

When they got to the terminus a tap was expertly put on to the cables and concealed in such a way that only a careful inspection would reveal it. The wire went out to the American side through a steel door on which the C. I. A. had printed in Russian: "No admittance by order of the Commanding Officer."

The C. I. A. spent several rewarding months listening to the telephone conversations of the Soviet Military headquarters, until the tap was finally discovered by a Russian technician.

Moscow sent an indignant note to Washington demanding punishment of the perpetrators of this "subterranean espionage". But a certain amount of admiration was mingled with the indignation, and the Soviet and East German Press, though denouncing this violation of their sovereign rights, referred to it as a "bold, skilful and audacious operation". The Russians opened the tunnel to the public and invited Western correspondents to come and view the latest exploit of the iniquitous C. I. A.

Charles Franklin: *Spies of the Twentieth Century*, London 1967
By permission of the publishers, Odhams Books

VOCABULARY. *C. I. A.*: Central Intelligence Agency (United States) — *junction*: place of joining — *pinpoint*: locate with the requisite precision — *terminus*: end of the line — *clay*: soft, sticky earth — *deceptive*: different from what it looks — *label*: a small written note — *crate*: box or packing-case — *excavator*: machine used for digging out — *corrugated iron*: sheets of iron shaped into waves — *tap*: device for listening secretly to messages — *admittance*: right to enter — *reward*: repay; recompense — *perpetrator*: person doing sth. wrong — *audacious*: daring; bold — *exploit*: daring deed — *iniquitous*: unjust; wicked.

150. School Libraries

A school library can never take the place of a public library, even when a boy or girl is still at school. The public library should always be able to offer a bigger and better choice. The function of school libraries is to give pupils the right attitude towards a library, and the knowledge of how to use it. In addition, they help people who want to form their own private libraries. Young people at school, or even after leaving, are sometimes seen wandering aimlessly in a library, not knowing what they want or how to find it, and too embarrassed to ask a librarian to help. Such people can easily be frightened away from libraries for life. But this will not happen if while they are at school they learn their way about a library.

A library can work properly only if it is treated as a place for tranquil work and study. Some school libraries are rather noisy places, because those using it have not learned respect for other people. The good library-user disturbs other people as little as possible; he replaces books and magazines exactly where he found them. Again some libraries are not as attractive as they ought to be, because the furniture and equipment are battered, and the books over-worn through ill-treatment. The good library-user has a respect for the books and furniture of the library, as well as for its users. Proper care of books means opening them carefully—especially new books—never putting a bulky object between their pages, never turning down the corner of a page, never marking a page, and never dropping them carelessly.

Denys Thompson and R. J. Harris: *Your English 2*, London 1963
By permission of the publishers, Heinemann Educational Books Ltd

VOCABULARY. *attitude*: manner of behaving — *aimless*: without plan or intention — *equipment*: outfit — *batter*: strike repeatedly so as to bruise or break — *ill-treatment*: bad dealing with — *bulky*: taking up much space.